DR. PRADEEP MEHENDIRATTA

PRADEEP

INDEX TO FELICITATION AND COMMEMORATION VOLUMES

Dr. Pradeep Mehendiratta Felicitation Volume

Edited by

JAGDISH S. YADAV

MANOHAR
AMERICAN INSTITUTE OF INDIAN STUDIES
1991

ISBN 81-85425-34-5

First published 1991

Published by Ajay Kumar Jain, Manohar Publications,
2/6 Ansari Road, Daryaganj, New Delhi 110 002
for
American Institute of Indian Studies
D-31 Defence Colony, New Delhi 110 024

Typeset by Tulika Print Communication Services Pvt. Ltd.
15/15 Sarvapriya Vihar, New Delhi 110 016

Printed at Rajkamal Electric Press
B35/9, GT Karnal Road Ind. Area, Delhi 110 033

DEDICATION

The Committee on Art and Archaeology and the Staff of the Center for Art and Archaeology of the American Institute of Indian Studies are proud to present this volume in honour of Dr. Pradeep Mehendiratta, Director of the Institute. With this small token, we hope to recognize Dr. Mehendiratta's tireless efforts on behalf of the Center over the years. Without his care and attention to every matter, from the minutest details to the broadest concerns, the Center could not have flourished as it has. This volume is dedicated with our deepest thanks to Dr. Mehendiratta on the occasion of the seminar 'Perceptions of India's Past from Ancient to Modern Times' held at the Center's premises 17-21 December 1989.

Committee for Art and Archaeology:

Susan L. Huntington, Chair

Catherine B. Asher

Thomas Metcalf

Walter M. Spink

Michael W. Meister, ex officio

Center Staff:

M. A. Dhaky

V. R. Nambiar

Suresh Vasant

Jagdish Yadav

R. Sharma

FOREWORD

It gives me extraordinary pleasure to be asked by Jagdish Yadav to write a foreword to this Bibliography, both because such a Bibliography is a worthy undertaking in itself (there often being no way except accident to recover exceptional scholarship from the rapidly increasing library of Festschriften and memorial collections) and because it has been prepared in honor of my long-time friend and colleague Dr. P.R. Mehendiratta. That such a valuable aid to scholarship should have been prepared in his name is particularly appropriate, for I can say without fear of contradiction that he himself has been the greatest aid to American scholarship on India—and not a little to Indian scholarship on India—ever. Nearly every American student and scholar who has visited India in the past quarter of a century is deeply in his debt, though a few of us more deeply enmeshed in *maya* than others do not always recognize the truth of that. Directly, through his long association with, and ultimate Directorship of, the American Institute of Indian Studies, he has provided an all-important structure in India for American scholars. No less importantly, he has provided a shoulder to cry on in emergency, a calm efficiency in crisis, an open purse in necessity: in general, a generosity of spirit that is so very rare in any time or place, and so particularly important in times of stress. Every one needs a friend, but especially young people on their own, often for the first time, in an unfamiliar culture.

It is a source of mild amusement to me to listen to conversations, sometimes querulous ones, among contemporary students and scholars, concerning minor inconveniences for which the Institute is blamed, although the problem nearly always lies elsewhere. When a student or scholar came to India thirty years ago (assuming he or she could get support to come here in the first place, there being available only Fulbright grants and the limited and ad hoc programs of the Ford and Rockefeller Foundations), the situation was quite different. One gathered one's own information, and made one's own arrangements for, visas, innoculations, research assistance etc. When finally in India, one made one's own banking arrangements, stood in long lines for travel tickets and at the Post Office, found one's own doctors and housing, and most of all one hoped that somewhere on the horizon a light would appear to help one navigate in a disorienting, seemingly chaotic and often genuinely hostile sea. For the first several months of any stay, all of one's time was spent on getting settled, especially if one had a family. All in all, it was an instructive way into India, but it was also frustrating, inefficient, and sometimes depressing to the point of intellectual catatonia. The American diplomatic missions were, I can say from personal experience, of little help, nor were the Fulbright offices, unless one happened to hold a Fulbright grant. One depended entirely on the few names and letters of introduction one could glean in the States. Pradeep Mehendiratta, through the American Institute of Indian Studies—and in these areas the two are synonymous—has changed all that.

He and I have both grown up with the Institute, intimately involved since its founding. And I have watched with more than a little awe and admiration as he has developed the structure that is the American Institute in India today. Not only has he dealt imaginatively with such problems as those mentioned above, but he has had the foresight to anticipate structural problems, sometimes years ahead, the wisdom to be flexible as situations have changed, the diplomatic and administrative skill to establish networks and channels within the governmental and academic bureaucracies, and the patience, shrewdness, and acumen to judge situations with the long-term interest of the Institute clearly in view. There have been occasions when American colleagues, perhaps thinking of days long past when numbers of American scholars of India were small and when India was still feeling her way towards the establishment of a bureaucracy, have impatiently and with arrogance demanded that the Institute call the attention of one Minister or another to one situation or another. Pradeep, wisely, has consistently urged that proper channels be followed, understanding that although any bureaucracy sometimes moves more ponderously than might be wished, the channels have a purpose, and that purpose must be respected. He has been, in my experience, invariably right.

Some of this perceptiveness is, perhaps, related to

Pradeep's period of service to the Government of India, from which post he came to the Institute in 1962; not everyone, however, has the sensitivity to assimilate, learn from, and use such experience in varying situations. In a similar way, part of his humanity is perhaps rooted in the fact that, having lost all material goods in Multan during the Partition, he began again, with incredible courage, to put his life together by working as a porter on a Railway platform. Such circumstances, of course, are also not guaranteed to increase sensitivity and human understanding: more usual would be bitterness and anger, or discouragement and apathy. Pradeep is a man of extraordinary personal courage, both moral and physical. This has been seen again, more recently, during the hijacking of the Pan American flight in Karachi, his injury during that awful time and his recovery from it, and by his sense of perspective during and following a serious heart attack. In such ways he has been an example and source of strength to many of us personally, and such qualities have had their effect, in increased admiration and loyalty, throughout the organisation. A creation must share in the qualities of its creator, and the Institute, especially in India, is largely his creation.

Since he had lost everything during the Partition, it also fell upon Pradeep to educate himself (he was in his very early teens in 1947), and this, with the help of a benefactor, he did, following courses in accounting, management, economics, and English. This formal education, together with practical experience, won him an MBA from Delhi University in 1965, and, in 1979, a Ph.D.; his dissertation was "University Administration in India and the United States" (it has been published by Oxford & IBH under that title, with the sub-title "Case Studies of Delhi University and the University of Illinois"). It is a painstaking and perceptive study, and shows, as one reviewer said, "an understanding of complex issues". Anyone who is reading this Foreword will understand the drive and discipline it took to write a dissertation while working—literally—fifteen hours a day to develop and preserve the Institute. Such discipline is characteristic of the whole organization in India, and throughout the organization one senses not only loyalty, but the unity and sense of purpose that only comes from working for and with a man both compassionate and himself efficient.

It has been my privilege and pleasure to work with this same man for some thirty years, and I know whereof I speak. If by some magic I could transform these inadequate words into a garland of flowers, it would be the most colorful and fragrant of garlands. Pradeep, with his customary modesty, would immediately remove it from his neck. But—and I speak for Trustees both past and present, and for the legion of scholars whom he has helped—I hope the traditional gesture will have conveyed its message of the profound esteem and gratitude we intend it to signify.

New Delhi
February 1990

EDWARD C. DIMOCK, JR.
Chair, AIIS Board of Trustees

PREFACE

In all disciplines of learning, apart from books, repositories of scholarly articles and other communications are journals and works like felicitation and commemoration volumes. Their importance in research and advancement of knowledge hardly needs any emphasis. The number of these journals and felicitation and commemoration volumes has increased so much that if contributions contained therein are not properly indexed they escape the attention of scholars and remain buried unused. Most of the standard learned journals have their own indexes and some are taken care of in various bibliographies. But unfortunately independent felicitation and commemoration volumes, which are not published as part of journals, have rarely been indexed particularly those belonging to the field of Indian studies. One such index entitled *Indexes to Papers in Commemoration Volumes* was published by the Bhandarkar Oriental Research Institute. It includes papers in Indian studies published up to 1957. Since then many felicitation and commemoration volumes containing valuable research on Indology have appeared. But no Index to them is available. Hence the present *Pradeep: Index to Felicitation and Commemoration Volumes* has been prepared to supplement the bibliographical literature relating to Indology published during the period 1960 to 1988. It covers one hundred Felicitation and Commemoration Volumes published during the period in India and abroad.

The Index is divided into three parts in the following sequence:

i) Classified Subject Index
ii) Author Index
iii) Key-Word Index

CLASSIFIED SUBJECT INDEX: All articles have been classified according to the subjects mentioned in the 'Contents'. Each entry in this part has been serialised for cross reference in indexes (ii) and (iii). The names of authors in each subject-group are alphabetically arranged beginning with the surname followed by name (in full or in initials). All Felicitation and Commemoration Volumes indexed have been given a serial number and are listed in the beginning. Hence, in the entries, instead of repeating full details of the Felicitation/Commemoration Volume containing the particular article, only their serial numbers are given. Complete details of the volumes are given in the list. The entries have been organised in the following manner/order:

Author's surname is followed by the first name, title of the article, serial number of the Felicitation/ Commemoration Volume and pages. Where a Volume is published in two parts, the particular part's number is given in parenthesis after its serial number. Examples of a few entries in the Classified Subject Index are presented below:

> ASHER, FREDERICK.
> On Stone and Artistic Production.
> **33:** 63-68.

Frederick Asher is the author of the article, 'On Stone and Artistic Production', published in the Felicitation Volume, Serial Number **33** of the list, on pages 63 to 68. The Felicitation Volume listed at Serial Number 33 is:

> CASE, Margaret and BARRIER, N. Gerald, ed.
> *Aspects of India: Essays in honor of Edward Cameron Dimock, Jr.* New Delhi, American Institute of Indian Studies, 1986.

Another example:

> MEISTER, Michael W.
> The Hero as Yogin: A Virastambha from Chittor. **46(1):** 283-286.

Michael W. Meister is the author of the article, 'The Hero as Yogin: A Virastambha from Chittor', which is published in the Felicitation Volume listed at Serial Number **46** on pages 283 to 286. **46(1)** refers to Part 1 of the work appearing at number **46**. The Felicitation Volume listed at Serial Number **46** is:

> LOKESH CHANDRA and JAIN, Jyotindra, ed.
> *Dimensions of Indian Art: Pupul Jayakar Seventy.* Delhi, Agam Kala Prakashan, 1986. 2 Vols.

AUTHOR INDEX: An Author Index is provided to find out an author's contributions irrespective of any subject-group. The names of the authors have been alphabetically arranged by surname followed by first name. The entries have been numbered serially in the Classified Subject Index and these entry numbers are mentioned against the name of each author. For example:

> Mukherjee, B.N., 304, 668-669, 1132, 1182, 3095-3096, 3258-3261, 3554, 3593, 3808, 4217, 4332
>
> Vatsyayan, Kapila, 334, 363, 1207, 3378-3380, 3964-3965, 4099

All the articles by B.N. Mukherjee and Kapila Vatsyayan are listed at serial numbers mentioned against their names in the Classified Subject Index.

KEY-WORD INDEX: The Classified Subject Index has been supplemented by a Key-Word Index. Sometimes it is difficult to classify an article, particularly when it deals with more than one subject. To help scholars find an article on any subject covered in this Index, this part should prove very useful. Important key-words from the titles of the articles listed in this volume have been selected and listed in an alphabetical order. This is not done if the key-word and subject-group are the same. For example, if epigraphy is the key-word and this article is listed in the subject-group Epigraphy, then the key-word epigraphy has not been selected because all the articles dealing with epigraphy will be found in the subject-group Epigraphy. But if the key-word is epigraphy and this article is not listed in the subject-group Epigraphy, then this key-word is selected. Against each key-word, serial numbers of the Classified Subject Index are given. For example:

> Asoka, 610–611, 666, 724, 746, 1000, 2354, 3007, 3012, 3080, 3085, 3095–3096, 3110, 3148, 3166, 3171
>
> Guptas, 9, 606, 609, 616, 626, 641, 661, 673, 696, 705, 720, 725, 1066, 2097, 3019, 3088, 3131, 3145, 3186, 3216, 3220, 3228, 3258, 3280, 3293, 3401, 3495, 3500, 3517, 3559, 3563, 3574, 3579, 3622, 3663, 3857, 4260, 4287
>
> Mathura, 1001, 2985, 3057, 3172, 3180, 3284, 3333, 3371, 3615, 3641, 3658, 3668, 3789
>
> Vishnu, 491, 1263, 1602, 2048, 3134, 3464, 3737, 3755, 3757, 3761, 3765, 4360

Hopefully, this work will be found useful by scholars working on such aspects of India as biographies, geography, history, social and economic history, sociology, anthropology, religion, philosophy, language, literature, archaeology, epigraphy, numismatics, art, architecture, sculpture and terracottas, iconography, painting, museology, music, dance, drama, and cultural relationships between India and the world; it also includes entries in the field of cultural aspects of countries other than India.

Dr. Pradeep Mehendiratta, the able and dynamic director of the American Institute of Indian Studies, has rendered valuable service to the academic community. The Committee on Art and Archaeology and the staff of AIIS presented this Felicitation Volume to him in recognition of his tireless efforts in assisting scholars from India, USA and other countries in their academic pursuits. His first name, 'Pradeep', which means 'Light' thus appears appropriate as the title of the volume for this brings to light 4459 articles covering a wide range of subjects appearing in felicitation and commemoration volumes.

I consider it an honour to edit this Volume. I pray to God to bestow upon him and his family all the health and happiness so that he may continue to direct the Institute in the coming years with unfailing dedication.

15 December 1990

JAGDISH S. YADAV
Editor

ACKNOWLEDGEMENTS

I am very grateful to the AIIS for sponsoring this volume and to Prof. Susan Huntington of the Ohio State University, Chair of the Institute Committee on Art and Archaeology for her valuable suggestions during compilation of the volume. Thanks are due to Dr. Catherine B. Asher and other members of the Committee for their sustained support, and to Prof. Edward C. Dimock, Chair of Trustees for writing the Foreword. I am thankful to all my colleagues at the Center for their help and cooperation. Mr. D.N. Pandey and Mr. V.K. Venkatavardhan typed the manuscript in a very short time for which I am grateful to them. I record my sincere thanks to Ramesh Jain of Manohar for his valuable suggestions and help in the publication of this volume. My wife Nirmala not only helped me in compilation of the volume but also took care of the children and the household thus enabling me to devote my full time and effort to this work. I am grateful to her and our son Yogesh and daughter Shikha.

Jagdish S. Yadav

CONTENTS

Foreword vii

Preface ix

Acknowledgements xi

List of Felicitation and Commemoration Volumes 3

CLASSIFIED SUBJECT INDEX 13

Biography 13

Abhedananda 13
Agrawal, Jagannath 13
Ashraf, K.M. 13
Bajpai, K.D. 14
Barani, Zia-ud-din 14
Barua, B.K. 14
Basavesvara 14
Basham, A.L. 16
Bhandarkar, D.R. 16
Bhatta, Asadhara 16
Bhatta, Kumarila 16
Bhatta, Narayana 16
Bhattacharyya, Kalidas 16
Bhavabhuti 16
Bhuyan, S.K. 16
Bishndas 17
Boner, Alice 17
Bose, Nandalal 17
Brown, W. Norman 17
Callaway, John 17
Charudeva Shastri 17
Chattopadhyaya, K.C. 17
Chattopadhyaya, Sudhakar 18
Chhabra, B. Ch. 18
Chitraoshastri, M.M. 18
Conze, Edward 18
Coomaraswamy, Ananda 18
Dandekar, R.N. 18
Datta, D.M. 18
De, S.K. 19
Desai, P.B. 19
Deshpande, M.N. 19
Dhanapala 19
Dignaga 19
Dikshit, G.S. 19
Dimock, Edward C., Jr. 19

Elphinstone, Mountstuart 19
Elwin, Verrier 19
Fleet, J.F. 19
Foote, R.B. 19
Galanos, Demetrius 19
Gangoly, O.C. 20
Gaurinath Sastri 20
Ghosh, A. 20
Gode, P.K. 20
Goetz, Hermann 20
Gonda, J. 20
Gorakhnath 20
Guenther, H.V. 21
Gunaratna Suri 21
Handiqui, K.K. 21
Jani, A.N. 21
Javadekar, A.G. 21
Jayakar, Pupul 21
Jayaswal, K.P. 21
Jha, A.N. 22
Kant, I. 22
Kashyap, Bhikkhu Jagdish 22
Kavindracarya Sarasvati 22
Kaviraj, Gopinath 22
Kesarcodi-Watson, Ian 23
Kipling, Lockwood 23
Kosambi, D.D. 23
Kuppuswami Sastri, S. 24
Madhvacarya 24
Mainkar, T.G. 24
Majumdar, Khitindranath 24
Majumdar, R.C. 24
Mirashi, V.V. 24
Mishra, L.N. 24
Mishra, Umesha 24
Misra, Godavara 25
Misra, Vacaspati 25
Mola Ram 25
Mookerjee, Satkari 25
Moraes, G.M. 25
Morley, Grace 25
Murti, T.R.V. 25
Nilakanta Sastri, K.A. 25
Pandey, Lochan Prasad 25
Pant, G.B. 25
Paranavitana, Senarat 25
Paranjpe, V.G. 26
Parvanikar, Sitarama 26
Pawar, A.G. 26
Raghavan, V. 26

Rajasekhara 26
Ramachandra Rao, S. 26
Ramakrishna 26
Ramaraya, Bellamkonda 26
Rao, S.R. 26
Ray, Niharranjan 26
Sankalia, H.D. 26
Saraswati, S.K. 26
Sarma, E.R. Sreekrishna 27
Sarma, K.V. 27
Satya Prakash 27
Saunaka 27
Sen, Keshab Chandra 27
Shastri, D.N. 27
Singhal, S.P. 28
Sinha, B.P. 28
Sircar, D.C. 28
Sivaramamurti, C. 28
Srikantha Sastri, S. 28
Srinivasan, K.R. 28
Sternbach, Ludwik 29
Stokes, H.N. 29
Su 29
Subhaganada 29
Udayacandra 29
Udayanacarya 29
Udayavira Shastri 29
Upadhyaya, Jagannath 30
Vamkalakacarya 30
Velankar, H.D. 30
Vivekananda 30
Yagnik, Mulshankar 30
Yazdani, Ghulam 30

Geography 31

History 33
Historiography 33
Indus Valley Civilization 34
Ancient 36
Medieval 41
Modern 43
States 44
Andhra Pradesh 44
Assam 45
Bihar 45
Delhi 46
Gujarat 46
Haryana 46
Himachal Pradesh 46
Jammu and Kashmir 46

Karnataka 46
Kerala 48
Madhya Pradesh 48
Maharashtra 48
Orissa 49
Punjab 49
Rajasthan 49
Tamilnadu 49
Uttar Pradesh 51
West Bengal 51

Social History 53

Economic History 55
Ancient 55
Medieval 56
Modern 56

State, Government and Political Thought 58

Sociology 59

Anthropology 61

Psychology 62

Religion 63
Hinduism 63
Vedic 67
Upanisad 75
Epics 75
Ramayana 75
Mahabharata 76
Gita 77
Puranas 78
Buddhism 79
Jainism 84
Christianity 85
Islam 85
Sikhism 85
Zoroastrianism 85

Philosophy 86
Hindu 91
Buddhist 97
Jaina 99

Language 100
Apabhramsa 100
Assamese 100
Bengali 101
Brahui 101
Dravidian 101
English 101

Hindi 101
Indo-Aryan 101
Indo-European 102
Kannada 102
Khamti 102
Konkani 102
Ladakhi 102
Lepcha 102
Malayalam 102
Munda 102
Oriya 102
Pali 102
Prakrit 103
Sanskrit 103
Santali 107
Sinhalese 107
Tamil 107

Literature 108
Arabic 108
Assamese 108
Bengali 108
Dravidian 109
English 109
Hindi 109
Kannada 109
Indo-Persian 109
Khotanese 110
Marathi 110
Oriya 110
Pali 110
Persian 110
Prakrit 110
Sanskrit 110
  Poetry 114
  Drama 117
  Fiction 118
Sinhalese 118
Tamil 118
Urdu 118

Archaeology 119
Andamans 122
Andhra Pradesh 122
Bihar 122
Chandigarh 122
Gujarat 122
Haryana 123
Himachal Pradesh 123
Jammu and Kashmir 123
Karnataka 123

Madhya Pradesh 124
Maharashtra 124
Punjab 125
Rajasthan 125
Tamilnadu 126
Uttar Pradesh 126
West Bengal 127

Epigraphy 128

Numismatics 136

Art 140

Architecture 143
Hindu 143
Andhra Pradesh 144
Bihar 144
Goa 144
Gujarat 144
Himachal Pradesh 145
Karnataka 145
Kerala 145
Madhya Pradesh 146
Maharashtra 146
Orissa 146
Rajasthan 147
Tamilnadu 147
Uttar Pradesh 148
West Bengal 148
Buddhist 148
Jaina 148
Islamic 149
Christian 149

Sculpture 150
Hindu 150
Buddhist 153
Jaina 154
Animal 154

Iconography 155
Hindu 155
Buddhist 158
Jaina 159

Terracottas 160

Painting 162
Ajanta 162
Bengal 163
Bihar 163
Deccan 163
Malwa 163

Mughal 163
Pahari, Kangra and Mandi 164
Punjab 164
Rajasthan 165
Illustrated Manuscripts 165
Jaina 166

Handicrafts 167
Textile 167

Preservation and Conservation 168

Museum and Museology 169

Music 171

Dance 172

Drama 173

Education 174

Games 175

Astronomy 176

Mathematics 177

Botany 178

Medical Science 179

Science and Technology 180

Military Science 181

Library and Archives 182

India and the World 183

Other Countries 186
Asia 186
Afghanistan 186
Bangladesh 186
China 186
Japan 187
Mongolia 187
Nepal 187
Pakistan 188
Sri Lanka 188
Tibet 189
South-East Asia 189
Burma 190
Cambodia 190
Indonesia 190
Laos 191
Thailand 191
Vietnam 192

Iran	192
Israel	192
Lebanon	192
Siberia	192
Central Asia	192
Czechoslovakia	193
France	193
Germany	193
Turkey	193
United Kingdom	193
Egypt	193
South Africa	193
Australia	193
North America	194
United States of America	194
Mexico	194
South America	194
AUTHOR INDEX	195
KEY-WORD INDEX	221

LIST OF FELICITATION AND COMMEMORATION VOLUMES

1. **ABHEDANANDA**
   Mazumdar, Amiya Kumar and **Prajanananda,** Ed.
   The bases of Indian Culture; commemoration volume of Abhedananda. Calcutta, Ramakrishna Vedanta Math, 1971.

2. **ACHARYA, PARAMANANDA**
   Das, Binod S., Ed.
   Paramananda Acharya commemoration volume: Life & Culture in Orissa. Calcutta, Minerva Associates, 1984.

3. **AGRAWAL, JAGANNATH**
   Gupta, Dharmendra Kumar, Ed.
   Jagannath Agrawal felicitation volume: Recent studies in Sanskrit and Indology. Delhi, Ajanta Publications, 1982.

4. **ASHRAF, KUNWAR MOHAMMAD**
   Kruger, Horst, Ed.
   Kunwar Mohammad Ashraf: An Indian scholar and revolutionary 1903-1962. Delhi, People's Publishing House, 1969.

5. **BAJPAI, K.D.**
   Shastri, A.M. and others, Ed.
   Vajapeya: Essays on evolution of Indian art and culture: K.D. Bajpai felicitation volume. Delhi, Agam Kala Prakashan, 1987. 2 vols.

6. **BANERJEA, J.N.**
   J.N. Banerjea volume: A collection of articles by his friends and pupils presented on his retirement from Carmichael Professorship of Ancient Indian History and Culture. Calcutta, University of Calcutta, 1960.

7. **BARUA, BIRINCHI KUMAR**
   Neog, Maheshwar and **Sharma, Mukunda Madhava,** Ed.
   Professor Birinchi Kumar Barua commemoration volume. Gauhati, Local Committee, XXII Session All India Oriental Conference, 1966.

8. **BASAVESVARA**
   Wodeyar, S.S., Ed.
   Sri Basavesvara eighth centenary commemoration volume. Bangalore, Government of Mysore, 1967.

9. **BASHAM, A.L.**
   Maity, S.K. and others, Ed.
   Studies in Orientology: Essays in memory of Prof. A.L. Basham. Agra, Y.K. Publishers, 1988.

10. **BASHAM, A.L.**
    Mukherjee, S.N., Ed.
    India: History and thought; essays in honour of A.L. Basham. Calcutta, Subarnarekha, 1982.

11. **BHANDARKAR, D.R.**
    Bandyopadhyaya, Samaresh, Ed.
    Acarya vandana; D.R. Bhandarkar birth centenary volume. Calcutta, University of Calcutta, 1984.

12. **BHATTACHARYYA, KALIDAS**
    Sengupta, Pradip Kumar, Ed.
    Freedom, transcendence and identity: Essays in memory of Professor Kalidas Bhattacharyya. New Delhi, Indian Council of Philosophical Research, 1988.

13. **BHUYAN, SURYYA KUMAR**
    Neog, Maheswar and **Barpujari, H.K.,** Ed.
    Suryya Kumar Bhuyan commemoration volume, Gauhati, All India Oriental Conference, 1966.

14. **BONER, ALICE**
    Baumer, Bettina, Ed.
    Rupa pratirupa: Alice Boner commemoration volume. New Delhi, Biblia Implex, 1982.

15. **BROWN, W. NORMAN**
    Bender, Ernest, Ed.
    Indological studies in honor of W. Norman Brown. New Haven, American Oriental Society, 1962.

16. **CHARUDEVA SHASTRI**
    Charudeva Shastri felicitation volume presented to Charudeva Shastri on the occasion of his seventy-fifth anniversary by his friends and admirers. Delhi, Charudeva, Shastri Felicitation Committee, 1974.

17. **CHATTERJI, B.R.**
Buddha Prakash, Ed.
Studies in Asian history and culture: Presented to Dr. B.R. Chatterji on his eightieth birthday. Meerut, Meenakshi Prakashan, 1970.

18. **CHATTERJI, SUNITI KUMAR**
Mallik, Bhakti P., Ed.
Suniti Kumar Chatterji commemoration volume. Burdwan, University of Burdwan, 1981.

19. **CHATTOPADHYAYA, K.C.**
K.C. Chattopadhyaya memorial volume. Allahabad, Department of Ancient History, Culture & Archaeology, Allahabad University, 1975.

20. **CHATTOPADHYAYA, SUDHAKAR**
Jash, Pranabananda, Ed.
Religion and society in ancient India: Sudhakar Chattopadhyaya commemoration volume. Calcutta, Roy & Chowdhury, 1984.

21. **CHHABRA, B. CH.**
Ramesh, K.V. and others, Ed.
Svasti Sri: B. Ch. Chhabra felicitation volume. Delhi, Agam Kala Prakashan, 1984.

22. **Chhavi. Varanasi, Bharat Kala Bhavan**
Vol. 1: Golden Jubilee volume. Edited by Ananda Krishna and Chandramani Singh. 1971.
Vol. 2: Rai Krishnadasa felicitation volume. Edited by Anand Krishna and Kamal Giri. 1981.

23. **CHITRAOSHASTRI, M.M.**
Chinmulgund, P.J. and Mirashi, V.V., Ed.
M.M. Chitraoshastri felicitation volume; review of Indological research in last 75 years. Poona, Bharatiya Charitrakosha Mandal, (1967).

24. **CONZE, EDWARD**
Lancaster, Lewis, Ed.
Prajnaparamita and related systems: Studies in honour of Edward Conze. Berkeley, University of California, 1977.

25. **COOMARASWAMY, A.K.**
Dasgupta, Kalyan Kumar, Ed.
Ananda Coomaraswamy; a centenary volume. Calcutta, Calcutta University, 1981.

26. **COOMARASWAMY, A.K.**
Sheikh, Gulam Mohammed and others, Ed.
Paroksa: Coomaraswamy centenary seminar papers. New Delhi, Lalit Kala Akademi, 1984.

27. **DANDEKAR, R.N.**
Joshi, S.D., Ed.
Amrtadhara: R.N. Dandekar felicitation volume. Delhi, Ajanta Publications, 1984.

28. **DATTA, DHIRENDRA MOHAN**
Ramjee Singh, Ed.
World perspectives in philosophy, religion and culture: Essays presented to Dhirendra Mohan Datta. Patna, Bharati Bhawan, (1968).

29. **DE, S.K.**
Hazra, R.C. and Banerji, S.C., Ed.
S.K. De memorial volume. Calcutta, Firma K.L. Mukhopadhyay, 1972.

30. **DESAI, P.B.**
Ritti, Shrinivas and Gopal, B.R., Ed.
Studies in Indian history and culture; volume presented to Dr. P.B. Desai. Dharwar, Prof. P.B. Desai Felicitation Committee, 1971.

31. **DESHPANDE, M.N.**
Nagaraja Rao, M.S., Ed.
Madhu; recent researches in Indian archaeology and art history: M.N. Deshpande festschrift. Delhi, Agam Kala Prakashan, 1981.

32. **DIKSHIT, G.S.**
Narasimha Murthy, A.V. and Ramesh, K.V., Ed.
Giridharasri; essays on Indology: G.S. Dikshit felicitation volume. Delhi, Agam Kala Prakashan, 1987.

33. **DIMOCK, EDWARD CAMERON, Jr.**
Case, Margaret and Barrier, N. Gerald, Ed.
Aspects of India: Essays in honor of Edward Cameron Dimock, Jr. New Delhi, American Institute of Indian Studies, 1986.

34. **ELWIN, VERRIER**
Pradhan, M.C. and others, Ed.
Anthropology and archaeology: Essays in commemoration of Verrier Elwin, 1902-64. Bombay, Oxford University Press, 1969.

35. **FOOTE, ROBERT BRUCE**
Sen, D. and **Ghosh, A.K.**, Ed.
Studies in prehistory: Robert Bruce Foote memorial volume. Calcutta, Firma K.L. Mukhopadhyay, 1966.

36. **GANGOLY, O.C.**
Ganguli, Kalyan Kumar and **Biswas, S.S.**, Ed.
Rupanjali in memory of O.C. Gangoly. Calcutta, O.C. Gangoly Memorial Society, 1986.

37. **GAURINATH SASTRI**
A corpus of Indian studies: Essays in honour of Professor Gaurinath Sastri. Calcutta, Sanskrit Pustak Bhandar, 1980.

38. **GHOSH, A.**
Pande, B.M. and **Chattopadhyaya, B.D.**, Ed.
Archaeology and history: Essays in memory of Shri A. Ghosh. Delhi, Agam Kala Prakashan, 1987.
2 Vols.

39. **GODE, P.K.**
Hariyappa, H.L. and **Patkar, M.M.**, Ed.
Professor P.K. Gode commemoration volume. Poona, Oriental Book Agency, 1960.
3 parts bound together.

40. **GOETZ, HERMANN**
Deppert, Joachim, Ed.
India and the West; proceedings of a seminar dedicated to the memory of Hermann Goetz. New Delhi, Manohar Publications, 1983.

41. **GONDA, J.**
Ensink, J. and **Gaeffke, P.**, Ed.
India maior; congratulatory volume presented to J. Gonda. Leiden, E.J. Brill, 1972.

42. **GUENTHER, HERBERT V.**
Kawamura, Leslie S. and **Scott, Keith**, Ed.
Buddhist thought and Asian civilization: Essays in honor of Herbert V. Guenther on his sixtieth birthdav. California, Dharma Publishing, 1977.

43. **HANDIQUI, KRISHNA KANTA**
Shastri, Biswanarayan and **Choudhury, Pratap Ch.**, Ed.
Abhinandanabharati: Prof. Krishna Kanta Handiqui felicitation volume. Gauhati, Kamarupa Anusandhana Samiti, 1982.

44. **JANI, A.N.**
Datta, B. and others, Ed.
Aruna-Bharati: Professor A.N. Jani felicitation volume; essays in contemporary Indological research. Baroda, Professor A.N. Jani Felicitation Volume Committee, 1983.

45. **JAVADEKAR, A.G.**
Bhatt, S.R., Ed.
Reality, knowledge and value: Essays in honour of Professor A.G. Javadekar. Delhi, Bharatiya Vidya Prakashan, 1985.

46. **JAYAKAR, PUPUL**
Lokesh Chandra and **Jain, Jyotindra**, Ed.
Dimensions of Indian art: Pupul Jayakar seventy. Delhi, Agam Kala Prakashan, 1986.
2 Vols.
Vol. 1: Text.
Vol. 2: Plates.

47. **JAYASWAL, K.P.**
Jha, J.S., Ed.
K.P. Jayaswal commemoration volume. Patna, K.P. Jayaswal Research Institute, 1981.

48. **JHA, ADITYA NATH**
Samskriti: Dr. Aditya Nath Jha abhinandan-grantha. Delhi, Dr. Aditya Nath Jha Abhinandan-Grantha Sanyojan Samiti, 1969.
Vol. 3.

49. **KASHYAP, JAGDISH**
Narain, A.K., Ed.
Studies in Pali and Buddhism: A memorial volume in honor of Bhikkhu Jagdish Kashyap. Delhi, B.R. Publishing Corporation, 1979.

50. **KAVIRAJ, GOPINATH**
Kaviraj abhinandana grantha. Lucknow, Akhil Bharatiya Sanskrit Parishad, 1967.

51. **KESARCODI-WATSON, IAN**
Bilimoria, Purusottama and **Fenner, Peter**, Ed.
Religions and comparative thought: Essays in honour of the late Dr. Ian Kesarcodi-Watson. Delhi, Sri Satguru Publications, 1988.

52. **KHARE, G.H.**
Mate, M.S. and **Kulkarni, G.T.**, Ed.
Studies in Indology and medieval history: Prof. G.H. Khare felicitation volume. Poona, Joshi & Lokhande Prakashan, 1974.

53. **KOSAMBI, D.D.**
Gopal, Lallanji and others, Ed.
D.D. Kosambi commemoration volume. Varanasi, Banaras Hindu University, 1977.

54. **KOSAMBI, D.D.**
Science and human progress: Prof. D.D. Kosambi commemoration volume. Bombay, Popular Prakashan, 1974.

55. **KOSAMBI, D.D.**
Sharma, R.S. and **Jha, Vivekanand**, Ed.
Indian society: Historical probings in memory of D.D. Kosambi. New Delhi, People's Publishing House, 1977.

KRISHNADASA, RAI
See
Chhavi. Vol. 2, under S. No. 22.

56. **KUPPUSWAMI SASTRI, S.**
Janaki, S.S., Ed.
Kuppuswami Sastri birth-centenary commemoration volume. Madras, The Kuppuswami Sastri Research Institute, 1981-85.
2 Vols.

57. **MAINKAR, T.G.**
Deshpande, C.R. and **Chapekar, Nalinee**, Ed.
A homage to Dr. Mainkar; a glimpse into the research work done under his guidance. Dhule, The Editors, 1982.

58. **MAJUMDAR, R.C.**
Sarkar, Himansu Bhusan, Ed.
R.C. Majumdar felicitation volume. Calcutta, Firma K.L. Mukhopadhyay, 1970.

59. **MIRASHI, V.V.**
Deshpande, G.T. and others, Ed.
Felicitation volume: A collection of forty-two Indological essays presented to Dr. V.V. Mirashi. Nagpur, Vidarbha Samshodhan Mandal, 1965.

60. **MISHRA, L.N.**
Thakur, Upendra and **Mishra, Yugal Kishore**, Ed.
The heritage of India: L.N. Mishra commemoration volume. Bodh Gaya, L.N. Mishra Commemoration Volume Publication Committee, 1978.

61. **MISHRA, UMESHA**
Seksena, B.R., Ed.
Umesha Mishra commemoration volume. Allahabad, Ganganatha Jha Research Institute, 1970.

62. **MOOKERJI, SATKARI**
Sinha, B.P. and others, Ed.
Dr. Satkari Mookerji felicitation volume. Varanasi, The Chowkhamba Sanskrit Series Office, 1969.

63. **MORAES, GEORGE MARK**
De Souza, J.P. and **Kulkarni, C.M.**, Ed.
Historiography in Indian language: Dr. George Mark Moraes felicitation volume. Delhi, Oriental Publishers, 1972.

64. **MORLEY, GRACE**
Dwivedi, V.P. and **Pant, G.N.**, Ed.
Museums and Museology: New horizons (Essays in honour of Dr. Grace Morley on her 80th birthday). Delhi, Agam Kala Prakashan, 1980.

65. **MURTI, T.R.V.**
Coward, Harold and **Sivaraman, Krishna**, Ed.
Revelation in Indian thought: A festschrift in honour of Professor T.R.V. Murti. California, Dharma Publishing, 1977.

66. **NILAKANTA SASTRI, K.A.**
K.A. Nilakanta Sastri felicitation volume. Madras, Prof. K.A. Nilakanta Sastri Felicitation Committee, 1971.

67. **PANDEY, LOCHAN PRASAD**
Thakur, Vishnu Singh and others, Ed.
Kosala Kaumudi: Pt. Lochan Prasad Pandey, Sarma birth centenary volume; studies in Indology. Allahabad, Shanti Prakashan, 1988.

68. **PARANAVITANA, SENARAT**
Prematilleke, Leelananda and others, Ed.
Senarat Paranavitana commemoration volume. Leiden, E.J. Brill, 1978.

69. **PARANJPE, V.G.**
Chatterji, Suniti Kumar and others, Ed.
Commemoration volume of Dr. V.G. Paranjpe: Some aspects of Indo-Iranian literary and cultural traditions. Delhi, Ajanta Publications, 1977.

70. **PAWAR, A.G.**
Rao, V.D., Ed.
Studies in Indian history: Dr. A.G. Pawar felicitation volume. Kolhapur, Dr. Appasaheb Pawar Satkar Samiti, 1968.

71. **RAGHAVAN, V.**
Dandekar, R.N. and others, Ed.
Sanskrit and Indological studies: Dr. V. Raghavan felicitation volume. Delhi, Motilal Banarsidass, 1975.

72. **RAGHAVAN, V.**
Dr. V. Raghavan shashtyabdapurti felicitation volume: A souvenir of the 61st birthday celebrations and a collection of essays contributed in his honour by his friends, colleagues and students on that occasion. Madras, Dr. V. Raghavan Shashtyabdapurti Felicitation Committee, 1971.

73. **RAMACHANDRA RAO, S.**
Ramakrishna, G. Ed.
Studies in Indian culture: A volume of essays presented to Professor S. Ramachandra Rao. Bangalore, Professor S. Ramachandra Rao Felicitation Committee, 1986.

74. **RAO, S.R.**
Narasimha Murthi, A.V. and **Gururaja Rao, B.K.**, Ed.
Rangavalli; recent researches in Indology: S.R. Rao felicitation volume. Delhi, Sundeep Prakashan, 1983.

75. **RAY, NIHARRANJAN**
Chattopadhyaya, Debiprasad, Ed.
History and society: Essays in honour of Professor Niharranjan Ray. Calcutta, K.P. Bagchi & Company, 1978.

76. **RAY, NIHARRANJAN**
Ray, Amita and others, Ed.
Indian Studies: Essays presented in memory of Prof. Niharranjan Ray. Delhi, Caxton Publications, (n.d.).

77. **SANKALIA, H.D.**
Deo, S.B. and **Dhavalikar, M.K.**, Ed.
Studies in Indian archaeology: Professor H.D. Sankalia felicitation volume. Bombay, Popular Prakashan, 1985.

78. **SARASWATI, S.K.**
Chakrabarty, Jayanta and **Bhattacharyya, D.C.**, Ed.
Aspects of Indian art and culture: S.K. Saraswati commemoration volume. Calcutta, Rddhi-India, 1983.

79. **SARMA, E.R. SREEKRISHNA**
Surabhi: Sreekrishna Sarma felicitation volume. Tirupati, E.R. Sreekrishna Sarma Felicitation Committee, 1983.

80. **SARMA, K.V.**
Nair, S. Bhaskaran, Ed.
Bharati-bhanam (light of Indology) being K.V. Sarma felicitation volume. Hoshiarpur, Vishveshvaranand Vishva Bandhu Institute of Sanskrit and Indological Studies, 1980.

81. **SATCHIDANANDA MURTY, K.**
Balasubramanian, R. and **Bhattacharyya, Sibajiban**, Ed.
Freedom, progress and society: Essays in honour of Professor K. Satchidananda Murty. Delhi, Motilal Banarsidass, 1986.

82. **SATYA PRAKASH**
Srivastava, Vijai Shankar, Ed.
Cultural contours of India: Dr. Satya Prakash felicitation volume. New Delhi, Abhinav Publications, 1981.

83. **SEN, D.**
Ghosh, Asok, K., Ed.
Perspectives in palaeoanthropology: Professor D. Sen festschrift. Calcutta, Firma K.L. Mukhopadhyay, 1974.

84. **SHASTRI, DHARMENDRA NATH**
Pal, Keshav Ram, Ed.
Dr. D.N. Shastri felicitation volume: Indological studies presented to Dr. Dharmendra Nath Shastri in 85th year of his life by his students, admirers and friends. Ghaziabad, Vimal Prakashan, 1982.

85. **SINGHAL, S.P.**
Handa, Devendra, Ed.
Indological studies: Essays in memory of Shri S.P. Singhal. Delhi, Caxton Publications, 1987.

86. **SINHA, B.P.**
Sahai, Bhagwant, Ed.
History and culture: B.P. Sinha felicitation volume. Delhi, Ramanand Vidya Bhawan, 1987.

87. **SIRCAR, D.C.**
Bhattacharya, Gouriswar, Ed.
Deyadharma: Studies in memory of Dr. D.C. Sircar. Delhi, Sri Satguru Publications, 1986.

88. **SIRCAR, D.C.**
Dasgupta, K.K. and others, Ed.
Sraddhanjali: Studies in ancient Indian history (D.C. Sircar commemoration volume). Delhi, Sundeep Prakashan, 1988.

89. **SIRCAR, D.C.**
Maity, S.K. and **Thakur, Upendra**, Ed.
Indological studies: Prof. D.C. Sircar commemoration volume. New Delhi, Abhinav Publications, 1987.

90. **SIRCAR, D.C.**
Mukherjee, B.N. and others, Ed.
Sri Dinesacandrika; studies in Indology: D.C. Sircar festschrift. Delhi, Sundeep Prakashan, 1983.

91. **SIVARAMAMURTI, C.**
Nagaraja Rao, M.S., Ed.
Kusumanjali, new interpretation of Indian art & culture: C. Sivaramamurti commemoration volume. Delhi, Agam Kala Prakashan, 1987.
2 Vols.

92. **SRIKANTHA SASTRI, S.**
Srikanthika: Dr. S. Srikantha Sastri felicitation volume. Mysore, Geetha Book House, 1973.

93. **SRINIVASAN, K.R.**
Raman, K.V. and others, Ed.
Srinidhih; perspectives in Indian archaeology, art and culture: Shri K.R. Srinivasan festschrift. Madras, New Era Publications, 1983.

94. **STERNBACH, LUDWIK**
Sinha, J.P., Ed.
Ludwik Sternbach felicitation volume. Lucknow, Akhila Bharatiya Sanskrit Parishad, 1979.
2 parts.

95. **UDAYA VIRA SHASTRI**
Varma, K.C. and others, Ed.
Rtambhara; studies in Indology: Acharya Udaya Vira Shastri felicitation volume. Ghaziabad, Society for Indic Studies, 1986.

96. **UPADHYAYA, JAGANNATH**
Samtani, N.H., Ed.
Sramana vidya; studies in Buddhism: Prof. Jagannath Upadhyaya commemoration volume. Sarnath, Central Institute of Higher Tibetan Studies, 1987.
Vol. 1.

97. **VELANKAR, H.D.**
Gajendragadkar, S.N. and **Upadhyaya, S.A.**, Ed.
H.D. Velankar commemoration volume: A volume of Indological studies by his students presented to Prof. H.D. Velankar on the occasion of his seventy-second birthday on 3rd October 1965. Bombay, Prof. H.D. Velankar Commemoration Volume Committee, 1965.

98. **VIVEKANANDA**
Lokesh Chandra and others, Ed.
India's contribution to world thought and culture: Vivekananda commemoration volume. Madras, Vivekananda Rock Memorial Committee, 1970.

99. **WHEELER, MORTIMER**
Lal, B.B. and **Gupta, S.P.**, Ed.
Frontiers of the Indus civilization: Sir Mortimer Wheeler commemoration volume. New Delhi, Books & Books, 1984.

100. **YAZDANI, GHULAM**
Sherwani, H.K., Ed.
Studies in Indian culture: Dr. Ghulam Yazdani commemoration volume. Hyderabad, Maulana Abul Kalam Azad Oriental Research Institute, 1966.

CLASSIFIED SUBJECT INDEX

Biography

ABHEDANANDA

1. **Abhedananda**
   1: 2–11.
2. **Bagchee, Moni**
   Abhedananda: The patriot-saint of India. 1: 655–659.
3. **Chari, C.T.K.**
   Abhedananda and the parapsychological quest for the beyond. 1: 660–668.
4. **Litman, A.D.**
   Abhedananda on the relation between religion, philosophy and science. 1: 691–698.
5. **Lokeswarananda**
   Abhedananda's work in the west. 1: 678–690.
6. **Mitra, Sankar Prasad**
   Abhedananda. 1: 637–654.
7. *Spiritual teachings of Swami Abhedananda.* 1: 12–18.
8. **Sudhanshu, Brahmachari**
   Vedantic biogenesis and pan-psychism of Swami Abhedananda. 1: 669–677.

AGRAWAL, JAGANNATH

9. **Agrawal, Ashvini Kumar**
   Prof. Agrawal on the literary sources of the Gupta history. 3: xxiv–xxvi.
10. **Airi, Raghunath**
    Profile of a celebrated savant. 3: xv–xvii.
11. **Bharadwaj, O.P.**
    Prof. Agrawal: A scholar and a teacher. 3: xviii–xx.
12. *List of publications of Prof. Jagannath Agrawal.* 3: 273–278.
13. **Mittal, Kewal Krishan**
    Prof. Agrawal contribution to Buddhist studies. 3: xxi-xxiii.

ASHRAF, K.M.

14. **Ali, Aruna Asaf**
    (K.M. Ashraf). 4: 378–379.
15. **Anand, Mulk Raj**
    An undelivered letter. 4: 230–231.
16. **Bhawalpuri, Azad**
    (K.M. Ashraf). 4: 375–377.
17. *Condolence meeting.* 4: 386.
18. **Iqbal Singh**
    (K.M. Ashraf). 4: 357–362.
19. *Interview with K.M. Ashraf dated 27th October 1960, recorded by N.L. Gupta.* 4: 412–421.
20. *K.M. Ashraf on himself.* 4: 389–398.
21. *Dr. K.M. Ashraf s Presidential address to the fourth session of the All India Students' Federation held in Calcutta on the 1st January 1939.* 4: 399–402.
22. **Kruger, Horst**
    (K.M. Ashraf). 4: 380–385.
23. **Latifi, Danial**
    (K.M. Ashraf). 4: 368–370.
24. **Namboodiripad, E.M.S.**
    (K.M. Ashraf). 4: 363–364.
25. *Presidential address to the Medieval section of the Indian History Congress, Aligarh, 1960.* 4: 403–411.
26. **Rahbar, Hansray**
    (K.M. Ashraf). 4: 365–367.
27. **Sankrityayan, Rahul**
    (K.M. Ashraf). 4: 349–354.
28. **Sarup Singh**
    (K.M. Ashraf). 4: 371–374.
29. **Tonki, Saiyed Mohammad**
    (K.M. Ashraf). 4: 340–348.
30. **Zaheer, S. Sajjad**
    (K.M. Ashraf). 4: 355–356.

BAJPAI, K.D.

31. *Blessings.* **5 (1):** xii–xvii.
32. *Brief information about Prof. K.D. Bajpai.* **5 (1):** xix–xxi.
33. *Select publications of Prof. K.D. Bajpai.* **5 (1):** xxiii–xxviii.

BARANI, ZIA-UD-DIN

34. **Ray, Sukumar**
    India's historians of old: Barani. **6:** 220–224.

BARUA, B.K.

35. **Agrawala, Bharat Bhushan**
    Bharatiya sahitya ke aatmiya: Dr. Barua. **7:** xxvii–xxx. (Hindi)
36. **Bargohain, Bipin Kumar**
    Birinchi Barua: Reminiscences. **7:** xxxiii–xxxiv.
37. **Barthakur, Anil Ratan**
    Dr. Barua and the W.U.S. **7:** lxxv–lxxvi.
38. **Barua, Bhaben**
    An elegy. **7:** lxxvii.
39. ———
    Jivanar Batat: The story of a society. **7:** xliv–lxiv.
40. ———
    A note on Sevji Patar Kahini and the short stories. **7:** lxv–lxvi.
41. **Barua, Rohini Kanta**
    Dr. B.K. Barua—my reminiscences and a tribute. **7:** xix–xxii.
42. **Basham, A.L.**
    Respect for the memory of Professor Barua. **7:** xvi.
43. **Borooah, Devkanta**
    A writer of the people. **7:** xviii.
44. **Chaudhury, P.D.**
    Birinchi Kumar Barua as I saw him. **7:** xxxviii–xxxix.
45. **Dorson, Richard M.**
    Birinchi Kumar Barua. **7:** xv.
46. **Goswami, Golockchandra**
    B.K.B.: An ex-pupil's reminiscences. **7:** lxxi–lxxiv.
47. **Goswami, Praphulladatta**
    Dr. Barua as a student of folk culture. **7:** xl–xliii.
48. **Kabir, Humayun**
    A leading humanist and scholar. **7:** xvii.
49. **Kakati, Satish Chandra**
    Dr. B.K. Barua as an American saw him. **7:** xxxi–xxxii.
50. **Kripalani, K.R.**
    A humble tribute. **7:** xxvi.
51. **Lahkar, B.C.**
    Dr. Barua as an organiser of educational activities. **7:** lxvii–lxviii.
52. **Machwe, Prabhakar**
    Tribute to a scholar and creative artist. **7:** xxiii–xxv.
53. **Neog, Maheswar**
    A bibliography of the works of Birinchi Kumar Barua. **7:** ix–xiv.
54. ———
    Professor Birinchi Kumar Barua: A life-sketch. **7:** i–viii.
55. **Saikia, Jogendranath**
    Reminiscences of Dr. B.K. Barua. **7:** xxxv–xxxvii.
56. **Sharma, Mukunda Madhava**
    Sri Birinchi Kumar Barua sanstava. **7:** lxxviii (Sanskrit).
57. **Talukdar, Phanindranath**
    Dr. Barua and his varied interests and activities. **7:** lxix–lxx.

BASAVESVARA

58. **Awalikar, Pandit**
    Basavesvara and Tukaram. **8:** 243–250.
59. **Basavaraja, K.R.**
    Basavesvara and his contributions. **92:** 258–266.

60. **Bhat, M. Mariappa**
Basava and Tiruvalluvar. **8:** 217–223.

61. **Chidananda Murty, M.**
Sri Basavesvara and his modern outlook on life. **8:** 109–115.

62. **Desai, P.B.**
Historical places pertaining to Basaveswara. **8:** 459–483.

63. **Diwakar, R.R.**
Message of Sri Basavesvara. **8:** 77–81.

64. **Gajendragadkar, P.B.**
Homage to Basava. **8:** 159–161.

65. **Ganganna, G.M.**
Basavesvara: Saviour of the downtrodden. **8:** 491–494.

66. **Gokak, Vinayak Krishna**
Sri Basavesvara: The universal man. **8:** 43–47.

67. **Gunjal, S.R.,** Comp.
Bibliography. **8:** 497–509.

68. **Halappa, G.S.**
Sri Basavesvara and free thinking. **8:** 145–149.

69. **Hiranmaya**
Basava and Gorakhnath. **8:** 309–323.

70. **Hiremath, R.C.**
Sri Basavesvara: A biography. **8:** 3–30.

71. **Hondius, J.M.**
Significance of Sri Basavesvara's teachings to the world. **8:** 83–84.

72. **Hunashal, S.M.**
Basavesvara and democracy. **8:** 485–489.

73. **IM.**
Sri Basavesvara and Swami Vivekananda as social reformers. **8:** 251–261.

74. **Javali, V.K.**
Kayaka and dignity of labour. **8:** 139–144.

75. **Kalagate, B.M.**
Basava's immortal message. **8:** 163–168.

76. **Kalghatgi, T.G.**
Basava and Mahavira. **8:** 181–190.

77. **Kanavi, Channaveera**
Basavanna's vacanas as literature. **8:** 437–457.

78. **Krishnamoorthy, K.**
Sri Basavesvara and Bhagavadgita. **8:** 101–108.

79. **Kulkarni, V.G.**
Basavesvara and Gandhiji. **8:** 277–286.

80. **Kumara Swamiji**
Sri Basavesvara: A prophet. **8:** 49–59.

81. **Mallappa, T.N.**
Trend of thoughts in vedopanisads and Basavesvara's vacanas. **8:** 85–99.

82. **Malwad, S.S.**
Sri Basavesvara and Sri Aurobindo. **8:** 263–275.

83. **Marulasiddaiah, G.**
Basava the saint-ruler of Karnatak (Mysore). **13:** 232–237.

84. **Menezes, Armando**
Basava and Christ. **8:** 203–215.

85. **Nandimath, S.C.**
Basavesvara in Sanskrit literature. **8:** 409–419.

86. **Rechanna, G.N.**
Basava and Confucius. **8:** 191–201.

87. **Shapeti, S.B.**
The Buddha and Sri Basavesvara. **8:** 171–179.

88. **Shintri, Sarojini**
Basava and womanhood. **8:** 151–157.

89. **Somasundaram, S.**
Basavanna in Tamil literature. **8:** 421–429.

90. **Sunkapur, M.S.**
Sri Basavesvara: A social reformer. **8:** 133–137.

91. **Thammaiah, Bandaru**
Basavesvara in Telugu literature. **8:** 431–435.

92. **Theodore, A. Sunderaraj**
Basavesvara and Manickavasagar. **8:** 225–241.

93. **Tipperudraswamy, H.**
Basavesvara: The revolutionary saint of Karnataka. **92:** 249–257.

94. **Wadiyar, Jayachamaraja**
Sri Basavesvara: A mystic. **8:** 33–42.

95. **Yamunacharya, M.**
Sri Basavesvara's philosophy of life. **8:** 61–75.

BASHAM, A.L.

96. **Derrett, Duncan**
'Bash'—we miss him. **9:** 4–5.

97. *His ailment and death.* **9:** 392–394.

98. **Maity, S.K.**
Professor Arthur Llewellyn Basham—man and Indologist. **9:** 11–18.

99. **Mukherjee, S.N.,** Comp.
Publications of A.L. Basham. **10:** 326–331.

100. **Puri, B.N.**
My friend—Bash. **9:** 7–8.

101. **Puskas, Ildiko**
A.L. Basham—moments of meetings. **9:** 3–4.

102. **Saha, Sushil**
An absorbing moment of Prof. A.L. Basham. **9:** 5.

103. **Sinha, B.P.**
Dr. A.L. Basham—a tribute. **9:** 6–7.

BHANDARKAR, D.R.

104. *Bibliography of published writings.* **11:** 91–108.

105. *Centenary celebrations.* **11:** 111–124.

106. *Extracts from letters.* **11:** 85–88.

107. **Majumdar, R.C.**
D.R. Bhandarkar—the great Indologist. **11:** 29–32.

108. **Puri, B.N.**
D.R. Bhandarkar and Indian historiography. **47:** 419–423.

109. *Reminiscences and tributes.* **11:** 43–81.

110. **Sastri, Sakuntala Rao**
D.R. Bhandarkar as a scholar, archaeological officer and University professor. **11:** 5–28.

111. **Sircar, D.C.**
Epigraphic and numismatic contributions of Devdatta Ramkrishna Bhandarkar. **11:** 33–40.

BHATTA, ASADHARA

112. **Shah, Umakant P.**
A note on Asadhara Bhatta and his works. **71:** 351–359.

BHATTA, KUMARILA

113. **Upadhyaya, Vachaspati**
Kumarila Bhatta—his date, place and works. **37:** 177–184.

BHATTA, NARAYANA

114. **Salomon, Richard**
Biographical data on Narayana Bhatta of Benares. **11:** 326–336.

BHATTACHARYA, KALIDAS

115. **Majumdar, Santwana,** Comp.
List of publications of Professor Kalidas Bhattacharyya. **12:** 212–220.

BHAVABHUTI

116. **Mirashi, V.V.**
Dr. Kane on Bhavabhuti and Umbeka. **13:** 91–94.

BHUYAN, S.K.

117. **Bargohain, Bipin Kumar**
A debt of gratitude which every Assamese owes. **13:** 51–54.

118. **Barua, Bhaben**
S.K. Bhuyan: The poet and the historian. **13:** 59–69.

119. **Bhuyan, Laksheswari**
Remembering my husband. **13:** 45–50.

120. **Bhuyan, Nakulchandra**
Looking back: with Dr. Bhuyan. **13:** 55–58.

121. **Cantlie, Keith**
A tribute. **13:** 37.

122. **Chaudhury, P.D.**
Dr. Bhuyan's association with Kamarupa Anusandhan Samiti and the State Museum. **13:** 70–72.

123. **Dutta, S.K.**
Last days of Dr. Bhuyan. **13:** 39–41.

124. **Kabir, Humayun**
A fine scholar and ardent nationalist. **13:** 38.

125. **Kakati, Banikanta**
Dr. Bhuyan's literary and historical output. **13:** 31–35.

126. **Kripalani, K.R.**
Humble tribute to the noble memory. **13:** 42.

127. **Machwe, Prabhakar**
Tribute to a historian and thinker. **13:** 43–44.

128. **Neog, Maheswar,** Comp.
Bibliography of the writing of Dr. Suryya Kumar Bhuyan. **13:** 10–19.

129. **Neog, Maheswar**
How it struck his contemporaries: Learned opinions about Professor Bhuyan. **13:** 20–30.

130. ———
Professor Suryya Kumar Bhuyan: A life-sketch. **13:** 1–9.

131. **Parija, Prankrishna**
My reminiscences of Dr. Suryya Kumar Bhuyan. **13:** 36.

132. **Sharma, Mukunda Madhava**
Sri Sri Suryya Kumar Bhuyan samarttitarpanam. **13:** 73. (Sanskrit).

BISHNDAS

133. **Das, Asok Kumar**
Bishndas. **22 (1):** 183–191.

BONER, ALICE

134. *Bibliography Alice Boner.* **14:** 7–8.

135. **Danielou, Alain**
Alice Boner and the Indian arts. **14:** 9.

136. **Wuerfel, Alfred**
Alice Boner (1889–1981): On her life and work. **14:** 1–6.

BOSE, NANDALAL

137. **Bhattacharya, Asok K.**
Nandalal Bose and Indian art tradition. **46 (1):** 21–25.

BROWN, W. NORMAN

138. *Bibliography of W. Norman Brown's writings.* **15:** ix–xx.

CALLAWAY, JOHN

139. **Reynolds, C.H.B.**
John Callaway in Ceylon. **68:** 181–190.

CHARU DEVA SHASTRI

140. **Gupta, D.K.**
Creative and critical writings of Prof. Charu Deva Shastri: A critique. **16:** xxv–lix.

141. *Professor Charu Deva Shastri: A biographical sketch.* **16:** xv–xx.

142. **Satya Vrat**
Shastri ji - a scholar and a ṣaint. **16:** xxiii–xxiv.

143. **Triloki Nath**
Homage to a savant. **16:** xxi–xxii.

CHATTOPADHYAYA, K.C.

144. **Sharma, G.R.**
In memoriam. **19:** vii–viii.

145. **Srivastava, V.C.**
Select articles of Pt. K.C. Chattopadhyaya. **19:** ix–xii.

CHATTOPADHYAYA, SUDHAKAR

146. **Banerjee, Tarasankar**
Professor Sudhakar Chattopadhyaya: The man and the scholar. **20:** 17–23.

147. **Jash, Pranabananda**
Sudhakar Chattopadhyaya: The historian. **20:** 1–16.

148. *Principal works of Prof. Sudhakar Chattopadhyaya.* **20:** xi–xii.

CHHABRA, B. CH.

149. **Agam Prasad**
Dr. B. Ch. Chhabra: A biographical sketch. **21:** xiii–xv.

150. *Some outstanding literary contributions of Dr. Chhabra.* **21:** xvii–xxiii.

CHITRAOSHASTRI, M.M.

151. **Bhide, N.K.**
M.M. Chitraoshastri; an appreciation. **23:** iii–x.

152. **Chinmulgund, P.J.**
M.M. Chitraoshastri; a sanskrit scholar. **23:** xvii–xxii.

153. **Dhadphale, G.R.**
M.M. Chitraoshastri; a vedic philosopher. **23:** xxiii–xxviii.

154. **Sankalia, H.D.**
M.M. Chitraoshastri; a born 'Koshakara'. **23:** xi–xv.

CONZE, EDWARD

155. *The works of Edward Conze.* **24:** 421–433.

COOMARASWAMY, ANANDA

156. **Anand, Mulk Raj**
Coomaraswamy darshan. **26:** 8–14.

157. **Ghosh, Nirmal K.**
Ananda K. Coomaraswamy. **1:** 580–584.

158. **Jag Mohan**
Contemporary relevance of Ananda Coomaraswamy. **26:** 164–167.

159. **Kapur, Geeta**
On the vocation of the artist. **26:** 148–153.

160. **Ranganathan, A.**
The relevance of Coomaraswamy and Goetz to the history of ideas—some aesthetic considerations. **40:** 25–43.

161. **Ray, Niharranjan**
The life of Coomaraswamy: An interpretation. **26:** 3–7.

162. **Subramanyan, K.G.**
The significance of Coomaraswamy's ideas in our times. **26:** 15–19.

DANDEKAR, R.N.

163. *Ramachandra Narayan Dandekar.* **27:** v–vii.

164. *Writings of Professor R.N. Dandekar.* **27:** viii-xviii.

DATTA, D.M.

165. **Jha, Hari Mohan**
At the feet of the great guru. **28:** xxiv–xxviii.

166. **Ramjee Singh**
Dhirendra Mohan Datta. **28:** xvii–xxiii.

167. **Wadia, A.R.**
Dr. D.M. Datta: An appreciation. **28:** xxix–xxx.

DE, S.K.

168. *Bibliography of the published writings of S.K. De.* **29:** ix–x.

169. **Guha, P.K.**
Dr. S.K. De as a teacher of English literature. **29:** 254–257.

170. **Majumdar, R.C.**
Susil Kumar De: A reminiscence. **29:** 1–9.

171. *S.K. De: Biographical notes.* **29:** vii–viii.

DESAI, P.B.

172. *Books and articles of Dr. P.B. Desai: A select list.* **30:** 569–579.

173. *Dr. P.B. Desai—a biographical sketch.* **30:** 549–568.

DESHPANDE, M.N.

174. **Dhavalikar, M.K.**
Shri M.N. Deshpande—a biographical sketch. **31:** ix–x.

175. *Shri M.N. Deshpande's literary contributions.* **31:** xi–xii.

DHANAPALA

176. **Gogna, Kamal**
Dhanapala—a literary study. **16:** 429–442.

DIGNAGA

177. **Sankaranarayanan, S.**
Date of Dignaga—fresh light. **87:** 201–208.

DIKSHIT, G.S.

178. **Ritti, Shrinivas**
A teacher par excellence. **32:** 307–312.

179. **Sundara, A.**
Dr. G.S. Dikshit; his work and publications. **32:** 313–320.

DIMOCK, EDWARD C., Jr.

180. **O'Flaherty, Wendy**
Envoi. **33:** 172–173.

ELPHINSTONE, MOUNTSTUART

181. **Datta, V.N.**
Mountstuart Elphinstone: His training, method and intellectual system. **4:** 176–186.

ELWIN, VERRIER

182. **Pradhan, M.C.**
Bibliography of Verrier Elwin. **34:** 311–318.

183. ———
Verrier Elwin as anthropologist. **34:** 1–39.

FLEET, J.F.

184. **Nagaraju, S.**
The place of J.F. Fleet in western contributions to Indological studies **73:** 327–337.

FOOTE, R.B.

185. *Robert Bruce Foote.* **35:** vii–viii.

GALANOS, DEMETRIUS

186. **Zannas, Eliki**
Greek contribution to Sanskrit studies; Demetrius Galanos 1760–1833. **56 (2):** 269–278.

GANGOLY, O.C.

187. **Anand, Mulk Raj**
Dear good friend—O.C. Gangoly. **36:** 17–18.

188. **Bose, Sudha**
O.C. Gangoly, the master as I saw him. **36:** 23–34.

189. **Chattopadhyay, Kamaladevi**
O.C. Gangoly—a tribute. **36:** 13–15.

190. **Chunder, P.C.**
O.C. Gangoly, Esq., Attorney-at-law. **36:** 35–36.

191. **Datta, Bimal Kumar**
O.C. Gangoly as I saw him as Professor. **36:** 19–21.

192. **Gangoly, Srihari**
O.C. Gangoly: The man and his contribution to art and culture. **36:** 9–12.

GAURINATH SASTRI

193. **Basham, A.L.**
A tribute. **37:** 413–414.

194. *Short life-sketch & a selected bibliography of the works of Professor Gaurinath Sastri.* **37:** 415–416.

GHOSH, A.

195. **Jain, S.P.**
Remembering A. Ghosh. **38 (1):** liii–lv.

196. **Joshi, M.C.**
Memories of Shri A. Ghosh. **38 (1):** xlv–xlvii.

197. **Khanna, Amar Nath**
Life, publications and some views of Shri Amalananda Ghosh. **38 (1):** xli–xliv.

198. *List of publications of Shri A. Ghosh.* **38 (1):** xxxv–xxxix.

199. **Srinivasan, L.K.**
Shri A. Ghosh—a lovable personality. **38 (1):** xlix–li.

GODE, P.K.

200. *Bibliography of the published writings of P.K. Gode.* **39:** xix–xlvi.

201. **Kunhan Raja, C.**
Gode pancakam. **39:** liii. (Sanskrit).

202. ———
Message of greetings. **39:** lii.

203. **Patkar, M.M.**
Parashuram Krishna Gode. **39:** xiii–xviii.

204. **Raghavan, V.**
Prof. P.K. Gode. **39:** l–li.

205. **Rangaswami Aiyangar, K.V.**
Professor P.K. Gode—an appreciation. **39:** xlviii.

206. **Sahu, L.N.**
P.K. Gode. **39:** lvii–lix.

207. **Sarma, R. Nagaraj**
Acarya-Gode-prasasti-padya-naksatramala. **39:** liv–lvi. (Sanskrit).

208. **Vishva Bandhu**
An appreciation of Professor P.K. Gode. **39:** lx–lxi.

GOETZ, HERMANN

209. **Kulke, Hermann**
Life and work of Hermann Goetz. **40:** 13–23.

210. **Ranganathan, A.**
The relevance of Coomaraswamy and Goetz to the history of ideas—some aesthetic considerations. **40:** 25–43.

GONDA, J.

211. **Chemparathy, G.**
Bibliography of publications by J. Gonda. **41:** 1–40.

GORAKHNATH

212. **Chaturvedi, Parashu Ram**
Guru Gorakhnath ke samaya ka nirupana. **50:** 385–394. (Hindi)

GUENTHER, H.V.

213. *Herbert V. Guenther's publications.* **42:** xiii–xviii.

GUNARATNA SURI

214. **Matilal, Bimal Krishna**
Gunaratna Suri as a commentator of Sasadhara. **11:** 297–302.

HANDIQUI, K.K.

215. **Sattar, Abdus**
Professor Krishna Kanta Handiqui as a man and a scholar. **43:** 201–206.

216. **Sharma, Jajneswar**
Professor Handiqui's writings in Assamese. **43:** 207–210.

217. **Shastri, Biswanarayan**
Professor Handiqui's contribution to the study of Indology. **43:** 211–228.

218. **Talukdar, Nanda**
Professor Krishna Kanta Handiqui: A bio-bibliographical note. **43:** 229–232.

JANI, A.N.

219. *A.N. Jani: A profile.* **44:** xvii–xviii.

220. *List of important publications.* **44:** xix–xxii.

JAVADEKAR, A.G.

221. *Prof. A.G. Javadekar's publications.* **45:** 247–258.

222. **Javadekar, Pradnya Anant**
Prof. A.G. Javadekar's bio-data. **45:** 235–246.

JAYAKAR, PUPUL

223. **Anand, Mulk Raj**
Journey into the interior. **46 (1):** xxi–xxii.

224. **Bhattacharya, Ruby**
A bibliography of Smt. Pupul Jayakar's works. **46 (1):** xliii–xliv.

225. **Brook, Peter**
All roads lead to Pupul Jayakar. **46 (1):** xxiii.

226. **Jha, L.K.**
Pupul Jayakar: An explorer. **46 (1):** xxv–xxix.

227. **Malvika Singh**
The tapestry of her life. **46 (1):** xv–xix.

228. **Martand Singh**
Pupul Jayakar: A banyan tree. **46 (1):** xli.

229. **Nehru, B.K.**
Pupul Jayakar: A distinguished citizen of India. **46 (1):** xxxi.

230. **Norman, Dorothy**
The radiance of Pupul Jayakar. **46 (1):** xxxiii–xxxiv.

231. **Patwardhan, Achyut**
The two streams. **46 (1):** xxxv–xxxvi.

232. **Rao, Raja**
Pupul. **46 (1):** xxxvii–xxxviii.

233. **Sethi, Rajiv**
A tribute to Mrs. Pupul Jayakar. **46 (1):** xxxix.

JAYASWAL, K.P.

234. **Dinkar, Ramdhari Singh**
Punyashlok Jayaswalji. **47:** 13–22. (Hindi).

235. **Jayaswal, Sushila**
Mere Pujya pita Sri Kashi Prasad Jayaswal. **47:** 56–58. (Hindi).

236. *Late Dr. K.P. Jayaswal: Tribute paid by the Patna University Senate.* **47:** 73–79.

237. **Manuk, P.C.**
Dr. K.P. Jayaswal—the barrister and man: A character sketch. **47:** 46–53.

238. **Rajendra Prasad**
Kashi Prasad Jayaswal. **47:** 44–45.

239. **Rajendra Ram**
Life and work of Kashi Prasad Jayaswal (27 November 1881—4 August 1937). **47:** 59–72.

240. **Sankratyayana, Rahul**
Dr. Kashi Prasad Jayaswal. **47:** 1–12. (Hindi).

241. ———
Dr. Kashi Prasad Jayaswal. **47:** 54–55. (Hindi).

242. **Sinha, B.P.**
Kashi Prasad Jayaswal. **47:** 31–43.

243. **Sinha, Chitta Ranjan Prasad**
Works of K.P. Jayaswal. **47:** 80–84.

244. **Sinha, Sachidananda**
Kashi Prasad Jayaswal. **47:** 27–30.

245. **Uma Shankar**
Dr. Kashi Prasad Jayaswal (1881–1937). **47:** 23–26. (Hindi).

JHA, A.N.

246. *Adityanath Jha.* **48:** 14–15.

247. **Bipin Chandra**
Some personal glimpses. **48:** 11–13.

248. **De Mellow, Melville**
Tribute to Mr. A.N. Jha. **48:** 6–8.

249. **Deshmukh, C.D.**
A model administrator. **48:** 5.

250. **Gopi Nath**
Dr. Aditya Nath Jha. **48:** 9.

251. **Rao, Chalapati**
Dr. Jha: A sketch. **48:** 3–4.

252. **Sahay, Vishnu**
Michael Angelo of Indian Civil Service. **48:** 10.

253. **Singh, P.N.**
H.E. Dr. A.N. Jha—Some reminiscences of a friend of the family. **48:** 16–18.

KANT, I.

254. **Kruse, Cornelius**
Immanuel Kant as a spokesman for philosophy's concern for perpetual peace. **28:** 172–188.

KASHYAP, BHIKKHU JAGDISH

255. **Narain, A.K.**
Bhikkhu Jagdish Kashyap: A biography. **49:** xv–xxxii.

KAVINDRACARYA SARASVATI

256. **Chanana, Dev Raj**
Kavindracarya Sarasvati—a problem of scholarship and personal integrity. **62:** 242–254.

KAVIRAJ, GOPINATH

257. **Bhattacharya, S.**
Kaviraj ji as I know him. **50:** 511–515.

258. **Chaturvedi, Narmadeshwar, Ramashram** and **Bhattacharya, Ram Shankar,** Comp.
Works of Dr. Gopinath Kaviraj. **50:** 593–611.

259. **Dravid, Rajeshwar Shastri**
Sriguru sharanam. **50:** 516–517. (Sanskrit).

260. **Jha, Aditya Nath**
Sraddhaya Kaviraja ji—some memories. **50:** 542.

261. **Malaviya, Ram Kuber**
Abhinandanam. **50:** 587–589. (Sanskrit).

262. **Mishra, Baldeva**
Kaviraj ji: Katipaya sansmaran. **50:** 524–529. (Hindi).

263. **Mukhopadhyay, Govind Gopal**
Gopinath Kaviraj: Reminiscences. **50:** 543–546.

264. **Pandey, Yogesh**
Kaviraj ji ki mahta. **50:** 540–541. (Hindi).

265. **Sampurnanand**
Sanskrit-jagat ki vibhuti Pandit Gopinath Kaviraj. **50:** 523. (Hindi).

266. **Shastri, Dharmendra Nath**
Kaviraj ji: Ek Vidwan ke rup me. **50:** 585–586. (Hindi).

267. **Shukla, Govardhan Nath**
Mahamahopadhyaya Gopinath Kaviraj ji ka vidya-vayasan. **50:** 522. (Hindi).

268. **Singh, Bhagwati Prasad**
Ghane prem taru tale. **50:** 537–539. (Hindi).

269. ———
Kaviraj ji: Jivan aur Sadhana **50:** 547–573. (Hindi).

270. **Sinha, Gopal Chandra**
Mahamahopadhyaya Pandit Gopinath Kaviraj—a life sketch. **50:** 574–584.

271. **Tripathi, Rammurti**
Jaiye, bhajan kijie. **50:** 534–536. (Hindi).

272. **Upadhyaya, Baldeva**
Kaviraj ji ke katipaya sansmaran. **50:** 530–531. (Hindi).

273. **Varma, Vishwanath Prasad**
Apaar gyanrashi ke sath hi sadhana ke dhani—Kaviraj ji. **50:** 532–533. (Hindi).

KESARCODI-WATSON, IAN

274. **Bailey, Greg**
Introduction: Random reflections on Ian Kesarcodi-Watson. **51:** ix–xiii.

275. **Bilimoria, Purusottama** and **Bailey, Greg**
Bibliography of Dr. Ian Kesarcodi-Watson. **51:** xv–xvii.

KIPLING, LOCKWOOD

276. **Archer, Mildred**
Lockwood Kipling: Champion of Indian arts and crafts. **46 (1):** 7–12.

KOSAMBI, D.D.

277. **Arguimbau, Lawrence B.**
"Baba" of Harvard days. **54:** 318–321.

278. **Banerjee, A.K.**
D.D.K.: A rough diamond. **54:** 311–317.

279. **Basham, A.L.**
"Baba" : A personal tribute. **55:** 16–19.

280. **Bernal, J.D.**
D.D. Kosambi. **54:** 331–334.

281. **Birkhoff**
Extract from the tribute. **54:** 349.

282. **Deshmukh, C.D.**
Extract from the tribute. **54:** 344.

283. **Gokhale, V.V.**
Damodar Dharmanand Kosambi. **54:** 361–364.

284. ———
Damodar Dharmanand Kosambi. **55:** 1–15.

285. **Habibullah**
Tramping with Kosambi through history. **54:** 327–330.

286. **Ingalls, Daniel H.H.**
My friendship with D.D. Kosambi. **55:** 20–33.

287. **Khan, Namdar**
Extract from the tribute. **54:** 345–348.

288. **Madgavkar, Kusum**
Kosambi's world view. **54:** 350-355.

289. **Nene, R.P.**
Bibliography of Kosambi's writings. **54:** 365–375.

290. **Prasad, B.K.R.**
Notes and reminiscences about Prof. D.D. Kosambi. **54:** 322–326.

291. *Prof. D.D. Kosambi: A brief chronology of major events.* **54:** 309–310.

292. **Riepe, Dale**
D.D. Kosambi: Father of scientific Indian history. **55:** 34–44.

293. **Saklatwala, Beram**
A tribute in verse. **54:** 356–360.

294. **Sankalia, H.D.**
The late Prof. D.D. Kosambi. **54:** 335–337.

295. **Seidel, W.**
Extract from the tribute. **54:** 343.

296. **Siddiqi, M. Raziuddin**
Some personal reminiscences of Prof. Kosambi. **54:** 340–342.

297. **Vasudeva Murthy, A.R.**
Kosambi's approach to human problems. **54:** 338–339.

KUPPUSWAMI SASTRI, S.

298. **Raghavan, V.**
Prof. S. Kuppuswami Sastri. **56 (1):** iii–xiii.

299. **Ramakrishna Bhat, N.**
Gurucaritam. **56 (1):** iii–xlviii. (Sanskrit).

MADHVACARYA

300. **Venkatarayacharya**
Srimadhvacaryajivanakalavicarah. **39 (3):** 219–223. (Sanskrit).

MAINKAR, T.G.

301. **Chapekar, Nalinee**
A homage. **57:** xv–xx.

302. *T.G. Mainkar: Biodata and bibliography.* **57:** xxi–xxvii.

MAJUMDAR, KHITINDRANATH

303. **Appasamy, Jaya**
Khitindranath Majumdar. **22 (1):** 218–223.

MAJUMDAR, R.C.

304. **Mukherjee, B.N.**
Acarya Sri Rames Candra Majumdar: A biographical sketch. **58:** v–viii.

305. *A select list of the published works of R.C. Majumdar.* **58:** 269–282.

MIRASHI, V.V.

306. **Aney, M.S.**
A few words about Mirashi **59:** xxviii–xxx.

307. *Bibliography of Dr. Mirashi's writings.* **59:** xlix–lxx.

308. **Deshpande, Y.K.**
Dr. Mirashi's sckolarship. **59:** xxxiii–xxxviii.

309. *Mahamahopadhyaya-Mirashi-prashasa-taya.* **59:** xli–xliv. (Sanskrit).

310. **Niyogi, M. Bhavanishankar**
Dr. Mirashi at work. **59:** xxxi–xxxii.

311. **Shastri, Ajay Mitra**
A life sketch of Mahamahopadhyaya Dr. V.V. Mirashi. **59:** xxi–xxvii.

312. *Text of the Copper plate presented to Dr. Mirashi.* **59:** xxxix–xxxx. (Sanskrit).

313. *What scholars say.* **59:** xlv–xlviii.

MISHRA, L.N.

314. **Das, Jata Shankar**
Lalit Narayan Mishra—a tribute. **60:** 35–36.

315. **Jain, Dharam Chand**
Lalit Narayan Mishra—as I knew him. **60:** 30.

316. **Jha, Ramakant**
Lalit—my comrade-in-arms. **60:** 37–38.

317. **Mishra, Jagannath**
Lalit Babu: A tribute to his memory. **60:** 25–29.

318. **Mishra, Madaneshwar**
The Lalit Babu I knew. **60:** 31–34.

319. **Mishra, Yugal Kishore**
A leading light: A brief life-sketch of L.N. Mishra. **60:** 15–23.

320. **Thakur, Upendra**
Shri Lalit Narayan Mishra. **60:** 7–14.

MISHRA, UMESHA

321. *A list of the works of Mahamahopadhyaya Dr. Umesha Mishra.* **61:** xi–xvi.

322. *Important dates in the life of Mahamahopadhyaya Dr. Umesha Mishra.* **61:** 1–3.

323. *Messages and tributes.* **61:** 7–22.

MISRA, GODAVARA

324. **Das, Sridhar**
Life and works of Pandita Godavara Misra. **39:** 63–67.

MISRA, VACASPATI

325. **Sankaranarayanan, S.**
Date and patron of Vacaspati Misra—a new study. **32:** 227–234.

MOLA RAM

326. **Mukandi Lal**
Documentary evidence on Mola Ram. **48:** 51–67.

MOOKERJEE, SATKARI

327. **Jaiswal, O.P.**
Dr. Satkari Mookerjee. **62:** xxv–xxix.

MORAES, G.M.

328. **David, M.D.**
A bibliography of the works of Dr. Moraes. **63:** 265–270.

329. ———
Dr. George Mark Moraes; a biographical sketch. **63:** vii–xiv.

MORLEY, GRACE

330. **Banerjee, P.**
Dr. Grace Morley as the Director of the National Museum, New Delhi (1960–1966). **64:** 317–321.

331. **Dwivedi, V.P.** and **Pant, G.N.**
Dr. Grace Morley: Post-National Museum period (1966–1979). **64:** 323–324.

332. **Sharma, S.**
List of Dr. Grace Morley's publications. **64:** 325–330.

333. **Sivaramamurti, C.**
Dr. (Mrs.) Grace L. McCann Morley as I know her. **64:** 313–316.

334. **Vatsyayan, Kapila**
Dr. Grace Morley: Some personal glimpses. **64:** 309–312.

MURTI, T.R.V.

335. *Complete bibliography of the writings of Professor T.R.V. Murti.* **65:** 191–193.

336. **Coward, Harold G.**
Academic biography of Professor T.R.V. Murti. **65:** xii–xvii.

NILAKANTA SASTRI, K.A.

337. *About Professor K.A. Nilakanta Sastri.* **66:** i–v.

338. *Prof. Sastri's contributions.* **66:**vii–xxiv.

PANDEY, LOCHAN PRASAD

339. **Thakur, Vishnu Singh** and **Tiwari, Nand Kishor**
Late Pt. Lochan Prasad Pandey: A biographical sketch. **67:** i–xi.

PANT, G.B.

340. **Jha, A.N.**
A tribute to Pandit Govind Ballabh Pant. **48:** 39–40.

PARANAVITANA, SENARAT

341. **Goonetileke, H.A.I.**
A bibliography of the published writings of Senarat Paranavitana. **68:** 1–19.

342. *Senarat Paranavitana.* **68:** ix–xi.

PARANJPE, V.G.

343. **Mainkar, T.G.**
Dr. Vasudeva Gopal Paranjpe. **69:** 1–4.

PARVANIKAR, SITARAMA

344. **Sarma, M. Madhava Krishna**
Sitarama Parvanikar. **39 (3):** 181–184.

PAWAR, A.G.

345. **Ithape, Usha**
Dr. A.G. Pawar: A biographical sketch. **70:** xi–xvi.

RAGHAVAN, V.

346. **Anjaneyulu, D.**
An integrated scholar. **72:** 353–359.

347. **Bowers, Faubion**
Books: Four by Raghavan. **72:** 348–352.

348. *Dr. V. Raghavan.* **72:** ix–x.

349. *Dr. V. Raghavan: Work and bibliography 1969.* **71:** 541–573.

350. **Khoroche, Peter**
Dr. V. Raghavan—a profile. **71:** 537–540.

351. **Satya Vrat**
His other poems. **72:** 325–347.

352. **Venkatarama Aiyar, T.L.**
Raghavan—the poet. **72:** 317–324.

RAJASEKHARA

353. **Shastri, Ajay Mitra**
Rajasekhara, Tripuri and the Kalacuris. **11:** 347–360.

RAMACHANDRA RAO, S.

354. *A portrait of our Professor.* **73:** 339–351.

RAMAKRISHNA

355. **Chakraborty, Nirod Baran**
Sri Ramakrishna and his spiritual message. **1:** 612–619.

356. **Gambhirananda**
Sri Ramakrishna: Humanity's past, present and future. **1:** 605–611.

RAMARAYA, BELLAMKONDA

357. **Lalye, P.G.**
Bellamkonda Ramaraya: An introduction to a twentieth century poet. **44:** 309–313.

RAO, S.R.

358. **Nagaraj Rao, Nalimi**
Dr. S.R. Rao and career. **74:** 335–338.

359. **Raghunath Bhat, H.R.**
Dr. S.R. Rao and his works. **74:** 339–343.

360. *Reports, books and articles by Dr. S.R. Rao.* **74:** 345–347.

RAY, NIHARRANJAN

361. *An interview with Niharranjan Ray.* **75:** 613–632.

362. *Bibliography of Niharranjan Ray.* **75:** 633–640.

363. **Vatsyayana, Kapila**
Niharranjan Ray (1903–1981). **76:** 3–6.

SANKALIA, H.D.

364. *Bio-data of Professor H.D. Sankalia.* **77:** i–xv.

SARASWATI, S.K.

365. **Chakrabarti, Jayanta**
A profile of the scholar. **78:** xii–xiv.

366. **Gupta, D.P.**
A personal reminiscence. **78:** xiv–xv.

367. **Nag, Dilip Kumar**
A short life-sketch. **78:** ix–xii.

368. ———
Select Publications. **78:** xv–xviii.

SARMA, E.R. SREEKRISHNA

369. *E.R. Sreekrishna Sarma.* **79:** 1–4.

SARMA, K.V.

370. **Bindra, Trilochan Singh**
Bibliography of the writings of Dr. K.V. Sarma. **80:** 7–12.

371. **Nair, S. Bhaskaran**
Dr. K.V. Sarma: A profile. **80:** 3–6.

SATYA PRAKASH

372. **Bedekar, V.H.**
An ideal museologist. **82:** 88–89.

373. *Bibliography of publications of Dr. Satya Prakash.* **82:** 159–182.

374. **Chaturvedi, P.D.**
An ideal teacher. **82:** 101–102.

375. **Chaturvedi, Yugal Kishore**
Hindi ke ananya sevi evam sahityakar-kavi roop me. **82:** 103–105. (Hindi).

376. **Dwivedi, V.P.**
An ideal museologist. **82:** 91.

377. **Harinarayana, N.**
An ideal museologist. **82:** 93.

378. **Jagdhari, A.K.**
Contribution: Dr. Satya Prakash—Museums of Rajasthan. **82:** 59–70.

379. **Khan, Shaukat Ali**
The beacon of Rajasthan's history. **82:** 96–98.

380. **Krishna Prakash Lal** and **Gyan Prakash**
Our father: Biographical profile. **82:** 1–18.

381. **Mathur, M.S.**
An ideal museologist. **82:** 92.

382. **Mehta, J.S.**
A dedicated life in the preservation of Rajasthan's cultural heritage. **82:** 94–95.

383. **Morley, Grace**
An ideal museologist. **82:** 87–88.

384. *Personal reminiscences: Bouquet of sweet memories.* **82:** 109–158. (Hindi, English and Sanskrit).

385. *Dr. Satya Prakash as research-guide.* **82:** 183–185.

386. **Sharma, Hazari Lal**
Sanskriti ke udghoshak roop me. **82:** 106–107. (Hindi).

387. **Sharma, R.G.**
Contribution: Dr. Satya Prakash—History and culture. **82:** 75–86.

388. **Srivastava, Vijai Shankar**
Contribution: Dr. Satya Prakash—archaeology and art. **82:** 47–58.

389. **Tiwari, Lalit Shankar**
An ideal research guide. **82:** 99–100.

390. **Varma, D.N.**
An ideal museologist. **82:** 89–91.

391. *Contribution: Dr. Satya Prakash—Salar Jung Museum.* **82:** 71–74.

SAUNAKA

392. **Sharma, Umesh Chandra**
Acarya Saunaka. **44:** 183–187.

SEN, KESHAB CHANDRA

393. **Nath, Dwijendra Lal**
Brahmananda Keshab Chandra Sen. **1:** 439–444.

SHASTRI, D.N.

394. *Articles of Dr. D.N. Shastri.* **84:** xxxv–xxxvi.

395. **Pal, Keshav Ram**
Shastri ji ke vyaktittva evam krititva se samabandhit katipay ullekhniya tathya. **84:** xxvii–xxxiv. (Hindi).

396. **Pramod Kumar**
Life and works of Dr. Dharmendra Nath Shastri. **84:** xiii–xviii.

397. **Tyagi, B.S.**
Dr. Shastri's magnum opus. **84:** xix–xxiv.

398. **Ved Vyas**
Dr. Dharmendra Nath Shastri. **84:** xxv–xxvi.

SINGHAL, S.P.

399. **Shastri, Ajay Mitra**
Late Shri Swadesh Prasad Singhal: A friend's tribute. **85:** xxvii–xxviii.

400. **Tiwari, S.P.**
A biographical sketch of Sh. S.P. Singhal. **85:** xxiii–xxv.

SINHA, B.P.

401. **Jamuar, Bipin Kumar**
Publications of Dr. B.P. Sinha. **86:** xxxv–xl.

402. **Sinha, Chitta Ranjan Prasad**
Dr. B.P. Sinha—career and contributions. **86:** xxii–xxxiv.

SIRCAR, D.C.

403. **Bhattacharyya, Pranab Kumar**
Dr. Dinesh Chandra Sircar (1907–1985). **88:** 1–8.

404. **Bhattacharyya, P.K.**, Comp.
List of papers by D.C. Sircar on inscriptions and epigraphy & palaeography. **88:** 411–428.

405. *Dineschandra Sircar: A biographical sketch.* **90:** 1–63.

406. **Maity, S.K.**
Professor D.C. Sircar: Man and Indologist. **89:** 151–187.

407. **Sohoni, S.V.**
Dr. D.C. Sircar—a tribute. **89:** 149–150.

408. **Thakur, Upendra**
Reminiscences. **89:** 189.

SIVARAMAMURTI, C.

409. **Anand, Mulk Raj**
A letter to an illustrious friend. **91 (1):** 5–7.

410. **Chattopadhyay, Kamaladevi**
Dr. Calambur Sivaramamurti: A tribute. **91 (1):** 9–10.

411. **Morley, Grace**
C. Sivaramamurti—scholar, writer and Museum professional. **91 (1):** 1–3.

412. **Soundara Rajan, K.V.**
Unique upasaka of Bharati—Shri Sivaramamurti: A profile in tribute. **91 (1):** 11–13.

SRIKANTHA SASTRI, S.

413. **Ananthanarayana, S.**
The votary of truth. **92:** 351–369.

414. *Bibliography.* **92:** 383–392.

415. **Gopal, B.R.**
Dr. Sastri's works in Kannada **92:** 378–382.

416. **Murthy, P.N.N.**
Dr. S. Srikantha Sastri—a biographical sketch. **92:** 345–350.

417. **Sheik Ali, B.**
Dr. Srikantha Sastri as a historian. **92:** 370–377.

SRINIVASAN, K.R.

418. **Banerjee, N.R.**
Helpful colleague. **93:** 479–480.

419. **Deshpande, M.N.**
The tallest among art historians. **93:** 477–478.

420. **Khanna, Amar Nath**
An expert conservationist. **93:** 487–489.

421. *K.R. Srinivasan: A brief sketch.* **93:** 473–475.

422. *K.R. Srinivasan: Bio-data.* **93:** 467.

423. *K.R. Srinivasan: List of publications.* **93:** 469–472.

424. **Raman, K.V.**
A scientist turned archaeologist. **93:** 481–483.

425. **Sthapathy, Ganapathy**
A great teacher. **93:** 485–486.

STERNBACH, LUDWIK

426. **Altuchow, Nicholas**
Three encounters. **94 (1):** 5–7.

427. **Bhargava, P.L.**
My reminiscences of Professor Sternbach. **94 (1):** 9–10.

428. **De Mora, Juan Miguel**
Ludwik Sternbach. **94 (1):** 11.

429. **Lacombe, Olivier**
My reminiscences about the great scholar Dr. L. Sternbach. **94 (1):** 13–14.

430. **Pobozniak, T.**
My reminiscences about Dr. Ludwik Sternbach. **94 (1):** 15–16.

431. **Satyavrat Shastri**
Poland ke ek vyovrdha Bharatiya vidya—vishesajna: Prof. Ludwik Sternbach. **94 (1):** 17–19. (Hindi).

432. **Sinha, Gopal Chandra**
A few hours with Prof. Sternbach. **94 (2):** 921–923.

433. **Sinha, J.P.**
Bibliography of works by Dr. Ludwik Sternbach. **94 (1):** 25–26.

434. ———
Prof. Sternbach—as I know him. **94 (1):** 21–24.

435. ———
Supplement to the bibliography of works by Dr. L. Sternbach. **94 (2):** 925–926.

436. **Tripathi, Ram Narayana**
Abhinandanam. **94 (1):** 1. (Sanskrit).

STOKES, H.N.

437. **Santucci, James A.**
H.N. Stokes' early contact with the Theosophical Society. **9:** 340–353.

SU

438. **Thaplyal, Kiran Kumar**
King Su of the Maukhari dynasty. **11:** 386–390.

SUBHAGANANDA

439. **Sarma, K.V.**
Subhagananda Natha alias Sri Kantha: A Kerala tantricist of the 17th century. **39 (3):** 185–188.

UDAYACANDRA

440. **Mahalingam, T.V.**
Udayacandra—a great Pallava general. **11:** 286–296.

UDAYANACARYA

441. **Thakur, Anantalal**
Udayanacarya and his contribution. **16:** 400–406.

UDAYAVIRA SHASTRI

442. **Bharatiya, Bhawani Lal**
Pt. Udayavira Shastri ki saaraswata—saadhana. **95:** 12–13. (Hindi).

443. **Pandeya, Sangam Lal**
Udaya Vira Shastri: Hindi manisha ki praudhta. **95:** 14–17. (Hindi).

444. **Rai, Jaya Chandra**
Acarya Udaya Vira Shastri: Jiwana-parichaya. **95:** 3–7. (Hindi).

445. **Tanaji, B.**
Sansamarniyame Acharyavayah. **95:** 10–11. (Sanskrit).

446. **Vohra, Durga Devi**
Acarya ji meri drishti mein. **95:** 8–9. (Hindi).

UPADHYAYA, JAGANNATH

447. *A dialogue between J. Krishnamurti and Pandit Jagannath Upadhyaya.* **96:** 5–15.

447A. **Jayakar, Pupul**
Panditji. **96:** 3–4.

448. *Professor Jagannath Upadhyaya: Academic profile.* **96:** 385–390.

449. *Published works of Professor Jagannath Upadhyaya.* **96:** 391–396.

450. **Samtani, N.H.**
Upadhyayaji: Acarya extraordinary. **96:** 16–19.

VAMKALAKACARYA

451. **Upadhye, A.N.**
Vamkalakacarya: A forgotten authority on astrology. **39 (3):** 203–208.

VELANKAR, H.D.

452. **Gajendragadkar, S.N.**
Prof. H.D. Velankar: An appreciation. **97:** 1–3.

VIVEKANANDA

453. **Avinashilingam, T.S.**
Swami Vivekananda on education. **98:** 677–684.

454. **Das Gupta, Santwana**
Socio-religious thoughts of Swami Vivekananda. **1:** 385–414.

455. **Gambhirananda, Swami**
Worship of the God in man. **98:** 685–691.

456. **Joshi, M.C.**
Self-renewal in Indian history and Swami Vivekananda. **98:** 692–702.

457. **Ranganathananda, Swami**
Swami Vivekananda: India's emissary to the west. **98:** 649–676.

YAGNIK, MULSHANKAR

458. **Jani, A.N.**
Mulshankar Yagnik—his life and works. **3:** 147–149.

YAZDANI, GHULAM

459. **Devkar, V.L.**
Dr. Yazdani's contribution to the Salar Jung Museum. **100:** 33–34.

460. **Joshi, R.M.**
Dr. Yazdani's contribution to archaeology. **100:** 16–25.

461. **Yazdani, Ali**
Life sketch of Dr. Yazdani, his family history and tributes from well known personages. **100:** 3–15.

462. **Yazdani, Masood**
A select bibliography of Dr. Yazdani's works. **100:** 26–32.

Geography

463. **Agrawala, V.S.**
Ancient Indian geography. **23:** 235–247.

464. ———
Narayana as ocean (Narayana Maharnavah). **17:** 180–183.

465. **Ahmad, Enayat**
Occupational structure of the Himalayan population. **60:** 98–102.

466. **Awasthi, A.B.L.**
Ancient Indian cartography. **62:** 275–278.

467. **Bajpai, K.D.**
The location of Ramagiri. **89:** 31–34.

468. **Bhattacharje, Aparna**
River communication in north Bihar a hundred years ago. **60:** 92–97.

469. **Chauhan, D.V.**
Bhaskaracharya's Vijjalavida is Bid town. **52:** 42–48.

470. **Deshpande, Madhav**
Rajasekhara on ethnic and linguistic geography of India. **84:** 312–327.

471. **Jain, K.C.**
Identification of the ancient Bhaddilapura. **5 (1):** 103–104.

472. **Katti, Madhav N.**
Thoughts on the historical geography of the South. **36:** 133–134.

473. **Kotraiah, C.T.M.**
Pampa Sarassu and Hampi. **36:** 239–243.

474. **Law, Bimal Churn**
The river Aciravati. **39:** 233–235.

475. **Manager Prasad**
Sugar industry in Bihar—a geographical survey. **60:** 113–120.

476. **Mehendale, M.A.**
Mount Nadoda—old name of Ramagiri. **71:** 251–256.

477. **Mehta, R.N.** and **Jamindar, Rasesh**
Precursors of Ahmadabad: Asaval and Karnavati. **85:** 355–359.

478. **Mirashi, V.V.**
The birth-place of Bhavabhuti. **17:** 184–191.

479. ———
Location of Devagiri described in Kalidasa's meghaduta. **50:** 418–422.

480. **Mohinder Singh**
The five villages demanded by the Pandavas. **85:** 347–354.

481. **Pande, Shyam Narain**
Identification of the ancient land of Uttara Kuru. **61:** 725–735.

482. **Pandey, Lochan Prasad**
Ancient Sarabhapura. **67:** 294–296.

483. ———
Antiquity of Mahakosala. **67:** 297–304.

484. ———
Mahanandi—the famous river of Mahakosala. **67:** 313–316.

485. ———
Six lacs and ninety-six villages of Kosala. **67:** 317–320.

486. ———
Topographical position of Mahakosala and Trikalinga from inscriptions. **67:** 338–341.

487. **Paul, R.K.**
Historical geography of South Panchala—a cultural analysis. **5 (1):** 105–106.

488. **Ramaswami, N.S.**
Where was Sopatma?. **46 (1):** 355–358.

489. **Sankalia, H.D.**
Historical geography from inscriptions. **23:** 249–288.

490. **Sarma, Dimbeswar**
Extent of the ancient Pragjyotisa kingdom (from the data in the Ramayana and the Mahabharata). **88:** 397–401.

491. **Singhal, G.D.**
The cultural evolution of Hindu Gaya, the Vishnu Dham. **60:** 83–91.

492. **Upadhyay, R.** and **Pandey, J.N.**
Morphological analysis of surface land forms of the Rohtas plateau. **60:** 103–112.

493. **Upadhye, A.N.**
References to Sindhu durga and Vijaya durga in some Prakrit works. **70:** 377–382.

494. **Vishnu-Mittre**
Climate vs. biotic factor: Pollen evidence in the post-glacial history of northwest India. **83:** 25–31.

History

495. **Agrawala, V.S.**
Indology and research. **39:** 1–5.

496. **Bhat, S.S.**
Causation in History. **30:** 344–347.

497. **Bhattacharya, Ananta Kumar**
Histrir bhabadhara. **6:** 93–95. (Bengali).

498. **Chapekar, N.G.**
The Indian's lack of historical sense. **70:** 1–4.

499. **Das, Sukumar**
Raw materials for history. **9:** 382–385.

500. **Dhavale, D.G.**
The astronomical method and Indian chronology. **54:** 184–189.

501. **Ghosh, Biplab Ranjan**
Sister Nivedita on Indian history. **9:** 354–364.

502. **Habib, Irfan**
Problems of Marxist historical analysis. **54:** 34–47.

503. **Haldar, Gopal**
Recent trends in the study of Indian history of India. **4:** 224–229.

504. **Joshi, P.M.**
Further India. **23:** 289–350.

505. **Kosambi, D.D.**
Combined methods in Indology. **54:** 1–27.

506. **Kulkarni, Chidambara**
Indian approach to history. **30:** 197–205.

507. **McLeod, W.H.**
History: "An academic amusement". **9:** 90–94.

508. **Maloney, Clarence**
Dynastic drift: A process of cultural universalization. **66:** 89–107.

509. **Nilakanta Sastri, K.A.**
History and its writing. **7:** 1–4.

510. **Ray, Niharranjan**
Truth, objectivity and science in history. **20:** 24–33.

511. **Saksena, Dwarika Prasad**
Jal-palavan-ek etihasik ghatna **61:** 747–755. (Hindi).

512. **Saran, Parmatma**
History: Its conception and methodology. **95:** 140–146.

513. **Sreedhar, B.H.**
The Hindu view of history. **30:** 348–349.

514. **Thapar, Romila**
The mouse in the ancestry. **27:** 427–434.

515. **Uberoi, J.P.S.**
The structural concept of the Asian frontier. **75:** 67–77.

HISTORIOGRAPHY

516. **Basavaraja, K.R.V.**
History in Kannada literatur. **63:** 125–137.

517. **Bhattacharya, N.N.**
Epigraphical and literary sources in Bengali. **63:** 34–40.

518. ———
Historical works in Bengali. **63:** 157–164.

519. ———
Research in progress in Bengali. **63:** 233–237.

520. **Chavda, V.K.**
Literary sources for the early history of Gujarat down to 18th century. **63:** 138–147.

521. **Desai, P.B.**
The national role of Karnataka inscriptions. **63:** 120–124.

522. **Dhavalikar, M.K.**
Epigraphical sources in Marathi. **63:** 24–33.

523. **Fauza Singh**
Sources of history in Panjabi. **63:** 41–54.

524. **Gaṇḍa Singh**
History in Panjabi. **63:** 165–179.

525. **Gopal, B.R.**
Historical works in Kannada. **63:** 213–232.

526. **Kirpal Singh**
Historical research in Panjabi. **63:** 238–253.

527. **Kulkarni, A.R.**
Marathi sources of Maratha history. **63:** 1–23.

528. **Kurup, K.K.N.**
Historical writings in Malayalam. **63:** 201–212.

529. **Mahalingam, T.V.**
Inscriptions in Tamil Nadu. **63:** 81–87.

530. **Namboodiri, P.E.D.**
Literary sources in Malayalam. **63:** 112–119.

531. **Narayanan, M.G.S.**
Epigraphical sources of history in Malayalam. **63:** 98–111.

532. **Pathak, N.R.**
Research and writing of history in Maharashtra. **63:** 148–156.

533. **Pillay, K.K.**
Literary sources in Tamil. **63:** 88–97.

534. **Ramachandran, C.E.**
A brief account of research in Tamil. **63:** 254–264.

535. **Sanjivi, N.** and **Thirunavakkarasu, K.D.**
Historical writings in Tamil since 1947. **63:** 192–200.

536. **Yasoda Devi**
Epigraphical and literary sources in Telugu. **63:** 55–80.

537. **Yasoda Devi, V.**
Historical works in Telugu. **63:** 180–191.

INDUS VALLEY CIVILIZATION

538. **Agrawal, D.P.**
Harappan chronology; a re-examination of the evidence. **35:** 139–148.

539. ———
Metal technology of the Harappans. **99:** 163–167.

540. **Agrawala, R.C.**
Aravalli, the major source of copper for the Indus and Indus-related cultures. **99:** 157–162.

541. **Allchin, Bridget**
The Harappan environment. **99:** 445–454.

542. **Allchin, F.R.**
The northern limits of the Harappan culture zone. **99:** 51–54.

543. **Ashraf, Jaweed**
Smoking tradition in the Indus Valley civilization: The structural argument. **38 (1):** 235–240.

544. **Caspers, Elizabeth During**
Sumerian trading communities residing in Harappan society. **99:** 363–370.

545. **Chakrabarti, Dilip K.**
Origin of the Indus civilization: Theories and problem. **99:** 43–50.

546. ———
Seals and an evidence of Indus-West Asia interrelations. **75:** 93–116.

547. **Chitalwala, Y.M.**
The problem of class structure in the Indus civilization. **99:** 211–215.

548. **Dales, George F.**
The mythical massacre at Mohen-jo-daro. **95:** 70–73.

549. ———
Sex and stone at Mohen-jo-daro. **99:** 109–115.

550. **Dhavalikar, M.K.**
Sub-Indus cultures of Central and Western India. **99:** 243–251.

551. **Dikshit, K.N.**
Late Harappa in Northern India. **99:** 253–269.

552. **During Caspers, E.C.L.**
Singular aspects of Indus Valley artistry. zation. **82:** 35–38.

553. **Fairservis, Walter A., Jr.**
The Harappan civilization according to its writing: A model for the decipherment of the script. **38 (1)**: 187–211.

554. **Fentress, Marcia**
Time and process at Harappa and Mohenjo–daro. **99**: 99–104.

555. **Francfort, H.P.**
The Harrappan settlement of Shortughai. **99**: 301–310.

556. **Goyal, S.R.**
Socio-religious aspect of the Indus civilization. **82**: 35–38.

557. **Gupta, S.P.**
Internal trade of the Harappans. **99:** 417–424.

558. **Jansen, M.**
Architectural remains in Mohenjo-daro. **99:** 75–88.

559. **Jettmar, Karl**
Westerners beyond the great Himalayan range: Rock carvings and rock inscriptions in the Indus Valley near Chilas. **40:** 159–164.

560. **Joshi, J.P., Madhu Bala** and **Jassu Ram**
The Indus civilization: A reconsideration on the basis of distribution maps. **99:** 511–530.

561. **Kennedy, K.A.R.**
Trauma and disease in the ancient Harappans. **99:** 425–436.

562. **Kenoyer, Jonathan M.**
Chipped stone tools from Mohenjo-daro. **99:** 117–132.

563. **Kesarwani, Arun**
Harappan gateways: A functional reassessment. **99:** 63–73.

564. **Knorozov, Yu., Volchok, B.** and **Gurov, N.**
Some groups of proto-religious inscriptions of the Harappans. **99:** 169–171.

565. **Konishi, Masatoshi A.**
'Pre' or 'early' Harappan culture: A conceptual battle. **99:** 37–42.

566. ———
Writing materials during the Harappan period. **38 (1):** 213–217.

567. **Lamberg-Kar Lovsky, C.C.**
An idea or pot-luck. **99:** 347–351.

568. **Mainkar, V.B.**
Metrology in the Indus civilization. **99:** 141–151.

569. **Malik, S.C.**
Harappan social and political life. **99:** 201–209.

570. **Mate, M.S.**
Harappan fortifications: A study. **77:** 75–84.

571. **Meadow, R.H.**
A camel skeleton from Mohenjo-daro. **99:** 133–139.

572. **Mehta, R.N.**
Valabhi—a station of Harappan cattle-breeders. **99:** 227–230.

573. **Misra, V.N.**
Climate, a factor in the rise and fall of the Indus civilization—evidence from Rajasthan and beyond. **99:** 461–489.

574. **Momin, K.N.**
Village Harappans in Kheda district of Gujarat. **99:** 231–234.

575. **Nigam, J.S.**
The religion of the Harappans in Rajasthan. **82:** 32–34.

576. **Pande, B.M.**
Harappan art: An experiment in third dimension. **99:** 105–107.

577. ———
Missing cultural components between Harappan and early historical: Some observations based on microstudy. **38 (1):** 241–244.

578. ———
A note on the Harappan ring-kernoi. **66:** 231–233.

579. **Possehl, Gregory L.**
Archaeological terminology and the Harappan civilization. **99:** 27–36.

580. **Raghunath, S.N.**
Varsus: Latest Harappan post in Dhule district, Maharashtra. **31:** 17–18.

581. **Raikes, R.L.**
Mohenjo-daro environment. **99:** 455–460.

582. **Ramachandran, K.S.**
Dating the Indus civilization. **99:** 538–539.

583. **Rao, S.R.**
Religion of the Harappans. **5 (2):** 267–270.

584. **Ray, Amita**
Harappan art and life: Sketch of a social analysis. **75:** 117–131.

585. **Sali, S.A.**
Late Harappan settlement at Daimabad. **99:** 235–242.

586. **Sankalia, H.D.**
Expectations from the excavation of a new site of the Indus civilization. **99:** 539–540.

587. ———
Indus or the Harappan civilization in Gujarat. **76:** 35–38.

588. **Sarma, A.V.N.**
Decline of Harappan cultures: A re-look. **66:** 280–296.

589. **Serge, Cleuziou**
Oman Peninsula and its relations eastward during third millennium. **99:** 371–394.

590. **Sinha, B.P.**
Harappan fall-out (?) in the mid-gangetic valley. **47:** 103–105.

591. **Soundararajan, K.V.**
Kutch Harappan—a corridor of the Indus phase. **99:** 217–226.

592. **Srivastava, K.M.**
The myth of Aryan invasion of Harappan towns. **99:** 437–443.

593. **Stacul, Giorgio**
Harappan post-urban evidence in the Swat valley. **99:** 271–275.

594. **Thapar, B.K.**
Six decades of Indus studies. **99:** 1–25.

595. **Varma, Kailash Chandra**
Antiquity of the Indus civilization. **48:** 97–135.

596. **Vedavyasa**
Harappan wars of seven generations. **80:** 451–454.

597. **Vij, Brij Bhusan**
Linear standard in the Indus civilization. **99:** 153–156.

598. **Weiner, Sheila**
Hypotheses regarding the development and chronology of the art of the Indus Valley civilization. **99:** 395–415.

ANCIENT

599. **Aalto, Pentti**
Marginal notes on the Meluhha problem. **66:** 234–238.

600. **Agrawal, Ashvini**
The Murunda problem re-examined. **80:** 461–464.

601. **Agrawal, J.N.**
Some historical verses reconsidered. **59:** 400–405.

602. **Agrawal, Jagannath**
Lineage of Yasovarman. **85:** 17–21.

603. ———
Some new light on the Hindu Sahis of Kabul and Udbhandapura. **80:** 427–434.

604. **Ahmed, Nisar**
A re-examination of the genealogy and chronology of the Vakatakas. **77:** 149–164.

605. ———
History of the Sungas of Kosala. **53:** 104–115.

606. **Aquique, Md.**
Notes and queries on successors of Budha Gupta. **60:** 257–265.

607. **Arasaratnam, S.**
Francois Valentijn's description of Coromandel. **66:** 1–8.

608. **Auboyer, Jeannine**
A note on "the feet" and their symbolism in ancient India. **91 (1):** 125–127.

609. **Banerjee, Manabendu**
Religious horoscope of the Bengal land-grants of the time of the Gupta monarchs. **37:** 353–368.

610. **Basham, A.L.**
Emperor Asoka. **89:** 1–5.

611. ———
Religious concept of emperor Asoka. **9:** 64–70.

612. **Basu, Jogiraj**
The coronation ceremony in ancient India. **13:** 82–90.

613. **Bharadwaj, O.P.**
Pururava's pratisthana. **80:** 455–460.

614. ———
Vedic sites of Northern India **95:** 100–105.

615. **Bhargava, P.L.**
Names, order and chronology of pre-Mauryan kings according to the puranas. **3:** 161–170.

616. **Bhattacharya, S.C.**
Some aspects of female names in eastern India of Gupta and post-Gupta periods. **19:** 127–136.

617. **Buddha Prakash**
A new approach to Kalacuri-Rastrakuta relations. **59:** 406–423.

618. ———
Cyrus the great and the Indus Valley region. **62:** 133–140.

619. ———
Samudragupta's Southern expedition: A new interpretation. **66:** 15–31.

620. **Chatterjee, Asoke**
New light on Devapala's conflict with Dravidanatha. **37:** 343–352.

621. **Chattopadhyaya, B.D.**
Transition to the early historical phase in the Deccan: A note. **38 (2):** 727–732.

622. **Chattopadhyaya, Sudhakar**
Gautamiputra Satakarni. **62:** 92–96.

623. **Chaudhary, Radhakrishna**
Nature of feudalism in early medieval India (c. A.D. 600–1200). **47:** 470–476.

624. ———
Pre-feudal India. **60:** 295–310.

625. **Dahiya, B.S.**
Sanskritisation and historical clans. **80:** 465–472.

626. **Dandekar, R.N.**
Some aspects of the Gupta civilization. **39:** 50–62.

627. **Das, Binod S.**
Dynamics of changes in the social frame-work, religion and language in eastern India (8th–12th century). **2:** 27–41.

628. **Das, Sukla**
Harsa, the litterateur king. **60:** 275–283.

629. **Deo, S.B.**
Ancient Indian history. **23:** 159–191.

630. ———
Jaina data on the Satavahanas. **38 (2):** 733–736.

631. **Dikshit, R.K.**
Public services in Kamandakiya. **60:** 287–291.

632. **Dixit, Sadhna**
Espionage in the administration of the Mauryas. **5 (2):** 395–396.

633. **Eggermont, Pierre H.L.**
Sanchi-Kakanada and the Hellenistic and Buddhist sources. **87:** 11–27.

634. **Ghosh, Oroon K.**
Folk movements in ancient India. **48:** 488–507.

635. **Ghoshal, U.N.**
The alleged Achaemenid and Hellenistic influences upon the administration of the Maurya Empire. **6:** 76–85.

636. **Gopal, Krishna Kanti**
Pancamahasabda. **59:** 392–399.

637. **Gopal, Lallanji**
Administration of justice in villages in ancient India. **71:** 127–132.

638. ———
Early Greek writers on writing in India. **53:** 41–54.

639. _______
Megasthenes on writing and smritis. **88:** 117–129.

640. **Goyal, S.R.**
Did Harsha ever embrace Buddhism as his personal religion? **47:** 373–393.

641. _______
The problem of the Baladityas in the Gupta period. **13:** 100–114.

642. **Gupta, P.L.**
The beginning of the Satavahana rule. **52:** 101–112.

643. **Gupta, S.K.**
The Aryan problem. **61:** 737–742.

644. **Jai Narain** and **Tiwari, Ramakant**
Lalitaditya Muktapida, the first antiquarian king of India. **88:** 194–196.

645. **Jamindar, Rasesh C.**
Were the Western Ksatrapas Viceroys of the Kusanas? **61:** 703–708.

646. **Joshi, P.M.**
Foreign travellers. **23:** 193–231.

647. **Kamalapur, J.N.**
The Aryan problem and domesticated animals. **30:** 206–214.

648. **Karashima, Noboru**
Relations between South India and China in Chola times. **66:** 69–71.

649. **Kesarwani, Arun**
The problem of Indo-Aryan and the west Asian documents with reference to Boghazkoi tablet and Kikkuli text. **95:** 128–133.

650. **Krishna Deva**
Sattra in Indian epigraphy and art. **90:** 317–322.

651. **Krishnamoorthy, K.**
Indra-Dhvaja: A historical-critical survey. **91 (1):** 89–92.

652. **Krishnamurthy, K.**
Origin of Caitya. **85:** 45–48.

653. **Kumar, Suman**
The social evolution of Indian market. **86:** 306–312.

654. **Kuppuswami Sastri, S.**
Problems of identity in the cultural history of ancient India. **56 (1):** 1–8.

655. **Lorenzen, D.**
Imperialism and the historiography of ancient India. **10:** 84–102.

656. **Mahadevan, Iravatham**
Pallavas and the 'jar' legends. **66:** 84–88.

657. **Mahalingam, T.V.**
Genesis and nature of feudalism under the Pallavas of Kanchi. **89:** 89–96.

658. **Majumdar, R.C.**
Digvijaya and aggressive militarism in ancient India. **100:** 179–184.

659. **Mankad, D.R.**
Nabhagarista (?) genealogy. **29:** 173–189.

660. **Mazumdar, B.P.**
Polity of the Andhakavrsni Sangha. **62:** 206–216.

661. **Mirashi, V.V.**
D.R. Bhankarkar on the relations of the Guptas and Vakatakas. **91 (1):** 85–88.

662. _______
Further light on Yasodharman-Visnuvardhana. **80:** 405–426.

663. _______
New light on Yasodharman. **94 (2):** 665–673.

664. **Mishra, V.B.**
The remunerative sequel of dana in the epigraphs and literature of early mediaeval India. **7:** 207–211.

665. **Misra, V.N.**
Prehistory & protohistory. **23:** 353–415.

666. **Mohan, Mehta Vasishtha Dev**
The Mauryas after Asoka. **3:** 171–178.

667. _______
The Sunga victory on the Sindhu. **5 (2):** 307–311.

668. **Mukherjee, B.N.**
Cults of the emperor and empire in the Kusana dominions. **10:** 127–138.

669. _______
Religious policy of the imperial Kushanas. **20:** 280–286.

670. **Nagaraju, S.**
Chalukya Vinayaditya's intervention in Cambodian politics. **30:** 222–225.

671. **Nagaswamy, R.**
Pandya Arikesari and Pandikkovai. **66:** 108–111.

672. **Narain, A.K.**
The five Yabgus of the Yueh-Chih. **10:** 174–185.

673. **Narayanan, M.G.S.**
A reappraisal of Samudra Gupta's digvijaya. **90:** 283–293.

674. **Nilakanta Sastri, K.A.**
A note on administrative statistics in ancient India. **4:** 3–4.

675. **Ojha, Kailas Chandra**
The Hunas in the Gangetic Basin. **50:** 423–424.

676. **Om Prakash**
Pleasures and pastimes in India in the eleventh and twelfth centuries A.D. **62:** 263–274.

677. **Pandey, C.B.**
The break-up and fall of the Mauryan empire—a reappraisal. **44:** 315–327.

678. ———
Indo-Greek invasion during the time of Pusyamitra Sunga. **48:** 136–147.

679. **Pandey, V.C.**
Kautilya and Harishena (A comparative study of some of their contents). **47:** 356–360.

680. ———
Public opinion in ancient India. **3:** 203–207.

681. **Parpola, Asko**
The Todas of the Nilgiris: Hypothesis of a two fold origin—pre-Tamil and Saka. **27:** 319–336.

682. **Pathak, V.S.**
The navasahasankacarita: Itihasa under the shadow of a symbolist. **59:** 424–432.

683. **Phadke, H.A.**
Pratihara Ramabhadra. **48:** 148–153.

684. **Prajnananda**
Prehistoric civilization and music in prehistoric times. **1:** 477–494.

685. **Prasad, S.N.**
Dhruvadevi ki jaati. **61:** 757–762. (Hindi).

686. **Puri, B.N.**
Aspects of socio-economic changes in Northern India between the eighth and eleventh centuries A.D. **89:** 97–101.

687. ———
The Kusanas and the Asian cultural ethos. **95:** 9–12.

688. ———
Religion—a challenging force in Indian history between the 8th-10th century A.D. **20:** 268–272.

689. **Ramachandran, K.S.**
The personality of Rajasimha: An assessment of his Birudas. **48:** 160–165.

690. **Rama Rao, M.**
Visnukundin Vikramendravarman II. **71:** 311–314.

691. **Ramesh, K.V.**
Chalukya Pulakesi I. **30:** 215–221.

692. ———
Kadamba-Pallava-Ganga relationship. **85:** 23–30.

693. **Rau, Heimo**
The image of India in European antiquity and the middle ages. **40:** 197–208.

694. **Rocher, Ludo**
Notes on the technical term sahasa "fine, pecuniary penalty". **71:** 515–531.

695. **Roy, Brajdeo Prasad**
The Indian teachers of Hiuen-Tsiang. **86:** 419–425.

696. **Roy, Udai Narain**
A fresh investigation of the imperial Gupta capital. **47:** 361–372.

697. ———
Prachin Bharatiya nagar tatha nagarsannivesha. **50:** 447–456. (Hindi).

698. **Roy, Upendra Nath**
Parikshita Nandantara Nirnaya. **95:** 29–33. (Hindi).

699. **Ruben, Walter**
The development of the town in ancient India. **75:** 229–237.

700. ———
Some problems of the ancient Indian republics. **4:** 5–29.

701. **Sahay, S.N.**
Amusements in the Mauryan period. **47:** 308–314.

702. **Sankaranarayanan, S.**
Yavana conquest of the Madhyadesa—fresh light. **79:** 207–224.

703. **Sexena, K.S.**
Advent of Mauryans in Kashmir. **94 (2):** 687–692.

704. **Sengupta, R.**
On the identity of the "Mlechchas" **66:** 180–186.

705. **Sethna, K.D.**
Hiuen-Tsang on the time of the imperial Guptas. **95:** 45–50.

706. **Shah, Kirit K.**
Social structure in Candella charters. **85:** 229–237.

707. **Sharan, Mahesh Kumar**
Origin of republics in India with special reference to the Yaudheya tribe. **90:** 241–252.

708. **Sharma, Dasharatha**
The Bhadanakas. **59:** 433–437.

709. ———
Some new light on the route of Mahmud Ghaznavi's raid on Somanatha: Multan to Somanatha and Somanatha to Multan. **62:** 165–168.

710. **Sharma, Pushpa**
The military system of the Mongols. **82:** 359–363.

711. **Sharma, R.S.**
Early Indian feudalism (c. 400–1200 A.D.). **4:** 39–43.

712. ———
Material progress, taxation and state formation in the age of the Buddha. **86:** 245–274.

713. ———
Satavahana polity. **62:** 108–121.

714. ———
Stages in state formation in ancient India. **73:** 180–203.

715. **Sharma, Ram**
Extinction of Paramara rule from Malwa. **85:** 223–227.

716. **Shastri, Ajay Mitra**
The Pandavas of Mekala. **86:** 472–491.

717. ———
Closing phase of the Satavahana power and allied issues. **3:** 185–193.

718. ———
Kalachuri-Rashtrakuta relations in the Viddha-salabhanjika. **60:** 266–274.

719. **Shrivastava, M.C.P.**
Public opinion in the vedic period. **46 (1):** 427–438.

720. **Singh, Jai Prakash**
The religious leanings of the Guptas. **53:** 73–103.

721. **Singh, Y.B.**
Status and condition of workers in the Mauryan state. **47:** 315–320.

722. **Sinha, B.P.**
The slump in the creativity in ancient India. **9:** 187–191.

723. **Sinha, Gopal Chandra**
An ancient Indian law of partnership and its application to the priests officiating at a vedic sacrifice. **84:** 369–376.

724. **Sinha, Surendra Prasad**
Asoka and the break-up of the Mauryan empire. **86:** 459–468.

725. **Sohoni, Shridhar V.**
Samudragupta's vidyatsabha—verse 3 in Harisena's prasasti. **95:** 78–82.

726. **Soundararajan, K.V.**
Three empires and a culture. **86:** 241–24[illegible].

727. **Sternbach, L.**
Place and time of king's counsel with ministers according to the Dharmasastras, arthasastras and subhasita-samgrahas. **41:** 200–207.

728. **Surya Kanta**
The historical aspect of the Harsacarita. **50:** 465–474.

729. **Tewari, S.P.**
Why monkeys were kept inside the royal stable? **32:** 203–205.

730. **Thakur, A.L.**
Republics in India. **47:** 350–355.

731. **Thakur, Upendra**
The second phase of the Huna invasion of India. **62:** 181–205.

732. ———
Some problems of Huna history. **61:** 695–702.

733. **Thakur, Vijay Kumar**
The concept of urban revolution—a theoretical study of the second urbanization of India. **60:** 321–335.

734. ———
Literary references to fortification in ancient India (c. 300 B.C.—A.D. 500) **32:** 15–20.

735. ———
Role of guilds in ancient Indian urban administration (c. 200 B.C.—A.D. 600). **76:** 217–222.

736. ———
Towns in early medieval India. **93:** 389–397.

737. ———
Urban status of the later vedic society: An inquiry. **9:** 54–63.

738. **Thapar, B.K.**
The Aryans: A reappraisal of the problem. **98:** 147–164.

739. **Thapar, Romila**
Epigraphic evidence and some Indo-Hellenistic contacts during the Mauryan period. **89:** 15–19.

740. ———
Origin myths and the early Indian historical tradition. **75:** 271–294.

741. **Trautmann, Thomas R.**
Elephants and the Mauryas. **10:** 254–281.

742. **Vanaja, R.**
History of the Mitra kings from Numismatic and epigraphic evidences. **91 (1):** 77–84.

743. **Varma, Kailash Chandra**
Some Western Indologists and Indian civilization. **98:** 165–180.

744. **Varma, Vishwanath Prasad**
Some dimensions of Hindu political institutions and thought. **86:** 275–305.

745. **Verma, O.P.**
Different traditions of Hemadri. **59:** 438–443.

746. **Wayman, Alex**
Asoka and Upagupta-Moggaliputta. **47:** 300–307.

MEDIEVAL

747. **Ambasthya, B.P.**
Ilahdad Faizi Sarhindi's Akbarnamah and its importance. **47:** 508–511.

748. **Arjun Dev**
India in the eyes of early Muslim scholars. **98:** 589–596.

749. **Ashrafyan, Klara Z.**
The historical significance of the Turkish conquest of northern India. **4:** 67–83.

750. **Askari, S.H.**
Amir Khusrau as a social historian: An appraisal. **47:** 482–496.

751. **Bedekar, D.K.**
Review of interpretations on Shivaji's achievements. **54:** 77–86.

752. **Bhatnagar, G.D.**
The Banaras farman of Aurangzeb. **53:** 227–232.

753. **Dighe, V.G.**
Maratha political system: Theory and practice. **70:** 5–18.

754. **Dikshit, G.S.**
A new portrait of Shivaji and fresh light on an incident in his Karnatak expedition. **70:** 19–24.

755. **Gokhale, Kamal**
Chhatrapati Sambhaji and Shahajada Akbar. **52:** 72–85.

756. **Gopal, Krishna Kanti**
Defining feudalism in the context of early medieval India. **53:** 116–122.

757. **Gorekar, N.S.**
Cultural affinity between the Mughals and Safvids. **13:** 212–220.

758. **Haq, S. Moinul**
Shaykh Nizam al-Din Awliya. **100:** 196–202.

759. **Hasan, Mohibbul**
Lacunae in the study of medieval Indian history. **4:** 116–122.

760. ———
A note on the assassination of Sher Afgan. **100:** 192–195.

761. **Husaini, S.A.Q.**
Early Muslim fiefs in India. **4:** 44–61.

762. **Jauhri, R.C.**
Ghiyathu'd-Din Tughluq—his original name and descent. **4:** 62–66.

763. **Joshi, P.M.**
Ala-ud-Din Khalji's first campaign against Devagiri. **100:** 203–211.

764. ———
Asad Beg's return from Bijapur and his second mission to the Deccan, 1604–06. **70:** 136–155.

765. **Joshi, P.S.**
Chhatrapati Rajaram (1670–1700 A.D.): A reappraisal. **30:** 238–248.

766. **Kalyan Krishna**
Akbar kaal me sanskritik punruthan, Akbar ka samnavavaad aur Bharatiyata ki aur jhukav. **82:** 332–338. (Hindi).

767. **Karimashil, K.S.**
The political ideas of Candesvara—a medieval Indian political thinker. **62:** 446–457.

768. **Khan, Iqtidar Alam**
A note on the conception of Akbar's religious policy. **75:** 455–465.

769. **Kulkarni, A.R.**
Rajgad: The first capital of Shivaji. **70:** 156–171.

770. ———
Shivaji and the Portuguese. **32:** 189–201.

771. **Kulkarni, G.T.**
A new phase in the Mughal intelligence system. **52:** 118–131.

772. **Kunte, B.G.**
Aurangzeb's siege of Panhala. **70:** 172–189.

773. **Madhav Rao, P. Setu**
Ahwal-i-Khawaqin. **70:** 207–252.

774. **Naudou, Jean**
An example of engineering in mediaeval India. **66:** 224–230.

775. **Nizami, K.A.**
Attitude of Muslim mystic toward society and state during the Sultanate period. **48:** 539–558.

776. **Oturkar, R.V.**
Mediaeval period of Indian history, its duration, nature and content. **70:** 201–206.

777. **Prasad, Rajiva Nain**
The Ujjainiya rajputs of Bhojpur and the power politics of the Mughal empire. **60:** 311–320.

778. **Radhey Shyam**
The succession states and Indo-Muslim cultural synthesis in the Deccan. **52:** 171–189.

779. **Ray, Aniruddha**
French attitude to Sivaji: Some observations. **75:** 467–478.

780. **Ray, Sukumar**
Bairam Khan in Persia. **4:** 84–94.

781. **Rizvi, S.A.A.**
The Maktab Khana. **48:** 166–185.

782. **Saksena, Banarsi Prasad**
Modern administration in the light of medieval experience. **60:** 500–503.

782A. **Saletore, G.N.**
The conflict at Mayakonda during 1748–49. **39:** 340–346.

783. **Sarkar, J.N.**
Some aspects of military engineering in medieval India. **52:** 223–239.

784. **Somasundara Rao, C.**
The battle of Penukonda and its date. **90:** 235–240.

785. **Suresh Singh, K.**
A study in state-formation among tribal communities. **55:** 317–336.

786. **Yadava, B.N.S.**
Social significance of the main religious trends and ideologies during the medieval period. **19:** 39–49.

MODERN

787. **Ansari, Hasan Nishat**
The Momins: Population and nationalism. **47:** 555–563.

788. **Awasthi, D.**
A critical assessment of the activities of a forgotten English administrator. **66:** 9–14.

789. **Bajpai, S.C.**
Historical genesis of the trouble on the Northern borders of India. **48:** 220–229.

790. **Bidya Nand**
A leaf from Indo-Bhutanese relations. **60:** 504–511.

791. **Bipan Chandra**
The Indian capitalist class and imperialism before 1947. **55:** 390–420.

792. ———
Jawaharlal Nehru and the capitalist class: 1936. **75:** 513–538.

793. **Birendra Prasad**
Indian public opinion and Indo-Chinese freedom movement. **60:** 512–518.

794. **Chaudhury, V.C.P.**
The British policy towards Indian princes and aristocracy in the era of nationalism. **13:** 252–280.

795. **Datta, K.K.**
Modern India and World fellowship. **62:** 7–18.

796. **De, Barun**
Complexities in the relationships between nationalism, capitalism and colonialism. **75:** 479–512.

797. **De Souza, J.P.**
Edwin Montagu's visits to India and his impressions of Bombay. **70:** 304–321.

798. **Durai Raja Singam, S.**
Coomaraswamy and Indian nationalism. **25:** 119–122.

799. **Embree, Ainslie T.**
The diplomacy of dependency: Content and style in nineteenth-century foreign relations in India. **33:** 134–152.

800. **Ganda Singh**
The Maratha-Sikh relations. **70:** 93–135.

801. **Goswami, R.B.L.**
Indo-Pakistan relations: 1965–1972. **95:** 90–93.

802. **Gune, V.T.**
An outline of the administrative institutions of the Portuguese territories in India and the growth of their Central Archives at Goa—16th to 19th century A.D. **70:** 47–92.

803. **Gupta, P.C.**
The Bible chapati and the greased cartridge. **6:** 250–265.

804. **Jha, A.N.**
Can President Ayub talk of self-determination. **48:** 41–45.

805. **Kabir, Humayun**
India: One and many. **28:** 166–171.

806. **Kemp-Ashraf, P.M.**
India and Internationalism: A note on the early working class movement. **4:** 187–223.

807. **Kohli, Manorama**
India's Himalayan policy: A historical perspective. **76:** 293–303.

808. **Krishnamurthi, V.G.**
Mackenzie and his collections. **92:** 179–186.

809. **Krishnaswamiengar, B.S.**
The spirit of 1857. **30:** 255–257.

810. **Maitra, K.**
Swami Vivekananda and the terrorist movement in Bengal. **48:** 197–202.

811. **Majumdar, R.C.**
The price of our freedom. **78:** 1–7.

812. **Misra, J.P.**
Auckland Colvin's hostility towards the Congress. **53:** 261–267.

813. **Mukerjee, Hiren**
Hindu-Muslim unity. **4:** 271–273.

814. **Niyogi, Sumanta**
Henry Fawcett: India's friend in the Gladstone Ministry 1880–1884. **86:** 503–508.

815. *The proclamations of the leaders of the struggle of 1857.* **48:** 21–28.

816. **Ray, Aniruddha**
Tipu Sultan and the invasion of Zaman Shali: The English reaction. **76:** 279–292.

817. **Roy, Somnath**
Early Congress and growth of public opinion. **60:** 471–479.

818. **Sankhdher, B.M.**
The Annual Register: A spectrum of British attitudes towards India during the East India Company's administration. **48:** 203–219.

819. **Sar Desai, D.R.**
Indian intervention in Indo-China—Imbroglio, 1954. **70:** 266–303.

820. **Saswadkar, P.L.**
Was Brahmendraswami a politician? **30:** 249–254.

821. **Singh, S.B.**
Early British religious policy in India. **62:** 230–241.

822. **Srivastav, N.M.P.**
Patna Yuvak Sangh and India's liberation. **60:** 480–486.

823. ———
Struggle for freedom: The Gaya trial of revolutionaries. **86:** 509–522.

824. **Varma, Birendra**
Ahmad Shah Abdali's ninth invasion and its repercussion on East India Company. **62:** 322–326.

825. **Venkataramani, M.S.**
The United States and the release of Mahatma Gandhi, May 1944: A preliminary note. **70:** 371–376.

HISTORY—STATES

Andhra Pradesh

826. **Alam, Manzoor**
The growth of Hyderabad city: A historical perspective. **100:** 212–220.

827. **Mazumdar, B.P.**
Observations on the chief priests of early medieval temples in Andhra Pradesh (based on inscriptions of A.D. 1000–1325). **90:** 125–130.

828. **Mirashi, V.V.**
The date of Vishnukundin Madhavavarman I. **21:** 1–3.

829. **Rama Rao, M.**
Calukyan conquest of the East Coast. **13:** 97–99.

830. **Reddy, P. Chenna**
Pekkandru—the guild of merchants in mediaeval Andhradesa. **85:** 373–377.

831. **Sadyojata Swamiji**
Three brothers of Lepakshi. **30:** 298–301.

832. **Sarkar, H.**
Emergence of urban centres in early historical Andhradesa. **38 (2):** 631–641.

833. **Shastri, Ajay Mitra**
Vasishthiputra Sivasri Pulumavi. **74:** 151–162.

834. **Venkataramanayya, N.**
The Matli chiefs of Siddavatam. **71:** 475–498.

835. **Vittal Rao, Y.**
Some thoughts on Western impact (education) in Hyderabad in the Company period. **32:** 163–167.

Assam

836. **Acharyya, N.N.**
Chaopha Su-hum-mung, the Assamese Napoleon. **7:** 138–144.

837. ———
Civilisation of Assam—a study. **9:** 336–339.

838. ———
Human sacrifice in Assam and adjoining regions. **88:** 197–202.

839. **Chaudhury, P.D.**
Land and people of ancient Kamarupa. **50:** 395–399.

840. **Choudhury, R.D.**
Cultural background of Jonai region, Assam. **5 (2):** 403–406.

841. **Dasgupta, Sanghamitra**
Brahmanical education in Kamarupa (c. 6th–12th centuries A.D.) as known from inscriptions. **88:** 70–74.

841A. **Goswami, Praphulladatta**
Bhatheli or Sori. **7:** 221–224.

842. ———
Folk tales of the Miris. **61:** 775–778.

843. **Mohanty, Banshidhar**
The cultural relation of Assam and Orissa. **13:** 162–167.

844. **Sankalia, H.D.**
From history to prehistory in Assam. **82:** 1–5.

845. **Singh, Jai Prakash**
Earthquakes in medieval Assam. **88:** 230–235.

846. ———
On Brajanatha Simha of Assam. **90:** 79–82.

Bihar

847. **Ahmad, Qeyamuddin**
Regional study of medieval Bihar: Some new aspects and sources. **47:** 477–481.

848. **Altekar, A.S.**
New light on the history of Bihar and the origin of Lakshmana samvat. **6:** 110–115.

849. **Ansary, Hasan Nishat**
Political organisation of Bihar under the Turks A.D. 1203–1412/A.H. 599–815. **86:** 426–441.

850. **Athavale, Sadashiv**
A sidelight on the decline and fall of the Republic of Vaishali. **52:** 13–21.

851. **Chaudhary, V.C.P.**
Vernacular newspapers as the organs of historiography: A case study of the history of modern Bihar. **47:** 538–554.

852. **Choudhary, Radha Krishna**
Social structure in medieval Mithila (c. A.D. 1200–1600). **55:** 217–234.

853. **Jha, J.C.**
Tribal unrest in Chota Nagpur in the late eighteenth century. **47:** 525–532.

854. **Mazumdar, B.P.**
Some aspects of the historicity of the Nibandhas of North Bihar (c. A.D. 1097–1526). **88:** 82–91.

855. **Pandey, Lochan Prasad**
The Chauhan king, Baijaladeva II of Patna state. **67:** 260–266.

856. **Sharma, R.S.**
Early medieval society in Bihar (c. A.D. 600–1200). **71:** 383–390.

857. **Sinha, B.K.**
Some facts about the famine of 1770 in Bihar. **47:** 520–524.

858. **Thakur, Upendra**
Maithila Panditas beyond the frontiers of Mithila. **90:** 229–234.

859. ———
Socio-economic life in Mithila under the Khandavalas or Darbhanga raj. **50:** 483–498.

860. **Thakur, Vijay Kumar**
The Panji—prabandha and its impact on Maithila society. **94 (2):** 715–720.

Delhi

861. **Deshpande, M.N.**
Delhi after Chrit. **48:** 75–79.

862. **Lal, B.B.**
How old is Delhi? **48:** 70–74.

Gujarat

863. **Majumdar, A.K.**
An approach to the study of the socio-economic history of Gujarat. **20:** 431–443.

864. **Mehta, R.N.**
Urban centres of Western India and the western world. **40:** 139–148.

865. **Sankalia, H.D.**
Patronage of Sanskrit by a zealous Muslim king of Gujarat Mahmud Begada. **20:** 72–74.

866. **Shastri, H.G.**
Ancient cultural relations between Gujarat and Malwa. **5 (2):** 339–342.

Haryana

867. **Banerji, Adris**
Culture sequence in Hariyana. **62:** 122–126.

868. **Haye, Chowdhry Abdul**
The freedom movement in Mewat and Dr. K.M. Ashraf. **4:** 291–336.

869. **Phadke, H.A.**
Haryana: The landmarks in historical growth. **85:** 31–43.

Himachal Pradesh

870. **Kaul Deambi, B.K.**
Political history of ancient Chamba as gleaned from her inscriptions. **3:** 221–230.

Jammu and Kashmir

871. **Das, Sukla**
Jonaraja and Dvitiya Rajatarangini. **89:** 61–64.

872. **Dutta, Kali Kumar**
A peep into a story in the Rajatarangini. **13:** 127–135.

873. **Hangloo, Rattan Lal**
Social background of religious conversion in 14th and early 15th century Kashmir. **88:** 360–374.

874. **Shrivastava, M.C.P.**
Kashmir politics and the role of public opinion on the basis of Kalhana's Rajatarangini. **86:** 492–502.

875. **Singh, Y.B.**
Rajadharma in early medieval Kashmir—analysis of a regional peculiarity in national context. **88:** 49–52.

876. ———
The study of regional history: Problems and possibilities. **32:** 103–108.

877. **Topdan**
Zanskar—a brief historical study. **38 (2):** 699–707.

878. **Ved Kumari**
Debates and discussions in ancient Kashmir. **3:** 209–220.

879. **Yun-Hua, Jan**
Hui Ch'ao's record on Kashmir. **48:** 154–159.

Karnataka

880. **Basavaraja, K.R.**
The Council of Ministers in medieval Karnataka. **30:** 331–336.

881. **Chitnis, K.N.**
Glimpses of Dharwar during the Peshwa period. **30:** 262–269.

882. **Dikshit, G.S.**
Popular participation in early Indian governments with special reference to Karnataka. **30:** 302–306.

883. ———
Social and religious conditions of Karnatak before Basava. **8:** 117–132.

884. **Filliozat, Vasundhara**
Vijayanagar and Portuguese chronicles. **40:** 165–171.

885. **Gai, G.S.**
The early Sendrakas of Karnataka. **92:** 108–110.

886. **Gopal, B.R.**
State of trade and towns in Karnataka (600–1200 A.D.). **93:** 451–457.

887. **Gurav, R.N.**
Mahamandalesvara Anantapala. **30:** 229–237.

888. **Gururajachar, G.**
Vachana literature: A historical note. **92:** 171–178.

889. **Gururajachar, S.**
Irrigation in medieval Karnataka. **73:** 304–307.

890. ———
The Vira-Bananjus of Karnataka (1000–1300 A.D.). **30:** 307–313.

891. **Halappa, G.S.**
Literary history of Karnataka. **30:** 467–476.

892. **Kamath, Jyotsna**
Preceptors of medieval Karnataka. **30:** 294–297.

893. **Katti, Madhav N.**
More light on early Chalukyan history. **92:** 111–113.

894. **Kotraiah, C.T.M.**
Hampi before founding of Vijayanagara. **93:** 381–387.

895. **Krishnamurthy, C.**
Some minor dynasties of Kolar district (1179–1338 A.D.). **66:** 72–83.

896. **Krishnan, K.G.**
Rattapadi—seven and a half lakhs. **30:** 270–274.

897. **Krishnappa, M.V**
Weights and measures in early medieval Karnataka. **74:** 185–187.

898. **Krishnayya, D.N.**
Nayaks of Ikkeri and the Haleri Rajahs of Coorg—their interrelation. **92:** 149–151.

899. **Marulasiddaiah, H.M.**
Sectarian and secular bases of social welfare and their consequences. **92:** 322–327.

900. **Mehta, R.N.**
Some Dravidian toponyms in Gujarat. **93:** 411–413.

901. **Muddachari, B.**
Shahji in Karnataka. **92:** 127–134.

902. **Nagaraju, S.**
Karnataka's contacts with Ceylon. **92:** 152–163.

903. **Narasimha Murthy, A.V.**
A Chalukya feudatory of Varuna. **30:** 226–228.

904. ———
Karnataka origin of the Savunas. **66:** 112–116.

905. **Paramashivaiah, J.S.**
Folklore traditions in Mysore city. **92:** 227–231.

906. **Ramachandra Rao, C.V.**
Rayavacakamu; its date and historicity. **32:** 291–305.

907. **Ramanna, H.S.**
The economic condition of medieval Karnataka as reflected in travel accounts of Caesar Frederic 1563–1581. **74:** 199–202.

908. **Ramesh, K.V.**
Kongu in South Indian History. **93:** 323–327.

909. ———
Notes on some imperial dynasties of Karnataka. **92:** 99–107.

910. ———
Rashtrakutas of Manyakheta—a study. **36:** 129–132.

911. **Rao, B.V.**
Ministers in Hoysala polity. **30:** 337–340.

912. **Rao, T.R.**
Development of astrological thought in Karnataka. **92:** 328–331.

913. **Ritti, Shrinivas**
A note on the genealogy of the Seunas. **92:** 114–120.

914. ———
A Sanskrit document relating to the Adil Shahis of Bijapur. **30:** 110–120.

915. **Sampath, M.D.**
New light on Nolambas. **66:** 165–179.

916. **Shantakumari, Leela**
Agraharas in ancient Karnataka. **30:** 288–293.

917. **Shastri, Ajay Mitra**
Vakatakas in Karnataka. **9:** 242–246.

918. **Shastry, A.K.**
Relation between the Sringeri matha and the Keladi rulers. **32:** 137–141.

919. **Sheik Ali, B.**
Mysore and the Confederacy of 1780. **92:** 135–142.

920. **Shivaganesha Murthy, R.S.**
Sources of the history of Karnataka in Sanskrit literature. **92:** 164–170.

921. **Shivanna, K.S.**
Some aspects of the agrarian system during the Hoysala period. **92:** 292–298.

922. **Shripaty Sastry, K.**
The first session of the Mysore Representative Assembly 1881. **32:** 177–181.

923. **Sircar, D.C.**
Karnatas outside Karnata. **6:** 211–219.

924. **Surendra Rao, B.**
James Mill's views on the necessity of Wellesley's war against Tipu Sultan. **92:** 143–148.

925. **Varadaraja Rao, G.**
Kaifiyats in Kannada. **92:** 187–194.

926. **Vasantha, R.**
Tonnur—its importance in the history of Karnataka. **92:** 121–126.

927. **Venkataramanayya, N.**
Mir Jumla's conquest of Karnataka (from Telugu sources). **100:** 221–227.

928. **Venkataratnam, A.V.**
Mysore Representative Assembly (1881–1947). **32:** 183–188.

929. **Wodeyar, Sadashiva**
Two ancient towns of Karnataka. **30:** 258–261.

Kerala

930. **Sankarankutfy Nair, T.P.**
Resistance to British power in Kerala in the pre-mutiny period of Indian history. **90:** 261–267.

931. **Trumalai, R.**
The Venad rulers and the medieval Pandyas. **5 (2):** 353–362.

Madhya Pradesh

932. **Bajpai, K.D.**
New light on the early history of Central India. **13:** 115–120.

933. **Jha, V.D.**
Identification of the Dahala king defeated by Yadava Simhana. **5 (2):** 343–345.

934. **Pandey, Lochan Prasad**
Mahakosala (Chhattisgarh) and its ancient capitals. **67:** 347–362. (Hindi).

935. ———
Was Ujjain ever in Mahakosala? **67:** 325–326.

936. **Reu, Bisheswar Nath**
Kachchhapaghat (Kachhavaha) vamsha. **50:** 436–446. (Hindi).

937. **Shastri, Ajay Mitra**
Chronology of the Panduvamsins of South Kosala. **5 (2):** 313–327.

Maharashtra

938. **Chitnis, K.N.**
Marathas and Lakshmeshwar Desais. **52:** 49–58.

939. ———
The pedigree of the Lakshmeshwar Desais based on a Modi genealogy. **32:** 143–147.

940. **Conlon, Frank F.**
Indian renaissance beyond Bengal: The awakening in Maharashtra. **33:** 80–97.

941. **D'costa, Anthony**
The East India Company and the common folk of Bombay. **48:** 186–196.

942. **Joshi, S.N.**
Masala. **39:** 186–188.

943. **Mate, M.S.**
Pandharpur: Myth and reality. **52:** 132–138.

944. **Pawar, A.G.**
Palace revolution at Kolhapur 1714 A.D. **52:** 159–170.

945. **Rao, V.D.**
The Chhatrapatis of Kolhapur. **70:** 334–370.

946. **Sankalia, H.D.**
Sanjan—a miniature Bombay in c. A.D. 980. **90:** 209–213.

947. **Thosar, H.S.**
New light on the history of the early Rashtrakutas. **21:** 191–200.

Orissa

948. **Biswas, Dilip Kumar**
A note on the first Sonpur grant of Yayati Mahasivagupta I. **6:** 289–291.

949. **Das, Binod S.**
The land and people of Orissa. **2:** 1–26.

950. ———
Social changes in modern India—a case study of Orissa from the middle of 18th to the middle of the 20th century. **2:** 119–131.

951. **Jit, Nabin Kumar**
Resistance movements in the native states of Orissa. **2:** 179–195.

952. **Mahapatra, L.K.**
The role of Hindu princes in the caste system in Orissa. **2:** 42–60.

953. **Mazumdar, Kanchanmoy**
British Baptist missionaries in Orissa 1822–58: A study in western impact on nineteenth century society. **2:** 108–118.

954. **Mohanty, Gopinath**
Fading outlines in tribal culture. **2:** 196–224.

955. **Panda, Shishir Kumar**
Nayaka system in medieval Orissa. **88:** 92–107.

956. **Pandey, Lochan Prasad**
C.U. Wills on the Sambalpur Atharagarh. **67:** 276–282.

957. **Shastri, Ajay Mitra**
Genealogy and chronology of later Somavamsins. **38 (2):** 649–662.

958. ———
Trikalinga. **46 (1):** 417–423.

959. **Tripathy, Snigdha**
Rashtrakuta ruling families of Orissa. **74:** 189–194.

Punjab

960. **Barrier, N. Gerald**
Punjab politics and the press, 1880–1910. **33:** 118–133.

961. **Chopra, S.N.**
Punjab's contribution to Indian culture abroad. **20:** 88–96.

962. **Handa, Devendra**
Some ancient cities and towns of Punjab. **85:** 303–345.

Rajasthan

963. **Bhargava, Nondita**
The murder of Major Burton and the revolt of 1857 in Kota. **60:** 340–348.

964. **Bhargava, P.L.**
Rajasthan: The cradle of Indo-Aryan civilisation. **82:** 39–41.

965. **Kachhawaha, O.P.**
A note on the development of the famine policy in Rajasthan. **82:** 401–404.

966. **Khare, G.H.**
Rajasthanchi Bikaner yethil lekhyashala. **70:** 15–23. (Marathi).

967. **Nigam, S.B.P.**
Account of Rajasthan in the Waqiat-i-Azfari. **82:** 384–388.

968. **Pilania, G.P.**
Sawai Jai Singh as high priest of reformation. **82:** 392–395.

969. **Rahurkar, V.G.**
The Rajaprasastimahakavya of Bhatta Ranachoda. **13:** 121–126.

970. **Sahai, Yaduendra**
Pink city: Its original colour and allied problems. **82:** 396–400.

971. **Sharma, B.D.**
Amir Khan—an unrecognized genius. **60:** 336–339.

972. **Sharma, Ravindra Kumar**
Military system of the Rajput states during "grand anarchy" (A.D. 1707 to 1857). **90:** 253–260.

973. ———
The Rajput elephant corps: An assessment. **82:** 389–391.

974. **Sinha, B.C.**
Foreign origin of the Rajputs: A misnomer. **82:** 357–358.

975. **Srivastava, Vijai Shankar**
The story of archaeological, historical and antiquarian researches in Rajasthan before independence. **82:** 19–46.

Tamilnadu

976. **Ganesan, Saw**
Fresh light on Pallava history. **66:** 474–478.

977. **Gurumurthy, S.**
The Ghatika at Kanchi. **72:** 151–158.

978. **Karashima, Noboru**
Declining phase Brahmadeya of Ukkal. **93:** 351–356.

979. **Kasinathan, Natana**
Sankarappadiyar. **93:** 377–379.

980. **Murton, Brian J.**
Towns and markets in Salem in the eighteenth century. **93:** 399–409.

981. **Perumal, V.**
The Tamil society of the Sangam age. **61:** 381–395.

982. **Pillay, K.K.**
Schwartz and the Maratha kings of Tanjavur. **70:** 253–257.

983. **Raghotham, Venkata**
Tamil vamsavalis as a source for the study of the political structure of medieval Tamil country. **21:** 339–357.

984. **Rajayyan, K.**
Balance of forces in the Nayaka polity of Madurai. **61:** 677–683.

985. **Ramachandran, K.S.**
The madhyastha in the village administration of medieval Tamilnadu. **74:** 179–183.

986. **Ramamurthy, V.**
The Pallavas and the Kadavas. **93:** 333–338.

987. **Ramanujam, Chidambaram S.**
The Madras revolution. **66:** 131–158.

988. **Somasundara Rao, C.**
The loyalty of the Nayaks of Tanjore to the Vijaynagara empire. **32:** 133–135.

989. **Spencer, George W.**
When queens bore gifts: Women as temple donors in the Chola period. **93:** 361–373.

990. **Srinivasan, K.R.**
Cultural contacts with Kambuja (part played by Tamilnadu). **38 (2):** 679–684.

991. **Srinivasan, S.**
The battle of Takkolam: A reappraisal. **93:** 459–464.

992. ———
The Velaikkarar in the Tamil country. **30:** 320–324.

993. **Subbarayalu, Y.**
The place of ur in the economic and social history of the early Tamilnadu from A.D. 750 to 1350. **74:** 171–177.

994. ———
Sidelight on Chola officialdom. **93:** 357–360.

995. **Subbiah, G.**
Habitat and society: A study of Neytal region in early Tamil literature. **20:** 444–456.

996. **Swaminathan, S.**
Land transactions at Srinivasanallur. **93:** 375–376.

997. ———
Tiruvorriyur as an economic entity. **21:** 161–171.

998. **Thiruvenkatachari, S.**
The city of Madurai in classical times. **66:** 461–466.

999. **Tirumalai, R.**
The Brahmadeyas of Pudukkottai district. **93:** 339–350.

Uttar Pradesh

1000. **Bajpai, K.D.**
Fresh light on the post-Asokan history of Kausambi. **50:** 373–377.

1001. **Gaur, R.C.**
Mathura-Govardhana region: An archaeological assessment in historical perspective. **89:** 103–113.

1002. **Joshi, M.C.**
The Khasas in the history of Uttarakhand. **21:** 371–376.

1003. **Joshi, Maheshwar P.**
Perspectives in social history of Kumaon. **38 (2):** 709–726.

1004. **Sullerey, S.K.**
Significance of Kalanjara Fort in the history of Candellas. **5 (1):** 107–109.

1005. **Thakur, Umakant**
An account of Varanasi as depicted in the Skandapurana. **62:** 681–684.

West Bengal

1006. **Banerjee, Tarasankar**
Nationalist historiography in Bengal: A response to imperialist historiography in the 19th century. **32:** 169–176.

1007. **Bhattacharya, Sabyasachi**
Positivism in 29th century Bengal: Diffusion of European intellectual influence in India. **55:** 337–355.

1008. **Bhattacharya, Swapna**
On the concept of samantas in early medieval Bengal (c. 5th–13th centuries A.D.). **88:** 75–81.

1009. **Chakravarti, Ranabir**
Economic measures of Ramapala in Varendri. **78:** 217–219.

1010. **Dikshit, K.N.** and **Pandeya, R.G.**
Ancient maritime contacts of West Bengal—literary and archaeological evidence. **60:** 232–237.

1011. **Ganguli, Kalyan Kumar**
Bangalir itihas: A departure in Indian historiography. **76:** 7–11.

1012. **Ghosh, Asok K.**
History of the Bengalees: The unrecorded period. **75:** 419–432.

1013. **Guha, Arti**
British imperialism and education in Bengal. **60:** 349–355.

1014. **Gupta, Chitrarekha**
Early Brahmanic settlement in Bengal—pre-Pala period. **90:** 215–224.

1015. **Husain, Shahanara**
Village life in early medieval Bengal: A study based on the Subhasitaratnakosa. **75:** 311–316.

1016. **Imam, Abu**
Bengal in history. **10:** 71–83.

1017. **Jha, J.C.**
Barabhum in the early British period. **13:** 281–284.

1018. **Mukherjee, S.N.**
Gauriya Samaj: A literary society of the bhadralok. **10:** 139--173.

1019. **Ray, Amita**
Urbanisation in early Bengal. **76:** 271–277.

1020. **Sanyal, Hitesranjan**
Literary sources of medieval Bengali history: A study of few mangalkavya texts. **76:** 205–215.

1021. **Sircar, D.C.**
The Kamboja rulers of Bengal. **43:** 107–112.

Social History

1022. **Basu, Jogiraj**
Recognition of merit in caste system in ancient India. **61:** 685–694.

1023. **Bhattacharya, Sibesh**
Social mobility in ancient and early mediaeval India—some issues. **53:** 172–186.

1024. **Bongard-Levin, G.M.**
Some problems of the social structure of ancient India. **75:** 199–227.

1025. **Chakraborti, Haripada**
Cross-Cousin marriage in ancient India. **20:** 398–404.

1026. **Chapekar, Nalinee**
Social reality as depicted in the Gathasaptasati of Hala. **57:** 53–72.

1027. **Chaudhary, Radhakrishna**
Social classes in ancient India. **20:** 390–397.

1028. **Deppert, Joachim**
East or West—the precedent: The Aryan schism. **40:** 45–138.

1029. **Dwivedi, R.K.**
A critical study of the changing social order at yuganta: Or the end of Kali age with special reference to the Mahabharata. **53:** 276–297.

1030. **Guha, Amalendu**
Geography behind history: An introduction to the socio-economic study of North-east India. **54:** 87–116.

1031. **Jaiswal, Suvira**
Studies in the social structure of the early Tamils. **55:** 124–155.

1032. **Jha, Vivekanand**
From tribe to untouchable: The case of Nisadas. **55:** 67–84.

1033. **Naqvi, S.**
Marx on pre-British Indian society and economy. **54:** 48–76.

1034. **Negi, J.S.**
Some light on the institution of slavery from the Likhanavali of Vidyapati. **19:** 93–96.

1035. **Oberai, K.**
Toilet in ancient India. **30:** 505–507.

1036. **Ojha, A.P.**
Position of potters in the socio-regional stratification of early medieval India. **86:** 366–376.

1037. **Om Prakash**
King and brahmanas vis-a-vis prayascita and danda. **19:** 97–107.

1038. **Oommen, T.K.**
Towards reconciling traditional and modern experiment. **40:** 253–263.

1039. **Parabrahma Sastry, P.V.**
Tambula: A forgotten Hindu custom. **90:** 167–171.

1040. **Patkar, M.M.**
Professional castes in the dharmasutras. **59:** 225–239.

1041. **Puri, B.N.**
Aspects of socio-economic changes in Northern India between the 8th and 11th centuries A.D. **86:** 377–382.

1042. **Roy, U.N.**
Ancient India village and city—a relational assessment. **5 (1):** 97–101.

1043. ———
Dohada—a folk-custom of ancient India. **86:** 104–111.

1044. **Ruben, Walter**
Outline of the structure of ancient Indian society. **55:** 85–94.

1045. **Sarkar, V.C.**
Marriage with courtesans in ancient India. **39:** 347–349.

1046. **Sharma, R.S.**
The Kali age: A period of social crises. **10:** 186–203.

1047. **Sivaramamurti, C.**
The charm of feminine coiffure. **22 (1):** 316–321.

1048. **Sreenivasa Murthy, H.V.**
Changing patterns in social stratification during Vijayanagara. **32:** 129–132.

1049. **Thapar, Romila**
Social mobility in ancient India with special reference to elite groups. **55:** 95–123.

1050. **Tomas, Jindrich**
D.D. Kosambi's conception of slavery and feudalism in the light of some recent investigation. **53:** 1–14.

1051. **Venkateswara Rao, K.V.**
The native culture of Andhras as depicted in the Srngararasodaya-Bhana. **80:** 388–393.

1052. **Viney Kumar**
A note on the origin of the Devadasi custom. **80:** 394–395.

Economic History

ANCIENT

1053. **Aquique, Md.**
Credit transaction in early Indian literature. **53:** 196–201.

1054. **Chakravarti, Ranabir**
Rajasresthi. **38 (2):** 671–678.

1055. **Chanana, Dev Raj**
Data on agriculture around Varanasi in the 12th cent. A.D. **71:** 81–87.

1056. **Chhabra, B. Ch.**
Gold through the ages. **72:** 304–315.

1057. **De Silva, Anil**
The spice and silk roads. **98:** 299–304.

1058. **Dhavalikar, M.K.**
The Lampsacos Dish—a reconsideration. **46 (1):** 127–131.

1059. **Gopal, Lalanji**
Credit laws in ancient India. **59:** 444–458.

1060. ———
Economic pursuits in ancient Indian life. **50:** 405–417.

1061. ———
Economic self-sufficiency of ancient Indian villages. **61:** 763–768.

1062. ———
Honey industry in ancient India. **62:** 255–262.

1063. ———
Indian shipping in early mediaeval period. **98:** 108–122.

1064. ———
Mining and metallurgy in early medieval India. **86:** 356–365.

1065. **Gupta, P.L.**
Roman trade in India. **62:** 169–180.

1066. **Jha, D.N.**
Forced labour in post-Maurya and Gupta times. **62:** 443–445.

1067. **Kangle, R.P.**
Kautilya and Yajnavalkya. **59:** 240–253.

1068. **Margabandhu, C.**
Ancient sea-ports of South India—their trade relationship with the Western world during the first century B.C. to second century A.D. **90:** 185–202.

1069. **Mehta, M.J.**
The agate industry of Cambay. **32:** 109–122.

1070. **Muzumdar, B.P.**
Guilds in early medieval North India (c. A.D. 606–1206). **78:** 48–55.

1071. **Niyogi, Puspa**
The economy of land measurement in ancient Bengal—c. A.D. 800–1200. **60:** 557–570.

1072. **Ramachandran, K.S.**
Ancient Indian maritime ventures. **98:** 71–82.

1073. **Rao, S.R.**
Shipping in ancient India from the earliest times to 600 A.D. **98:** 83–107.

1074. **Roy, Brajdeo Prasad**
Banabhatta's notices of economic life in a Vindhyan forest village. **47:** 394–400.

1075. ———
Foreign trade during the vedic period. **60:** 521–532.

1076. **Sampath, M.D.**
The Chitrameli. **30:** 314–319.

1077. **Sarkar, K.R.**
Concept of budget in the economic thought of ancient India. **9:** 386–391.

1078. **Sarma, Sreeramula Rajeswara**
Varnamalika system of determining the fineness of gold in ancient and medieval India. **44:** 369–389.

1079. **Shanmugam, P.**
Aspects of the Chola revenue system in Karnataka. **32:** 123–127.

1080. **Shivanna and Rangaswamiah, G.R.**
Agriculture during the Ganga period. **92:** 299–303.

1081. **Shrivastava, M.C.P.**
Employer and employee relationship in ancient India. **47:** 401–408.

1082. **Singh, Hari Sahay**
Pracheen Bharatiya arthatantra main swayatshasi sansthaon ki bhumika. **86:** 321–329. (Hindi).

1083. **Singh, Madan Mohan**
Early Indian trade with West Asia. **60:** 549–552.

1084. **Srivastava, O.P.**
Sulka in ancient and early medieval India. **86:** 335–355.

1085. **Thakur, Upendra**
Corruption in early Indian trade. **60:** 533–548.

1086. ———
Some aspects of corruption in early Indian trade. **53:** 24–40.

1087. **Thakur, Vijay Kumar**
Economic changes in early medieval India (c. A.D. 600–1200). **53:** 187–195.

1088. **Thapar, Romila**
The impact of trade c. 100 B.C.—300 A.D. in India. **4:** 30–38.

MEDIEVAL

1089. **Gopal, Lallanji**
Agricultural technique in medieval India; its Central Asian contacts. **32:** 235–251.

1090. **Gopal, Surendra**
Indian trades in Russia in the XVIIth century. **62:** 291–300.

1091. ———
Merchants in Western India in the sixteenth-seventeenth centuries. **55:** 235–247.

1092. **Irfan Habib**
The social distribution of landed property in pre-British India: A historical survey. **55:** 264–316.

1093. **Rashid, A.**
Merchants and artisans in medieval north Indian economy (1206–1526). **62:** 313–321.

1094. **Sangar, S.P.**
India's textile exports to South-east Asia in the 17th century. **52:** 190–213.

1095. **Saran, Paramatma**
Insurance during medieval India. **82:** 369–375.

1096. **Sarkar, Jagadish Narayan**
Indigo as a form of commercial agriculture in India during the first half of the seventeenth century. **62:** 45–91.

1097. ———
Marketing organisation in Mughal India. **47:** 512–519.

1098. **Satish Chandra**
Shivaji and the Maratha landed elements. **55:** 248–263.

1099. **Sherwani, H.K.**
Some economic aspects of the reign of 'Abdu'llah Qutb Shah (1626–1672). **4:** 95–115.

1100. **Srivastava, Hari Shanker**
Famines in medieval India (1200–1526). **47:** 497–507.

MODERN

1101. **Fukazawa, H.**
A note on the corvee system (Vethbegar) in the eighteenth century Maratha kingdom. **54:** 117–130.

1102. **Gupta, P.S.**
Notes on the origin and structuring of the industrial labour force in India—1880 to 1920. **55:** 421–441.

1103. **Habib, Sayera I.**
The state sector in the Indian economy. **54:** 131–136.

1104. **Mishra, L.N.**
The present situation. **60:** 78–80.

1105. ———
Railway budget 1973–74. **60:** 45–57.

1106. ———
Restoring financial health of Railways. **60:** 62–77.

1107. ———
Zonal Railway Service Commission. **60:** 58–61.

1108. **Prasad, Deo Muni**
Technique of accounting present system and some suggestions. **60:** 593–598.

1109. **Prasad, Kunwar Deo**
Principles of taxation—ancient and modern. **60:** 553–556.

1110. **Rangaswamy, C.V.**
Some aspects of village economy in ex-Bombay Karnataka (18–20 cent.) from British settlement reports and daftars. **32:** 149–161.

1111. **Saran, Pramatma**
Trade and life assurance during the pre- and early British period in India. **100:** 228–236.

1112. **Singh, C.D.**
Agricultural finance and the nationalized bank. **60:** 571–577.

1113. **Singh, Ghanshyam Narain**
Dynamism of the Marxian economy. **60:** 599–603.

1114. **Singh, Nawal Kishore**
Government control and the cooperative movement in Bihar. **60:** 586–592.

1115. **Sinha, Satya Prakash**
Trade union rivalry—a threat to trade unionism. **60:** 578–585.

1116. **Srivastava, Dharma Bhanu**
Failure of early British land settlements in Uttar Pradesh 1775–1833. **82:** 405–412.

1117. **Syamchaudhuri, N.K.**
Indigenous irrigation of Assam: An eco-cultural trait. **13:** 295–301.

State, Government and Political Thought

1118. **Agrawal, K.M.**
Religious offences in the Arthasastra of Kautilya. **94 (1):** 163–168.

1119. **Bongard-Levin, G.M.** and **Vigasin, A.A.**
Society and state in ancient India. **94 (1):** 169–180.

1120. **Botto, O.**
Dvaidhibhava in the Kautiliyarthasastra and in other texts. **41:** 46–56.

1121. **Dandekar, R.N.**
Sources of ancient Indian polity: "Checks on monarchy: Popular Assemblies": Atharvaveda VII.12. **13:** 77–81.

1122. **Das, R.M.**
Manu's theory of punishment. **94 (1):** 181–187.

1123. **Dikshit, R.K.**
Kamandaka's conception of state. **59:** 254–263.

1124. ———
Law and justice in Kamandakiya nitisara. **62:** 162–164.

1125. **Ewing, A.C.**
The concept of democracy. **28:** 94–108.

1126. **Ezhuthachan, K.N.**
The bhasakautaliyam. **71:** 105–111.

1127. **Harihara Sastri, G.**
Kautalya's arthasastra—some textual problems. **71:** 315–324.

1128. **Jha, Dayadhar**
Inviolability of the mission and the right to diplomatic asylum. **60:** 487–499.

1129. **Kangle, R.P.**
The steelyard in Kautilya. **39:** 189–193.

1130. **Litman, A.D.**
Mahatma Gandhi on progress and peace. **81:** 161–166.

1131. **Moghe, S.G.**
A new interpretation of the Kautiliya arthasastra III.14.29 & 34. **84:** 342–347.

1132. **Mukherjee, B.N.**
A note on the date of the Arthasastra. **5 (2):** 303–305.

1133. **Mukherjee, S.N.**
The social implications of the political thought of Raja Rammohum Roy. **55:** 356–389.

1134. **Ojha, K.C.**
The date of the Arthasastra. **61:** 743–746.

1135. **Pande, G.C.**
The conception of ancient Indian state. **5 (2):** 373–377.

1136. **Prabhu, Joseph**
Dharma as an alternative to human rights. **9:** 174–179.

1137. **Samozvantsev, A.M.**
Some observations on the evolution of ancient Indian law (the property). **94 (1):** 215–230.

1138. **Shah, K.K.**
Polity from the Pratimanataka. **5 (2):** 379–381.

1139. **Shapeti, S.B.**
Principles and practices in Indian polity. **30:** 341–343.

1140. **Singh, K.S.**
Religion and morality in Kautilya and Machiavelli. **47:** 447–454.

1141. **Sinha, Atul Kumar**
Ethical tone of the arthasastra of Kautilya. **86:** 413–418.

1142. **Sinha, Tarkeshwar Nath**
Salient feature of the functions of local government in ancient India. **62:** 466–468.

1143. **Sternbach, Ludwik**
Juridical studies in ancient Indian law. **39:** 396–425.

1144. **Tyagi, N.C.**
The ideals of the ancient Indian state. **84:** 276–280.

Sociology

1145. **Agrawal, Govind**
Sati-pratha—ek adhyayan aur vivechan. **85:** 405–428. (Hindi).

1146. **Aiyappan, A.**
Sociology of friendship. **72:** 242–261.

1147. **Apte, Usha M.**
Vedic Hindu and tribal marriage. **57:** 223–230.

1148. **Bose, D.**
Utilisation of social and cultural anthropology in historical research: The case of the impact of agriculture on some South Indian societies. **75:** 25–45.

1149. **Breckenridge, Carol Appadurai**
The social use of everyday objects in Hindu South India. **46 (1):** 57–66.

1150. **Das, Sudhir Ranjan**
Some aspects of the nineteenth century Bengali society. **6:** 271–283.

1151. **Forbes, Geraldine**
From patronage to partisanship: The beginnings of the women's movement in India. **33:** 98–117.

1152. **Furer-Haimendorf, Christoph von**
Morality and prestige among the Nagas. **34:** 154–181.

1153. **Ganguly, P.G.**
Separatism in the Indian polity; case study. **34:** 58–107.

1154. **Ghosh, O.K.**
The kayasthas. **95:** 13–16.

1155. **Gopal, Lallanji**
Proprietary rights of the village community in northern India. **29:** 145–155.

1156. **Gough, Kathleen**
Political party conflict in a Kerala Village. **34:** 127–141.

1157. **Gould, Harold A.**
A theory of social stratification and the case of Indian society. **34:** 142–153.

1158. **Gune, Vithal Triumbak**
The social development in Maharashtra. **39:** 147–150.

1159. **Jayakar, Pupul**
The human challenge. **36:** 39–41.

1160. **Jena, Kurana C.**
Human sacrifices in Ganjam (1837–1861). **32:** 259–264.

1161. **Jha, Jata Shankar**
An early attempt at marriage reform in Mithila. **47:** 533–537.

1162. **Kosambi, D.D.**
Development of the gotra system. **39:** 215–224.

1163. **Malhotra, K.C., Khomne, S.B., Hulbe, S.K. and Kolte, S.B.**
A nomadic caste-cluster in a new culture setting: A study in culture adaptation. **53:** 298–308.

1164. **Meenakshisundaran, T.P.**
Varadaksina, its rise and results. **7:** 38–42.

1165. **Neog, Maheswar**
The role of tambula in Assam's social life. **39:** 270–281.

1166. **Peter, H.R.H. Prince of Greece and Denmark**
Patterns of polyandry in Tibet and India. **34:** 40–57.

1167. **Raghuvanshi, V.P.S.**
The Institution and working of caste in the latter part of the eighteenth century from European sources. **4:** 147–175.

1168. **Rajamani, M.B.**
A study of 'Garuda' tradition in the light of Emile Durkheim's sociological theory. **32:** 253–257.

1169. **Ramasubramanian, N.**
Personal name study—Madras Hindu female names. **30:** 519–530.

1170. **Roy Choudhury, P.C.**
What a tribal woman can teach us. **62:** 127–132.

1171. **Saberwal, Satish**
Oral data, religious literature and history: Notes from a sociologist. **75:** 15–24.

1172. **Sengupta, Nilakshi**
Symbolism in ancient Indian marriage rituals. **6:** 313–317.

1173. **Shashi, S.S.**
The Gujjar women. **85:** 147–150.

1174. **Visswanathan, E. Sa**
The emergence of Brahmans in South India with special reference to Tamil Nadu. **10:** 282–325.

Anthropology

1175. **Abbie, A.A.**
Indian and the Australian aborigines. **83:** 87–94.

1176. **Das, Bhuban M.**
Variations among Bodo populations of Assam. **7:** 230–233.

1177. **Ferreira, John V.**
Finitude, complementarity and dependence in primitive societies. **34:** 182–202.

1178. **Fuchs, Stephen**
Applied anthropology in India. **34:** 258–271.

1179. **HSU, Francis L.K.**
Christianity and the anthropologist. **34:** 203–228.

1180. **Hutton, J.H.**
The Naga tribes in the Tarikh-i-Assam. **13:** 95–96.

1181. **Miller, Beatrice Diamond**
Revitalization movements; theory and practice as evidenced among the Buddhists of Maharashtra. **34:** 108–126.

1182. **Mukherjee, Bratindra Nath**
The import of the term "Maccocalingae". **6:** 318–325.

1183. **Mukherjee, Swapan K.**
Gypsies: Inhabitants from lost land. **76:** 201–204.

1184. **Pradhan, M.C.**
Some aspects of the Jat religion and ethics. **34:** 229–257.

1185. **Sarkar, S.S.**
The Indo-Aryan or Indo-Caspian head form. **50:** 457–464.

1186. **Singh, L.P.**
The concept of man: Some modern critiques and the Indian archetypal evidence. **9:** 180–186.

1187. **Sontheimer, Gunther D.**
Field research in Maharashtra and Karnatak: The history of some Pastoral communities and their cults. **52:** 246–261.

Psychology

1188. **Dhammaratna, U.**
A study of the nature of dream—consciousness with special reference to its explanation given in the Pali literature. **62:** 529–540.

1189. **Dinesh Chandra Shastri**
A study of Indian psychology. **1:** 249–260.

1190. **Krishnamoorthy, K.**
Sanskrit psychological terminology. **39:** 225–232.

Religion

1191. **Bedar, A.R.**
The wisdom of India in the seventeenth century: A study based on Diwan-e-Mubad; a rare manuscript in Khuda Bakhsh Library. **82:** 364–368.

1192. **Bhattacharya, Kamaleswar**
The criterion of orthodoxy in India and the case of Jainism and Buddhism. **96:** 101–109.

1193. **Bhattacharyya, N.N.**
Coomaraswamy and Indian religious history. **25:** 101–110.

1194. **Chatterjee, Bhaskar**
Foreign immigrants influence on Indian religion. **20:** 287–305.

1195. **Devaraja, N.K.**
Religion and philosophy. **16:** 354–358.

1196. **Habibullah, A.B.M.**
An early Arab report on Indian religious sects. **75:** 433–443.

1197. **Jaiswal, Suvira**
Syncretism of the doctrine of incarnation. **62:** 410–416.

1198. **Mashi, Y.**
The nature of religion. **28:** 205–218.

1199. **Puskas, Ildiko**
Indian religions in classical sources. **9:** 166–173.

1200. **Ramakrishna, G.**
Religion, science and society. **73:** 49–64.

1201. **Ranganathananda**
Scientific approach to religion. **1:** 351–362.

1202. **Roth, Phil. Gustav**
The birth of a saviour related in Buddhist, Christian, Islamic and Jaina traditions. **47:** 455–469.

1203. **Sengupta, Santosh**
Study of mystical experience. **1:** 371–384.

1204. **Sharma, R.S.**
Material milieu of tantricism. **55:** 175–189.

1205. **Sircar, D.C.**
An aspect of early Indian religious life. **47:** 424–427.

1206. **Smart, Ninian**
The convergence of religions. **51:** 247–256.

1207. **Vatsyayan, Kapila**
Goddesses and women in Indian myth and art. **84:** 281–295.

HINDUISM

1208. **Agnihotri, P.D.**
Idol and idol worship in the mahabhasya of Patanjali. **3:** 178–184.

1209. **Agrawala, R.C.**
Sakti cult in ancient Rajasthan: Some interesting aspects. **89:** 57–60.

1210. **Anantharangachar, N.**
Saranas and Alwars. **8:** 299–307.

1211. **Arunachalam, M.**
Gandaraditta and his Tiru-isaippa. **93:** 229–232.

1212. **Bagchi, Subhendu Gopal**
The rituals of the pitha of Kalighata. **20:** 257–267.

1213. **Bailey, G.M.**
Brahma's role as a protector. **11:** 127–136.

1214. **Bajpai, K.D.**
Vasudeva-Krsna cult—the early phase. **90:** 149–151.

1215. **Balasubrahmanyam, S.R.**
The Skanda cult. **66:** 326–334.

1216. **Banerjee, Nitya Narayan**
Peace through Hinduism. **62:** 417–429.

1217. **Banerji, Sures Chandra**
Kali in Bengal tantra. **84:** 191–194.

1218. **Basham, A.L.**
Notes on the origins of Saktism and Tantricism. **20:** 148–154.

1219. **Bhat, G.K.**
Affection—motive in animal sacrifice. **11:** 187–190.

1220. **Bhatt, G.H.**
Muralidharadasa's commentary on the Sandilya bhakti sutras. **50:** 72–75.

1221. **Bhattacharya, Dinesh Chandra**
The tantrasara of Krsnananda Vagisa. **39:** 27–33.

1222. **Bhattacharya, Vishnupada**
The evolution of Bhakti-cult in Aryavarta: The revival of Bhakti-cult in South India. **29:** 156–172.

1223. **Bhattacharyya, N.N.**
The cult and rituals of Dharma Thakur. **75:** 327–340.

1224. **Biardeau, M.**
The ball-game: Myth and rite. **94 (2):** 875–881.

1225. **Bongard-Levin, G.M.**
Hindustan in the 3rd-1st Millennia B.C.: Some problems of ethnic history (archaeology and linguistics). **78:** 81–91.

1226. **Brockington, J.L.**
Mountains and suns. **56 (2):** 63–74.

1227. **Buddha Prakash**
Krsna. **39 (3):** 36–57.

1228. **Chakraborti, Haripada**
The cult of Jagannatha in Indian culture. **60:** 451–458.

1229. **Chakravarti, Chintaharan**
A few ritualistic terms current in Bengal. **71:** 77–79.

1230. ———
A note on the study of feasts and festivities of the Hindus. **61:** 771–773.

1231. **Chatterji, Suniti Kumar**
A brahmanical deity in Indo-China and Indonesia. **6:** 86–92.

1232. **Chattopadhyaya, K.**
Hinduism. **48:** 275–280.

1233. **Chawdhry, Radha Krishna**
Position of the Brahmanas in ancient India. **39:** 43–49.

1234. **Chidananda Murthy, M.**
Nilapatas—a relatively unknown religious sect of medieval India. **32:** 217–221.

1235. **Clothey, Fred W.**
Some aspects of Arunagiri's significance for Tamil bhakti. **93:** 261–265.

1236. **Creel, Austin B.**
The sources of Hindu dharma. **20:** 97–108.

1237. **Dandekar, R.N.**
What is Hinduism? **71:** 89–96.

1238. **Dange, Sadashiv A.**
The birth of Ganapati. **44:** 1–7.

1239. **Dasgupta, Kalyan Kumar**
The Bauls and the Pasupatas. **6:** 339–352.

1240. **Derrett, J. Duncan M.**
Professions of faith: A zero-value in Hinduism. **9:** 21–30.

1241. **Deshpande, G.T.**
Saivism and Saktism. **23:** 624–657.

1242. **Devasenapathi, V.A.**
Obeisance to all persons born in Tiruvarur. **72:** 166–169.

1243. **Dhal, U.N.**
Viraja-Ksetra—a sakta pitha. **44:** 67–76.

1244. **Ensink, Jacob**
Hindu pilgrimage and Hindu sacrifice. **94 (1):** 105–117.

1245. **Ganguli, Kalyan Kumar**
Krishna cult in Rajasthan. **20:** 235–252.

1246. ———
The other Krsna. **78:** 21–30.

1247. **Gaurinath Sastri**
Worship of the clay image of Durga. **6:** 266–270.

1248. **Gopal, Lallanji**
Devala on dana. **21:** 245–255.

1249. **Goswami, Asha**
The monogamist Krsna. **16:** 443–450.

1250. **Goswami, Krishnagopal**
The manava principal in Manu and Nietzche's appraisal. **62:** 685–695.

1251. **Hara, Minoru**
Atidana, atiyajana and atitapas. **43:** 34–43.

1252. ———
A note on the Pasupata concept of purity (saucha). **21:** 237–244.

1253. **Jeyechandrun, A.V.**
The temple danseuses. **32:** 65–73.

1254. **Jha, D.N.**
Temples as landed magnates in early medieval South India (c. A.D. 700–1300). **55:** 202–216.

1255. **Joshi, M.C.**
The cult of Sri or Srividya and its association with temporal kingship. **88:** 22–28.

1256. **Karan Singh**
Hinduism challenge and response. **91 (1):** 35–37.

1257. **Kashikar, C.G**
The area of Syenaciti in the apastamba tradition. **56 (2):** 21–26.

1258. **Khiste, Batuknath Sastri**
Agama-sastriyah pujakramah. **44:** 83–86. (Sanskrit).

1259. **Kopf. David**
Keshub and Chaitanya: Brahmo evangelism and the indigenous modernization of Vaishnavism in Bengal. **33:** 69–79.

1260. **Krishan, Y.**
Anti-karma. **21:** 225–235.

1261. **Krishnan, K.G.**
A forgotten deity. **92:** 245–248.

1262. **Krishna Rao, M.V.**
Saranas and Haridasas. **8:** 287–297.

1263. **Kuiper, F.B.J.**
The three strides of Visnu. **15:** 137–151.

1264. **Kulkarni, B.S.**
Virasaivism and Jainism. **8:** 399–406.

1265. **Kuppuswami Sastri, S.**
Srimukapancasati. **56 (1):** 208–209.

1266. ———
Sri Ramakrishna and the message of Hinduism. **56 (1):** 203–205.

1267. ———
Sri Visnusahasranama stotra. **56 (1):** 206–207.

1268. **Lokesh Chandra**
Hellenistic echoes in the legend of Krsna. **40:** 149–154.

1269. **Lorenzen, David N.**
The Kalamukha background to Virasaivism. **9:** 278–293.

1270. **McLean, M.D.**
Ramakrishna: The greatest of the Saktas of Bengal? **51:** 151–172.

1271. **Mahapatra, Sitakant**
Art and ritual: A study of Saora pictograms. **46 (1):** 265–277.

1272. **Mahapatra, Sitakanta**
The ecstasy of love and communitas: A note on Jagannath culture. **2:** 61–69.

1273. **Maity, P.K.**
Folk-cults of West Bengal. **9:** 309–327.

1274. **Majumdar, R.C.**
Impact of Islam on Hinduism. **4:** 265–270.

1275. **Malledevaru, H.P.**
The authority (pramanya) of the Saivagamas. **73:** 224–234.

1276. ———
Virasaivism and Saivasiddhanta. **8:** 345–361.

1277. **Marulasiddiah, G.**
Virasaiva literature during the Vijayanagara empire (A.D. 1400–1800). **50:** 136–139.

1278. **Mirashi, V.V.**
Further light on the identification of Kalapriyanatha. **71:** 257–260.

1279. **Mishra, V.B.**
The retribution of karma in the Prakrita and Samskrita literature of the early medieval India. **13:** 136–141.

1280. **Mitra, Sisir Kumar**
A document relating to the worship at the Puri temple. **6:** 284–288.

1281. **Mukherjea, Sushil**
Mystical Lord Jagannatha. **2:** 70–86.

1282. **Mukhia, Harbans**
The ideology of the Bhakti movement: The case of Dadu Dayal. **75:** 445–454.

1283. **Nagaraja Rao, P.**
Humanism of Sri Madhva and the saint singers of Karnataka. **92:** 272–274.

1284. **Nagaswamy, R.**
Nataraja and the Urdhva Saivas. **91 (1):** 241–248.

1285. **Nakamura, Hajime**
The historico-social attitude of the Brahma sutras. **16:** 373–378.

1286. **Namjoshi, Vijayalaxmi S.**
The concept of Rudra-Siva in the light of its nama-literature. **57:** 41–49.

1287. **Nandi, R.N.**
Origin and nature of Saivite monasticism: The case of Kalamukhas. **55:** 190–201.

1288. **Nigam, M.L.**
The homeland of emotional bhakti of Krsna. **5 (2):** 271–277.

1289. **Pandey, D.P.**
The pre-procreational sanskars of Hindus. **7:** 217–220.

1290. **Parpola, Asko**
Reconstructing the Harappan Hinduism—sources and methods. **66:** 335–344.

1291. **Paul, Harendra Chandra**
An approach to the mystic philosophy in the Candi. **13:** 238–247.

1292. **Potdar, Mrinalini K.**
Relationship between the Gandharvas and Apsarases. **30:** 477–482.

1293. **Puri, Baijnath**
Ganesa and Ganapati cult in India and South-east Asia. **48:** 9–17.

1294. **Puri, B.N.**
Krishna and Krishnaism across India. **74:** 311–315.

1295. **Raghavachar, S.S.**
Classical Hinduism. **73:** 141–148.

1296. ———
Virasaivism and Vaisnavism. **8:** 369–379.

1297. **Rajagopalachar, K.**
Relevance of mythology to modern times. **73:** 172–179.

1298. **Rajendra Prasad, B. and Sambaiah, O.**
Brahmanayudu and Viravaishnavism. **93:** 239–242.

1299. **Raman, K.V.**
Karuppu—the village deity of Southern Tamilnadu. **32:** 265–266.

1300. **Ramaswamy, S.**
Siva consciousness in Indian literature: A comparative view. **73:** 40–48.

1301. **Ranjit Singh**
Dharm ke Hindu siddhanta ki utapatti evam vikas. **61:** 301–329. (Hindi).

1302. **Ray, Amita**
House-building rituals in ancient India. **6:** 298–312.

1303. **Rocher, L.**
Schools of Hindu law. **41:** 167–176.

1304. **Rolland, Piere**
Le ceremonial d'exclusion de la caste dans l'Inde ancienne. **66:** 487–497. (French).

1305. **Roychowdhury, Jyotsna**
Religious syncretism in ancient India: A conceptual approach. **88:** 203–210.

1306. **Rudrappa, J.**
Virasaivism and Kashmir Saivism. **8:** 327–343.

1307. **Sardesai, S.G.**
The peculiarities of Hinduism. **73:** 149–158.

1308. **Seetharamaiah, M.V.**
Goravas of Karnataka, **92:** 316–321.

1309. **Sen, S.**
On Yaksa and Yaksa worship. **41:** 187–195.

1310. **Sengupta, Bratindra Kumar**
An appraisal of the doctrine of bhakti. **7:** 199–206.

1311. ———
Towards a synthesis of the Saiva doctrines with the Bhakti cult. **13:** 227–231.

1312. **Shanmugam, P.**
The Saptamatri cult during Chola times. **93:** 257–260.

1313. **Sharma, B.N.**
Ganesa. **48:** 18–21.

1314. **Sharma, M.R.**
Human values in ancient India. **5 (2):** 279–281.

1315. **Shastri, Ajay Mitra**
Vaisnavism. **23:** 595–623.

1316. **Shastri, Balacharya Khuperkar**
Manavajanamache saphlaya. **52:** 280–285. (Marathi).

1317. **Shivarudrappa, A.L.**
Virasaivism and advaita. **8:** 363–368.

1318. **Shraddhananda**
The Ramakrishna movement in the west. **1:** 620–632.

1319. **Shulman, David**
Notes on the Kalantaka myth at Tirukkadavur. **93:** 267–274.

1320. **Singh, Sheo Bahadur**
Pasupata—Saivism in Haryana. **21:** 99–103.

1321. **Singh, Y.B.**
Jajmani system: Socio-economic transformation of a religious practice. **86:** 330–334.

1322. **Sircar, D.C.**
Kali worshipped in Bengal. **36:** 49–53.

1323. ———
The Narasimha cult. **62:** 42–44.

1324. ———
Rise of Kulinism in Mithila and Bengal. **66:** 349–359.

1325. **Sontheimer, Gunther D.**
The Mallari Khandoba myth as reflected in folk art and ritual. **40:** 237–251.

1326. ———
Some notes on Biroba, the Dhangar god of Maharashtra. **54:** 167–175.

1327. **Soundararajan, K.V.**
God in nature and its laws: The Indian syndrome. **91 (1):** 25–30.

1328. **Srivastava, V.C.**
The antiquity of the Pasupata sect. **19:** 109–125.

1329. ———
Historiography of Ganesa—cult in ancient India. **19:** 137–157.

1330. **Staal, J.F.**
Language and ritual. **56 (2):** 51–61.

1331. **Subramani Aiyar, N.**
Sakti-worship in the south. **1:** 334–340.

1332. **Thakur, Upendra**
The Ganga and Indian culture. **9:** 71–82.

1333. ———
Religion and culture: A study in Hindu ethics. **20:** 333–343.

1334. **Thipperudraswamy, H.**
Virasaivism and Buddhism. **8:** 379–398.

1335. **Thiruvengadathan, A.**
Tamil movement in Srivaisnavism. **56 (2):** 119–130.

1336. **Tiwari, A.R.G.**
Evolution of the Brahmanical pantheon: A study. **44:** 9–21.

1337. **Tripathi, Gaya Charan**
Die vorstellung der damonen im Indischen glauben. **94 (2):** 989–1002. (German).

1338. ———
Indo-European elements in Greek and Indian mythologies. **5 (2):** 297–302.

1339. **Vishva Bandu Shastri**
Some harmonising tendencies in ancient Hindu culture. **66:** 345–348.

VEDIC

1340. **Agrawala, P.K.**
Vedic evidence on betel-eating. **53:** 258–260.

1341. **Agrawala, V.S.**
Gauri. **15:** 1–7.

1342. ———
Purusa-sukta. **59:** 7–23.

1343. **Aithal, K.P.**
Asvalayana and his works. **79:** 75–82.

1344. **Amar Nath Shastri**
Vratya-samiksha. **50:** 36–41. (Hindi).

1345. **Apte, P.P.**
Pancaratra-samhitas—a study. **57:** 81–93.

1346. **Apte, V.M.**
Apropos of Rgveda 11.1.1a. **16:** 1–4.

1347. **Awasthi, Brahmamitra**
Vidya aura avidya ka svaroopa. **95:** 54–58. (Hindi).

1348. **Bailey, H.W.**
Atharva-veda makaka. **41:** 41–45.

1349. **Bandyopadhyay, Santi**
Some linguistic aspects of the Satapatha Brahmana. **37:** 383–387.

1350. **Betal, R.S.**
State of criminal law in Manusmrti. **61:** 279–300.

1351. **Bhagwan Singh**
Rigvedic pura. **95:** 67–74. (Hindi).

1352. **Bhandari, V.S.**
Vedic legend of Cyavana and Sukanya. **59:** 108–112.

1353. **Bhanj Deo, Prafulla Chandra**
"Om mani—padme hum". **39:** 90–94.

1354. **Bharadwaj, O.P.**
Naubandhana. **3:** 231–238.

1355. **Bhargava, P.L.**
The Adityas in the Rgveda. **80:** 15–18.

1356. ———
The comparative antiquity of Indra and Varuna. **94 (1):** 59–61.

1357. **Bhat, G.K.**
Marriage of Surya (Rgveda X.85). **94 (1):** 63–75.

1358. **Bhattacharya, Rabindra Kumar**
Scientific and philosophical wisdom in the vedic literature. **95:** 57–61.

1359. **Bhide, V.V.**
Praisa proksanir asadaya . . . at the darsapurnamasa sacrifices. **3:** 43–49.

1360. **Bhise, Usha**
Divine character of speech in the Rgveda. **97:** 11–15.

1361. **Bodewitz, H.W.**
Jaiminiya Brahmana I, 153–155 on the kaleya saman. **79:** 179–191.

1362. ———
The raising of Central pillar (made of udumbara wood) of Sadas hut by the Udgatr according to Jaiminiya Brahmana I.70-72. **94 (1):** 77–82.

1363. ———
Rgveda 10, 146: The hymn to Aranyani. **84:** 3–15.

1364. ———
What did Indra do with the Yatis? **27:** 65–72.

1365. **Bose, Abinash Chandra**
Approach to the vedic world. **72:** 1–13.

1366. **Bronkhorst, Johannes**
Further remarks on Bhartrhari's vedic affiliation. **73:** 216–223.

1367. **Brown, W. Norman**
Duty as truth in the Rigveda. **41:** 57–67.

1368. **Buhler, G.**
Note on Professor Jacobi's age of the veda on Professor Tilak's orion. **95:** 106–116.

1369. **Chakrabarti, Samiran Chandra**
Sabha in the vedic literature. **37:** 61–68.

1370. **Chakravarti, Chintaharan**
Interesting developments in vedic rituals. **50:** 1–2.

1371. **Chapekar, N.G.**
Two Rgvedic personalities. **39:** 38–42.

1372. **Chattopadhyaya, Debiprasad**
Scientific thought in the vedic age. **73:** 81–112.

1373. ———
Sources of Indian idealism. **75:** 239–270.

1374. **Chaudhuri, Korak K.**
'Ayas' in vedic literature. **88:** 321–326.

1375. **Dandekar, R.N.**
Some aspects of vedic exegesis. **56 (2):** 1–13.

1376. ———
Sources of ancient Indian polity: "Election of a king": Atharvaveda III.4. **7:** 32–37.

1377. ———
Universe in vedic thought. **41:** 91–114.

1378. ———
Vedic religion and mythology. **23:** 561–593.

1379. ———
The vena-sukta in the Atharvaveda. **59:** 24–30.

1380. **Dange, S.A.**
Adornment as a protective measure in vedic ritual. **59:** 87–103.

1381. ———
Cosmo-sexualism in the vedic ritual. **16:** 23–44.

1382. ———
Crying worlds (krandasi). **3:** 9–16.

1383. ———
Folk-traditions and rain-imagery of the vedic seers. **84:** 16–26.

1384. ———
Garta and Garta-aruk in the Rgveda. **94 (1):** 83–87.

1385. ———
The kuntapa hymns and the silpa. **27:** 85–93.

1386. ———
Pururavas: A research for identity. **37:** 52–60.

1387. ———
The riddle of the black antelope. **43:** 27–33.

1388. ———
Ritual-variations from the Brahmanas. **95:** 3–6.

1389. ———
Sisna-Deva and the vedic cult of the nude. **80:** 22–25.

1390. ———
Yama-Yami, the cosmic twins. **69:** 24–37.

1391. **Dange, Sindhu S.**
Yaska on widow's share. **80:** 385–387.

1392. **Demora, Juan Miguel**
Vac. **27:** 281–284.

1393. **Deore, Vijaya**
The socio-legal position of women in the smrtis of Manu and Yajnavalkya. **57:** 1–17.

1394. **Derrett, J. Duncan M.**
Forbidden occupations in smrti and their aftermath. **94 (1):** 189–197.

1395. ———
"Mother-in-law v. daughter-in-law": A translation of the anonymous Svasru-Snusa-dhana-samvada. **61:** 261–277.

1396. **Deshpande, G.T.**
Sala-suktas in the Atharvaveda. **59:** 37–55.

1397. **Devasthali, G.V.**
The correct reading of Rgveda 8.35.13–15c D. **94 (1):** 89–96.

1398. ———
The form and the arrangement of the Atharva-Veda. **7:** 43–53.

1399. ———
The krama-patha unit. **27:** 105–113.

1400. ———
Madhava's mantrarthanukramani. **79:** 193–198.

1401. ———
Panini as an aid to Rgvedic interpretation. **97:** 20–26.

1402. ———
The status of the Atharvaveda. **50:** 3–13.

1403. ———
Vedic literature. **23:** 29–54.

1404. **Dharmadhikari, T.N.**
On the untraced kalpa—citations in Sayana's commentary on the taittiriya samhita. **56 (2):** 27–32.

1405. **Dumont, P.E.**
The manuscript of the Rgveda of the M.A. Stein collection. **15:** 51–55.

1406. **Dwivedi, R.C.**
Jara in the Rgveda. **3:** 17–22.

1407. **Edgerton, Franklin**
Atharva-veda 13.1.10. **15:** 56–58.

1408. **Elizarenkova, T.Y.**
About some archaic peculiarities of the Rgvedic syntax. **27:** 125–132.

1409. ———
To the interpretation of the spell Atharvaveda VI, 117. **84:** 27–31.

1410. **Elizarenkova, T.Y. and Toporov, V.N.**
Vedic vanku. **94 (1):** 97–104.

1411. **Esteller, A.**
The Rgveda samhita—"palimpsest" and its complete deciphering code. **37:** 6–30.

1412. ———
The Rgveda-samhita "Palimpsest" in VIII. 46. **16:** 45–76.

1413. ———
The udatta as key-stone of the deciphering code for the Rgveda-samhita-"palimpsest". **94 (2):** 929–947.

1414. **Ganguly, J.**
Influence of Bengali smrti writers on Maithila smrti. **29:** 369–378.

1415. **Godbole, G.H.**
Prajapati in the Brahmanas. **97:** 45–56.

1416. **Gonda, J.**
Balinese hymns addressed to god Akasa. **66:** 404–415.

1417. ———
The Gods of the godana ceremony (AVS. 6, 68). **27:** 153–158.

1418. ———
The highest principle in the early veda: Some critical notes. **91 (1):** 19–23.

1419. ———
The mantras of Taittiriya-Brahmana 1, 5, 5. **43:** 1–17.

1420. ———
Mind and moon. **87:** 147–160.

1421. ———
Rgveda 1.36.13 and 14. **56 (2):** 15–20.

1422. ———
Rgveda 10.40.10. **15:** 78–86.

1423. ———
Rgveda-samhita 8, 18. **20:** 143–147.

1424. ———
Some notes on optional rites. **3:** 23–41.

1425. ———
Suci. **94 (1):** 119–127.

1426. **Gopal, Lallanji**
Devaladharmasutra on varnas and jatis. **27:** 239–245.

1427. **Gopalaswamy Iyengar, T.K.**
The place of the vedas in Vatsyayana's nyayabhasya. **7:** 130–137.

1428. **Goswami, Kunja Govinda**
Vedic cult (circa B.C. 200 to A.D. 500). **37:** 31–41.

1429. **Gupta, M.N.**
The riddle of 'trisaptah' of Atharvaveda I.1.1 in relation to symbolism on seals from Mohenjo-daro in the Indus Valley (an archaeology aided solution). **44:** 155–181.

1430. **Hara, Minoru**
Miscellanea pasupatica. **50:** 55–65.

1431. **Hazra, R.C.**
A hitherto obscure vedic word on the vratyas—its derivation, interpretation and historical importance. **44:** 143–153.

1432. **Heesterman, J.C.**
The ritualist's problem. **27:** 167–179.

1433. **Hejib, Alaka**
Hermann Grassmann on Rgveda X.18.6a. **80:** 36–38.

1434. **Hoffmann, Karl**
J.B.III, 304: Arikseva lokam. **79:** 176–177.

1435. **Howard, Wayne**
Samaveda arcika recitation of the Namputiris. **79:** 145–169.

1436. **Jacobi, Hermann G.**
On the date of the Rgveda. **95:** 91–97.

1437. **Jani, A.N.**
On the matra and the mode of recitation of an independent svarita. **16:** 77–81.

1438. **Jog, K.P.**
Is Rgveda I.117 a composite hymn? **44:** 137–141.

1439. **Joshi, Rasik Vihari**
Methods of vedic interpretation in the west. **44:** 115–136.

1440. **Joshi, S.B.**
Is Indra, the vritrahan, supreme God in the Rigveda? **30:** 351–359.

1441. **Kansara, N.M.**
Rv. X.14.IA: A fresh approach. **61:** 517–519.

1442. ______
Vivarta and avikrta parinama in the vedanta mimamsa. **3:** 79–88.

1443. **Kantawala, S.G.**
Some remarks on the Naciketas-legend. **94 (1):** 293–302.

1444. **Kapadia, B.H.**
Atri, rbisa and saptavadhri. **16:** 82–89.

1445. ______
The word "garta" in the Rgveda. **61:** 521–526.

1446. **Karnik, H.R.**
Some derivative legends from the II, III and IV kandas of the Satapatha Brahmana. **97:** 64–71.

1447. **Kashikar, C.G.**
A critical study of the ritualistic sutras. **39:** 203–210.

1448. ______
Further notes on the Varaha srauta sutra I.1.3. **71:** 193–198.

1449. ______
The obscure in the vedic sacrificial rituals. **69:** 89–94.

1450. ______
A rare manuscript of the Varaha school. **50:** 14–16.

1451. ______
Varaha srutasutra III.1.1-2.2: Vajapeya and Dvadasaha; a critical and exegetical study. **27:** 195–200.

1452. ______
Yajnaparsve: An unpublished parisista of the Sukla Yajurveda school. **94 (1):** 135–142.

1453. **Katti, Madhav N.**
Antiquity of the Vedas. **30:** 421–424.

1454. **Kawthekar, P.N.**
The folk-lore in the Rgveda. **16:** 90–93.

1455. **Koller, John M.**
Ritual and world view in the Rgveda. **20:** 109–119.

1456. **Kramrisch, Stella**
Two: Its significance in the Rgveda. **15:** 109–136.

1457. **Krishna Lal**
Rigvede krida. **95:** 19–21. (Sanskrit).

1458. **Kuiper, F.B.J.**
The heavenly bucket. **41:** 144–156.

1459. ______
Vedic ayas—"not to be injured." **16:** 94–105.

1460. **Laddu, S.D.**
Sayana's authorship of the vedabhasyas. **3:** 61–65.

1461. **Lahiri, A.K.**
The pliancy of myth: A study of the Indra-vrtra myth in the later vedic literature. **20:** 120–142.

1462. **Limaye, V.P.**
Nagayajnopavitin. **27:** 509–511.

1463. **Mainkar, T.G.**
The kratu, the yajna and the yatu in the Rgveda. **37:** 1–5.

1464. **Maity, S.K.**
Women in the Rig vedic culture. **5 (2):** 383–387.

1465. **Mallison, F.**
A note on holiness allowed to women: Pativrata and sati. **94 (2):** 741–744.

1466. **Mankad, D.R.**
Divodasa. **71:** 211–219.

1467. **Mehendale, M.A.**
Anupa in nirukta. **59:** 104–107.

1468. ______
Atihayat (?) **80:** 19–21.

1469. ______
Nirukta notes XII (Vibhakti). **50:** 17–19.

1470. ______
Prakamodya—its relevance to the akhyana theory. **94 (1):** 143–144.

1471. ______
Sapta devalokah. **16:** 106–111.

1472. ______
Two vedic notes. **95:** 98–99.

1473. ______
Vanargu. **97:** 76–81.

1474. **Mishra, Hari Mohan**
Brahman: A semantic discussion. **16:** 112–115.

1475. **Misra, Vidya Niwas**
Vak legends in the Brahmana literature. **50:** 20–28.

1476. **Modak, B.R.**
The social and political conditions as reflected in the Atharvaveda-Parisishtas. **30:** 280–287.

1477. **Moghe, S.G.**
Significance of Vyaghrasmrti in dharmasastra. **57:** 33–40.

1478. **Mukhopadhyay, Biswanath**
Rsabha. **80:** 39–42.

1479. **Mus, Paul**
Du nouveau sur Rgveda 10–90? Sociologie d'une grammaire. **15:** 165–185. (French).

1480. **Mylius, Klaus**
Visvasrj, Visvasrjah and the problem of continuity in Indian religious history. **27:** 285–300.

1481. **Narahari, H.G.**
Eschatology in the later samhitas. **39 (3):** 129–132.

1482. **Nariman, Faribourz**
The emanation of spiritual authority and temporal power from Miora-Ahura/Mitravaruna. **95:** 62–66.

1483. **Narten, Johanna**
Jagat-im Rgveda. **41:** 161–166.

1484. **Ojihara, Yutaka**
Sur le nivartana, dit des cheveux: Addenda. **37:** 42–51. (French).

1485. **Palsule, G.B.**
Devanam-priyah: Has it any vedic antecedents? **27:** 313–317.

1486. ———
A unique case of a V-glide in the Taittiriya Brahmana (2.4.4.4). **69:** 118–121.

1487. **Pandey, Raj Bali**
The wheel of the state (Rastra-chakra) in the Atharvaveda. **59:** 31–36.

1488. **Pathak, R.A.**
An explanatory note on some vedic compounds. **53:** 268–275.

1489. **Patkar, M.M.**
Family law as observed in the smrtis of Narada, Brhaspati and Katyayana. **71:** 301–310.

1490. **Patyal, H.C.**
The Paippalada samhita (kanda III). **16:** 125–132.

1491. **Potdar, K.R.**
The mimamsa view about the daksina-sacrifice-relationship and its implication. **16:** 379–384.

1492. **Puri, Baij Nath**
Educational data from the Medhatithi. **7:** 160–162.

1493. **Rahurkar, V.G.**
Apropos the Rgveda V.40. **61:** 511–516.

1494. ———
Devapi and Santanu in the Rgveda. **39 (3):** 175–180.

1495. ———
A literary evaluation of the grtsamada-suktas. **50:** 29–31.

1496. **Ram Gopal**
The home and date of Durgacharya. **94 (1):** 129–134.

1497. ———
Rgvedic compounds formed from is-kr. **3:** 1–7.

1498. ———
The Rgvedic compound svar-drs. **27:** 337–342.

1499. **Rau, Wilhelm**
Sundry remarks on the printed text of Jaiminiya-Brahmana. **79:** 141–144.

1500. **Renou, Louis**
Sur la forme des Brahmasutra. **15:** 195–203.

1501. **Ritschl, Eva and Schetelich, Maria**
Sambhuyasamutthana. **94 (1):** 199–206.

1502. **Rocher, Ludo**
The definition of Vakparusya. **39:** 323–334.

1503. ———
The sutras and sastras on the eight types of marriage. **94 (1):** 207–214.

1504. **Sahasrabuddhe, Madhukar Tryambak**
Vedo me jyotivigyan ki dharsti se pinda aur brahmand ka pratipadan. **50:** 32–35. (Hindi).

1505. **Saklatwala, Beram**
Urvasi and Pururavas. **39:** 337–339.

1506. **Saloman, Richard**
Traditional Hindu concepts of tirtha and yatra as reflected in smrti literature. **20:** 327–332.

1507. **Sane, P.S.**
Use of mimamsa in dharmasastra. **97:** 112–132.

1508. **Saraswati, Vidyanand**
Vedartha ke moolabhoota siddhanta. **95:** 33–38. (Hindi).

1509. **Sarma, E.R. Sreekrishna**
Significance of Sankara's adhyasa-bhasya. **27:** 399–401.

1510. **Satyavrat Singh**
Mratuanjayamantrathavimarsha. **94 (1):** 151–159. (Sanskrit).

1511. ———
Sri Vaishnavadharmasaya darshan-ikprashtabhumi. **3:** 67–69. (Sanskrit).

1512. **Schlerath, B.**
Zur bedeutung von ved. samsa—und aw. sengha-, sanha—. **27:** 371–375. (German).

1513. **Schmidt, Hanns-Peter**
Akupara. **27:** 377–381.

1514. **Sehgal, S.R.**
The problem of Rigvedic khilas as re-examined through its own grihya sutras. **21:** 201–203.

1515. **Sen, Sukumar**
Dva suparna sayuja. **6:** 125–126.

1516. **Sen Sharma, Deba Brata**
Hamsa vidya—a study. **95:** 18–22.

1517. **Sharma, B.N.K.**
Importance and scope of the Brahmasutras. **71:** 361–367.

1518. **Sharma, B.R.**
Apah in vedic cosmogony. **39:** 350–357.

1519. **Sharma, K.L.**
Pratisakhyas and padapatha. **16:** 133–148.

1520. **Sharma, Mukund Madhava**
A note on the saying: Itihasa puranabhyam vedam samupabrmhayet. **44:** 237–244.

1521. **Sharma, Ram**
Panini's chatvarimsa Brahmana. **30:** 436–440.

1522. **Sharma, Umesh Chandra**
The legend of dirghatamas. **80:** 26–35.

1523. ———
Visvamitra in the vedic ancillaries. **16:** 149–152.

1524. **Shastri, D.N.**
Vedic conjugational system. **16:** 294–298.

1525. **Shende, N.J.**
Aditya and adityas in the Rgveda brahmanas. **59:** 56–86.

1526. ———
Teachers and their views in the Rgveda brahmanas. **97:** 133–153.

1527. **Shivaganesha Murthy, R.S.**
Vedic sacrifice—A conspectus. **16:** 116–124.

1528. **Sivaji Singh**
Lines oj approach to the problem of Smriti interpretation. **48:** 410–418.

1529. **Singh, Rajeshwar Prasad**
Varna, jati and technical occupations in the Dharmasastra. **90:** 295–309.

1530. **Singh, Satya Prakash**
Conscious introversion and divine intimations in the Rgveda. **50:** 44–54.

1531. **Sinha, K.P.**
A new light on the apauruseyatva, nityaatva and abhrantatva of the vedas. **43:** 18–26.

1532. **Sircar, D.C.**
An aspect of social life in the vedic age. **20:** 344–346.

1533. **Smith, R. Morton**
Embarrassed Brahmans. **94 (2):** 701–705.

1534. ———
Impotent Gods. **27:** 395–398.

1535. **Sreekrishna Sarma, E.R.**
Concept of man in the vedic and upanisadic literature. **43:** 56–61.

1536. **Sri Nivas**
Nyaya sutra tatha bhasya me gunavratti. **3:** 71–77. (Hindi).

1537. **Srivastava, Narendra Pratap**
Agni ka aviskaar kese hua? **94 (1):** 145–150. (Hindi).

1538. **Staal, Frits**
Moon chants, space fillers and flow of milk. **79:** 17–30.

1539. ———
Rgveda 10.71 on the origin of language. **65:** 3–14.

1540. ———
Ritual, mantras and the origin of language. **27:** 403–425.

1541. **Sternbach, Ludwik**
Indian tales and the smrtis. **80:** 371–380.

1542. ———
Manava-dharmasastra VII.99 and yajnavalkyasmrti I.317. **29:** 82–89.

1543. **Subrahmanian, N.**
Vedic sacrifices in Tamulaham in the sangam age. **72:** 177–179.

1544. **Subrahmanya Sastri, P.S.**
Aho Ahalaya. **50:** 42–43. (Sanskrit).

1545. **Subrahmanya Sastri, S.**
Eligibility for the study of 'vedanta'. **37:** 138–144.

1546. **Sundar Raj, M.**
Rgvedic mythology. **66:** 360–366.

1547. **Surya Kanta**
Is Weber's edition of the SBR final? **16:** 153–154.

1548. **Swaminathan, V.**
Ksetrajna of Manu. **71:** 401–424.

1549. **Thite, Ganesh**
Contribution of Western scholars to the study of vedic ritual. **80:** 43–57.

1550. ———
Result of sacrifice and Gods in the Brahmana texts. **3:** 51–53.

1551. **Tiwari, Ramanand**
Cultural argument in history and philology. **95:** 59–63.

1552. **Tripathi, Gaya Charan**
The legend of the destruction of Tripura and its vedic origin. **27:** 445–455.

1553. **Udaya Vira Shastri**
Sapta-Sindhava. **95:** 18–21. (Sanskrit).

1554. **Upadhyaya, S.A.**
Kariristi: A sacrifice to be performed for securing rain. **97:** 161–175.

1555. **Upreti, Jayadutt**
Rishinammantradrashtritvammantrakartritvam cha. **95:** 22–32. (Sanskrit).

1556. **Varma, K.C.**
Date of the vedic kalpasutras. **38 (2):** 601–619.

1557. **Varma, V.K.**
Vedic optimism and origin of the doctrine of karman. **3:** 55–60.

1558. **Velankar, H.D.**
Gharma and oman in the Arti legend. **15:** 228–238.

1559. ———
Visvamitra and Vasistha in the Rgveda. **59:** 1–6.

1560. **Varma, K.C.**
Date of Harisvami. **47:** 409–418.

1561. **Vidyalankar, Kailash Chandra**
Vratya: Ek Adhyayan. **84:** 32–39. (Hindi).

1562. **Vishva Bandhu**
Some indications of heterodoxy in the vedas. **16:** 5–7.

1563. **Woolner, A.C.**
The philological argument for an upper limit to the date of the Rgveda. **95:** 78–83.

UPANISAD

1564. **Banerjee, Hiranmay**
Impact of the upanisads on western thought. **11:** 157–165.

1565. **Bhatkhande, S.M.**
The chandogya upanisad and the brahmasutras of Badarayana—a comparative study. **57:** 94–108.

1566. **Bhatt, Vishnu Prasad**
The attitude of the upanisads towards sacrifices. **16:** 8–22.

1567. **Bhattacharyya, Ramaprasad**
Sankara, Mandana and Ramanuja on mantra XI, Isopanisad. **37:** 132–137.

1568. **Bucca, Salvador**
Word order and its stylistic value in the Isopanisad. **39:** 34–37.

1569. **Chattopadhyaya, Basanta Kumar**
Upanisads and vedic rituals. **62:** 341–347.

1570. **Gonda, J.**
Notes on the katha upanisad. **69:** 60–70.

1571. **Hacker, P.**
Notes on the Mandukyopanisad and Sankara's Agamasastravivarana. **41:** 115–132.

1572. **Kunst, Arnold**
Some notes on the interpretation of the Svetasvatara upanisad. **94 (1):** 565–572.

1573. **Kuppuswami Sastri, S.**
The Brhadaranyaka upanishad. **56 (1):** 9–13.

1574. **Mayeda, Sengaku**
The concept of avidya in the older upanisads. **81:** 197–208.

1575. **Mehta, Vasistha Dev Mohan**
The antiquity of the upanisads. **80:** 58–66.

1576. **Morgenroth, Wolfgang**
Principles of text-construction and interpretation: Some remarks on a new edition of the Chandogya upanisad under preparation. **27:** 493–499.

1577. **Nikam, N.A.**
Brahma arose. **72:** 314–316.

1578. **Raghunathan, N.**
The upeya-nama-viveka of Upanishad brahmayogin. **72:** 56–63.

1579. **Roy, Brajdeo Prasad**
Some aspects of the upanisadic educational system. **62:** 327–340.

1580. **Stone, James H.**
The problem of canon-formation in the aupanisadavada. **81:** 217–229.

1581. **Swaminathan, V.**
In defence of a Prabhakara standpoint. **79:** 115–129.

1582. **Varenne, J.**
The Garuda upanisad. **41:** 222–231.

EPICS

1583. **Bhargava, P.L.**
A fresh appraisal of the historicity of Indian epics. **95:** 107–114.

1584. **Gajendragadkar, S.N.**
Varuna in the epics. **97:** 27–40.

RAMAYANA

1585. **Agrawal, Jagannath**
The date of Valmiki's Ramayana. **95:** 67–69.

1586. **Bhattacharya, Bhabatosh**
The Ramayana and its influence upon the mediaeval digests of eastern India. **39:** 19–26.

1587. **Bhattacharyya, Sivaprasad**
The Bhusundopakhyana and its esoteric drift. **50:** 79–89.

1588. **Buck, Harry M.**
Two kraunca birds: A phenomenological and form-critical study of the opening slokas of Valmikiramayana. **66:** 368–380.

1589. **Chatterjee, Asim Kumar**
The Ramayana in the canonical and non-canonical texts of the Buddhists and Jains. **90:** 159–165.

1590. **Chaturvedi, Harish Kumar**
Ramayana in Asia. **98:** 181–188.

1591. **Deshpande, N.A.**
Boons and curses in the Ramayana. **7:** 212–216.

1592. **Hara, Minoru**
Valmiki, the singer of tales. **29:** 117–128.

1593. **Kibe, M.V.**
Lanka as described in Valmiki's Ramayana. **39 (3):** 93–107.

1594. **Kuppuswami Sastri, S.**
Valmiki-Ramayana. **56 (1):** 152–153.

1595. **Nagaraja Rao, P.**
Valmiki's message and his ideal hero Ramachandra, the God-man (dharmatma). **7:** 95–97.

1596. **Pandey, Lochan Prasad**
The Ramayana of Valmiki mentions two Kosalas. **67:** 271–275.

1597. **Pollock, S.**
Text-critical observations of Valmiki Ramayana. **94 (1):** 317–324.

1598. **Sadhu Ram**
Ramayana notes. **50:** 322–327.

1599. **Sankalia, H.D.**
Rama's paduka and finger ring. **11:** 337–340.

1600. **Schwartz, Susan L.**
The heroic epic of quest: A study of the Ramayana and the odyssey. **44:** 245–271.

1601. **Sen, Nilmadhav**
Irregular treatment of the augment in the Ramayana. **29:** 268–273.

1602. **Sharma, Kadambri**
Valmiki Ramayana me Visnu ke avataar. **82:** 242–248. (Hindi).

1603. **Shastri, Biswanarayan**
New light on the Ahalya-Indra story of the Ramayana. **88:** 345–352.

1604. **Sitaramayya, V.**
An episode in the Ramayana. **72:** 75–83.

1605. **Sivaramamurti, C.**
Kandarpa iva murtiman: Charming like cupid incarnate. **22 (2):** 1–4.

1606. **Soundar Rajan, K.V.**
Ramayana story and its original scene of location—some arguments. **47:** 321–330.

1607. **Sternbach, Ludwik**
Ramayana verses in Canakya's compendia. **50:** 328–339.

1608. **Thapar, Romila**
The Ramayana: Theme and variation. **10:** 221–253.

1609. **Vyas, S.N.**
A brief survey of Ramayana culture. **39:** 462–467.

MAHABHARATA

1610. **Arora, U.P.**
Birth of Karna. **19:** 69–78.

1611. **Bahura, Gopal Narayan**
Sanchipaat par likhit Mahabharat ke parva. **82:** 265–271. (Hindi).

1612. **Bedekar, V.M.**
A hymn to the Sun in the Mahabharata 3.3: Its analysis and implications. **7:** 57–67.

1613. **Bharadwaj, O.P.**
Is there Kuruksetra—Kutsana in the Mahabharata? **85:** 295–301.

1614. **Chatterjee, Asim Kumar**
Historicity of Vasudeva Krsna. **5 (2):** 389–392.

1615. **Deshpande, C.R.**
Studies in recensions and versions of the Mahabharata. **57:** 18–32.

1616. **Dwivedi, R.K.**
The Sarasvati river complex in the Mahabharata. **19:** 158–175.

1617. **Goswami, Asha**
The historicity of the Mahabharata. **80:** 148–151.

1618. **Hara, Minoru**
Expressions for "numberless" in the Mahabharata. **54:** 154–163.

1619. **Kalyanov, V.I.**
On the military code of honour in the Mahabharata. **27:** 187–194.

1620. **Kawthekar, P.N.**
Fables in the Mahabharata. **59:** 122–129.

1621. **Krishnamoorthy, K.**
Interpretation of the Mahabharata heroes: Madhvacarya's perspective. **27:** 211–218.

1622. **Maheshwari Prasad**
Varaha-katha in the Mahabharata. **5 (2):** 289–291.

1623. **Mainkar, T.G.**
The Mahabharata war; its nature and significance. **59:** 113–121.

1624. **Mehendale, M.A.**
Nemesis and some Mahabharata episodes. **27:** 273–279.

1625. **Mirashi, V.V.**
The date of the original Harivamsa. **30:** 425–435.

1626. **O'Flaherty, Wendy**
Horses and snakes in the Adi Parvan of the Mahabharata. **33:** 16–44.

1627. **Pusalker, A.D.**
Social world in the Mahabharata. **61:** 575–580.

1628. **Ram Gopal**
Vedic sources of the Sarngaka legend of the Mahabharata. **61:** 397–401.

1629. **Sadhu Ram**
Derivations of certain names as recorded in the Adi-parvan of the Mahabharata (Gita Press edition). **48:** 405–409.

1630. **Vaidya, P.L.**
The so-called kutaslokas in the Karnaparvan. **39 (3):** 209–218.

1631. **Van Buitenen, J.A.B.**
On the structure of the sabhaparvan of the Mahabharata. **41:** 68–84.

GITA

1632. **Bailey, G.M.**
An essay on the Bhagavadgita as an impediment to the understanding of Hinduism. **51:** 113–122.

1633. **Chatterjee, Bhaskar**
Conception of lokasamgraha in the Bhagavad-Gita. **37:** 165–171.

1634. **Gangadharan, N.**
The Gita and the Garudapurana. **72:** 218–220.

1635. **Hutchings, P.AE. and Bilimoria, P.**
On not having regards for fruits: Kant and the Gita. **51:** 353–367.

1636. **Jaideva Singh**
The first verse of the Bhagavadgita. **50:** 213–214.

1637. **Jezic, Mislav**
The first yoga layer in the Bhagavadgita. **94 (1):** 545–557.

1638. **Jha, Harihar**
The concluding ten lines of the Gita. **60:** 423–425.

1639. **Katre, Sadashiva L.**
Krsna, Gopas, Gopis and Radha. **39 (3):** 83–92.

1640. **King, Ursula**
The Bhagavad Gita within the image world of modern Hinduism. **46 (1):** 221–235.

1641. **Krishna Warrier, A.G.**
The role of Jnana in the Bhagavadgita. **79:** 93–98.

1642. **Mainkar, T.G.**
The early antecedents of the vibhuti-yoga in the Bhagavadgita Ch. X. **97:** 72–75.

1643. **Masson, J. Moussaieff**
Did Freud comment on the Bhagavadgita? **37:** 112–114.

1644. **Misra, Satya Swarup**
Linguistic chronology of Srimadbhagwadgita. **95:** 75–77.

1645. **Modak, B.R.**
Bhagavadgita—the philosophy of transcendence. **73:** 252–254.

1646. **Modi, P.M.**
Brahmasutrakara: As interpreter of the Gita. **61:** 139–150.

1647. **Nagaraja Rao, P.**
The message of Bhagavadgita. **73:** 204–209.

1648. **Paradkar, M.D.**
Similes in Sankara's bhasya on the Gita. **97:** 91–107.

1649. **Satyavrat Shastri**
Thoughts on the Gita. **94 (1):** 607–614.

1650. **Sharan, Mahesh Kumar**
The Gita for the man of devotion. **80:** 334–348.

1651. **Sharma, Ganesh Datta**
Bhagvadgita me yajna ka swaroop. **84:** 244–249. (Hindi).

1652. **Sharpe, E.J.**
The Bhagavad Gita and the West. **51:** 285–292.

1653. **Singh, A.D.**
The path of love—the Gitaway of personality integration. **48:** 314–325.

1654. **Smith, R. Morton**
Statistics of the Bhagavadgita. **61:** 39–46.

1655. **Vajpeyi, Raghavendra**
Varna-samkara crisis and the Bhagavad Gita. **95:** 102–106.

PURANAS

1656. **Agrawala, V.S.**
Vaman purana ke anusar Shaiva sampradaya. **50:** 69–71. (Hindi).

1657. **Chatterji, Suniti Kumar**
Purana apocrypha: A "Manipura-purana." **15:** 28–41.

1658. **Datta, B.**
The manuscript evidence on some of the important interpolated passages in the Visnu purana. **44:** 283–290.

1659. **Filliozat, Jean**
Les dates du Bhagavatapurana et du Bhagavatamahatmya. **15:** 70–77. (French).

1660. **Ganguli, Kalyan Kumar**
Govindabhisheka—a significant episode in the puranic tradition of Krishna. **88:** 33–44.

1661. **Gupta, Anand Swarup**
The South Indian version of the Varaha purana. **94 (1):** 531–535.

1662. **Gupta, Hira Lal**
Manusmritti ki apratim mahta ka rahsya. **86:** 313–320. (Hindi).

1663. **Kane, P.V.**
Paurana-dharma. **39 (3):** 70–82.

1664. **Kantawala, S.G.**
Matsya-purana: A brief review. **80:** 152–165.

1665. ———
The pupil the embryo. **16:** 471–475.

1666. ———
Puranas and Dharmasastra: Some observations. **95:** 3–4.

1667. **Karmarkar, A.P.**
Crafts and professions in the puranic period. **39:** 194–198.

1668. **Khan, Mohd. Israil**
The puranic episode of Brahma and Sarasvati. **84:** 214–220.

1669. **Mazumdar, B.P.**
Some aspects of the social milieu and the puranas. **9:** 192–209.

1670. **Mehta, R.N.** and **Jamindar, Rajesh**
Chronology of uttarakhanda of Padma purana. **95:** 34–37.

1671. **Pal, Pratapaditya**
The gift of books according to the Devipurana. **91 (1):** 49–52.

1672. **Pusalker, A.D.**
Puranic studies. **23:** 689–773.

1673. **Raghavan, V.**
The date of the Narasimha purana. **41:** 239–240.

1674. **Roy, S.N.**
Analysis of a Purana passage in historical perspective. **86:** 469–471.

1675. ———
The dynastic account of the Vayu purana: An analysis of its authenticity. **19:** 79–83.

1676. **Sarma Biswas, A.T.**
On some vedic and archaic words in the Bhagavata-purana. **7:** 154–159.

1677. **Schreiner, Peter**
Bhakti in the Visnu purana. **44:** 273–282.

1678. **Shastri, Biswanarayan**
Katha-sarit-sagara and the Pauranic literature: The Skandapurana (Some common folk-motifs). **43:** 158–166.

1679. **Upadhye, P.M.**
Mysticism in the Puranas. **30:** 376–282.

1680. **Usha Dev**
References to animal and human sacrifices in the Kalika purana. **16:** 424–428.

BUDDHISM

1681. **Almond, Philip C.**
Buddhism and the Oriental mind in the nineteenth century. **51:** 293–317.

1682. **Aronson, Harvey B.**
Equanimity (upekkha) in Theravada Buddhism. **49:** 1–18.

1683. **Bailey, H.W.**
The Bodhisattva in the Prajna-paramita. **68:** 20–21.

1684. ———
Mahaprajnaparamitasutra. **24:** 153–162.

1685. **Bajpai, K.D.**
South Kosala and Buddhism. **88:** 29–32.

1686. **Banerjee, Anukul Chandra**
Buddhism—its basic teachings. **94 (1):** 463–466.

1687. ———
The Theravada School of Buddhist thought. **49:** 19–23.

1688. **Bapat, P.V.**
Chinese madhyamagama and the language of its basic text. **62:** 1–6.

1689. ———
Khanti: Kanti: Ksanti. **16:** 635–642.

1690. ———
Vohara: Vyahara: Vyavahara. **71:** 27–33.

1691. **Bareau, Andre**
Benares et le Bouddhisme antique. **94 (1):** 471–478. (French).

1692. **Barua, Dipak Kumar**
Buddhism: Revelation and message. **96:** 359–364.

1693. ———
Early Buddhist concept of matter. **11:** 174–186.

1694. **Basak, Radhagovinda**
Indian life as revealed in the Buddhist work, the Mahavastu-Avadana. **6:** 1–70.

1695. **Bechert, Heinz**
The Chakmas, an ancient Buddhist population in the Indian subcontinent. **43:** 130–132.

1696. ———
A collection of "minor texts" from the Buddhist sanskrit canon. **3:** 89–94.

1697. ———
Contemporary Buddhism as a major factor of social and political change. **16:** 329–336.

1698. ———
Mahayana literature in Sri Lanka: The early phase. **24:** 361–368.

1699. ———
Remarks on four Buddhist Sanskrit works composed in Sri Lanka. **49:** 25–27.

1700. **Beyer, Stephan**
Notes on the vision quest in early Mahayana. **24:** 329–340.

1701. **Bhattacharya, Dipak**
The scheme of four in early Buddhism. **80:** 291–298.

1702. **Bhattacharya, Kamaleswar**
Brahman in the Pali canon and in the Pali commentaries. **9:** 95–112.

1703. **Biley, H.W.**
The profession of prince ɪcum-Ttehi. **15:** 18–22.

1704. **Bollee, W.B.**
A note on evil and its conquest from Indra to Buddha. **24:** 371–381.

1705. **Bond, George D.**
The nature and meaning of the netti-pakarana. **49:** 29–39.

1706. **Buddhadatta Bhikshu**
Secular activities of Buddhist monks. **7:** 195–198.

1707. **Carter, John Ross**
The notion of "refuge" (sarana) in the Theravada Buddhist tradition. **49:** 41–42.

1708. **Chandra-Ngarm, Saeng**
The Buddhist tolerance. **96:** 223–232.

1709. **Chandra Shekhar Prasad**
Meat-eating and the rule of Tikotipar-isuddha. **49:** 289–295.

1710. **Chinchore, Mangala R.**
Dinnaga's criticism of Vasubandhu. **96:** 47–63.

1711. **Dalai Lama, H.H.**
Arya Tara. **48:** 559–560.

1712. **De Jong, J.W.**
The background of early Buddhism. **53:** 55–65.

1713. ———
Notes on Prajnaparamita texts: The Suvikrantavikramipariprccha **24:** 187–199.

1714. **Derrett, J. Duncan M.**
Maithuna-virati: The Buddhist novice's dilemma. **79:** 45–53.

1715. ———
A quotation from the Dhammapada in Jayaraksita's Srighanacara-sangraha-tika. **89:** 21–23.

1716. ———
Sumptuary laws for Buddhist novices. **56 (2):** 283–291.

1717. **Deshpande, Madhav M.**
Introducing the Milindapanha-atthakatha of 'Thaton Mingun Zetawun Sayadaw. **27:** 95–103.

1718. **Dow Ling, Thomas L.**
Karma doctrine and sectarian development. **49:** 83–92.

1719. **Dutt, Nalinaksha**
Contribution of Buddhism to letters. **6:** 116–124.

1720. **Emmerick, R.E.**
The concluding verses of the Khotanese Vajracchedika. **24:** 83–92.

1721. **Franke, Herbert**
Three Mongolian Buddhist fragments from Turfan. **48:** 468–472.

1722. **Gogoi-Chutia, Laksahira**
The concept of upacara in the Vijnaptima-tratasiddhi. **43:** 88–92.

1723. **Gokhale, Balkrishna Govind**
On Buddhist historiography. **49:** 99–108.

1724. ———
On the Buddhist concept of attha. **20:** 47–59.

1725. **Gokhale, V.V.**
Buddhist studies. **23:** 659–672.

1726. **Gomez, Luis O.**
The Bodhisattva as wonder-worker. **24:** 221–261.

1727. **Govinda, Lama Anagarika**
The origin of the Buddhist Mandala. **14:** 49–55.

1728. **Gunawardana, R.A.L.H.**
A Buddhist manuscript in the Sinhala language from the Sa-Skya monastery in Tibet. **47:** 199–206.

1729. **Handurukande, Ratna**
The benefit of caitya worship. **68:** 75–77.

1730. **Hanumantha Rao, S.**
Buddhism in the Deccan. **100:** 185–191.

1731. **Hirabayashi, Jay** and **IIDA, Shotaro**
Another look at the madhyamika vs. yogacara controversy concerning existence and non-existence. **24:** 341–360.

1732. **Horner, I.B.**
The Buddha's Co-natals. **49:** 115–120.

1733. **Hurvitz, Leon**
Hsuan-Tsang (602–664) and the Heart Scripture. **24:** 103–121.

1734. ———
The light deliverances. **49:** 121–161.

1735. **Ichimura, Shohei**
Sunyata and paradigm-shift: Dialogue between Buddhism and science. **96:** 81–100.

1736. **Inagaki, Hisao**
Haribhadra's quotations from Jnanaparbha's anantamukha-nirharadharani-tika. **42:** 132–144.

1737. **Indrapala, K.**
Buddhism among the Tamils, c. 300 B.C.—A.D. 600. **32:** 207–216.

1738. **Isri, R.**
Jivaka—the physician to Lord Buddha. **60:** 284–286.

1739. **Jaini, Padmanabh S.**
Prajna and drsti in the Vaibhasika Abhidharma. **24:** 403–417.

1740. **Jan, Yun-hua**
A ninth-century Chinese classification of Indian Mahayana. **49:** 171–182.

1741. ———
Rajadharma ideal in yogacara Buddhism. **20:** 221–234.

1742. **Jiyu, Ren**
Buddhism and Chinese culture. **81:** 118–124.

1743. **Joshi, L.M.**
The meaning of nirvana. **49:** 189–195.

1744. **Kajiyama, Yuichi**
Mahayana Buddhism and the philosophy of prajna. **49:** 197–206.

1745. ———
"Thus spoke the blessed one. . .". **24:** 93–99.

1746. **Karan Singh**
The Hindu renaissance. **81:** 1–8.

1747. **Kher, C.V.**
Buddhism and the non-philosophical Brahmanical literature. **49:** 207–216.

1748. **Kher, Chitrarekha**
Buddhism as presented by the Brahmanical systems. **57:** 120–130.

1749. **Krishan, Y.**
Buddhist challenge and Hindu response. **49:** 217–227.

1750. **Krishna Murthy, K.**
Vestiges of Hariti worship in Andhra. **76:** 57–58.

1751. **Kunst, Arnold**
Some aspects of the ekayana. **24:** 313–326.

1752. **Kuppuswami Sastri, S.**
The padyacudamani of Buddhaghosha. **56 (1):** 154–157.

1753. ———
Problems of identity in the cultural history of ancient India: Aravanavatikal in the Sangam age. **56 (1):** 217–227.

1754. **Lancaster, Lewis**
A study of a Khotanese Prajnaparamita text: After the work of Sir Harold Bailey. **24:** 163–183.

1755. **Lancaster, Lewis R.**
The editing of Buddhist texts. **42:** 145–151.

1756. **Lethcoe, Nancy R.**
The Bodhisattva ideal in the Asta and Panca Prajnaparamita sutras. **24:** 263–280.

1757. **Ling, Trevor**
Buddhism in India: Residual and resurgent. **49:** 229–241.

1758. ———
Buddhist Bengal and after. **75:** 317–325.

1759. ———
The non-political character of early Buddhism. **20:** 209–220.

1760. **Lokesh Chandra**
Nilakantha Lokesvara as the Buddhist apotheosis of Hari-Hara. **3:** 95–106.

1761. ———
The structure of the Garbhadhatu Mandala. **46 (1):** 255–264.

1762. ———
The tripitaka—translator Pao-ssu-Wei (Cintamani). **96:** 283–286.

1763. **Mahalingam, T.V.**
Mahinda's route to Ceylon. **90:** 181–184.

1764. **Maity, P.K.**
Buddhism at Tamralipta. **89:** 135–139.

1765. **Mallik, Madhusudan**
Brahmanas as depicted in Pali canon. **20:** 414–419.

1766. **Marathe, M.P.**
Dharmakirti on drstanta. **96:** 65–80.

1767. **Masefield, Peter**
The origin and development of the preta in early Buddhism. **51:** 47–69.

1768. **Mishra, Kameshwar Nath**
Reflections on the Tibetan etymologies of the Sanskrit synonyms of Buddha. **96:** 197–209.

1769. **Mizuno, Kogen**
Dharmapadas of various Buddhist schools. **49:** 255–267.

1770. **Mukherjee, Biswadeb**
On the genesis and some early developments of the Skandhaka. **20:** 376–389.

1771. **Nakamura, Hajime**
A process of the origination of Buddhist meditations in connection with the life of the Buddha. **49:** 269–277.

1772. ———
Aspects of original Buddhism. **94 (1):** 573–578.

1773. **Neog, Maheswar**
A Mahavagga narrative and an incident from Assamese Gurucarita. **43:** 102–106.

1774. **Niyogi, Puspa**
Chinese pilgrims on academic regulations and activities of monasteries in ancient Bengal and Bihar. **88:** 60–69.

1775. **Norman, K.R.**
An epithet of nibbana. **96;** 23–31.

1776. **Oates, L.R.**
Buddhist thought reflected in Asian landscape art. **51:** 71–86.

1777. **Parrinder, Geoffrey**
Mystery and mysticism. **24:** 395–402.

1778. **Pas, Julian F.**
The Kuan-wu-liang-shou-Fo-ching: Its origin and literary criticism. **42:** 194–218.

1779. **Pathak, S.K.**
A note on the Lokayatikas from the Lankavatara sutra. **47:** 442–446.

1780. ———
Prajna and Karuna in Buddha-yana. **96:** 349–358.

1781. **Perera, L.P.N.**
The gramani (gamani) in ancient India: An addendum. **68:** 169–171.

1782. **Pobozniak, T.**
The problem of dream in Milinda-panha. **94 (2):** 675–678.

1783. **Prasad, H.S.**
A critique of the samskrtalaksana. **96:** 151–159.

1784. **Pratap Chandra**
Nature of continuity in early Buddhism. **96:** 139–150.

1785. **Prebish, Charles S.**
Recent progress in Vinaya studies. **49:** 297–306.

1786. **Pye, Michael**
The Heart sutra in Japanese context. **24:** 123–134.

1787. **Rahula, Walpola**
Zen and the taming of the bull: Brief comparison of Theravada and Zen. **49:** 307–315.

1788. **Raman, N.S.S.**
Some comments on anatmavada in early Buddhism. **53:** 202–206.

1789. **Rawlinson, Andrew**
The position of the Astasahasrika Prajnaparamita in the development of early Mahayana. **24:** 3–34.

1790. **Remon, Joaquin Perez**
Anattavada in the sutta-pitaka. **57:** 73–77.

1791. **Richardson, Hugh E.**
"The dharma that came down from heaven": A Tun-huang fragment. **42:** 219–229.

1792. **Roth, Gustav**
Mangala-symbols in Buddhist Sanskrit manuscripts and inscriptions. **87:** 239–249.

1793. ———
Notes on the introduction of the Bhiksu-pratimoksa-sutra of the Arya-Mahasamghika-Lokottaravadin. **49:** 317–326.

1794. **Ruegg, D. Seyfort**
The gotra, ekayana and tathagatagarbha theories of the Prajnaparamita according to Dharmamitra and Abhayakaragupta. **24:** 283–312.

1795. **Samtani, N.H.**
Buddha: The teacher extra-ordinary. **49:** 341–346.

1796. **Sander, Lore**
Om or Siddham—remarks on openings of Buddhist manuscripts and inscriptions from Gilgit and Central Asia. **87:** 251–261.

1797. **Schmithausen, Lambert**
Textgeschichtliche Beobachtungen zum 1. Kapitel der Astasahasrika Prajnaparamita. **24:** 35–80. (German).

1798. **Sen Majumdar, Gayatri**
A brief note on the laity as depicted in the Anguttara Nikaya. **88:** 327–330.

1799. **Sharma, Arvind**
The Surangama-sutra: A study in internal consistency. **80:** 285–290.

1800. **Shukla, Bhawani Shanker**
The concept of metta in Buddhism. **96:** 183–196.

1801. **Shukla, Karunesha**
Vajrayana tradition and Kambalapada. **47:** 234–241.

1802. **Siridhamma, Ven. L.**
Humanistic and scientific aspects of Buddhism. **44:** 99–105.

1803. **Smith, Bardwell L.**
Religious assimilation in early medieval Sinhalese society. **49:** 347–368.

1804. **Sprung, Mervyn**
Non-Cognitive language in Madhyamika Buddhism. **42:** 241–253.

1805. **Srivastava, Avinash Kumar**
Nature and significance of the silence of Buddha. **86:** 398–409.

1806. **Steinkellner, Ernst**
Jnanassimitra's Sarvajnasiddhih. **24:** 383–393.

1807. ———
Some Sanskrit—fragments of Jinendrabuddhi's visalamalavati. **37:** 96–105.

1808. **Tatz, Mark**
Candragomin's twenty verses on the Bodhisattva vow. **11:** 367–372.

1809. **Templeman, David R.**
A study of Buddhist tantric hagiography. **51:** 87–100.

1810. **Thakur, Anantalal**
Udayana's reference to some less-known Buddhist acaryas. **13:** 221–226.

1811. **Thakur, Vijay Kumar**
Origins of Buddhism: A resurvey of material factors. **20:** 206–208.

1812. ———
Origins of Buddhism: A resurvey of material factors. **89:** 53–56.

1813. **Tiwari, Lakshmi Narayan**
Some observations on tantric practices in Buddhist canon. **96:** 365–384.

1814. **Tripathi, Ram Shankar**
Process of change: The sautrantika view. **96:** 41–46.

1815. **Tulku, Doboom**
Tathagatagarbha. **96:** 329–334.

1816. **Upasak, C.S.**
The role of Uruvela Kassapa in the spread of Buddhism. **49:** 369–374.

1817. **Varma, Vishwanath Prasad**
Early Buddhism and the methodology of social and political research. **62:** 141–158.

1818. ———
Political values in the Buddhist Sanskrit literature. **47:** 180–196.

1819. **Waldschmidt, Ernst**
A contribution to our knowledge of Sthavira Srona Kotivimsa. **29:** 107–116.

1820. **Warder, A.K.**
Feudalism and Mahayana Buddhism. **55:** 156–174.

1821. **Wayman, Alex**
Secret of the Heart sutra. **24:** 135–152.

1822. ———
The twenty reifying views (sakkayaditthi). **49:** 375–380.

1823. **Weiler, Royal W.**
The Buddhist act of compassion. **15:** 238–250.

1824. **Yuyama, Abira**
The first two chapters of the Prajna-paramita-ratna-guna-samucaya-gatha (Rgs). **24:** 203–218.

1825. ———
The six perfections and the Bodhisattva in the lotus sutra: An example of philological and philosophical questions. **96:** 33–40.

1826. ———
Svalpaksara prajnaparamita. **42:** 280–301.

1827. **Zelinsky, A.N.**
The Buddhistic cosmos and Tibetan tradition. **49:** 383–387.

1828. **Zelliot, Eleanor**
The Indian rediscovery of Buddhism, 1855–1956. **49:** 389–406.

1829. **Zwilling, Leonard**
The Visesastva of Udbhattasiddhasvamin. **49:** 407–414.

JAINISM

1830. **Alsdorf, L.**
Namipavvajja: Contributions to the study of a Jain canonical legend. **15:** 8–17.

1831. **Bhattacharya, Mandira**
Jainism during the Pala-Sena period. **88:** 45–48.

1832. **Deshpande, N.A.**
Jaina concept of an ideal teacher. **97:** 16–19.

1833. **Dhaky, M.A.**
Apropos of Mahavacaka Arya Nandi Ksamasramana. **90:** 141–147.

1834. ———
A propos of Vacaka Asvasena. **5 (2):** 233–234.

1835. **Dwivedi, R.C.**
Jaina definitions of the pramana. **27:** 115–124.

1836. **Jain, K.C.**
Early Jainism and archaeological cultures. **90:** 135–140.

1837. **Jha, Shaktidhar**
Hindu deities in the Jaina puranas. **62:** 458–465.

1838. **Khadabadi, B.K.**
The vow of Samadhimarana in early Karnataka. **30:** 383–387.

1838A. **Malvania, D.D.**
Fundamentals of the Jaina code of conduct. **47:** 428–437.

1839. **Misra, Radhey Shyam**
Jain apabhransha puran aur mahapuran. **95:** 22–27. (Hindi).

1840. **Nakamura, Hajime**
The vedanta as noticed in mediaeval Jain literature. **15:** 186–194.

1841. **Raghava Varier, M.R.**
Socio-economic functions of the Jain temples in Kerala. **21:** 173–186.

1842. **Sen, Amulyachandra**
Jainism. **1:** 323–325.

1843. **Sharma, I.K.**
Western Ganga Jaina vestiges at Tippuru, district Mandya. **74:** 233–240.

1844. **Sharma, Jagdish P.**
The Jainist dream-world: A tentative analysis. **53:** 123–159.

1845. **Singh, Ram Bhushan**
The Jaina puranas as a source of social history. **60:** 292–294.

1846. **Sircar, D.C.**
Jaina contribution to Indian culture. **94 (2):** 693–700.

1847. **Thakur, Upendra**
The Ramayana of Valmiki and the Jaina puranas. **76:** 245–250.

1848. **Upadhye, A.N.**
Jaina studies. **23: 673–688.**

1849. ———
On the meaning of Yapaniya. **92:** 197–198.

1850. **Upadhye, P.M.**
The word 'ahacca' in the Uttaradhyayanasutra. **97:** 176–179.

1851. **Venkatachala Sastry, T.V.**
A note on the word 'Kundakunda'. **32:** 223–226.

CHRISTIANITY

1852. **De Smet, Richard V.**
The nature of Christian philosophy. **28:** 362–368.

1853. **Gupta, Lina** and **Gupta, Satadal Kar**
Jesus, the non-mythical messiah. **9:** 294–308.

1854. **Khan, Benjamin**
The Christian theory of moral obligation and inclination. **45:** 75–80.

1855. **Painter, John**
The purpose and Christology of the fourth gospel. **51:** 387–406.

ISLAM

1856. **Chopra, Hira Lall**
Sufism. **1:** 305–310.

1857. **Habib-ur-Rahman Shastri**
Upanisad aur Sufi-mat. **50:** 207–212. (Hindi).

1858. **Masud, S.A.**
Islam and its broad principles. **1:** 300–304.

1859. **Mujeeb, M.**
Sufis and Sufism. **48:** 281–307.

SIKHISM

1860. **Arora, Raj Kumar**
The concept of God in the Guru Grantha. **80:** 315–333.

1861. **McLeod, W.H.**
The problem of the Panjabi rahit-names. **10:** 103–126.

1862. **Uberoi, J.P.S.**
Sikhism and Islam: A structural analysis. **76:** 223–230.

ZOROASTRIANISM

1863. **Mehendale, M.A.**
On the significance of the name Zarathustra. **69:** 113–117.

Philosophy

1864. **Acharya, K.V.**
Sri Madhvacharya: His period. **92:** 283–286.

1865. **Aldrich, Virgil C.**
Tragedy west and east. **28:** 1–15.

1866. **Ali, B. Sheik**
An analysis of Spengler and Kroeber on culture growth. **30:** 531–539.

1867. **Anand, Mulk Raj**
Tradition and innovation. **72:** 35–41.

1868. **Arapura, J.G.**
The relevance of a fundamental mode of Western philosophy's self-understanding for East-West philosophy. **51:** 197–210.

1869. ———
Some perspectives on Indian philosophy of language. **65:** 15–43.

1870. **Athavale, Sadashiv V.**
Origin and growth of materialistic thought in ancient India. **30:** 367–375.

1871. **Bagchi, Kalyan Kumar**
Moksa and science. **12:** 105–115.

1872. **Balasubramanian, R.**
Philosophy for liberation. **81:** 22–44.

1873. **Banerjee, Hiranmay**
Coomaraswamy on philosophy and aesthetics. **25:** 71–79.

1874. ———
Theism in Indian philosophy. **29:** 206–211.

1875. **Banerjee, S.P.**
Structure of human action. **81:** 277–299.

1876. **Barlingay, S.S.**
Experience and expression. **45:** 1–8.

1877. ———
Some thoughts on the beginnings of religion, philosophy and culture in the Indian context. **51:** 1–7.

1878. ———
The theory of meaning in Indian grammar system. **81:** 300–311.

1879. **Basu, Manoranjan**
Sri Aurobindo on integral consciousness: Where the East meets the West. **12:** 45–55.

1880. **Bhadra, Mrinial Kanti**
The ontology of freedom. **12:** 31–44.

1881. ———
Truth as correspondence—an existentialist view. **45:** 9–16.

1882. **Bhartiya, M.C.**
Problem of original cause in Indian thought. **95:** 31–34.

1883. ———
Upadana—karana and samavayi—karana: A comparison. **84:** 201–204.

1884. **Bhattacharya, B.K.**
Nature and validity of inference. **1:** 261–296.

1885. **Bhattacharya, Kamaleswar**
Ratnakarasanti and Ratnakirti. **79:** 131–140.

1886. **Bhattacharyya, Kalidas**
Concept of philosophy. **1:** 21–37.

1887. **Bhattacharyya, Sibajiban**
The navya-nyaya theory of abstraction. **81:** 312–329.

1888. ———
Some Indian theories of the body. **12:** 176–212.

1889. **Bhavani, Sudhindra**
Is Arjuna a madhyamadhikarin? **30:** 412–415.

1890. **Bool Chand**
Ahimsa view of the origins of human society. **48:** 326–330.

1891. **Bose, S.K.**
Determinism and free will. **45:** 43–48.

1892. **Burnier, Radha**
Social values and spiritual insight. **81:** 364–371.

1893. **Burtt, Edwin A.**
A problem in comparative philosophy. **28:** 16–30.

1894. **Chandel, Bhuvan**
Mandelbaum's theory of moral judgements—a critical analysis. **81:** 372–379.

1895. **Chandrasekharan, K.**
We the civilised. **72:** 42–48.

1896. **Chatterjee, Chinmayi**
Notes on the doctrine of emanation (vyuha). **37:** 145–152.

1897. **Chatterjee, S.C.**
The real, the unreal and the illusory.

1898. **Chatterji, Margaret**
The concept of commitment: Some clarifications. **75:** 599–611.

1899. **Chattopadhyaya, D.P.**
Sri Aurobindo and the Marxist on civilisation and culture. **75:** 539–570.

1900. **Chattopadhyaya, Debi Prasad**
An introductory note on Indian idealism. **4:** 243–264.

1901. **Choudhury, Roma**
Sufism and vedanta. **1:** 311–322.

1902. **Chubb, J.N.**
The problem of truth. **28:** 71–80.

1903. **Coward, Harold G.**
Bhartrhari's Dhvani: A central notion in Indian aesthetics. **65:** 65–85.

1904. **Das, R.**
My god and my religion. **28:** 81–93.

1905. **Das Gupta, N.**
Aesthetics. **95:** 35–42.

1906. **Derrett, J. Duncan M.**
Prayascita without fault. **84:** 307–311.

1907. **De Smet, Richard**
Man's integral dynamism and his quest for values. **45:** 133–142.

1908. **Devaraja, N.K.**
Ethical disagreement. **28:** 138–156.

1909. **Dhebar, U.N.**
Relevance of Gandhiji's teachings to the modern time. **48:** 308–313.

1910. **Dikshit, K.K.**
A perspective for the study of Indian philosophy. **62:** 541–544.

1911. **Dubey, Rajendra Prasad**
Bhramasathal me pratiti ke siddhanta aur Vacaspati Misra. **84:** 205–213. (Hindi).

1912. **Frankena, William K.**
Ethics in an age of science. **28:** 109–124.

1913. **Franklin, R.L.**
Evil and faith. **51:** 369–385.

1914. **Ganguly, Jayadev**
Vayu rupabhavavan—how do we know it? **37:** 79–84.

1915. **Ganguly, Swati**
Sarvastivad—vijnanavad controversy on prapti and aprapti in the Cheng wei Shih Lun of Hsuan-Tsang. **88:** 353–359.

1916. **Garnett, A.C.**
Creativity and value. **28:** 125–137.

1917. **Gibson, A. Boyce**
Suffering and its conquest. **28:** 157–165.

1918. **Goel, D.** and **Sarin, Indu**
Value, intention and action. **45:** 53–58.

1919. **Gopal, Lallanji**
Devala on aristas. **89:** 141–142.

1920. ———
Devaladharmasutra on Aisvaryas. **90:** 153–158.

1921. **Gopalacharya, M.R.**
Sixtieth birthday. **30:** 540–547.

1922. **Gupta, Suman**
Some aspects of methodology in the context of Indian philosophy. **73:** 123–140.

1923. **Haldar, Aruna**
Common assumptions of Indian systems. **62:** 655–662.

1924. **Hanumantha Rao, G.**
Sermons on universal toleration in stone. **92:** 275–279.

1925. **Haque, Intisar-ul**
Culture, progress and peace. **81:** 139–152.

1926. **Harsh Narain**
A transmaterialistic interpretation of dialectical materialism. **53:** 207–217.

1927. **Hassan, S. Mahdi**
The genesis of the four elements; Air, water, earth and fire. **100:** 251–256.

1928. **Jaini, Padmanabh S.**
Values in comparative perspective: Sivadharma versus ahimsa. **96:** 111–112.

1929. **Jha, U.N.**
The concept of immortality—an analytic approach. **60:** 446–450.

1930. **Joshi, H.M.**
Reality and value. **45:** 59–68.

1931. **Joshi, Rasik Vihari**
Validity of knowledge in Indian logic. **71:** 175–191.

1932. **Joshi, Umashankar**
The problem of tragic pleasure: The enjoyment of pathetic emotion. **72:** 84–89.

1933. **Kapadia, B.H.**
Padmapada as an interpreter and as an independent thinker. **97:** 57–63.

1934. **Kar, Bijayananda**
An examination of Sri Aurobindo's views on reason and religion. **45:** 69–74.

1935. **Khwaja, Jamal**
Knowledge and truth. **81:** 351–363.

1936. **Klostermaier, Klaus**
Ecological dimensions of ancient Indian thought. **20:** 347–360.

1937. ———
Man carries the power of all things in his mouth: Jacob Boehme's ideas on word and language. **65:** 87–98.

1938. ———
A universe of feelings. **51:** 123–139.

1939. **Kucuradi, Ioanna**
Freedom and social freedom. **81:** 153–160.

1940. **Kulkarni, B.R.**
Ethical and religious aspects of absolutistic philosophy. **16:** 365–372.

1941. **Kunjunni Raja, K.**
Bhartrharir dinnagasca. **79:** 35–40. (Sanskrit).

1942. **Lal, B.B.**
Whither are we drifting? Our future prospect. **60:** 459–463.

1943. **Lewis, Boniface**
Sankara and Christianity. **30:** 416–420.

1944. **McKibbin, Penelope M.**
The personalities of prakrti—keys to a feminist predicament. **51:** 265–284.

1945. **McLean, George F.**
The person as subject of self-consciousness and freedom. **81:** 167–179.

1946. **Mahadevan, T.M.P.**
Faith and human personality. **28:** 189–194.

1947. **Malkani, G.R.**
Philosophy of the will. **28:** 195–204.

1948. **Malledevaru, H.P.**
The theory of changeless transformation (Avikrita-parinamavada). **30:** 388–392.

1949. **Marneffe, J. de S.J.**
Michael Polanyi on knowledge and value. **45:** 81–92.

1950. **Matilal, Bimal Krishna**
Dinnaga's remark on the concept of anumeya. **61:** 151–159.

1951. ———
On dogmas of orientalism. **88:** 15–21.

1952. **Mazumdar, Amiya Kumar**
Maharshi Debendranath Tagore as a philosopher. **12:** 15–30.

1953. **Mohanty, J.N.**
Concept of intuition. **1:** 203–208.

1954. **Moitra, Shefali**
Alternative standpoints: At the foundation and culmination of Kalidas Bhattacharyya's philosophy. **12:** 1–14.

1955. **Mokashi-Punekar, Shankar**
Notes on the sixth chapter of Siddhasiddhantapaddhati. **30:** 400–411.

1956. **Moore, Charles A.**
The practical aspect of western philosophy. **28:** 219–238.

1957. **Mullatti, L.C.**
Necessity and universality in Kant. **45:** 97–104.

1958. **Nagaraja Rao, P.**
God in Whitehead's philosophy. **39:** 300–313.

1959. ———
Science, philosophy and religion. **72:** 49–55.

1960. ———
Trends in contemporary Indian philosophy. **28:** 291–298.

1961. **Nakada, Naomichi**
On the three aspected logical reason in Asanga's Madhyantanugamasastra. **54:** 164–166.

1962. **Nakamura, Hajime**
Mistranslations by some Western scholars and the significance of traditional ways of thinking. **20:** 34–36.

1963. **Namboodiry, C.P.M.**
The secularism of communalism. **45:** 105–112.

1964. **Nath, Bhupendra**
Gandhi's quest for truth. **60:** 440–445.

1965. **Nayak, G.C.**
Man and religion in Tagore's philosophy. **12:** 158–164.

1966. **Nilakanta Sastri, K.A.**
Freedom and organisation in Indian culture. **39:** 364–372.

1967. **Northrop, F.S.C.**
The philosophical roots and validity of Tagore's genius. **28:** 255–278.

1968. **Pande, G.C.**
The upanisads and Buddhavacana. **81:** 209–216.

1969. **Pandey, A.N.**
The philosophy of Pancasikha. **84:** 221–227.

1970. **Pandey, Jagdishwar**
The Ambhiyas—a Lokayata sect. **47:** 438–441.

1971. **Pande, S.L.**
Obligation, inclination and wisdom. **45:** 125–132.

1972. **Pandeya, Ramchandra**
Knowledge and validity. **48:** 331–346.

1973. **Panikkar, R.**
Words and terms. **81:** 330–350.

1974. **Pavlov, Yuri**
Social progress and its criteria. **81:** 180–189.

1975. **Peris, Merlin**
The tunnel-maker and the labyrinth-builder. **68:** 145–165.

1976. **Perrett, Roy W.**
Tagore on art and religion. **51:** 173–195.

1977. **Potdar, K.R.**
Concept of God-hood (devatatva) according to the Mimamsakas. **30:** 360–366.

1978. **Potter, Karl H.**
The logical character of the causal relation in Indian philosophy. **28:** 279–287.

1979. **Rajagopala Shastri, S.**
Philosophy of tripurarahasya. **1:** 341–347.

1980. **Rajendra Prasad**
The emotivist Hume. **12:** 165–175.

1981. ———
Three types of ethical analysis. **28:** 288–290.

1982. **Ramakrishna Rao, K.B.**
Sri Vidyaranya—the impersonal person. **92:** 280–282.

1983. **Raman, N.S.S.**
Indian and German idealism. **40:** 221–235.

1984. **Ram Anant, L.B.**
Saundarya chetna ki avadhaarna. **95:** 25–30. (Hindi).

1985. **Ramanna, Raja**
Logic, Sankara and Subrahmanya Iyer. **81:** 61–72.

1986. **Ramanujacharyya, Yatindra**
Essentials of Vishishtadvaita philosophy. **1:** 235–246.

1987. **Rama Rao Pappu, S.S.**
Authority and obligation in Indian thought. **20:** 311–326.

1988. **Ramjee Singh**
Some reflections on the problem of omniscience and freedom. **28:** 453–457.

1989. **Ray, Annada Sankar**
An east-west synthesis. **88:** 9–14.

1990. **Reyna, Ruth**
Spirit of Indian philosophy. **1:** 38–42.

1991. **Riepe, Dale**
Influence of Indian thought upon that of the United States. **28:** 313–338.

1992. **Rimtlen, Fritz-Joachim von**
Existentialism and the modern mood in Europe: Martin Heidegger. **28:** 299–312.

1993. **Rinpoche, Tarthang Tulku**
A new vision of reality. **42:** 268–279.

1994. **Roy, J.K.**
Groundworks of mathematical philosophy in the Bhashaparichcheda. **1:** 223–234.

1995. **Roy, S.S.**
The meaning and vision of immediacy in Bradley's philosophy. **50:** 182–197.

1995A. **Rule, Paul**
Dialogue and monologue. **51:** 241–245.

1996. **Saraswati, Pratyagatmananda**
Mantra, yantra and tantra. **1:** 329–333.

1997. **Sastri, P.S.**
The causal relation. **61:** 115–127.

1998. **Saxena, Lakshmi**
Possibility of third reflection. **45:** 143–154.

1999. **Sengupta, Pradip Kumar**
Transcendence in visual art: Perspectives in the experiments of Rabindranath Tagore. **12:** 124–157.

2000. **Seshadri, C.**
Value education—the axionoetic standpoint. **45:** 155–158.

2001. **Shanbhag, D.N.**
Madhva's definition of pramana and the position of memory. **30:** 393–399.

2002. **Sharma, B.N.K.**
Sri Chaitanya and Prakasananda. **30:** 443–446.

2003. **Sharma, R.N.**
Priesthood—origin. **95:** 59–68.

2004. **Shastri, Raja Ram**
Secularism mundane and supra-mundane. **96:** 177–181.

2005. **Shaw, J.L.**
Singular existential sentences: Contemporary philosophy and the nyaya. **51:** 211–240.

2006. **Shukla, Karunesha**
Some missing portions of the Gotra-bhumi. **61:** 129–137.

2007. **Shute, Clarence**
A phenomenological study of "Providence". **1:** 209–222.

2008. **Sinari, Ramakant**
An emergence from nothing. **12:** 56–65.

2009. ———
The way toward moksa. **81:** 45–60.

2010. **Singh, Umrao Bist**
Language and reality. **45:** 185–196.

2011. **Sinha, Ajit Kumar**
The nature of space, time and causality according to Sankara and F.H. Bradley. **50:** 215–223.

2012. **Sinha, Debabrata**
The atman model and the question of human person. **12:** 73–84.

2013. **Sivaramamurti, C.**
Standards of Dharma. **68:** 265–267.

2014. **Sivaraman, K.**
The word as a category of revelation. **65:** 45–64.

2015. **Slater, Robert Lawson**
Movements of religious life and thought and religious diversity. **65:** 185–190.

2016. **Smirnov, G.L.**
Marxist conception of personality: Theory and practice. **81:** 73–88.

2017. **Sogani, Kamal Chand**
Ahimsa and the good. **45:** 167–174.

2018. **Spellman, J.W.**
Development and Indian cultural values. **10:** 204–220.

2019. **Srinivasan, G.**
Some aspects of the teaching of the Haridasas. **92:** 267–271.

2020. **Sriniwas Shastri**
Manava jivana ke rina: Ek sameekshatmaka anusheelana. **95:** 43–46. (Hindi).

2021. **Srivastava, J.S.**
Ontological commitment. **45:** 159–166.

2022. **Subrahmanya Sastri, Vepattur**
Anuvadavaicitri. **79:** 1–7. (Sanskrit).

2023. **Sudarshan, E.C.G.**
The seer and the seen. **46 (1):** 491–493.

2024. **Sundara Rajan, R.**
Man and nature: Religion and the crisis of secularization. **45:** 175–184.

2025. **Suryanarayana Sastri, Peri**
Dhatvarthamukhyavisesyakasabdadodhah. **79:** 9–21. (Sanskrit).

2026. **Sylvan, R.** and **Griffin, N.**
Unravelling and meanings of life? **51:** 407–459.

2027. **Tatia, Nathmal**
Materialism versus spiritualism. **7:** 54–56.

2028. **Thakur, Anantalal**
Members of pararthanumana: Later phase. **37:** 123–131.

2029. **Tipnis, S.N.**
The concept of madhura bhakti in Indian philosophy. **77:** 235–238.

2030. **Tripathi, C.L.**
Democracy and Satyagraha. **45:** 197–216.

2031. **Tripathi, R.K.**
The unspeakable in metaphysics. **65:** 171–183.

2032. **Vahiduddin, Syed**
Man's consciousness of death. **81:** 9–21.

2033. **Varadachari, K.C.**
Visistadvaita: A philosophy of religion. **39:** 442–448.

2034. **Varma, Siddheshwar**
Sensation in Indian philosophy. **50:** 241–244.

2035. **Verma, S.K.**
Metaphysics and poetry. **60:** 464–468.

2036. **Vyas, N.J.**
The ecological dilemma. **45:** 217–224.

2037. **Weedon, William S.**
The dialectic of atomism. **28:** 426–445.

2038. **Werkmeisters, W.H.**
Dr. Datta and the comprehensiveness and practicality of philosophy. **28:** 446–452.

2039. **Yajnik, J.A.**
Prof. A.G. Javadekar's contribution to philosophy. **45:** 225–234.

2040. **Yogendra, Jayadeva**
Emotion, art and yoga. **97:** 190–196.

2041. **Yun-Shah, Tan**
A study of ancient Chinese philosophy and its similarities to Indian philosophy. **28:** 369–394.

HINDU

2042. **Acharya, Ram Krishna**
Brahmasutrakar Badrayan ka Mohabharakkar Vedavyasa Krishnadvapayana se bhinnatava. **84:** 177–190. (Hindi).

2043. ———
Brahmasutro ka Badarayanekakrtaktava. **61:** 193–205. (Hindi).

2044. **Androssov, V.P.**
Mayavada according to the Ratnavali of Nagarjuna. **81:** 190–196.

2045. **Barlingay, S.S.**
Sankara on prescriptive and descriptive sentences. **84:** 195–200.

2046. **Basu, Arabinda**
Paramasiva and Bhagavan. **29:** 190–205.

2047. **Baumer, Bettina**
Purusa and the origin of form. **14:** 27–34.

2048. **Bharadwaj, K.D.**
The pancaratra: A tantra on the worship of Lord Visnu. **44:** 59–66.

2049. **Bharati, Agehananda**
The Kulakundalini template: Analysis or reverie? **20:** 162–205.

2050. **Bhatt, S.R.**
The concept of pramanya in navya-nyaya school. **45:** 17–28.

2051. ———
The navya-nyaya theory of jati and samanya. **44:** 23–33.

2052. **Bhattacharjee, Devaprasad**
Advaita views on causality. **1:** 177–193.

2053. **Bhattacharya, Bhakti**
Bhakti cult with special reference to acintyabhedabheda. **62:** 626–638.

2054. **Bhattacharya, Gopikamohan**
The concept of paksata in navyanyana. **16:** 337–343.

2055. ———
Narahari upadhyaya—the naiyayika. **37:** 210–220.

2056. **Bhattacharya, Kalidas**
Man as transcendence. **45:** 29–42.

2057. **Bhattacharya, Kamaleswar**
Nagarjuna's arguments against motion; their grammatical basis. **37:** 85–95.

2058. ———
On a passage of the Siddhantalaksana Jagadisi. **94 (1):** 479–483.

2059. **Bhattacharya, R.S.**
What is the means other than the Isvarapranidhana. **94 (1):** 485–489.

2060. **Bhattacharya, Ram Shankar**
Causes of duhkha. **16:** 348–353.

2061. ———
Vyasbhasya ke rachnakaal ka jnapak: Ek pathantar. **95:** 23–24. (Hindi).

2062. **Bhattacharya, S.**
The visesa and the a-visesa. **62:** 487–499.

2063. **Bhattacharya, Vibhuti Bhooshan**
Outlines of Hindu dynamics. **48:** 347–365.

2064. **Bhattacharyya, Ramaprasad**
Vacaspati, the follower of Mandana. **16:** 344–347.

2065. **Bokil, V.P.**
Spiritualism—its place in life and education. **72:** 21–34.

2066. **Bruckner, Heidrun**
Revelation and argumentation: Some references to the relation of sruti and tarka in Samkara's Brhadaranya-kopanisadbhasya. **40:** 209–220.

2067. **Chakravarti, Tapo Nath**
Matter according to the Samkhya system of thought. **50:** 90–102.

2068. **Chakravarty, S.J.**
From samkhya to Buddhism. **12:** 66–72.

2069. **Chatterjee, Chinmoy**
Problems of abstract thinking. **50:** 103–108.

2070. **Chatterjee, S.C.**
The vedantic way of life. **28:** 65–70.

2071. **Chaudhuri, Roma**
Vedantic conception of Brahman as Sachchidananda. **1:** 161–176.

2072. **Chemparathy, George**
The doctrine of Isvara as exposed in Nyayakandali. **61:** 25–38.

2073. ———
Nature and role of apta in the nyaya-vaisesika thought. **91 (1):** 39–47.

2074. ———
Theism and early vaisesika system. **50:** 109–125.

2075. **Clooney, Francis X.**
The concept of dharma in the mimamsa sutras of Jaimini. **56 (2):** 175–187.

2076. **Cogni, Giulio**
From pranagnihotra to eucharist. **94 (1):** 523–529.

2077. **Coward, Harold G.**
Bhartrhari versus Sankara on the overcoming of error. **42:** 1–15.

2078. **Dixit, Prabha**
The political and social dimensions of Vivekananda's ideology. **95:** 115–127.

2079. **Dravid, N.S.**
Sankara's justification of philosophical inquiry. **59:** 302–305.

2080. **Dviveda, Vrajavallabh**
Satvatiyo yogah. **44:** 87–94. (Sanskrit).

2081. **Dwivedi, Srimannarayan**
Mithila tatha tantra: Ek tippani. **61:** 249–258. (Hindi).

2082. **Esnoul, A.M.**
Notes sur le pancaratra. **94 (1):** 515–522. (French).

2083. **Garg, R.K.**
A discourse on Saccidananda. **61:** 65–80.

2084. **Gopal, Lallanji**
Sankhya darshana mein dasha moolikaartha. **95:** 3–9. (Hindi).

2085. **Gopalaswamy Iyengar, T.K.**
Pre-Sankara upanisadic philosophy as expounded by Kalidasa. **61:** 179–186.

2086. **Goswami, Krishan Gopal**
Incarnation of law from mimamsa standpoint. **16:** 359–364.

2087. **Goswami, Mahaprabhu Lal**
Vidhiswaroop vimarshanam. **62:** 643–654. (Sanskrit).

2088. **Goswami, Sitanath**
Self-luminosity. **62:** 545–559.

2089. **Govinda, Lama Anagarika**
H.V. Guenther as interpreter of the tantric view of life. **42:** 39–46.

2090. **Halbfass, Wilhelm**
Prasastapada's concept of substance (dravya). **94 (1):** 537–544.

2091. ———
Vyomasiva on sattasambandha. **73:** 65–80.

2092. **Hayes, Glen A.**
On the concept of vastu in the Vaisnava-sahijiya tradition of medieval Bengal. **51:** 141–149.

2093. **Inamdar, V.B.**
Dvaita school of vedanta. **57:** 109–119.

2094. **Iyengar, H.R.R.**
Interpretation of an old karika. **39:** 169–174.

2095. **Jha, Kishor Nath**
Nyayadarshane trilochana-matvimarsha. **61:** 207–213. (Sanskrit).

2096. **Joshi, Hem Chandra**
Udayana's arguments for God's existence. **62:** 614–625.

2097. **Joshi, M.C.**
Sakta-tantrism in the Gupta age. **44:** 77–81.

2098. **Joshi, Rasik Vihari**
The three qualities of sankhya system. **50:** 126–135.

2099. ———
Treatment of fallacy in Indian logic. **50:** 270–301.

2100. **Kedam, Michael**
Sat-cakrani concept and Lalitasahasranamabhasya of Bhaskararaya. **11:** 265–271.

2101. **Khiste, Batuk Nath Shastri**
Sri Bhaskar Rai Dixitana darshiniki dristi. **94 (1):** 559–564.

2102. **Krishnamoorthy, K.**
Impact of Bhagavata cult on Indian aesthetics. **79:** 99–113.

2103. **Krishna Warriar, A.G.**
Advaitic ethics—a re-examination. **71:** 499–508.

2104. **Kulkarni, E.D.**
The vidyabodhini of unmattananda on Srisukta. **16:** 571–578.

2105. **Kunjunni Raja, K.**
Mimamsa and linguistic problem. **56 (2):** 188–194.

2106. ———
A so-called view of Mandana on world-meaning discussed by the navya-nyaya school. **50:** 180–181.

2107. **Kuppuswami Sastri, S.**
Abrahmajijnasa. **56 (1):** 94. (Sanskrit).

2108. ———
Bodhayana and Dramidacarya—two old vedantins presupossed by Ramanuja. **56 (1):** 14–22.

2109. ———
Compromises in the history of advaitic thought. **56 (1):** 74–88.

2110. ———
Mandana's brahmasiddhi. **56 (1):** 23–65.

2111. ———
Nyaya-Vaisesika—origin and development. **56 (1):** 104–118.

2112. ———
The Prabhakara school of karma-mimamsa. **56 (1):** 95–103.

2113. ———
Purnaism in Indian philosophy—the wholism of ancient India. **56 (1):** 89–93.

2114. ———
Ravana-bhasya. **56 (1):** 119–121.

2115. ———
Vibhramaviveka of Mandana Misra. **56 (1):** 66–73.

2116. **Larson, Gerald James**
The pratyaya-sarga or "intellectual creation" in classical samkhya as interpreted by the yuktidipika. **20:** 60–71.

2117. **Mahadevan, T.M.P.**
The advaita view of time. **62:** 500–503.

2118. **Manoranjan Shastri**
Advaitavada or philosophy of nondualism in Kamarupa. **7:** 116–126.

2119. **Markandeya Sastry, C.**
Daksinamurti stotra and manasollasa. **56 (2):** 89–98.

2120. **Matilal, Bimal Krishna**
A note on 'the difference of difference'. **37:** 69–78.

2121. **Meenakshisundaram, T.P.**
The agamic conception of tattvas. **71:** 231–250.

2122. **Mishra, Adya Prasad**
Samkhya darshan ke dukhvada ka mul evam adhar. **50:** 140–145. (Hindi).

2123. **Mishra, Satya Deva**
The advaitic concept of Abhasa. **71:** 267–289.

2124. **Misra, Srinarayana**
Nyaya-vaisesikyo smrte apramatavam. **62:** 594–599. (Sanskrit).

2125. **Mode, Heinz**
Ancient Indian thought. **87:** 137–145.

2126. **Moghe, S.G.**
Milankantha as a mimamsaka. **61:** 87–99.

2127. **Mookerjee, Jatil Coomar**
The nature and classification of philosophical enquiry. **62:** 520–523.

2128. ———
Vitanda or Wrangling. **50:** 146–150.

2129. **Mudaliar, N. Murugesa**
The quintessence of Tamil philosophic thought. **72:** 170–176.

2130. **Mukerji, A.C.**
The renaissance of Indian thought. **50:** 151–158.

2131. **Mukhopadhyaya, Bhakti Sudha**
Samkhya darshan-samiksha. **62:** 600–613. (Sanskrit).

2132. **Mumme, Patricia**
Jivakartrtva in visistadvaita and the dispute over prapatti in vedanta desika and the tenkalai authors. **56 (2):** 99–118.

2133. **Nakamura, Hajime**
The particular nature of the vedanta. **50:** 159–165.

2134. ———
Vedanta philosophy in philosophical and religious works. **61:** 47–63.

2135. ———
Vedanta philosophy in pure literary works. **29:** 129–144.

2136. ———
The vedantic thought as represented in the Dharmasastra and Arthasastra. **54:** 137–153.

2137. **Nandi, Sudhir**
Aesthetic approach: Indian and Western. **36:** 245–251.

2138. **Narahari, H.G.**
On some important citations in the Nyayamanjari of Jayantabhatta. **61:** 111–113.

2139. **Narain, Harsh**
Anviksiki as dialectic. **94 (1):** 579–592.

2140. **Narasimhachary, M.**
Yamunacarya's influence on Ramanuja. **72:** 191–194.

2141. **Narayanaswami, V.**
Yogasanas to maintain health and cure diseases. **72:** 262–267.

2142. **Naresh Kumar**
Yoga-therapy and Kundalini-yoga. **84:** 348–360.

2143. **Nayak, G.C.**
Transcendental secularism—a study in one characteristic aspect of the Hindu system of values. **45:** 113–118.

2144. **Padoux, Andre**
About japa. **94 (1):** 593–601.

2145. **Pandey, Sangam Lal**
Authentic works of Samkaracarya. **61:** 161–177.

2146. **Pandeya, R.C.**
Indian attitude towards nature. **45:** 119–124.

2147. **Pandeya, Rewati Raman**
Samagra poornataa evam samagra yoga. **95:** 47–50. (Hindi).

2148. **Pandeya, Yogesh**
Sankar vedanta me Isvaravaad. **61:** 215–247. (Hindi).

2149. **Pandurangi, K.T.**
Concept of svarupabheda in Prabhakara and Dvaita. **79:** 170–175.

2150. **Paranjpe, V.G.**
A relative chronology of the six Brahmanical systems and early Buddhism. **71:** 291–299.

2151. **Prabhavananda**
Upanishadic thoughts and essence. **1:** 43–76.

2152. **Prajnananda**
Indefinable maya in advaita vedanta. **1:** 139–160.

2153. **Prasad, S.K.**
Yoga and literary criticism. **60:** 393–400.

2154. **Raghavachar, S.S.**
Karnataka and vedanta. **92:** 239–244.

2155. **Rajeevalochana, K.**
Acarya Ramanuja and vedanta desika. **73:** 268–271.

2156. **Ramachandra Sastry, S.**
The place of bhakti in advaita. **73:** 240–244.

2157. **Ramakrishna Rao, K.S.**
The philosophy of Rabindranath Tagore: Truth through beauty. **80:** 358–368.

2158. **Ramaswamy Sastri, V.A.**
Mantras or the mimamsaka conception of mantrapramanya. **39:** 373–377.

2159. **Rastogi, Navjivan**
Kramtattva par Kaviraj ji se ek varta. **50:** 518–521. (Hindi).

2160. **Redington, James D.**
The siddhantamuktavali or the pearl necklace of doctrines. **57:** 131–155.

2161. **Rocher, Ludo**
A note on Sad-gunya. **11:** 319–325.

2162. **Rucinski, Tomasz**
Some notes about the reading of Brahmasutras teaching. **94 (1):** 603–606.

2163. **Sadananda Giri**
Spiritual practice of advaita vedanta. **1:** 97–104.

2164. **Sampatkumaran, M.R.**
Ramanuja and prapatti. **72:** 64–74.

2165. **Sarat Chandran, K.**
The doctrine of maya. **7:** 234–237.

2166. **Sarma, R. Thangaswami**
Pramanas in purvamimamsa. **56 (2):** 155–174. (Sanskrit).

2167. **Sastry, M.P.L.**
Sadhana in advaita. **73:** 319–326.

2168. **Satswarupananda**
A critique of advaita philosophy. **1:** 87–96.

2169. **Sen, Deba Brata**
Panca kosa & panca kancuka—a study in comparison. **16:** 385–391.

2170. **Sen, Indra**
Reconstruction of Indian social thought. **72:** 14–20.

2171. **Sen Gupta, Anima**
Samkhya on validity and invalidity of knowledge. **1:** 79–86.

2172. **Sen Sharma, Debabrata**
The concept of purnahamta in the trika philosophy of Kashmir. **37:** 153–164.

2173. ———
The conception of tattva—a study. **50:** 198–201.

2174. ———
The nature of the ignorance in the trika philosophy of Kasmira. **84:** 237–243.

2175. **Seshagiri Rao, K.L.**
On truth: A vedantic perspective. **91 (1):** 15–18.

2176. **Shanbhag, D.N.**
Vadiraja—the dvaita poet. **73:** 159–163.

2177. **Sharma, R.K.**
The role of mind (citta) in the yogasutras. **27:** 383–389.

2178. ———
Siddhis in the yogasutras and saundaryalahari. **79:** 55–61.

2179. **Sharma, Ram Murti**
The advaita and I-sense. **73:** 113–122.

2180. ———
Concept of Isvara. **84:** 250–253.

2181. ———
Liberation (mukti). **80:** 354–357.

2182. ———
Vedantic concept of liberation (mukti). **37:** 172–176.

2183. **Sharma, Ram Nath**
The status of reason and revelation in advaita vedanta. **95:** 14–17.

2184. **Shri Nivas Shastri**
Acarya Trilocana: His contribution to Indian philosophy. **50:** 202–206.

2185. **Shukla, Badri Nath**
Atitanagatajnanopayah. **62:** 516–519. (Sanskrit).

2186. **Shukla, J.M.**
The verbal cognition according to Vacaspati Misra. **44:** 207–224.

2187. **Singh, S.P.**
The fundamentals of vedanta. **60:** 426–430.

2188. **Sinha, Jadunath**
Jivagosvamin's conception of God. **50:** 224–233.

2189. **Subrahmanya Sastri, S.**
Purvamimamsabhasyam Sriprabhakaramisra ca. **79:** 23–29. (Sanskrit).

2190. **Subramania Iyer, K.A.**
Sabdadvaitavaad. **94 (1):** 449–461. (Sanskrit).

2191. **Subramanyam Sastri, A.**
Mimamsadarshanam Ishwarvadshach. **62:** 524–528. (Sanskrit).

2192. **Tanaji, B.**
Bharatiyadarshanasyadhunikasamaje auchityam. **95:** 10–13. (Sanskrit).

2193. **Tatacharya, D.T.**
The suksma visesas of Sankhya. **16:** 396–399.

2194. **Thakur, Anant Lal**
Members of an Indian syllogism. **94 (1):** 615–621.

2195. ———
Vacaspati Misra's nyayavarttikatatparyatika and the vaisesika system. **71:** 425–435.

2196. **Tripathi, Ram Murti**
Agamik Isvaradvavaad tatha Sankar advaitavaad ya Brahmavaad. **61:** 187–192. (Hindi).

2197. **Tripathi, Ram Narain**
Sankhya muktiswaroopam tadupayashacha. **50:** 234–236. (Sanskrit).

2198. **Udaya Vira Shastri**
Antiquity of the sankhya sutras. **95:** 31–43.

2199. ———
Darshan ki mool samasyayen. **95:** 22–30. (Hindi).

2200. **Varadachari, K.C.**
Purusa. **50:** 237–240.

2201. ———
Sri vedanta desika (1268 A.D.—1368 A.D.). **61:** 101–109.

2202. **Varadachari, V.**
Conditions for the rise of perceptual cognition. **13:** 248–251.

2203. ———
Finitized form of God in Ramanuja's system. **80:** 349–353.

2204. ———
On the interpretation of a karika of Irvora Krsna. **61:** 81–85.

2205. **Varma, Siddheshwar**
The basic philosophical approach of the vaisesika system. **16:** 407–409.

2206. **Vireswarananda**
A comparative study of the commentaries of the Brahmasutras. **1:** 105–138.

2207. **Wayman, Alex**
Some accords with the samkhya theory of tanmatra. **37:** 115–122.

2208. **Wezler, Albrecht**
Further references to the vaisesikasutra in the Patanjalayogastravivarana. **27:** 457–472.

2209. ———
A note on concept adrsta as used in the vaisesikasutra. **44:** 35–58.

2210. **Yudhistar Mimansak**
Poorvamimaansya rathakar adikaranam. **95:** 52–56. (Sanskrit).

BUDDHIST

2211. **Awasthi, A.B.L.**
Variety and unity of Buddhist thought and practice. **89:** 65–67.

2212. **Banerjee, Biswanath**
Karman-rebirth: Buddhism. **12:** 116–123.

2213. ———
A note on the mahasukhain Buddhism. **94 (1):** 467–470.

2214. **Bapat, P.V.**
Self and the in-effable in early Buddhism. **27:** 473–474.

2215. **Barlingay, S.S.**
The concepts of duhkha, trsna and vaira as found in Dhammapada. **96:** 161–176.

2216. **Chan, Wing-Tsit**
Wang Yang-Ming's criticism of Buddhism. **28:** 31–47.

2217. **Chattarjee, A.K.**
Insight and paradox in Buddhist thought. **65:** 141–151.

2218. **Corless, R.J.**
The garland of love: A history of religions hermeneutic of nembutsu theory and practice. **49:** 53–73.

2219. **Daye, Douglas Dunsmore**
Methodological remarks on 20th century studies of Buddhist inference (anumana). **49:** 75–82.

2220. **De Jong, J.W.**
The Bodhisattvavadanakalpalata and the Saddantavadana. **42:** 27–38.

2221. **Derrett, J. Duncan M.**
Mrsa-vada-virati: A piece of Buddhist casuistry. **80:** 277–284.

2222. **De Silva, Padmasiri**
Zen and the art of motorcycle maintenance. **96:** 211–222.

2223. **Devaraja, N.K.**
Contemporary relevance of Buddhism. **45:** 49–52.

2224. **Fenner, P.**
A therapeutic contextualisation of Buddhist madhyamika consequential analysis. **51:** 319–351.

2225. **Guenther, Herbert V.**
A structural analysis of the Abhidharmakosa: First Chapter. **49:** 109–113.

2226. ———
Trikaya in Buddhist philosophy: Tibetan and Chinese Hua-Yen interpretation. **65:** 119–139.

2227. **Hattori, Massaki**
The sautrantika background of the apoha theory. **42:** 47–58.

2228. **Hurvitz, Leon**
The abhidharma on the 'four aids to penetration'. **42:** 59–104.

2229. **Inaba, Shoju**
On the Chos-grub's translation of the Chieh-shen-mi-ching-shu. **42:** 105–113.

2230. **Jaini, Padmanabh S.**
Samskara—duhkhata and the Jaina concept of suffering. **65:** 153–157.

2231. **Jaiswal, O.P.**
The problem of error. **62:** 639–642.

2232. **Joshi, Shivnarain**
Upanisadic influence on Buddhist tantrism. **60:** 431–439.

2233. **Kajiyama, Yuichi**
Realism of the Sarvastivada school. **42:** 114–131.

2234. **Kalupahana, David J.**
The Buddhist tantric deconstruction and reconstruction: Their sutra origin. **96:** 305–327.

2235. **Korti, Vijaya**
Tantra worship during I-Tsing's period. **85:** 87–92.

2236. **Krishnamoorthy, K.**
Bhamaha and Buddhist logic. **37:** 106–111.

2237. **Lokesh Chandra**
Oddiyana: A new interpretation. **94 (1):** 491–514.

2238. **Matilal, Bimal Krishna**
Nyaya critique of the Buddhist doctrine of non-soul. **12:** 85–104.

2239. **Matsunaga, Yukei**
A history of tantric Buddhism in India with reference to Chinese translations. **42:** 167–181.

2240. **Nakamura, Hajime**
Analysis of the individual existence by way of Buddhist psychology. **81:** 230–242.

2241. ———
The fundamental standpoint of early Buddhists. **28:** 239–254.

2242. ———
The problem of self in Buddhist philosophy. **65:** 99–118.

2243. **Pande, G.C.**
The origin of Mahayana: A historical-cum-metapsychological study. **50:** 166–179.

2244. **Pandeya, Sri Jagdishvar**
Bodh dharm evam darshan main asanga ka yogdaan. **86:** 410–412. (Hindi).

2245. **Pramod Kumar**
Vaibhasik ke anusar nirvana ka swaroop. **84:** 228–236. (Hindi).

2246. **Prasad, H.S.**
Language and reality: A Buddhist approach. **51:** 39–46.

2247. **Rahula, Telwatte**
Buddhist attitude toward meat-eating and non-violence. **51:** 101–112.

2248. **Ramakrishna Rao, K.**
Psychology of transcendence: A study in early Buddhistic psychology. **81:** 243–276.

2249. **Saraswati, Baidyanath**
Man and culture: The exegeses of science and scripture. **96:** 233–252.

2250. **Sarkar, A.K.**
Dignaga and the four Buddhist schools. **28:** 339–357.

2251. **Shukla, Karunesha**
The abhidharma, the madhyamika and the yogacara idealism of Asanga. **16:** 392–395.

2252. **Shukla, N.S.**
On the concept of a trantric teacher. **16:** 579–587.

2253. **Someshwar Prasad**
The abhidhamma view of momentariness. **59:** 264–269.

2254. **Sprung, Mervyn**
Nietzsche and Nagarjuna: The origins and issue of scepticism. **65:** 159–169.

2255. **Srinivasa Shastri**
Vacaspati Misra: Baudh-nyaya me bahya vastu ka swaroop. **84:** 254–261. (Hindi).

2256. **Takeuchi, Shoko**
Phenomena and reality in vjnaptimatra thought (1): on the usages of the suffix 'ta' in maitreya's treatises. **42:** 254–267.

2257. **Tiwari, Mahesh**
Chittavithi. **62:** 581–589. (Sanskrit).

2258. **Tsering, Migmar**
An analysis of the two truths in paramitayana and vajrayana. **96:** 335–348.

2259. **Upadhyaya, Jagannath**
Vajrayana: System, perceptivity and practice. **46 (1):** 547–555.

2260. **Upadhyaya, K.N.**
God, the self and the Buddha's silence. **96:** 123–137.

2261. **Varma, Vishwanath Prasad**
Early Buddhist anatmavada. **28:** 402–425.

2262. **Vijaya Rani**
Import of word according to the Buddhist logic. **84:** 262–267.

2263. **Wayman, Alex**
A prajnaparamita-type scripture within a tantra. **96:** 287–303.

JAINA

2264. **Bhattacharyya, H.M.**
Omniscience (sarvajnata) and metaphysic of knowledge (adhigama) in Jainism. **50:** 76–78.

2265. **Law, B.C.**
Some problems of Jain philosophy. **62:** 471–486.

2266. **Mittal, Kewal Krishan**
Jaina view of knowledge: Naturalistic or non-naturalistic? **45:** 93–96.

2267. **Nagasaki, Hojun**
Transcendent perception in Jaina logic with special reference to Buddhist logic. **42:** 182–193.

2268. **Sharma, Arvind**
The Jain doctrine of sysdvada: Examination of some modern presentations. **51:** 9–22.

2269. **Tatia, Nathmal**
Jaina logic and logicians. **62:** 504–515.

2270. **Vyas, Nitin J.**
The concept of ahimsa in Jainism. **44:** 107–114.

Language

2271. **Akhmanova, Olga and Krasnova, Irina**
Word-formation as a linguostylistic category. **18:** 32–40.

2272. **Basu, G.C.**
Phonological study of the modern Indian vernaculars. **29:** 288–297.

2273. **Bhattacharya, Sudhibhushan**
Language and evolution. **29:** 212–219.

2274. **Biswas, Sukumar**
Scope of linguistics in the study of history. **13:** 182–190.

2275. **Chaudhary, Ang Raj**
Language and culture. **62:** 373–385.

2276. **Bykova, E.M.**
On language as a system. **18:** 75–80.

2277. **Chawhan, Devi Singh**
Amir khusro birut Bharatiya bhasha sarvekshan. **70:** 24–55. (Hindi).

2278. **Damsteegt, Theo**
Sarnami Verbs in—I (Y) A—**87:** 129–136.

2279. **Dasgupta, Probal**
Indexative functions of language. **18:** 89–100.

2280. **Goswami, Ashok Kumar**
On the concept of eternality of sabda. **43:** 167–171.

2281. **Hamp, Eric P.**
An amendment to Fortunatov's law. **18:** 106–112.

2282. **Heinrich, A. and Kulli, J.S.**
A short comment on the history of linguistic science. **30:** 488–499.

2283. **Hoenigswald, Henry M.**
Degrees of genetic relatedness among languages. **18:** 113–115.

2284. **Katre, S.M.**
General lingustics. **23:** 1–28.

2285. **Kuppuswami Sastri, S.**
Linguistic notes—Bhadanta. **56 (1):** 190.

2286. **Low, Ramesh Kumar**
Nirukta aur artha vijnana. **95:** 39–41. (Hindi).

2287. **Mallik, Bhakti P.**
Rabindra Nath Tagore's styles of pronunciation. **18:** 324–328.

2288. **Martinet, Andre**
Fricatives and spirants. **18:** 145–151.

2289. **Mimamsaka, Yudhishthira**
Bharatiya bhasha-vijanam. **94 (2):** 823–839. (Sanskrit).

2290. **Mishra, V.**
Linguistics in India. **89:** 115–119.

2291. **Pike, Kenneth L.**
Systematic planned distortion of text as a clue to translation problems—a query. **18:** 163–166.

2292. **Randle, H.N.**
Coincidence of syllabic pattern in different metrical contexts. **39:** 292–299.

2293. **Sitaraman, B.**
Asuvika and Ajivika. **30:** 483–487.

2294. **Srivastava, R.N.**
The lingua-aesthetic approach to art symbol. **18:** 237–248.

2295. **Thirujnanasambandhan, P.**
Problems of meaning. **72:** 183–187.

2296. **Ucida, Norihiko**
Sound change and speech variation. **18:** 265–280.

2297. **Upadhyaya, U.P.**
Role of culture in language teaching. **92:** 232–235.

APABHRAMSA

2298. **De Vreese, K.**
A Dravidian idiom in Apabhramsa. **39:** 101–105.

ASSAMESE

2299. **Goswami, Upendranath**
Assamese and the Carya songs. **7:** 98–104.

BENGALI

2300. **Chevkina, L.M.**
On the study of socio-linguistic problems in the Bengali language area. **18:** 81–88.

2301. **Das, Sisir Kumar**
Bengali linguistic historiography. **75:** 373–388.

2302. ———
Halhed: The morning star of British orientalism. **76:** 173–183.

2303. **Mukherji, Tarapada**
Bengali lexicography up to 1800. **29:** 90–106.

2304. **Smith, W.L.**
Three Bengali compound makers. **18:** 229–236.

BRAHUI

2305. **Emeneau, M.B.**
New Brahui etymologies. **15:** 59–69.

DRAVIDIAN

2306. **Agesthialiangom, S.**
Adjectives in Dravidian. **18:** 1–31.

2307. **Andronov, M.**
To the etymology of conditional verbal participles in Dravidian. **18:** 41–44.

2308. **Bhattacharya, Sudhibhushan**
Indo-Aryan loanwords in central Dravidian. **71:** 47–59.

2309. **Emeneau, M.B.**
Brahui laterals from proto-Dravidian. **18:** 101–105.

2310. **Subramoniam, V.I.**
The law of convertibility of surds and sonants of Caldwell—re-examined. **18:** 249–253.

ENGLISH

2311. **Gune, N.P.**
The discovery of English. **39:** 121–128.

HINDI

2312. **Barannikov, P.A.**
The problem of modern Hindi and Urdu in the light of the lexical synonym. **4:** 274–288.

2313. **Kurl, Shreeprakash**
Hindi slang expressions. **18:** 122–128.

2314. **Lienhard, Siegfried**
A note on adjectival phrases in modern Hindi. **18:** 129–133.

2315. **Mahdihassan, S.**
A comparative study of Devanagri and Arabic characters. **39:** 236–259.

2316. **Saksena, Baburam**
Fresh formations in Hindi. **50:** 293.

2317. **Sharma, D.D.**
Dardic elements in Central Pahari. **80:** 105–119.

2318. **Tiwari, Bhola Nath**
Artha-nirdharana aur artha-prastuti: Kosha-nirmana ke sandarbha mein. **95:** 7–16. (Hindi).

2319. ———
Navya Bharatiya arya bhashaon ka ek vivadasapad shabda 'janjaal'. **50:** 294–295. (Hindi).

2320. **Verma, Shivendra K.**
Some observations on thematization in Hindi. **18:** 281–297.

INDO-ARYAN

2321. **Burrow, T.**
Some Euphorbia names in Indo-Aryan. **94 (2):** 805–809.

2322. **Katre, S.M.**
Dantura—in new Indo-Aryan. **50:** 281.

2323. ———
Old Indo-Aryan vacam—and its cognates in new Indo-Aryan. **7:** 8.

2324. **Master, Alfred**
Initial cerebrals in Indo-Aryan. **39:**

2325. **Misra, Haripriya**
Linguistic chronology of middle Indo-Aryan. **95:** 84–87.

2326. **Patyal, Hukam Chand**
Prothetic h—in Indo-Aryan. **80:** 96–101.

2327. **Saksena, Baburam**
A suggestion to solve some etymological problems of middle Indo-Aryan. **39:** 335–336.

2328. **Sen, Nilmadhav**
Some mutual borrowings in Indo-Aryan and Indo-Tibetan. **18:** 196–202.

INDO-EUROPEAN

2329. **Polome, Edgar C.**
Indo-European verb morphology. **94 (2):** 851–861.

2330. **Suryakanta**
Indo-European and semitic. **39:** 426–441.

KANNADA

2331. **Bhat, M.M.**
Tatsamas in Kannada. **72:** 221–222.

2332. **Venkatachala Sastry, T.V.**
Semasiological problems in the Kannada lexicon. **73:** 272–278.

KHAMTI

2333. **Biswas, S.**
A note on the Khamtis and their language. **7:** 169–178.

KONKANI

2334. **Katre, S.M.**
A special causative pattern in Konkani verbal bases. **15:** 108.

LADAKHI

2335. **Singh, Udaya Narayan**
A phonological analysis of Ladakhi numerals. **18:** 203–215.

LEPCHA

2336. **Sinha, Prabhakar**
Derivation in Lepcha. **18:** 216–228.

MALAYALAM

2337. **George, K.M.**
The contribution of the west to the scientific study of Malayalam. **72:** 223–235.

2338. **Narayana Pillai, P.K.**
A few old Malayalam proper names derived from Sanskrit. **80:** 120–128.

2339. **Venkitasubramonia Iyer, S.**
The influence of Sanskrit on Malayalam language and literature. **80:** 129–134.

MUNDA

2340. **Zide, Norman H.**
Robert Needham Cust and the beginnings of comparative Kolarian (Munda) studies. **18:** 298–320.

ORIYA

2341. **Mahapatra, Khageswar**
Portuguese words in Oriya. **7:** 179–184.

PALI

2342. **Bapat, P.V.**
Karana—sampatti. **39:** 6–8.

2343. ———
Sammuti: Sammati: Samvrti. **69:** 5–8.

2344. **Bhattacharya, Sudhibhushan**
An aspect of Pali semantics. **61:** 527–530.

2345. **Chido, M. D'onza and Panattoni, E.**
On a rare word in Pali and its Dravidian etymology. **94 (2):** 811–818.

2346. **Fiser, Ivo**
Pali averam, Dhammapada 5. **49:** 93–97.

2347. **Hinueber, Oskar Von**
A difficult verb form in Pali and Buddhist Hybrid Sanskrit: Asiyati. **47:** 197–198.

2348. **Hinueber, Oskar V.**
A vedic verb in Pali: Udajita. **94 (2):** 819–822.

2349. **Mallik, Madhusudan**
Elision in Pali. **44:** 225–228.

2350. ———
Some poetical forms in Pali. **80:** 102–104.

2351. **Norman, K.R.**
Magadhisms in the Kathavatthu. **49:** 279–287.

2352. **Ravi Prakash**
Change in OIA 5th Conj. 9th Conj. in Pali. **61:** 565–566.

2353. **Wijesekera, O.H. de A.**
The etymology of Pali gotrabhu. **49:** 381–382.

PRAKRIT

2354. **Ghosal, S.N.**
A syntactical agreement between the Asokan Prakrt and Ardhamagadhi. **61:** 531–535.

2355. **Saha, Anima**
On some Prakrt forms; Pischel's editions of Sakuntalam. **37:** 369–377.

2356. **Shashi Kant**
The prakrit. **21:** 93–98.

SANSKRIT

2357. **ABHYANKAR, K.V.**
Dramatical pictorial and verbal representations of past events at the time of Patanjali. **50:** 257–261.

2358. **Ananthanarayana, H.S.**
Word in Sanskrit. **73:** 11–18.

2359. **Bailey, Harold W.**
Three Indic notes. **87:** 9–10.

2360. ———
Vedic ksumpa—and connected data. **27:** 17–20.

2361. **Balasubrahmanyam, M.D.**
An accentual note on vedic vodhave. **79:** 229–240.

2362. ———
On Panini VI.1.158. **44:** 189–198.

2363. ———
Panini 6.1.209–210. **16:** 189–193.

2364. ———
Subhagamkarani in AV 6, 139, 1. **27:** 21–27.

2365. **Bandyopadhyay, Pratap**
Sanskrit indeclinables (upasargas and nipatas) and their meaning. **18:** 45–74.

2366. **Bhat, G.K.**
Rasa—relish: A consideration of prerequisites. **27:** 31–36.

2367. **Bhat, M.S.**
Authorship of the Laghusabdaratna. **97:** 203–205.

2368. **Bhat, M. Ramakrishna**
Astrological elements in Panini. **56 (2):** 199–208.

2369. **Bhattacharya, Biswanath**
Critical observations on the morphological notes in the printed text of Brhaspati Misra's padacandrika on Amarsimha's namalinganusasana, 1.1.2d. **44:** 229–236.

2370. **Bhattacharya, Gopikamohan**
Syntex and word-meaning. **27:** 37–45.

2371. **Bhayani, H.C.**
The nominal suffix—OTA in Sanskrit. **97:** 4–10

2372. **Birwe, Robert**
Authors and works referred to in Mahendra's Anekartha-kairavakarakaumudi. **27:** 47–63.

2373. **Biswanarayan Shastri**
The kamarupa school of Sanskrit grammar; Prayogaratnamala-vyakarana of Purusottama. **37:** 236–244.

2374. **Brahmanand, Swami**
Varnasaphot-nirupan. **62:** 590–593. (Sanskrit).

2375. **Buddha Prakash**
On Panini's sutra V, 3, 99 jivikarthe capanye. **48:** 394–404.

2376. **Burrow, T.**
Miscellaneous notes on Sanskrit etymology. **56 (2):** 43–50.

2377. ———
Sanskrit karota-'bowl, basin, vessel'. **27:** 73–78.

2378. ———
Sanskrit amoda—fragrance perfume. **15:** 23–27.

2379. ———
Six notes on Sanskrit etymology. **29:** 45–52.

2380. ———
Some cases of alternation between c and s in Sanskrit. **69:** 9–11.

2381. **Cardona, George**
On Panini's metalinguistic use of cases. **16:** 305–326.

2382. ———
On the apisalasiksa. **37:** 245–256.

2383. ———
On the formulation of Astadhyayi 8.3.4: Anunasikat paro'nusvarah. **79:** 199–205.

2384. ———
On the mahabhasya evidence for a paniniya dhatupatha without meaning entries. **27:** 79–84.

2385. ———
On Yaska's etymology of dandya. **56 (2):** 33–42.

2386. **Chakravorty, Jagannath**
The problem of modernization of Sanskrit. **9:** 370–381.

2387. **Chattopadhyay, Dipak**
Induraja on bhavika. **37:** 271–276.

2388. **Chattopadhyaya, Kshetresachandra**
Did Panini envisage 'a' as a close (samvrta) vowel? **16:** 194–205.

2389. **Dandekar, R.N.**
Some recent German contributions to vedic philosophy. **69:** 12–23.

2390. **Dange, Sadashiv Ambadas**
Siprin and sipivista. **61:** 501–510.

2391. **Das, S.R.**
Karnasuvarna: Name and origins. **20:** 75–87.

2392. **Dash, Prafulla Chandra**
Candra and the 'Asamjnakam vyakaranam'. **84:** 43–52.

2393. **De Mora, Juan Miguel**
On the opposites in Sanskrit texts. **94 (2):** 841–850.

2394. **Devasthali, G.V.**
Panini and Rgvedic exegesis. **71:** 97–104.

2395. ———
Vakya according to the munitraya of Sanskrit grammar. **16:** 206–215.

2396. ———
Vedic hiatus nasalization and Panini. **69:** 38–46.

2397. **Dwivedi, R.C.**
Influence of Sanskrit on the Rajasthani language and literature. **16:** 216–232.

2398. **Filliozat, Pierre**
On the semantic use of the word sphota. **27:** 133–140.

2399. **Gajendragadkar, S.N.**
Kara, hasta; pani—a study in synonyms. **69:** 53–59.

2400. **Gangopadhyay, M.**
The study of speech sounds in ancient India. **51:** 23–38.

2401. **Gaur, V.L.**
Paniniya sathanayadeshvyavsatha ka bhasaveganik vishleshan. **84:** 53–59. (Hindi).

2402. **Ghatage, A.M.**
Uktarthanam aprayogah. **27:** 141–151.

2403. **Ghosal, S.N.**
The Sanskrit—conjuncts of two dissimilar class nasals and their transformation in Prakrit. **50:** 266–270.

2404. **Gonda, J.**
The meaning of vedic karu—**61:** 479–488.

2405. ———
Nimita. **16:** 233–240.

2406. ———
On the use of the absolutive in Sanskrit. **50:** 262–265.

2407. ———
Panini and modern linguistics. **68:** 54–60.

2408. **Guha, Dinesa Chandra**
Nimittakaranalaksanapariskarah. **79:** 31–34. (Sanskrit).

2409. **Hara, Minoru**
A note on the epic folk-etymology of Rajan. **61:** 489–499.

2410. **Hartman, Carl Gustav**
Development of the Sanskrit particle 'opi'. **50:** 271–275.

2411. **Jani, A.N.**
On the meaning of the word 'vali' (Megh 35). **50:** 276–277.

2412. **Jayadev, Jani**
Treatment of karaka in the Sarasvata school of grammar. **95:** 88–90.

2413. **Jha, V.N.**
The structure of a sabdabodha. **84:** 77–82.

2414. **Joshi, D.M.**
Sentence and transformation in Panini. **18:** 116–121.

2415. **Joshi, Rasik Vihari**
Sanskrit studies in Mexico. **72:** 285–289.

2416. **Joshi, S.D.**
Bhartrhari's concept of pratibha: A theory on the nature of language acquisition. **69:** 71–76.

2417. ———
Kaunda Bhatta on sphota. **37:** 221–235.

2418. ———
Kaunda Bhatta on the meanings of case-endings. **80:** 88–95.

2419. ———
Panini's rule 1.3.67. **79:** 63–74.

2420. ———
Panini's treatment of karaka-relations. **16:** 258–270.

2421. ———
The role of boundaries in the Astadhyayi. **27:** 181–186.

2422. **Kantawala, S.G.**
Puranic etymologies. **50:** 278–280.

2423. **Kapil Deva Shastri**
On the authenticity of parama-laghu-manjusa. **16:** 299–304.

2424. **Kiparsky, Paul**
A compositional approach to vedic word accent. **27:** 201–210.

2425. **Krishnamoorthy, K.**
Bhamaha's poetics. **69:** 95–103.

2426. **Kunjunni Raja, K.**
Etymology and interpretation in ancient India. **72:** 180–182.

2427. **Laddu, S.D.**
On the earliest handbook on derivation (prakriya) in Sanskrit grammar. **84:** 83–90.

2428. ———
The teaching of a classical language: An integrated method for the teaching of Sanskrit. **27:** 229–237.

2429. **Lekha, Indu**
Sanskrit aur Rusi bhasha me prayukta upsarg. **84:** 60–76. (Hindi).

2430. **Leumann, M.**
Der altindische kausative aorist ajijanat. **15:** 152–159. (German).

2431. **Limaye, V.P.**
The basis of Panini (8.1.59 and 65) in Rgveda. **50:** 282–288.

2432. **Majumdar, R.C.**
Sanskrit learning and liberalism. **72:** 290–295.

2433. **Makkai, Adam** and **Christie, William M., Jr.**
Whose intellectual ancestor was Panini—really? **18:** 134–144.

2434. **Matilal, Bimal Krishna**
Grammaticality and meaningfulness. **27:** 263–271.

2435. ———
Jagadisa's classification of grammatical categories. **71:** 221–229.

2436. **Menon, M.S.**
Subhadraharana—a vyakarana kavya. **79:** 225–228.

2437. **Ojihara, Yutaka**
On the word 'kutilik', "poker, pickaxe": Panini 4.4.18. **43:** 44–50.

2438. ———
On Vamana's kavyalamkarasutravrtti V.ii.89: 'Nisyanda' or 'Nispanda'? **29:** 64–74.

2439. **Pal, Keshav Ram**
Vishesharthak sesamanyarthak. **84:** 91–102. (Hindi).

2440. **Pandey, Ramavadha**
Sarasvatonadiparishilanam. **62:** 560–580. (Sanskrit).

2441. **Phadke, Hari Anant Shastri**
Unadisurtrani Paninishacha. **50:** 289–292. (Sanskrit).

2442. **Raghavan, V.**
How many grammars? **16:** 271–278.

2443. **Ramakrishna Rao, B.S.**
The paribhasas dealing with vasarupavidhi. **73:** 285–296.

2444. **Ramakrishna Sastry, M.**
The asraya of rasa—Vemabhupala's stand. **72:** 214–217.

2445. **Roodbergen, J.A.F.**
Slesa: The reconstruction of an argument. **27:** 359–369.

2446. **Rurrow, T.**
On the derivation of the Sanskrit word nimita. **43:** 51–55.

2447. **Sarkar, H.**
Introduction of Sanskrit at Nagarjunakonda. **48:** 419–424.

2448. **Sastri, Devudu Narasimha**
Mula samskrtam. **39:** 358–363.

2449. **Satya Vrat**
Some anomalies in the language of the Yogavasistha. **71:** 325–329.

2450. **Scharfe, Hartmut**
Forms of speech and thought. **69:** 126–131.

2451. **Sen, Nilmadhav**
A note on akka—a ghost word in Sanskrit. **71:** 341–349.

2452. **Shastri, D.N.**
A re-appraisal of Panini. **50:** 296–301.

2453. **Sheo Shanker Prasad**
Do the Sanskrit words kala (rest), vaja (feather) and stega (stag) belong to proto-Indo-European stock. **94 (2):** 869–871.

2454. **Shyam Prakash**
Genitive case-endings in new Indo-Aryan. **94 (2):** 863–867.

2455. **Singh, J.D.**
Panini's technique of description. **16:** 279–293.

2456. **Singh, R.S.** and **Vyas, V.D.**
On the identity of and Greek impact on the Paninian plant-name 'siddhraka' (Panini VIII.4.4). **44:** 357–368.

2457. **Sluszkiewicz, E.**
Some remarks on Sanskrit and Greeĸ absolute genitives. **41:** 196–199.

2458. **Sreeramamurti, P.**
The concept of mahavakya according to the Vaiyakaranas. **56 (2):** 195–198.

2459. **Sriyan, Ratna N.**
Study of the desya and the rare words from Puspadanta's mahapurana. **97:** 154–160.

2460. **Subramania Iyer, K.A.**
Bhartrhari on grammatical analysis (apoddhara). **80:** 69–79.

2461. ———
Bhartrhari on taddhitaformations involving comparison. **16:** 241–257.

2462. ———
Some lost works on vyakarana. **71:** 137–144.

2463. **Thieme, Paul**
Durona-n. **27:** 435–444.

2464. **Tiwari, Bholanath**
Sanskrit bhasa mein prayukta kucha pracheentam videshi shabda. **61:** 567–572. (Hindi).

2465. **Upadhyaya, P.**
An exposition of the essential nature of self-comparison. **62:** 677–680.

2466. **Vaidyanathan, S.**
Phonology of Sanskrit loanwords in modern Tamil. **71:** 453–460

2467. **Varma, Siddheshwar**
The place of the concrete in Sanskrit scientific terminology. **39:** 449–453.

2468. **Venkatacharya, T.**
The significance of the dictum: Yata evakaras tato' nyatra niyamah. **80:** 80–87.

2469. **Venkitasubramonia Iyer, S.**
The concept and scope of adhikarana in Sanskrit grammar. **71:** 145–162.

2470. ———
Variants in Paninisutras affecting accent. **79:** 11–16.

2471. **Vora, P.R.**
Some noteworthy words of Paninian system. **44:** 199–206.

SANTALI

2472. **Jha, Munishwar**
Echoism in Santali language. **7:** 163–168.

SINHALESE

2473. **De Vreese, K.**
A Dravidian idiom in Sinhalese. **41:** 232–238.

TAMIL

2474. **Sankaran, C.R.** and **Sundaram, R.M.**
A historical study of Caarpeluthu in Tamil grammars and their commentaries. **61:** 551–564.

Literature

2475. **Chaitanya, Krishna**
Poetic experience: The Indian view. **48:** 369–374.

2476. **Chattopadhyaya, Alaka**
Folk poets of medieval eastern India. **73:** 164–171.

2477. **Chaudhary, Narayan**
Literary scene today in West Bengal. **1:** 431–438.

2478. **Choudhary, Satya Dev**
Karuna rasa: Its nature of aesthetic pleasure. **94 (2):** 951–958.

2479. **Filliozat, Vasundhara**
Contents of kavya contradicted by epigraphs. **94 (1):** 267–275.

2480. **Gaur, Albertine**
Early missionaries as manuscript collectors. **66:** 385–391.

2481. **Janaki, S.S.**
The Purusavas-Urvasi theme in Indian poetry and drama. **72:** 118–121.

2482. **Krishnamoorthy, K.**
What is sahitya? **29:** 220–228.

2483. **Mishra, Gopal Chandra**
Literary trends in eastern India through ages. **2:** 87–107.

2484. **Mishra, Shrikrishna**
Rasa and the tragic spirit. **60:** 406–413.

2485. **Mode, Heinz**
Folk-tales of India & Ceylon. **58:** 98–120.

2486. **Pisani, Vittore**
On a poetic hyperbole in Indian literature. **39:** 282–285.

2487. **Ramaswami, S.**
The function of criticism: The western tradition. **72:** 90–94.

2488. **Sarma, Dimbeswar**
Aspects of Indian textual criticism. **43:** 189–198.

2489. **Serebryakov, I.D.**
In quest of methodology with special reference to Indian kavya. **75:** 55–65.

2490. **Shukla, Uma Kant**
Prasadaguna: mammata, Viswanatha aur Panditaraja Jagannatha ki drsti. **95:** 10–14. (Hindi).

2491. **Sreekantaiya, T.N.**
Meaning in poetry. **39:** 387–395.

2492. **Viswanathan, K.**
Character and patra. **72:** 95–105.

2493. **Watwe, K.N.**
The problem of the karuna rasa and its solution. **39:** 468–470.

ARABIC

2494. **Kokan, Yousuf**
India's contribution to Arabic literature. **72:** 296–303.

ASSAMESE

2495. **Bhattacharjee, Jatindra Mohan**
Two Assamese manuscripts. **13:** 208–211.

BENGALI

2496. **Banerjee, S.K.**
Dramatic element in Bankim Chandra. **76:** 169–171.

2497. **Bhattacharyya, Asutosh**
British people in Bengali folk literature. **29:** 258–267.

2498. **Datta, Bhabatosh**
Bankimchandra and Anandamath. **1:** 452–463.

2499. **Mukherjee, Arun Kumar**
Nineteenth century Bengali criticism. **1:** 445–451.

2500. **Mukhopadhyaya, Krishnalal**
Doors of perception: A study of Jibanananda's poetic imagery. **76:** 193–198.

2501. **Poddar, Arabinda**
Modern Bengali poetry in search of man and meaning. **76:** 185–191.

2502. **Smith, W.L.**
The Turkish conquest and the dark age of Bengali literature. **94 (2):** 707–713.

DRAVIDIAN

2503. **Sankaran, C.R.** and **Balasubramaniam, S.R.**
Ancient Dravidian literature. **23:** 137–156.

ENGLISH

2504. **Sengupta, Pallab**
Resistance movements in 19th century Indo-English & English literature. **76:** 305–312.

HINDI

2505. **Abidi, S.A.H.**
The story of Mina and Lurak in Indo-Persian literature. **13:** 152–157.

2506. **Chauhan, D.V.**
The dating of Ali-namah. **13:** 146–151.

2507. **Choudhary, Satya Dev**
Kavya ki atma. **50:** 355–369. (Hindi).

2508. **Hawley, John Stratton**
Echoes of love and creation in the poetry of Sur Das. **33:** 45–62.

2509. **Jha, Ramanatha**
Bhavaprita-sangeet or a new lyric note in Maithili poetry. **61:** 453–457.

2510. **Jha, Shailendra Mohan**
Amrtkar: A dramatist and his patron. **61:** 459–467.

2511. **Krishnamurthy, M.S.**
A Hoysala prince in a Hindi historical romance. **92:** 211–218.

2512. **Mainariya, Purshottam Lal**
Sri Kumbhakarna virdauli. **82:** 413–415. (Hindi).

2513. **Meghraj**
Mystic strain in mediaeval Rajasthani poetry. **82:** 376–383.

2514. **Mishra, Bhagirath**
Ancient Hindi literature. **23:** 105–125.

2515. **Mishra, Shiva Gopal**
Haricaritra: A premier Krsna-kavya. **5 (2):** 393–394.

2516. **Nagendra**
Gandhi's impact on Hindi literature. **60:** 414–422.

2517. **Pandeya, Trilochan**
Bharatiya lok gito ki ekta. **50:** 318–321. (Hindi).

2518. **Raghavan, V.**
Vopadeva and Hemadri on bhakti rasa. **61:** 793.

2519. **Srivastava, D.N.**
Kabir's concept of Bhakti. **7:** 145–153.

KANNADA

2520. **Kanavi, Channaveera**
The poetic quality in Purandaradasa's songs. **30:** 453–462.

2521. **Nayak, H.M.**
Mysore city and Kannada literature. **92:** 219–226.

2522. **Ramanujan, A.K.**
The prince who married his own left half. **33:** 1–15.

2523. **Upadhye, A.N.**
Further light on the date of the Kannada Vaddaradhane. **30:** 441–442.

2524. **Venkatachala Sastry, T.V.**
Sloka metre in Kannada literature. **92:** 199–205.

INDO-PERSIAN

2525. **Abidi, S.A.H.**
The story of Hir and Ranjha in Indo-Persian literature. **7:** 23–31.

KHOTANESE

2526. **Dresden, M.J.**
Note on Khotanese poetry. **15:** 42–50.

MARATHI

2527. **Babar, Sarojini**
Lok sahitya: Etihasik khuna. **52:** 263–266. (Marathi).

2528. **Pathan, U.M.**
Bahina baiche "swagat". **52:** 292–298.

2529. **Tulpule, S.G.**
Ancient Marathi literature. **23:** 127–135.

ORIYA

2530. **Chakravorty, Tapas Kumar**
The social content in Oriya literature of the late nineteenth century. **2:** 132–178.

2531. **Misra, Gopal Chandra**
Baramasi, a literary form in ancient Oriya literature. **13:** 176–181.

PALI

2532. **Banerjee, Dilip Kumar**
The Pali atthakathas—an estimate. **62:** 359–372.

2533. **Saddhatissa, H.**
Pali literature from Laos. **49:** 327–340.

PERSIAN

2534. **Ahmad, Nazir**
Some little-known Indo-Persian poets of the thirteenth century. **100:** 157–167.

2535. **Fazlullah, S.M.**
Some Persian poets of Transoxiana (beyond the Oxus) who migrated to India during the early Mughal period (10th century A.D./16th century A.D.). **71:** 113–126.

2536. **Naik, C.R.**
The interest evinced by the Hindus of Gujarat in the study of Persian language and their contribution to Persian literature. **7:** 185–194.

2537. **Nizami, K.A.**
Some newly acquired Persian manuscripts of the British Museum. **100:** 168–175.

2538. **Saksena, B.P.**
Char Chaman of Chandra Bhan. **48:** 455–463.

PRAKRIT

2539. **Bhayani, H.C.**
The Prakrit poets Harivrddha, Satavahana and Adhyaraja. **71:** 61–76.

2540. **Ghatage, A.M.**
Prakrit literature. **23:** 73–103.

2541. **Masson, J.L.** and **Patwardhan, M.V.**
The Dhvanyaloka and the Gaudavaho. **54:** 176–183.

2542. **Upadhye, A.N.**
Geographical background of the Kuvalayamala. **7:** 5–7.

2543. ———
A note on the Haramekhala. **69:** 158–159.

2544. **Vasantharaj, M.D.**
An outline of the contribution of Karnataka to Prakrta literature. **73:** 301–303.

SANSKRIT

2545. **Agrawala, V.S.**
A difficult passage in the panchatantra: Lakshmi-vidambanam. **6:** 178–189.

2546. **Aklujkar, Ashok**
The authorship of the vakya-kanda-tika. **16:** 165–188.

2547. **Baldissera, F.** and **Janaki, S.S.**
Of some epic echoes in bhanas. **56 (2):** 75–86.

2548. **Bandyopadhyay, Pratap**
On the meaning of the word 'mahajana'. **37:** 337–342.

2549. **Banerjee, Manabendu**
On some interesting post-colophon statements of Sanskrit manuscripts preserved in the Asiatic Society Library. **89:** 75–80.

2550. **Banerji, Sures Chandra**
Apocryphal works attributed to Kalidasa. **71:** 1–26.

2551. ———
Aspects of folklore in Sanskrit. **11:** 166–173.

2552. ———
Commentaries of Mallinatha. **29:** 298–368.

2553. **Batuk Nath**
Kalidasasayenk padya tadavayakhya cha. **3:** 131–132. (Sanskrit).

2554. **Bedekar, V.M.**
Kubera in Sanskrit literature, with special reference to the Mahabharata (from an earth-spirit to a God). **61:** 425–451.

2555. **Bharadwaj, Shiv Prasad**
Function of svabhavokti. **84:** 116–121.

2556. ———
The exponent of abhasa-concept in rasa theory. **16:** 413–417.

2557. **Bhattacharya, Bhabatosh**
Spirit of research in the 20th century. **71:** 35–45.

2558. **Bhattacharya, Biswanath**
A critical appraisal of the Gandi-stotra-gatha ascribed to Asvaghosa. **13:** 142–145.

2559. ———
A critical re-examination of the variants 'prathama-divase' and 'prasama-divase' in Kalidasa's meghaduta. **71:** 509–513.

2560. **Bhattacharyya, Sivaprasad**
Recent strides in the study of Sanskrit anthology. **6:** 127–147.

2561. **Bhide, Sudha S.**
Nature and scope of Sanskrit literary criticism as seen in Sanskrit commentaries. **57:** 169–173.

2562. **Buddha Prakash**
New light on the life and works of Rajasekhara. **61:** 367–375.

2563. **Caillat, Colette**
Stylistic notes on candagavejihaya. **41:** 85–90.

2564. **Chakravarti, Pulin Bihari**
'Anviksiki-sthapana' section in the arthasastra of Kautilya. **6:** 229–249.

2565. **Charudeva Shastri**
Kavi Harichandra. **80:** 166–179. (Sanskrit).

2566. **Chatterjee, Asim Kumar**
Date of Kalidasa. **95:** 17–20.

2567. **Chidananda Murthy, M.**
A note on "karkataka rajju" in Dandin. **73:** 249–251.

2568. **Choudhury, P.C.**
The royal patronage of Sanskrit learning in Assam. **13:** 168–175.

2569. **Das Gupta, R.K.**
Coomaraswamy's concept of alamkara. **25:** 93–100.

2570. **Dave, K.N.**
The bee-eaters (sarngas) in Sanskrit literature. **39:** 68–74.

2571. **De, S.K.**
Indian erotics (kama-sastra) in its origin and development. **39:** 75–89.

2572. **Derrett, J. Duncan M.**
The anonymous svatvavicara: A legal study by a seventeenth-century logician. **16:** 605–611.

2573. **Devasthali, G.V.**
Kalidasa—Isvarakrsna identity not tenable. **59:** 150–164.

2574. **Dhadphale, M.G.**
Dr. V. Raghavan and the kriyakalpa. **69:** 47–52.

2575. **Eimer, Helmut**
Two Sanskrit-Tibetan fragments from the Berlin turfan collection identified. **44:** 95–98.

2576. **Emmerick, Ronald E.**
Another fragment of the Sanskrit Sumukhadharani. **87:** 165–167.

2577. **Filliozat, Jean**
Sur quelques designations de texts Sanskrits. **94 (1):** 253–258. (French).

2578. **Ghosal, S.N.**
Some observations on the words Bambhana and Bamhana. **11:** 233–236.

2579. **Ghosh, Manomohan**
Chronological sequence of Kalidasa's works. **29:** 229–240.

2580. **Gopal, Lallanji**
Araghatta in early Indian texts. **94 (2):** 635–657.

2581. ———
Cultural material in the Gurusamhita. **20:** 361–370.

2582. ———
The date of the Gurusamhita. **74:** 317–329.

2583. **Gupta, Dharmendra Kumar**
Kalidasa kavya mein vasant-sushama. **94 (1):** 277–290. (Hindi).

2584. **Jai Dev Vidyalankar**
Origin of allegory in Sanskrit literature. **3:** 115–126.

2585. **Janaki, S.S.**
Pururavas and Urvasi. **71:** 163–173.

2586. **Janert, K.L.**
Writing on arrows in ancient India: Studies in Kalidasa. **79:** 5–10.

2587. **Jani, A.N.**
Garvoktis of Panditaraja Jagannatha. **37:** 277–280.

2588. ———
Some practical hints on preparing a critical text. **95:** 17–18.

2589. **Kalia, Ashok Kumar**
Cakravaak-mithuna aur Kalidasa. **94 (2):** 959–967. (Hindi).

2590. **Katre, Sadashiva L.**
Digambaramucara alias Dasopanta (1551–1616 A.C.): A voluminous bilingual saint author from Maharastra. **71:** 199–210.

2591. ———
Kirticandrodaya-kavya; its author, date and author's patron. **59:** 189–200.

2592. **Krishnamoorthy, K.**
Dhvani and rasa. **16:** 476–487.

2593. ———
Epic in Sanskrit. **80:** 137–147.

2594. ———
Landscape in Sanskrit literature and criticism. **73:** 1–10.

2595. ———
New light on Bharata's laksana and related concepts. **3:** 151–159.

2596. ———
A note on the problem of authorship of works ascribed to Sayana and Madhava Vidyaranya. **30:** 447–452.

2597. ———
Udbhata's original contribution to Sanskrit literary theory. **94 (1):** 303–311.

2598. ———
Western response to Sanskrit literature. **84:** 328–336.

2599. **Krishnamurty, P. Gopal**
The story on the name, Bharata. **13:** 158–161.

2600. **Kunjunni Raja, K.**
Social attitude in Bhasa's works. **94 (1):** 357–360.

2601. **Kuppuswami Sastri, S.**
Authorial polyonymy and homonymy in Sanskrit literature. **56 (1):** 186–189.

2602. ———
Highways and byways of literary criticism in Sanskrit. **56 (1):** 122–151.

2603. ———
Presidential address at All-India Sanskrit Conference, Calcutta, 1926. **56 (1):** 212–216. (Sanskrit).

2604. **Mainkar, M.G.**
Classical Sanskrit literature. **23:** 55–71.

2605. **Masson, J. Moussaieff**
The sahrdaya. **94 (1):** 313–316.

2606. **Mishra, Adya Prasad**
The uniqueness of Sanskrit. **84:** 337–341.

2607. **Misra, Jayamanta**
Acarya Abhinavaguptapadanashantarasa-visayak-vichar. **7:** 105–115. (Sanskrit).

2608. **O'Connell, Joseph T.**
Ragavartmacandrika of Visvanatha Cakravartin, translated with introduction. **37:** 185–209.

2609. **Pade, J.S.**
Jambira. **39 (3):** 133–140.

2610. **Pai, Swarnalatha G.**
Ramapanivada—a study of his works in Sanskrit and Prakrit. **57:** 189–203.

2611. **Pandey, A.N.**
Kalidasa and the caturbani. **16:** 496–498.

2612. **Pandey, C.B.**
The date of Harisvamin, the commentator of Satapatha Brahmana. **66:** 436–442.

2613. **Paradkar, M.D.**
Kalidasa's knowledge of astronomy. **84:** 361–368.

2614. ———
Kavindracarya Saraswati, a native of Maharastra. **61:** 377–380.

2615. **Pingree, David**
The karanavaisnava of Sankara. **16:** 588–600.

2616. **Porcher, Marie-Claude**
On prahelika. **94 (1):** 325–330.

2617. **Puri, Ramchandra**
Rasa—nisapatti ke sandarbha me Acarya Shankuk ki darshnik dharna. **84:** 126–132. (Hindi).

2618. **Pusalkar, A.D.**
Sarngadhara-paddhati and brhat-sarngadhara-paddhati. **39 (3):** 157–172.

2619. **Raghavan, V.**
A Kalidasa-reference in the locana of Abhinavagupta. **59:** 147–149.

2620. ———
The vidagdhamukhamandana of Dharmadasa. **39 (3):** 224.

2621. ———
Why was Jayanta Bhatta known as Vrttikara? **39 (3):** 173–174.

2622. **Rahurkar, V.G.**
The bhasa-yogavasisthasara of Kavindracarya Sarasvati. **59:** 210–224.

2623. **Rau, Wilhelm**
Three further karika-manuscripts of the vakyapadiya. **27:** 343–349.

2624. **Rocher, Ludo**
Dayabhagavyavasthasamksepah. **27:** 351–358.

2625. ———
The terms niyukta, aniyukta and niyoga in Sanskrit legal literature. **18:** 167–177.

2626. **Ruben, Walter**
About ancient Indian riddles. **94 (1):** 361–369.

2627. ———
The history of Sanskrit is a problem of the history of the ancient Indian culture. **18:** 178–195.

2628. **Satya Vrat**
Jayasekhara's indebtedness to Kalidasa. **80:** 193–203.

2629. **Scharpe, A.**
Additions to the Kalidasa basic text. **41:** 177–186.

2630. **Serebryakov, I.D.**
Some thoughts on the 'catalogue of Sanskrit poets' by Dr. L. Sternbach. **94 (2):** 911–916.

2631. **Sharma, Ganesh Dutt**
Kalidasakavya vedic darshanam. **95:** 45–51. (Sanskrit).

2632. **Sharma, Mukunda Madhava**
On the concept of padalalitya in literary criticism. **37:** 257–270.

2633. ———
On the implications of the statement: Kavyesu natakam ramyam. **43:** 70–77.

2634. ———
On the significance of the saying kavyesu natakam ramyam. **94 (1):** 399–407.

2635. ———
The three qualities of Magha. **7:** 238–242.

2636. **Sharma, Narendra Nath**
New light on the concept of love in Kalidasa. **16:** 510–516.

2637. **Sharma, P.V.**
Botanical observations of Bana Bhatta (7th cent. A.D.). **71:** 369-382.

2638. **Shivaganesha Murthy, R.S.**
Appayya Diksita and metrics. **73:** 235–239.

2639. **Shivaramiah, B.K.**
Mysore palace publications. **92:** 206–210.

2640. ———
Philosophical implications of the rasa-sutra interpretations. **73:** 308–314.

2641. **Sinha, Priti.**
Karuna rasa ki rasamiyata. **94 (2):** 981–986. (Hindi).

2642. **Sivaramamurti, C.**
Fragrance and parijatapaharana. **78:** 31–36.

2643. **Sluszkiewicz, Eugeniusz**
Some new subhasita-s. **94(1):** 409–413.

2644. **Sohoni, S.V.**
Historical data about the date of Kalidasa. **5(2):** 334–338.

2645 . ———
A reference to Kalidasa in yasas-tilaka. **72:** 106–107.

2646. **Sreekrishna Sarma, E.R.**
Further focus on Mandana-Suresvara problem. **56(2):** 87–88.

2647. **Sternbach, Ludwik**
Subhasita-sangrahas and the Kamandakiya-nitisara. **3:** 135–145.

2648. **Suryanarayana Rao, M.K.**
Origin and development of campus. **59:** 175–188.

2649. **Sushma**
Sanskrit ke laksan-granthon mein roopakalankaara: Udbhava aur vikas. **95:** 15–21. (Hindi).

2650. **Thieme, P.**
Chess and backgammon (tric-trac) in Sanskrit literature. **15:** 204–216.

2651. **Thrasher, Allen W.**
Some Sanskrit works on karmas and their results. **94(2):** 721–724.

2652. **Tilakasiri, J.**
Kalidasa and the dhvani theory. **71:** 437–440.

2653. **Tiwari, Pratibha**
Kshemendrakrit Brihatkathamanjari mein Bharatiya Sanskrit tatha samajik adhunik vichardhara. **61:** 469–475. (Hindi).

2654. **Tripathi, Chandrabhal**
Ramanand and his teacher Ramendravana. **71:** 441–447.

2655. **Tripathi, Ram Narain**
Pratibha-swaroop-vimarsha. **94 (1):** 415–437. (Sanskrit).

2656. **Unni, N.P.**
A survey of Bhasa manuscripts. **3:** 107–113.

2657. **Upadhye, A.N.**
On the two recensions of the kuvalayamala. **59:** 201–209.

2658. ———
A point for the text critic. **71:** 449–451.

2659. **Upasak, C.S.**
On the editing of manuscripts. **62:** 355–358.

2660. **Ved Kumari**
Ksemendra's grudge against indisciplined students of 11th cent. A.D. **16:** 488–495.

2661. **Venkatachalam, V.**
Pracinamalaka—its true meaning rediscovered. **71:** 461–473.

2662. **Venkatakrishna Rao, U.**
Kama through the ages. **48:** 508–513.

2663. **Venkatarayacharya, S.K.**
Vijayadhvajacharya—an erudite commentator. **30:** 463–466.

2664. **Warnekar, Shridhar Bhaskar**
Adhunik Sanskrit sahitya "caritam Raghunathsaya". **94 (1):** 439–445. (Sanskrit).

POETRY

2665. **Balasubrahmanya, N.**
A Sanskrit apologist for poetry. **73:** 210–215.

2666. **Bandyopadhyay, Pratap**
The figure of speech udatta in Sanskrit poetics. **80:** 232–242.

2667. **Basak, Radhagovinda**
The Ramacarita of Sandhyakaranandin and king Madanapala as depicted therein and in the Manahali copper–plate grant. **29:** 30–44.

2668. **Bhardwaj, Shiv Prasad**
Kavyashastre Chamatkarvaad. **80:** 246–266. (Sanskrit).

2669. **Bhat, G.K.**
An obscure apabhramsa verse quoted in the dasarupa. **97:** 197–202.

2670. **Bhattacharya, Biswanath**
Fresh data on Bhartrmitra's view on laksana. **80:** 243–245.

2671. **Bhattacharya, Sivaprasada**
The naisadhacarita in its bearing on the alankaracode. **39 (3):** 19–35.

2672. **Chandramouli, Jaya**
Commentaries on the Uttararamacarita: A critical study. **57:** 174–188.

2673. **Chandra Prabha**
A study of madhuravijaya. **16:** 502–509.

2674. **Chattopadhyaya, Siddheshwar**
On the opening verse of the Meghaduta. **94 (1):** 247–252.

2675. **Dwivedi, R.C.**
Concept of obscenity (aslilata) in Sanskrit poetics. **43:** 78–87.

2676. **Emeneau, M.B.**
Sriharsa's naisadhacarita and the Mahabharata critical edition. **39:** 106–112.

2677. **Ghatage, A.M.**
The author of Srngaravairagyatarangini. **97:** 41–44.

2678. **Gore, N.A.**
Indrajit—kavya of Sri Raghunatha-deva. **39 (3):** 58–69.

2679. **Gupta, Dharmendra Kumar**
Kalidasa's vision of the cloud in his meghaduta. **16:** 451–459.

2680. **Hazra, R.C.**
Is the yukti-kalpataru a work of Bhoja? **39:** 161–168.

2681. **Ingalls, Daniel H.H.**
Words for beauty in classical Sanskrit. **15:** 87–107.

2682. **Jha, Mangalpati**
Elucidation of the figure, self-comparison. **62:** 672–676.

2683. **Karambelkar, V.W.**
Bhavabhuti's philosophy of speech in the Uttararamacaritam. **59:** 165–174.

2684. **Karna Singh**
Shakuntalam me shaskiya adarsha. **84:** 122–125. (Hindi).

2685. **Krishnamoorthy, K.**
Vopadeva and Hemadri on bhaktirasa. **61:** 403–409.

2686. **Kulshreshtha, R.B.**
Return of Kalidasa's Rtu-Samhara. **61:** 411–415.

2687. **Kuppuswami Sastri, S.**
Nilakantha-vijaya camp. **56 (1):** 171–175.

2688. ———
Sri Harsa's naisadham. **56(1):** 169–170.

2689. **Lienhard, Siegfried**
Ghatakarpara und Meghaduta: Einige bemerkungen zum alter des botengedichts. **27:** 247–253. (French).

2690. ———
Palai poems in Sanskrit and prakrit. **66:** 416–422.

2691. **Mirashi, V.V.**
The udayasundarikatha of Soddhala. **66:** 423–435.

2692. **Misra, Vidyaniwas**
Foundations of Sanskrit poetics. **48:** 375–393.

2693. **Mohan, P. Sarasvati**
Udaharana: A minor composition in Sanskrit literature. **72:** 195–209.

2694. **Moorthy, A.N.**
A note on poetic imagery in the Meghaduta. **39(3):** 121–128.

2695. **Mukherjee, Ramaranjan**
Kuntaka's approach to the problem of poetic expression. **62:** 663–671.

2696. **Nar Singh, K.T.**
Bhasasu bharatee ramya. **95:** 5–9. (Sanskrit).

2697. **Pandey, Lochan Prasad**
Kosalananda kavyam. **67:** 283–289.

2698. ———
Ramabhyudaya-kavyam by poet Narayana. **67:** 330–332.

2699. **Parab, L.G.**
Vallabhadeva and Mallinatha as commentators of the Raghuvamsa. **97:** 82–90.

2700. **Pillai, Poovattoor Ramakrishna**
The Visakhavijaya—a historical poem of Kerala. **80:** 204–208.

2701. **Raghavan, V.**
The author of the Laghu-yogavasistha. **29:** 53–63.

2702. ———
Kriyakalpa—an old name of Sanskrit poetics. **69:** 122–125.

2703. **Rath, Banamali**
The Gitagovinda and its imitations. **80:** 180–192.

2704. **Sarkar, Ranajit**
Meghaduta: A study of the interplay of "dark" and "bright" images. **94 (1):** 371–397.

2705. **Sarma, Dimbeswar**
Intuitional totality in the Meghaduta. **7:** 84–94.

2706. **Satyavrat**
Sisyahitaisini-—a Jaina commentary of Meghaduta. **85:** 361–372.

2707. **Satyavrat Singh**
Magha krit bharverathragauravasaya pratyabhigyanam. **50:** 351–354. (Sanskrit).

2708. **Singh, Lal Rama Yadupal**
Bhavabhuteruttar Ramacaritasayangirasa samiksha. **50:** 340–350. (Sanskrit).

2709. **Sohoni, S.V.**
Four verses in Meghaduta. **48:** 425–428.

2710. **Sriramamurti, P.**
Prameyacarcamrta of Viddanacarya. **16:** 517–522.

2711. **Sternbach, Ludwik**
An additional note on Sundarapandya's Nitidvisastika. **61:** 333–365.

2712. ———
Bhartrhari's Vairagya and niti-sataka-s, the first Sanskrit text known in Europe. **84:** 144–154.

2713. **Subramania Iyer, K.A.**
The moon in Kalidasa. **50:** 311–317.

2714. **Sukhvir Singh**
Saundarnand mahakavya me prayukta subhasita. **84:** 155–162. (Hindi).

2715. **Uniyal, Indra Datt**
Panditraj—Jagannath rasacha. **80:** 270–274. (Sanskrit).

2716. **Unni, N.P.**
The heroine of sukasandesa. **56 (2):** 221–227.

2717. ———
Yamaka poems of Kerala. **80:** 211–225.

2718. **Upadhyaya, Ramji**
Dashrooplaksana—samiksha. **80:** 226–231. (Sanskrit).

2719. **Varadachari, V.**
Trivikramabhatta, the poet. **16:** 529–536.

2720. **Ved Kumari**
Anyoktimuktalata: A critical appraisal. **84:** 169–173.

2721. **Venkitasubramonia Iyer, S.**
The syananduraprabandha of Svati Tirunal. **56 (2):** 209–220.

2722. **Vijayan, K.**
Refutation of santa according to Singabhupala. **80:** 267–269.

2723. **Wani, M.B.**
The elements of poetry in the Yogavasistha (Books I and II). **57:** 204–219.

DRAMA

2724. **Ambardekar, R.R.**
A critical study of the meghaduta of Kalidasa in the light of Bharata's rasa-sutra. **57:** 159–168.

2725. **Banerjee, Biswanath**
King Sudraka and the role of Sakara in the mrcchakatikam. **37:** 281–294.

2726. **Bhargava, Purshottam Lal**
The mrcchakatikam and the carudattam. **50:** 305–310.

2727. **Chakravarty, Dhyanesh Narayan**
Identity of Sri Harsa, the dramatist. **37:** 295–303.

2728. **Chattopadhyaya, B.D.**
Rajasekhara, his royal household and its religion: A study of some aspects of the Karpuramanjari. **20:** 273–279.

2729. **Chattopadhyaya, Siddheswar**
Later phase of Sanskrit theatre in eastern India. **43:** 62–69.

2730. ———
Stage and stage–craft as revealed in abhijnanasakuntala, uttararamacarita and mudraraksasa. **37:** 304–328.

2731. **Datta, Kali Kumar**
Some facts about the term sthapana in some Sankrit dramas. **37:** 329–336.

2732. **Devasthali, G.V.**
Bharatavakya in the plays of Bhasa. **39:** 95–100.

2733. **Filliozat, Pierre**
Quotations of Ratnavali in Abhinavabharati. **94(1):** 259–265.

2734. **Ghosh, Abhijit**
The controversial verse from the Prabodha-Candrodaya. **18:** 321–323.

2735. **Govind Pai, M.**
The word vrsala in Mudra-raksasa. **39(3):** 141–150.

2736. **Gupta, Urmi B.**
Kalidasa and Shakespeare—their common dramatic tradition. **16:** 460–470.

2737. **Janaki, S.S.**
Svarnamukta—samvada (or vivada)—a unique drama. **56(2):** 253–260.

2738. **Jog, K.P.**
A fresh revaluation of the inner meaning of the Sakuntala. **97:** 206–213.

2739. **Kanjilal, Dileep Kumar**
The reconstruction of the text of the Abhijnanasakuntalam. **29:** 274–287.

2740. **Kantawala, S.G.**
The Sangamaniya gem episode in the Vikramorvasiyam. **61:** 417–423.

2741. **Krishnamoorthy, K.**
New light on Bharata's laksana and related concepts. **56(2):** 261–268.

2742. **Kuppuswami Sastri, S.**
Ascaryacudamani. **56(1):** 158–168.

2743. **Mainkar, T.G.**
The Prakrit verses in the fourth act of the vikramorvasiyam. **69:** 104–112.

2744. **Mirashi, V.V.**
The author and the date of the Kundamala. **62:** 34–41.

2745. ———
The chronological relation of the Uttararamacarita and the kundamala. **48:** 429–444.

2746. **Nair, D. Appukuttan**
Ascaryacudamani of Saktibhadra on the Kerala stage. **56(2):** 229–238.

2747. **Narayana Sastry, H.V.**
Sahodarasnehah. **39(3):** 189–203.

2748. **Oleksiw, Susan**
A new interpretation of the Mrcchakatika. **56(2):** 239–252.

2749. **Pandey, K.C.**
Chayanataka (shadow-play) in Sanskrit. **16:** 499–501.

2750. **Pandya, Vijay**
Is there more than one vita in the Mrcchakatika. **44:** 293–308.

2751. **Poddar, R.P.**
Irony in the Mrcchakatika. **72:** 108–117.

2752. **Pusalkar, A.D.**
Amudanka-nadaa and Amrdanga-natakanka. **97:** 108–111

2753. **Ram Gopal.**
The secular origin of Sanskrit drama. **84:** 133–137.

2754. **Ramanathan, C.**
The tragic parts in the plays of Bhasa. **73:** 263–267.

2755. **Sharma, Brahmadatta**
Date of Sagaramandin. **48:** 451–454.

2756. **Sharma, D.D.**
Participation of women in Sanskrit plays. **84:** 138–143.

2757. **Sohoni, S.V.**
Kalidasa and Candragupta Vikramaditya—evidence from Vikramorvasiyam. **9:** 365–369.

2758. **Subbanna, N.R.**
Bhoja's citation of the extra verses of the longer version of the Sakuntala. **72:** 210–213.

2759. **Unni, N.P.**
Identity of Aryaka (Gopaladaraka) in the Mrcchakatika. **84:** 163–168.

2760. **Upadhyaya, R.**
The meaning of Chayanataka. **16:** 523–528.

2761. **Ursekar, H.S.**
Court scene in Mrcchakatika. **97:** 180–189.

2762. **Viswanathan, K.**
Is there not the tragic in Sanskrit drama. **39:** 454–461.

FICTION

2763. **Adrados, Francisco R.**
The influence of Mesopotamia and Greece on the Pancatantra. **84:** 105–115.

2764. **Chhabra, B. Ch.**
Narayana: Author of hitopadesa. **66:** 381–384.

2765. **Maten, Erik P.**
The rogue as a moralist: The place of Dandin's Dasakumaracarita in Sanskrit literature. **94(2):** 969–979.

2766. **Randeva, S.P.**
A glimpse into modern prose writing in Sanskrit. **3:** 127–129.

2767. **Sanghasen Singh**
The sphutartha Srighanacarasangraha–tika: The title, authorship, date and language. **47:** 230–233.

SINHALESE

2768. **Raghavan, M.D.**
The sandesa kavyas of the Sinhalese and the sacred dance. **72:** 236–241.

TAMIL

2769. **Adippodi, Kamban**
Kambar's date. **93:** 417–418.

2770. **Parpola, Asko**
On the social background of Tiruvalluvar. **79:** 83–91.

2771. **Graefe, W.**
Legends as mile-stones in the history of Tamil literature. **39:** 129–146.

2772. **Rao, K.V.**
Political philosophy of Kural. **30:** 325–330.

URDU

2773. **Rajendra 'Jijnasu'**
Urdu mein vedic sahitya: Ek jhanki. **95:** 42–44. (Hindi).

Archaeology

2774. **Agrawal, D.P., Krishnamurthy, R.V. and Kusumgar, Sheela**
Arsenical coppers in the Indian bronze age. **31:** 9–16.

2775. **Allchin, F.R.**
The archaeological significance of a modern Indian potter's technique. **75:** 1–14.

2776. **Allchin, Raymond and Allchin, Bridget**
The relationship of neolithic and later settled communities with those of late stone age hunters and gatherers in Peninsular India. **55:** 45–66.

2777. **Alur, K.R.**
Archaeological animal remains: Their significance and interpretation. **30:** 31–37.

2778. ———
Wild life affinity of animal in archaeology. **32:** 13–14.

2779. **Asthana, Shashi**
The first phase of Indian civilization. **95:** 55–58.

2780. **Balakrishnan Nayar, T.**
The 'Indian figurines from Memphis. **72:** 122–134.

2781. **Banerjee, K.D.**
Stone age migrations in India. **38 (1):** 41–46.

2782. **Banerjee, N.R.**
The megalithic problem of India. **35:** 163–178.

2783. **Bharadwaj, O.P.**
Identification of vinasana and some consequential observations. **21:** 205–224.

2784. ———
Vedic sites of North India. **5(1):** 85–91.

2785. **Bhattacharya, D.K.**
Conditions of the emergence of agriculture. **38(1):** 11–17.

2786. **Chakrabarti, Dilip K.**
Beginning of iron in India: problem reconsidered. **83:** 345–356.

2787. ———
Further notes on the Arya hypothesis in Indian archaeology. **95:** 74–77.

2788. **Dart, Raymond A.**
The concurrence of mining and symbolism. **83:** 309–320.

2789. **Dasgupta, Nupur**
An evaluation of the evidences for animal domestication in India in the neolithic and chalcolithic periods. **9:** 40–51.

2790. **Deo, S.B.**
Some aspects of megalithic technology. **31:** 33–35.

2791. **Deraniyagala, P.E.P.**
A code of nomenclature for prehistory. **83:** 77–80.

2792. **Deshpande, M.N.**
Historical archaeology. **23:** 417–455.

2793. **Dikshit, K.N.**
The antiquity of iron in India. **46 (1):** 109–119.

2794. ———
Archaeology of Ganga-Yamuna doab. **95:** 51–54.

2795. ———
Megalithic typology and chronology—a restatement. **48:** 85–89.

2796. **Dikshit, Moreshwar G.**
Rotary querns in India: A re-assessment. **70:** 25–46.

2797. **Gaur, R.C.**
OCP culture and its association with the pre-Harappans. **86:** 33–42.

2798. ———
OCP culture and the Indo-Aryans. **9:** 31–39.

2799. **Ghosh, A.K.**
Implementiferous laterite in Eastern India. **35:** 149–162.

2800. **Ghosh, Asok K.**
Concept of chopper/chopping tool complex in India. **83:** 221–234.

2801. ———
Palaeoanthropology or prehistory: Selection of terminology in Indian context. **38(1):** 3–10.

2802. **Gupta, S.P.**
The problem of the vedic Aryans and archaeology. **95:** 87–89.

2803. **Harinarayana, N.**
Electrolytic restoration. **93:** 47–50.

2804. **Hegde, K.T.M.**
Scientific basis of the technology of three ancient Indian ceramic industries. **38(1):** 401–410.

2805. ———
Some important ancient Indian materials and their industries. **60:** 142–149.

2806. **Joshi, Jagat Pati**
The Mahabharata and Indian archaeology. **38(1):** 19–34.

2807. **Joshi, R.V.**
The characteristics of the pleistocene climatic events in Indian sub-continent—a land of monsoon climate. **77:** 53–63.

2808. **Joshi, R.V.** and **Deotare, B.C.**
Phosphate content of anthrosals (archaeological deposits) of different cultural periods in India. **38(1):** 377–381.

2809. **Kantawala, S.G.**
Sanskrit and archaeology. **3:** 261–271.

2810. **Koenigswald, G.H.R. von.**
Asia and the evolution of man. **35:** 23–27.

2811. **Lal, B.B.**
On brick-sizes in early historical India. **46(1):** 247–254.

2812. **Lamberg–Karlovsky, C.C.**
Historical continuity, stage and process: The development of a metallurgical technology. **83:** 331–344.

2813. **Lele, V.S.** and **Koti, N.N.**
Statistics in archaeology. **77:** 64–74.

2814. **Madhu Bala**
Bharatiya puratattvasya navinatana visheshopalabdhayah. **95:** 83–86. (Sanskrit).

2815. **Makkhan Lal**
Distribution of copper hoards and their ore correlation. **95:** 21–28.

2816. **Malik, S.C.**
Indian archaeology as anthropology—a plea. **83:** 81–86.

2817. **Margabandhu, C.**
Early transport vehicles from Ganga Valley. **74:** 163–169.

2818. **Mason, R.J.** and **Thompson, I.**
Scientific procedure in pre-historic archaeology. **83:** 47–63.

2819. **Mehta, R.N.**
Archaeology and Kanada. **91 (1):** 117–119.

2820. **Mehta, R.N.** and **Kantawala, S.G.**
Stone–tools in the Rgveda. **5(1):** 23–26.

2821. **Mujumdar, G.G.**
Pedological study of some fossil and modern soils from Western Deccan. **52:** 139–150.

2822. **Nag, Arun K.**
Identification and origin of the 'sprinkler' **90:** 389–395.

2823. **Nagaraja Rao, M.S.**
Iron age in South India: Fresh evidence on chronology. **83:** 357–362.

2824. **Paddayya, K.**
The relevance of experimental approach in Indian prehistory. **74:** 1–10.

2825. **Pal, A.C.**
A note on the Jhukar pottery. **90:** 399–400.

2826. **Pal, Jagannath**
Madhya Ganga ghati ki pashan yugin sanskritiya: Ek survekshan. **86:** 12–25. (Hindi).

2827. **Panchamukhi, R.S.**
Archaeology and Sanskrit literature. **50:** 425–435.

2828. **Pant, G.N.**
Daggers and knives from excavations. **93:** 37–45.

2829. **Pappu, Raghunath S.**
The plaistocene geomorphology of the upper Krishna basin. **77:** 191–204.

2830. **Piaskowski, Jerzy**
Metallographic examinations of ancient iron objects. **83:** 321–329.

2831. **Pruffer, Olaf H.**
Some reflections on the extinction of the pleistocene megafauna. **35:** 28–40.

2832. **Purushottam Singh**
Neolithic cultures of Northern and North-Western India. **38(1):** 255–263.

2833. **Rai, Subash**
A fresh study of N.B.P. Ware glaze. **5 (1):** 47–49.

2834. **Ramachandran, K.S.**
Megalithic zones in India. **66:** 244–254.

2835. **Rao, K.P.**
Anthropomorphism in megalithic culture. **85:** 13–16.

2836. **Rao, S.R.**
Mining and metallurgy of copper in ancient India. **38 (1):** 383–398.

2837. **Roy, T.N.**
The concept, provenance and chronology of the painted Grey Ware. **86:** 43–54.

2838. ———
A critical study of the technical investigation made on N.B.P. **74:** 63–70.

2839. ———
Sanitary arrangements in northern black polished ware period. **38 (1):** 341–349.

2840. **Sahay, S.N.**
Neolithic ceramic industries. **86**: 26–32.

2841. **Sankalia, H.D.**
Cultural traditions versus functional activities in stone age and other archaeological assemblages. **75:** 79–91.

2842. **Sarana, Gopala**
Archaeological interpretation and Anthropology. **30:** 47–56.

2843. **Sen, D.**
Rebble chopper; chopping tools and flakes in India and Pakistan: A review in the light of recent finds in Europe and Asia. **34:** 287–295.

2844. **Sharma, G.R.**
Seasonal migrations and mesolithic lake cultures of the Ganga Valley. **19:** 1–20.

2845. **Sharma, R.S.**
The later vedic phase and the painted Grey Ware culture. **75:** 133–141.

2846. **Sharma, T.C.**
The neolithic pattern of north-eastern India. **31:** 41–52.

2847. ———
A note on the microlithic industry of the Garo hills. **68:** 215–217.

2848. **Simons, Elwin L.**
On the discovery of Gigantopithecus in north India. **83:** 1–7.

2849. **Singh, R.C. Prasad**
Are Indian cultures at the receiving end? **60**: 150–153.

2850. **Singh, Ravindra N.**
Ancient South Indian metallurgy: A reappraisal. **88:** 189–193.

2851. **Sinha, B.P.**
Archaeology in India—some problems and suggestions. **60:** 123–136.

2852. **Sinha, H.P.**
Black slipped ware—a study. **86:** 55–58.

2853. **Soundararajan, K.V.**
In quest of man: Anthropological bias in archaeology. **31:** 1–7.

2854. **Suraj Bhan**
Pre-vedic and vedic cultures of the Sarasvati Valley. **85:** I–11.

2855. **Thapar, B.K.**
Fresh light on the neolithic cultures of India. **38(1):** 247–254.

2856. **Thapar, Romila**
Archaeological artifacts and literary data: An attempt at co-relation. **38(1):** 411–415.

2857. **Varma, R.K.**
A review of the lower palaeolithic industries of India with special reference to the Sohan culture. **19:** 29–38.

2858. **Yash Pal, Sahai, Baldev, Sood, R.K.** and **Agrawal, D.P.**
Remote sensing of the 'lost' Sarasvati river. **99:** 491–497.

Andamans

2859. **Dutta, P.C.**
The kitchen—middens of the Andaman archipelago. **35:** 179–194.

Andhra Pradesh

2860. **Allchin, F.R.**
Drumbeats from the past. **46(1):** 1–6.

2861. **Khan, Abdul Waheed**
Yeleswaram excavations. **100:** 43–49.

2862. **Madhusudhana Rao, V.V.**
Metrical analysis of Acheulian tools from Paleru Valley, coastal Andhra Pradesh. **74:** 11–17.

2863. **Murty, M.L.K.**
Blade-and-burin and late stone age industries around Renigunta, Chittoor district. **77:** 106–128.

2864. **Rami Reddy, V.** and **Bhaskar, S.**
Maratipalem and Chintalapalem: Two late acheulian sites in south-eastern Andhra Pradesh. **74:** 19–43.

2865. **Reddy, K. Thimma**
Vemula industry in Cuddapah basin. **77:** 227–234.

2866. **Subrahmanyam, B.R.**
Eastern Indian neolithic culture in north coastal Andhra Pradesh. **74:** 45–49.

2867. **Subrahmanyam, R.**
Musalimadugu and its antiquities. **90:** 177–180.

Bihar

2868. **Jayaswal, Vidula**
Bihar in the palaeolithic period. **47:** 85–91.

2869. **Narain, L.A.**
The chalcolithic settlements in Bihar. **31:** 53–58.

2870. **Roy, Sita Ram**
Balirajgarh—a unique historical site. **60:** 178–180.

2871. **Sharma, Krishna Kant**
A buried town at Katra. **90:** 109–114.

2872. **Singh, R.C. Prasad**
Economy of the upper palaeolithic people of Gaya district. **47:** 92–98.

2873. **Sinha, Chitta Ranjan Prasad**
Prehistoric art in Bihar. **60:** 173–175.

Chandigarh

2874. **Lalman**
Archaeology of Chandigarh. **85:** 379–400.

Gujarat

2875. **Agrawal, D.P.** and **Pant, R.K.**
Paleoenvironmental studies in Saurashtra. **60:** 137–141.

2876. **Bhowmik, Swarnakamal**
Evidences of ancient foundry and metal technology at Lothal. **46 (1):** 35–43.

2877. **Leshnik, Lawrence S.**
More microliths from Gujerat and some thoughts on Langhnaj. **83:** 249–258.

2878. **Mehta, R.N.**
Ahmedabad—a topographical, toponymical and archaeological perspective. **38 (1):** 363–374.

2879. **Mehta, R.N.**
Anhilwad Patan and Merutungacharya. **74:** 195–197.

2880. ———
Champaner: An experiment in mediaeval archaeology. **31**: 119–128.

2881. ———
An experiment in salvage archaeology of mediaeval period. **76**: 31–33.

2882. **Pandya, Suman**
Protohistoric floods at Lothal: A critical study. **38(1)**: 177–186.

Haryana

2883. **Agrawala, R.C.**
Celts from Hansi, Haryana. **91(1)**: 115–116.

2884. **Bisht, R.S.**
Further excavation at Banawali: 1983–84. **38(1)**: 135–156.

2885. ———
Structural remains and town-planning of Banawali. **99**: 89–97.

2886. **Manmohan Kumar**
Archaeological investigations in Kurukshetra. **5(1)**: 53–62.

2887. **Margabandhu, C. and Sharma, R.C.**
Khataoli—a protohistoric site in South Haryana. **38(1)**: 287–294.

Himachal Pradesh

2888. **Mohapatra, G.C.**
Lithic industries of Himachal Pradesh. **83**: 199–212.

2889. ———
Traces of neolithic in western sub-Himalaya at Ror, Kangra Valley. **78**: 123–134.

Jammu & Kashmir

2890. **Gaur, G.S.**
Semathan excavation: A step towards bridging the gap between the neolithic and the Kushan period in Kashmir. **38(1)**: 327–337.

Karnataka

2891. **Allchin, F.R.**
Antiquity of gold mining in the Gadag region—Karnataka. **31**: 81–83.

2892. ———
Pottery head-rests from Narasipur Sangam. **35**: 58–63.

2893. **Alur, K.R.**
Pre-historic cultural heritage of man and animals in Karnakata. **95**: 149–153.

2894. **Ansari, Z.D.**
Pebble tools from Nittur (Mysore State). **77**: 1–7.

2895. **Gururaja Rao, B.K.**
Socio-economic life in protohistoric Karnataka. **74**: 59–62.

2896. **Krishnamurty, C.**
The neolithic cultural remains in the Kaveri Valley, Mysore district. **30**: 4–12.

2897. **Nagaraja Rao, M.S.**
Earliest iron-using people in India and the megaliths. **31**: 25–32.

2898. ———
Significance of pottery head-rests from neolithic sites of Karnataka. **77**: 141–148.

2899. **Nagaraju, S.**
Middle and late stone age industries of the Amarja Valley, Gulbarga district, Mysore State. **66**: 218–223.

2900. **Narayanababu, P.**
A rare passage grave in Northern Karnataka. **30**: 38–41.

2901. **Paddayya, K.**
The blade-tool industry of Shorapur Doab, peninsular India. **77**: 165–190.

2902. **Seshadri, M.**
Chalcolithic culture at T. Narasipur. **30**: 1–3.

2903. ———
The polished stone axe-adze culture of Brahmagiri, Mysore State. **39**: 378–386.

2904. **Soundara Rajan, K.V.**
Pre-iron culture spectrum in Karnataka: An appraisal. **93:** 11–16.

2905. **Sundara, A.**
Chalcolithic phase of the upper Krishna Valley. **30:** 13–30.

2906. ———
New discoveries of ash mound in north Karnataka: Their implications. **66:** 308–314.

2907. ———
A new type of passage chamber tomb in Kaladgi, district Bijapur, Mysore State. **77:** 216–226.

2908. ———
Studies in ash mounds. **38 (1):** 313–325.

2909. ———
A two-thousand year old town and its architecture in Vadgaon-Madhavpur (Belgaum) in Karnataka. **31:** 87–98.

Madhya Pradesh

2910. **Bajpai, K.D.**
The archaeological wealth of Madhya Pradesh. **60:** 356–361.

2911. **Banerjee, N.R.**
Ujjayini and Kalidasa: Analysis of the archaeological data. **31:** 113–118.

2912. **Dhavalikar, M.K.**
A Malwa pottery kiln. **5(1):** 27–29.

2913. **Joshi, R.V.** and **Khare, M.D.**
Microlith-bearing deposit of Adamgarh rock-shelters. **35:** 90–95.

2914. **Joshi, R.V.** and **Pandey, R.P.**
Cultural ecology of early man in the upper Mahanadi basin. **5(1):** 1–13.

2915. **Khatri, A.P.**
Origin and evolution of hand-axe culture in the Narmada Valley (Central India). **35:** 96–121.

2916. **Krishna, C.**
Excavation at Pagara: 1981: **5(1):** 69–70.

2917. ———
Mahishmati. **32:** 267–271.

2918. **Misra, Om Prakash**
Excavations at Atudkhas (East Nimar)—1984–85. **5(1):** 81–83.

2919. **Misra, R.N.**
Urbanisation in Chalcolithic Central India and its aftermath. **46 (1):** 291–295.

2920. **Nigam, J.S.**
Animal cult in Chalcolithic Nagda. **48:** 80–94.

2921. **Sharma, R.A.**
Excavation at Sooron—1984. **5(1):** 73–79.

2922. **Sharma, R.K.**
Excavation at Kakrahta: 1984–1985. **5(1):** 63–67.

2923. **Singh, R.R.**
Excavations at Piplya Lorka (Raisen) 1983–84. **5(1):** 31–33.

2924. **Trivedi, C.B.**
Identification of Nadinagar and Namdinagar. **21:** 325–328.

2925. **Trivedi, H.V.**
The problem of the black-and-red ware with reference to Malwa. **31:** 63–66.

2926. **Wakankar, Vishnu Sridhar**
Daspur utkhanana upaiabdhiyan. **82:** 48–51. (Hindi).

Maharashtra

2927. **Bopardikar, B.P.**
Early stone age site at Manegaon on the Purna river, Jalgaon district, Maharashtra State. **77:** 8–12.

2928. **Corvinus, Gudrun**
The acheulian workshop at Chirki on the Pravara river, Maharashtra. **77:** 13–22.

2929. **Deo, S.B.**
The personality of Vidarbha megaliths. **77:** 23–31.

2930. **Dhavalikar, M.K.**
Chalcolithic burials of Inamgaon. **74:** 51–57.

2931. ———
Genesis of the Jorwe culture. **77:** 32–41.

2932. ——
The Malwa culture in Maharashtra. **93:** 17–21.

2933. **Gaur, R.C.**
The early megaliths in Poona and its neighbourhood. **53:** 15–23.

2934. **Majumdar, G.G.** and **Rajaguru, S.N.**
Environments as reflected in the river deposits around Poona. **35:** 131–138.

2935. **Rao, S.R.**
Excavations at Kanheri (1969). **30:** 43–46.

2936. **Sali, S.A.**
A potter's kiln of Jorwe culture from Daimabad. **31:** 59–62.

2937. ——
The Savalda culture of the Deccan with special reference to evidence from Daimabad. **38(1):** 295–311.

2938. ——
The sculptures and the human figurines of the chalcolithic from Daimabad. **46 (1):** 379–387.

2939. ——
Some geomorphic and tectonic observations in the central Tapti basin in Dhulia district. **77:** 205–215.

2940. **Sankalia, H.D.**
Early stone age in Poona. **35:** 77–89.

2941. ——
Prehistoric Ahmadnagar. **100:** 39–42.

2942. ——
The stone age man in and around Pune (Poona) or the habitation of early man in 'sat-chit-ananda'. **89:** 39–48.

2943. **Sankalia, H.D., Pappu, R.S., Rajaguru, S.N.** and **Mujumdar, G.G.**
Rock engravings near Poona. **54:** 28–33.

Punjab

2944. **Joshi, J.P.**
Settlement patterns in third, second and first millennia in India—with special reference to recent discoveries in Punjab. **95:** 134–139.

2945. **Manmohan Kumar**
A note on the excavation at Burj (1977) district Patiala. **21:** 319–323.

2946. **Sankalia, H.D.**
The handoxe industry in the Punjab. **83:** 213–219.

2947. ——
Panjab and the Aryans or prehistoric Panjab. **66:** 259–269.

2948. **Sharma, Y.D.**
Domeli: Fresh light on the neolithic culture of Panjab. **93:** 1–10.

2949. ——
Fresh light on the Bara culture from Mahorana. **38(1):** 157–176.

Rajasthan

2950. **Agrawala, R.C.**
Copper arrow-heads from Ganeshwar, Rajasthan. **86:** 5–7.

2951. ——
Fresh light on Ochre coloured pottery from Rajasthan. **31:** 77–80.

2952. ——
More copper celts from Rajasthan. **47:** 99–102.

2953. ——
Protohistoric copper objects from Rajasthan: New parameters. **82:** 25–31.

2954. **Dalal, Katy Feroze**
Binjor 1—a pre-Harappan site on the Indo-Pak border. **38(1):** 75–111.

2955. **Dikshit, K.N.**
Iron age in India and the Ahar evidence. **91(1):** 107–109.

2956. ——
The Sothi complex: Old records and fresh observations. **99:** 531–537.

2957. ——
The Sothi culture. **38(1):** 113–115.

2958. **Handa, Devendra**
A stone age site at Pokaran in the Thar desert. **5 (1):** 51–52.

2959. **Lal, B.B.**
Some reflections on the structural remains at Kalibangan. **99:** 55–62.

2960. **Mishra, Satya Prakash** and **Mishra, R.S.**
Newly discovered late stone age sites, Southwest Rajasthan. **82:** 12–16.

2961. **Misra, V.N.**
Early village communities of the Banas Basin, Rajasthan. **34:** 296–310.

2962. ———
Evidence for a new chalcolithic culture in South Rajasthan. **77:** 85–95.

2963. ———
Stone age research in Rajasthan. **35:** 122–130.

2964. **Misra, V.N.** and **Nagar, Malti**
The microlithic industry of Bagor, Rajasthan: A preliminary note. **82:** 6–11.

2965. **Naga, Malti**
Modern pottery in Mewar, Rajasthan. **77:** 129–140.

2966. **Saran, S.C.**
Old stone age tools and rock painting at Kisan Bilas and Kapil-Dhara, district Kota, Rajasthan. **86:** 8–11.

2967. **Sharma, R.P., Margabandhu, C.** and **Saxena, B.P.**
Prehistoric remains of the Bairat Valley. **21:** 363–366.

2968. **Sharma, Y.D.**
From Kalibangan to Ropar. **82:** 17–24.

2969. **Sinha, A.K.** and **Meena, B.R.**
Recent explorations in eastern Rajasthan. **21:** 313–317.

2970. **Sonawane, V.H.**
An engraved mesolithic core from Chandravati, Rajasthan. **38 (1):** 53–56.

Tamilnadu

2971. **Allchin, F.R.**
Pottery from graves in the Perumal hills near Kodaikanal. **83:** 299–308.

2972. **Foote, Robert Bruce**
On the occurrence of stone implements in lateric formations in various parts of the Madras and North Arcot districts. **35:** 1–22.

2973. **Gururaja Rao, B.K.**
Megalithic culture in Tiruchirapalli district. **66:** 202–205.

2974. **Nagaswamy, R.**
Roman sites in Tamil Nad: Recent discoveries. **31:** 337–339.

2975. **Narasimhiah, B.**
Pre-neolithic and neolithic cultures in Tamil Nadu. **31:** 19–22.

2976. **Sarma, I.K.**
Pre and protohistoric assemblages in Tamilnadu and Kerala: An appraisal. **88:** 290–310.

Uttar Pradesh

2977. **Agrawala, R.C.**
Unpublished copper celts with marks from Saharanpur, U.P. **38(1):** 281–286.

2978. **Allchin, Bridget**
Siddhapur and Barkachha: Two stone age factory sites in Uttar Pradesh. **83:** 235–248.

2979. **Dikshit, K.N.** and **Malik, D.K.**
Motifs on the painted grey ware from Allahapur. **93:** 23–36.

2980. **Gaur, R.C.**
One more copper hoard from the Ganga basin and a reassessment of the problem. **31:** 73–76.

2981. **Lal, B.B.**
An enquiry arising from chipping—marks noticed on weights from Ayodhya. **38(1):** 399–400.

2982. ———
Excavations at Hastinapura and their bearing on the Mahabharata. **94 (2):** 1005–1016.

2983. **Lal, B.B.** and **Dikshit, K.N.**
India's biggest and most unique tank ever revealed through archaeological excavations. **47:** 111–113.

2984. **Lal, B.B.** and **Srivastava, S.K.**
On some pot-forms worshipped as deities. **86:** 3–4.

2985. **Margbandhu, C.**
Archaeological evidence of Buddhism at Mathura—a chronological study. **21:** 267–279.

2986. **Misra, V.D.**
The chalcolithic cultures of Uttar Pradesh. **19:** 57–68.

2987. ———
The chalcolithic image of Eastern Uttar Pradesh with special reference to Varanasi district. **82:** 42–47.

2988. **Misra, V.D.** and **Misra, B.B.**
Megalithic cultures of South-eastern Uttar Pradesh. **53:** 309–320.

2989. **Misra, Vijaya Kant**
Sarnath ke naveen dhvanasavshesa. **47:** 114–116. (Hindi).

2990. **Mujumdar, G.G.** and **Rajaguru, S.N.**
Investigations of the pleistocene sediments from the Belan Valley, U.P. **77:** 96–105.

2991. **Nautiyal, K.P.**
Evidences of new cultural elements in the lesser Himalayan region of Garhwal; an appraisal. **31:** 67–72.

2992. **Negi, J.S.**
Nahush ka tila: A preliminary exploration. **19:** 51–56.

2993. **Saran, Satish Chandra**
Vikramsila University—a centre of tantricism. **47:** 117–122.

2994. **Sharma, D.P.** and **Sharma, Madhuri**
A reappraisal of the chronology of mesolithic and neolithic cultures of the Vindhyas and the middle Ganga Valley. **38 (1):** 57–66.

2995. **Sharma, R.C.**
Antiquarian wealth from Sonkh. **60:** 183–187.

2996. **Srivastava, K.M.**
The site of Buddha's Sarakupa and its location. **47:** 106–110.

2997. ———
Some interesting new finds from Kapilavastu. **38(1):** 359–362.

West Bengal

2998. **Bhattacharya, M.**
On the recent findings of ground and polished stone industries of South West Bengal. **90:** 103–107.

2999. ———
Stages of prehistoric culture in Rarh Bengal; a recent exploration. **38 (1):** 47–52.

3000. **Bose, Subhra**
The copper hoard culture of West Bengal. **5(1):** 39–43.

3001. **Chakrabarti, Dilip K.**
Pakbira, a Jaina site in Purulia District, West Bengal. **38(1):** 351–357.

3002. **Chakravarty, D.K.**
Disposal of the dead in ancient Bengal. **89:** 131–134.

3003. **Datta, Asok Kumar, Ray, Dilip Kumar** and **Samanta, Biswanath**
Chamargora, the microlithic site of Tarafeni Basin, dist. Midnapur. **76:** 21–30.

3004. **Ghosh, N.C.**
The chalcolithic background of West Bengal. **76:** 15–19.

3005. **Nag, Arun K.**
Spatial analysis of pre- and proto-historic sites in Ajay-Damodar Valley. **38 (1):** 265–280.

3006. **Sankalia, H.D.**
The earliest trace of man in Bengal. **52:** 214–222.

Epigraphy

3007. **Adrados, Francisco R.**
Asoka's inscriptions and Persian, Greek and Latin epigraphy. **27:** 1–15.

3008. **Agrawal, Ashvini**
Vajresvari Devi temple, Kangra, inscriptions of Samvat 1871 (A.D. 1814). **85:** 243–246.

3009. **Ahluwalia, M.S.**
Early medieval Jaisalmer: An assessment of the Turkish invasions. **82:** 134–137.

3010. **Ahmed, Sarharuddin**
On the characteristic features of the inscriptions of medieval Assam. **88:** 331–335.

3011. **Anandasivam, R.** and **Ramamurthy, K.K.**
Three inscriptions of the Pallava period: A study. **21:** 145–149.

3012. **Andersen, Paul Kent**
Preliminaries to a textual criticism of the minor rock edicts of Asoka. **87:** 1–7.

3013. **Bailey, H.W.**
The son of Kujula Katphisa. **94(2):** 625.

3014. **Bajpai, K.D.**
Identification of Vanga Vahlika in the Mehrauli iron pillar inscription. **59:** 355–361.

3015. **Bajpai, S.K.**
Pipalda copper plates of Bhojadeva of Samvat 1076. **5(1):** 147–149.

3016. **Bhadri, K.M.**
Two inscriptions of the time of Chandella Madanavarman. **21:** 137–140.

3017. **Bhattacharyya, Gouriswar**
The physician poets of Magadha. **88:** 53–59.

3018. **Bhattacharyya, Pranab Kumar**
Two eighteenth-century inscriptions from West Dinajpur. **88:** 144–147.

3019. **Chhabra, B. Ch.**
Beauties of the Bhitari inscriptions of Skandagupta. **59:** 362–371.

3020. **Chidanandamurthy, M.**
The meaning of "Palidhvaja": A reinterpretation. **92:** 85–88.

3021. **Choudhury, R.D.**
Art in the royal seals of the inscriptions from Assam. **88:** 236–242.

3022. **Chowdhury, Abdul Momin**
Pundra/Paundra-vardhana bhukti in early Bengal epigraphs. **75:** 295–310.

3023. **Chutia, D.**
The location of the Dijjinnavisaya mentioned in the epigraphs of early Assam. **43:** 123–129.

3024. **Dani, Ahmad Hasan**
Two Kusana inscriptions from Campbellpur district. **10:** 1–14.

3025. **Dasgupta, C.C.**
Some problems of Indian palaeography. **6:** 225–228.

3026. **Derrett, J. Duncan M.**
An inscription dated 1584 concerning reform of a matha. **30:** 91–103.

3027. ———
Two inscriptions concerning the status of Kammalas and the application of Dharmasastra. **66:** 32–55.

3028. **Desai, P.B.**
Vajra-baisanige: Derivation and interpretation. **92:** 89–91.

3029. **Desai, Z.A.**
A bilingual Tughluq inscription from Damoh district, Madhya Pradesh. **91(2):** 431–436.

3030. ———
Central Museum Indore bilingual inscription of Ghiyathu'd-Din Khalji of Malwa. **5(1):** 151–154.

3031. ———
Fresh light on the Mohils of Ladnun. **82:** 122–126.

3032. ———
A new inscription of Muhammad Bin Tughluq Shah from Basav Kalyan (Kalyani). **74:** 125–130.

3033. ———
A note on the Nagari inscription of Mughal emperor Babur from Gwalior fort. **90:** 67–71.

3034. ———
A note on the Telugu inscription of Abdullah Qutb Shah from Kaveripakkam. **93:** 311–319.

3035. ———
Two Tughluq inscriptions from Daulatabad. **100:** 77–83.

3036. **Dikshit, G.S.**
Mahanadu. **92:** 92–96.

3037. **Filliozat, Vasundhara**
Two small inscriptions from Hampi. **87:** 161–163.

3038. **Filliozat, Vasundara P.S.**
Three Kampannas of Vijayanagara. **66:** 56–59.

3039. **Filliozat, Vasundhara** and **Filliozat, Pierre–Sylvain**
A grant of Sriranga-Raya I dated 10th September 1585 A.D. Jean Filliozat. **87:** 209–230.

3040. **Ghosal, S.N.**
Some difficult words and passages in the Shinkot Steatite Casket inscription of the time of Menander. **29:** 241–253.

3041. ———
Some reflections on the Kosam stone inscription. **37:** 378–382.

3042. **Gokhale, Shobhana**
Matvan plates of the Traikutaka king Vikramasena K. 284. **52:** 86–94.

3043. ———
A new important inscription from Junnar. **88:** 315–317.

3044. ———
A note on Kusanamula. **90:** 225–227.

3045. ———
The Pandharpur stone inscription of the Yadava king Mahadeva, saka 1192. **77:** 42–52.

3046. **Gopal, B.R.**
Gudnapur inscription of Kadamba Ravivarma. **92:** 61–72.

3047. ———
Mudakkaru. **66:** 60–65.

3048. ———
Narayanabali and Mangalesa. **73:** 315–318.

3049. ———
A new Kadamba inscription. **30:** 57–62.

3050. ———
Three interesting sale-deeds of the 12th–14th centuries. **90:** 173–175.

3051. **Gopal, Lallanji**
On the origin of the Indian alphabet. **11:** 239–248.

3052. **Gunda Jois, K.**
Unpublished inscriptions of Keladi rulers. **32:** 99–101.

3053. **Gururajachar, S.**
Some revenue terms in medieval Karnataka epigraphs (A.D. 1000–1300). **66:** 66–68.

3054. **Handa, Devendra**
An interesting inscribed relief dated S. 1010 from Ladnun. **82:** 118–121.

3055. ———
Jaina temple torana inscription, Osian. **38(2):** 435–438.

3056. **Hanumantha Rao, M.**
Aprameya's Jayastambha inscription at Kaliyur. **92:** 79–84.

3057. **Hartel, Herbert**
An early coping stone inscription from Mathura. **87:** 101–110.

3058. **Jagadeb, Sri Lakshmi Narayana Harichandan**
The ancient statue and inscription in the Talcher (Orissa). **39:** 175–177.

3059. **Jai Prakash**
The guilds of oilmillers in ancient India. **21:** 307–312.

3060. **Joshi, M.C.**
An early inscriptional reference to Persian wheel. **66:** 214–217.

3061. **Joshi, M.P.**
Champawat copper plate of king Kalyana Chandra. **21:** 151–155.

3062. **Joshi, Maheshwar P.**
A newly discovered copperplate of king Bhishma Chandra of Kumaon. **80:** 444–450.

3063. **Joshi, N.P.**
Some aspects of Chalukya-Paramara conflict in Rajasthan. **82:** 127–133.

3064. **Katti, Madhav N.**
Gangas, Nolambas and Banas in Kongu country. **93:** 329–332.

3065. ———
Karnataka and South-East Asian epigraphy: A comparative study. **85:** 205–211.

3066. ———
Lakshmipur inscription of Rastrakuta Indra III. **21:** 329–334.

3067. ———
A note on Halebid inscription of Vira Ballala II, mentioning Kalachurya Bijjala. **90:** 91–93.

3068. **Khan, Ahmad Nabi**
The Indus Valley script: A survey of the attempts at its decipherment. **68:** 116–121.

3069. **Kolte, V.B.**
Hisse-Borala inscription of Vakataka king Devasena. **59:** 372–387.

3070. **Krishnamurthy, M.S.**
Date of five Kannada inscriptions at Kapalle. **92:** 73–78.

3071. **Krishnan, K.G.**
Date of the inscription from Pulankurchchi. **87:** 235–237.

3072. ———
Inscription from Udaiyarkoyil. **93:** 299–301.

3073. ———
Sanskrit in inscriptions of Tamilnadu. **21:** 21–23.

3074. ———
Two inscriptions on Kanyadana. **74:** 121–123.

3075. **Kuppuswamy, Gouri** and **Hariharan, M.**
A new theory on the Kudumiyamalai inscription. **85:** 247–252.

3076. **Lahiri, A.N.**
The occurrence of the title Maharaja in early Indian inscriptions and coins. **94(2):** 659–664.

3077. **Lakshminarayan Rao, N.**
The river 'Prehara'. **72:** 139–142.

3078. **Lal, B.B.**
Sindhu-sabhayata ki lipi: Ek anshik drishtipaat. **50:** 499–501. (Hindi).

3079. ———
Some observations on Harappan script. **98:** 189–202.

3080. **Lindtner, Christian**
An old error in Asoka's first pillar edict. **96:** 279–281.

3081. **Mahadevan, Iravatham**
An old Sinhalese inscription from Arikamedu. **56(2):** 279–282.

3082. **Mahajan, Malati**
Some curious place-names from inscriptions found in Maharashtra. **85:** 213–221.

3083. **Majumdar, R.C.**
New light on the interpretation of 'Atita-rajya-samvat'. **6:** 71–75.

3084. **Mangalam, S.J.**
Two copper plate inscriptions from Anegondi. **85:** 239–242.

3085. **Mehendale, M.A.**
Notes on Asoka's seventh and ninth rock edicts. **61:** 581–585.

3086. **Mirashi, V.V.**
Chinchani plates of the Arab feudatory Sugatipa. **6:** 96–109.

3087. ———
Epigraphical research. **23:** 505–529.

3088. ———
New light on the reigns of Kumaragupta and Skandagupta. **82:** 101–106.

3089. ———
A note on the Pandarangapalli grant of Avidheya. **100:** 73–76.

3090. ———
Pandarangapalli grant of Rashtrakuta Avidheya. **70:** 190–200.

3091. ———
Thalner plates of the Vakataka Harisena. **3:** 239–248.

3092. ———
Visnukundichya Indrapur danpatravar navin prakash. **52:** 286–291. (Marathi).

3093. **Mishra, R.S.**
Bharat Kala Bhavan copper-plate grant of Rajyapala. **22(2):** 221–230.

3094. **Misra, R.N.**
Village life and settlements in the light of Vakataka inscriptions. **38(2):** 643–647.

3095. **Mukherjee, B.N.**
Historical data in the Aramaic and Greek inscriptions of Asoka. **38(2):** 419–426.

3096. ———
A note on the Kandahar fragmentary aramaic inscription of Asoka. **90:** 407–410.

3097. **Mullick, C.C.**
Inscriptional evidences of Nalanda. **88:** 340–344.

3098. **Nagaswamy, R.**
Mahendra's inscription at Tiruchirapalli—a study. **72:** 135–138.

3099. **Nandimath, S.C.**
A broken stone inscription from Chaudadanapura. **30:** 76–84.

3100. **Nanjundaswamy, N.**
The Tekkalakota inscription of Brahmadhiraja, Saka 943. **90:** 83–85.

3101. **Narasimhamurthy, A.V.**
Epigraphical references to Pujyapada. **90:** 131–134.

3102. ———
Epigraphical references to Umasvati. **21:** 57–60.

3103. ———
Palaeographic features of the evolution of Kannada script. **86:** 221–225.

3104. ———
Pancamahasabdas. **73:** 245–248.

3105. **Nath, R.**
On identification of 'Kumbhaswamin-Alaya' of the Kirttistambha-prasasti. **82:** 165–169.

3106. **Nawani, N.P.**
Inscribed potsherds (A.D. 100–400): A cultural study. **21:** 87–92.

3107. **Negi, J.S.**
Two epigraphic notes. **19:** 21–28.

3108. **Neog, Meheswar**
The Barmurtiya-bil copper plate inscription, 1314 Saka. **88:** 402–407.

3109. ———
Origin and development of eastern Indian scripts. **13:** 191–195.

3110. **Norman, K.R.**
Asokan Sila-thambhas and Dhamma-thambhas. **11:** 311–318.

3111. **Padigar, Shrinivas V.**
Significance of Lad Khan temple inscription. **74:** 135–143.

3112. **Pandey, Lochan Prasad**
Arang plates of Maha-Sudevaraja. **67:** 43–54.

3113. ———
Chola-bula Someshwar Deva: The lord of Kosala (Mahakosala). **67:** 342–346.

3114. ———
A copper plate charter of the Haihaya king Maharanaka Ratnadeva II of the cedi year 878. **67:** 118–127.

3115. ———
Damaged Sripura plates containing the seal of Maha-Jayaraja of Sarabhapura dynasty. **67:** 28–35.

3116. ———
Date of the Narasinghanath inscription. **67:** 110–117.

3117. ———
An inscripton of Surya Verman of the Aswapati family. **67:** 290–293.

3118. ———
Kosala ratna-mala. **67:** 128–188.

3119. ———
Lodhia plates of Maha-Sivagupta: year 57. **67:** 88–105.

3120. ———
The longest and earliest Brahmi inscriptions in Mahakosala (Chhattisgarh, C.P.). **67:** 1–7.

3121. ———
Mahakosala in inscriptions. **67:** 305–312.

3122. ———
Mallar plates of Maha-Sivagupta. **67:** 63–86.

3123. ———
A new charter of Maha–Sudevaraja of Sarabhapura (from Sarangarh). **67:** 36–42.

3124. ———
A new copper charter of Maha Sivagupta Balarjuna, dated 57th year. **67:** 107–109.

3125. ———
Our latest find—Mallar plates of Maha Sivagupta (Balarjuna). **67:** 323–324.

3126. ———
Our startling discoveries. **67:** 321–322.

3127. ———
Pipardula copper-plate inscription of king Narendra of Sarabhapura. **67:** 13–27.

3128. ———
A short Brahmi inscription from Arang (C.P.). **67:** 8–12.

3129. ———
Thakurdiya copper charter of Maha-Pravaraja of Sarabhpura family. **67:** 56–62.

3130. ———
The title "Trikalingadhipati" the lord of three Kalingas. **67:** 333–337.

3131. **Pandey, V.C.**
The Bhitari pillar inscription of Skandagupta: A controversy. **80:** 435–438.

3132. ———
The Bhitari pillar—some observations. **60:** 161–165.

3133. **Parpola, Asko**
Interpreting the Indus script. **99:** 179–191.

3134. **Picron, Claudine Bautze**
Names of Visnu in the inscriptions from Bihar and Bengal: 9th to 13th centuries. **87:** 65–81.

3135. **Pillay, K.K.**
The Dalavaipuram plates of Parantaka Viranarayana. **72:** 159–165.

3136. **Poonacha, K.P.**
Discovery of Brahmi inscription at Brindavan (Madan Mohan Temple complex). **74:** 131–133.

3137. **Rajagopal, T.S.**
Two early inscriptions from South Kanara. **30:** 72–75.

3138. **Ramachandraiya, O. and Somasundara Rao, C.**
Munjeru plates of eastern Ganga Anantavarma. **66:** 117–124.

3139. **Ramachandra Murthy, S.S.**
Kanakadurga—Mallesvara temple inscriptions: A study. **93:** 307–310.

3140. ———
A note on the terms 'Inupa-edlu' and 'Velledlu'. **21:** 367–370.

3141. ———
Sirkurmanatha temple inscriptions: A study. **74:** 113–119.

3142. **Ramachandran, K. S.**
Process of Tamilisation of Sanskrit terms in medieval Tamil inscriptions. **21:** 141–144.

3143. **Raman, K.V.**
Some epigraphical gleaning on Vaishnava acharyas. **66:** 125–130.

3144. **Ramesh, K.V.** and **Subramonia Iyer, S.**
Rajpur copper plate grant of Paramara Naravarman. 74: 105–111.

3145. **Rana, S.S.**
King Candra of Mehrauli iron pillar inscription. **61:** 669–675.

3146. **Rao, S.R.**
New light on Indus script and language. **99:** 193–199.

3147. **Ritti, Shrinivas.**
A spurious (?) Kadamba Grant. **5 (1):** 121–124.

3148. **Roth, Gustav**
Observations on the languages of the inscriptions of Asoka including notes on the Bharhut—inscriptions. **86:** 201–211.

3242. ———
A unique potin coin of Rudrasimha I. **11:** 237–238.

3243. **Gunindra Singh, P.**
New light on Manipur history from the rare coins preserved in Mutua Museum. **88:** 254–259.

3244. **Gupta, Chandrashekhar**
The coinage of the Maharavela Lakshmanasingh of Banswara. **85:** 179–187.

3245. **Gupta, P.L.**
Chronology of the post-Kushana rulers and the allied tribes. **47:** 291–299.

3246. **Handa, Devendra**
Historicity of Vyaghra—the Naga king of Narwar. **76:** 323–325.

3247. **Jaiswal, O.P.**
The Apratigha-type of coin. **62:** 348–354.

3248. **Kasinathan, Natana**
Coins of Samara Kolahala and Bhuvanekavira. **66:** 322–324.

3249. **Lahiri, A.N.**
Coomaraswamy and Indian coins. **25:** 111–118.

3250. ———
Impact of Indo-Greek coins on succeeding issues of foreign and indigenous rulers. **88:** 220–229.

3251. ———
Silver-like coins and the trend of evolution of early silver punch-marked issues. **22(2):** 130–134.

3252. **Lahiri, Bela**
Religious affiliations of the medieval non-Muhammadan rulers of north-eastern states of India as reflected on their coins. **88:** 263–280.

3253. **Lal, A.**
Numismatic gleanings from Sanskrit Buddhist literature. **62:** 279–281.

3254. **Lawson, Simon.**
A curious Buddhist seal from the Ashmolean Museum. **87:** 169–177.

3255. **Maity, S.K.**
A note on coinage and culture of ancient India. **86:** 226–238.

3256. **Mangalam, S.J.**
A rare South Indian coin from Madura. **85:** 189–191.

3257. **Mirashi, V.V.**
A unique coin of the Visnukundins. **11:** 303–305.

3258. **Mukherjee, B.N.**
A note on Gupta numismatic art. **78:** 135–138.

3259. ———
The Paglatek hoard and the relation between Kamarupa and Samatata. **88:** 281–286.

3260. ———
Tiny coins of Malwa. **53:** 66–72.

3261. **Mukherjee, Bratindra Nath**
Obverse legend on the coins of Vainyagupta. **6:** 336–338.

3262. **Mukherjee, D.**
Glimpses into the temple architecture on some early indigenous coins of Northern India. **36:** 153–158.

3263. **Mukhopadhyay, Samir Kumar**
Four Rajghat seals in the Indian Museum collection. **76:** 243–244.

3264. **Nagaraja Rao, M.S.**
Early Byzantine Solidi from Karnataka. **91(2):** 441–445.

3265. **Narasimha Murthy, A.V.**
Ancient mints in Karnataka. **5 (1):** 161–163.

3266. ———
Numismatic data from Banavasi. **92:** 289–291.

3267. ———
Some problems of Karnataka coinage. **74:** 145–150.

3268. **Nigam, L.S.**
Numismatography of repousse gold coins. **5 (1):** 155–159.

3269. **Pandey, C.B.**
The Satavahana coinage. **61:** 637–656.

3270. **Pandey, Lochan Prasad**
Balapur stone seal stamp of Sri Balakesari. **67:** 216–218.

3271. ———
Balapur copper coins of Pratapamalladeva (A new discovery). **67:** 223–228.

3272. ———
Haihaya coins of Mahakosala. **67:** 239–242.

3273. ———
A note on the Hanumana type copper-coins of Prithvideva and Jalalladeva of Mahakosala. **67:** 229–233.

3274. ———
A silver coin of king Prasannamatra (with a legend in box-headed characters). **67:** 194–215.

3275. ———
Silver coins of the Haihaya princes of Mahakosala. **67:** 234–237.

3276. ———
Two unassigned coins of Balapur. **67:** 219–222.

3277. ———
Type and legends of Haihaya coins of Mahakosala. **67:** 243–259.

3278. ———
A unique Andhra coin attributed to Apilaka. **67:** 189–193.

3279. ———
A unique Andhra coin attributed to Apilaka. **67:** 327–329.

3280. **Pandey, M.S.**
The Candragupta-Kumaradevi type of coins. **62:** 282–285.

3281. **Phukan, J.N.**
Re-reading of the coins of Shu-Klen-Mung. **7:** 225–229.

3282. **Punekar, Shankar Mokashi**
Who is Kutra Trita Aptya? **85:** 197–203.

3283. **Raghunath Bhat, H.R.**
Kura coins Kerehalli—a note. **21:** 359–362.

3284. **Ray, Sunil C.**
Stratigraphic evidence of coins from excavations at Mathura. **88:** 375–384.

3285. **Reddy, D. Raja** and **Reddy, P. Suryanarayana**
Some observations on uninscribed coins of Andhra. **85:** 155–160.

3286. **Rhodes, N.G.**
On two north-eastern Indian coins. **88:** 140–143.

3287. **Roy, P.C.**
The coins of the Chahamana dynasty. **60:** 241–256.

3288. **Sali, S.A.**
A terracotta cylinder seal from Daimabad. **5(1):** 35–37.

3289. **Sankaranarayana, N.**
Medals in the Madras Government Museum. **88:** 318–320.

3290. **Saran, S.C.**
On a newly acquired Indus seal from Kalibangan. **5(1):** 45–46.

3291. **Sharma, I.K.**
Depiction of temple on Visnukundi coins. **90:** 337–343.

3292. **Shastri, Ajay Mitra**
A problem of Western Kshatrapa numismatics: The name of Svami-Jivadaman's son; a re-appraisal. **32:** 91–94.

3293. ———
Contemporary forgeries of silver coins of Kumaragupta I. **90:** 97–102.

3294. ———
Die-studies: Some observations. **85:** 151–153.

3295. ———
Note on a joint issue of Queen Machenes and King Maues. **21:** 187–189.

3296. ———
Satavahana Prince Saktikumara: Numismatic evidence. **91(2):** 447–453.

3297. **Shukla, S.P.**
Ahichchhatra sealing of the Kumbhakara guild. **85:** 193–195.

3298. **Singh, Sarjug Prasad**
Indological notes (2): Kinjar hoard of early Indian coins. **90:** 115–124.

3299. **Singh, Y.B.**
Perspective on coins of early medieval Kashmir. **38(2):** 439–442.

3300. **Suresh Vasant**
A new coin type of Vasisthiputra Mahaksatrapa from Junnar. **31:** 293–296.

3301. **Thaplyal, K.K.**
Some observations on Harappan and early historical seals. **31:** 37–40.

3302. ———
A sealing of a Kumaramatya of Kanyakubja. **47:** 125–127.

3303. **Varma, R.L.**
Silver punch-marked coin from Jangambadi (Gaya). **90:** 95–96.

Art

3304. **Agrawala, R.C.**
Rajasthan contribution to early Indian art and sculpture. **52:** 1–12.

3305. **Asher, Frederick**
On stone and artistic production. **33:** 63–68.

3306. **Bajpai, K.D.**
Indian art history: Some reflections. **86:** 83–90.

3307. ———
Source-material for Indian art history. **82:** 143–147.

3308. **Banerjee, N.R.**
The relevance of Indian art in the context of scientific and technological advances of modern times. **46 (1):** 13–19.

3309. **Bedekar, V.M.**
The process of casting metal images in the Mahabharata. **59:** 306–310.

3310. **Bhattacharya, Asok K.**
Coomaraswamy's approach to art. **25:** 6–10.

3311. ———
Medieval background of Indian art. **78:** 162–181.

3312. **Bhowmick, Atul Chandra**
Sola pithwork—an expression of folk-art in Bengal. **36:** 211–217.

3313. **Brajesh Krishna**
Politico-social backdrop of the Pratihara art. **85:** 111–121.

3314. **Chakrabarti, Jayanta**
Coomaraswamy's approach to Indian aesthetics: Its relevance today. **25:** 80–85.

3315. **Chakraborti, Kanchan**
Dialectics of art and Ananda Coomaraswamy. **25:** 86–92.

3316. **Chhabra, B. Ch.**
Patronage of arts in ancient India. **5(2):** 253–255.

3317. **Das, A.K.**
Style and symbolic motifs in the art of Arunachal. **36:** 207–209.

3318. **Dasgupta, Rajatananda**
Coomaraswamy and the Indian artist. **25:** 3–5.

3319. **Desai, Devangana**
Reflections on Coomaraswamy's approach to Indian art. **26:** 60–61.

3320. **Dhavalikar, M.K.**
Kirtimukha. **91 (2):** 349–354.

3321. **Donaldson, Thomas**
Naga images and the cult of Manasa in Orissan art. **14:** 99–108.

3322. **Dwivedi, V.P.**
Ivory carvings as a source of ancient art history. **60:** 196–203.

3323. **Ettinghausen, Richard** and **Henderson, Edward P.**
Jahangir's "Meteoritic" knife. **22 (2):** 38–42.

3324. **Goetz, H.**
Muslims in Vijayanagar: The record of monuments. **100:** 66–70.

3325. **Govind Chandra, Rai**
Symbols as sources of our beliefs and customs with special reference to the symbol of Chakra. **82:** 207–215.

3326. **Gros, Francoise**
Uttaramerur revisited. **66:** 191–201.

3327. **Gupta, S.P.**
The dharma approach to Indian art. **86:** 91–96.

3328. **Irwin, John**
Towards a humanist appreciation of Indian art. **4:** 235–242.

3329. **Jain, Jyotindra**
Significance of myth and ritual in Indian art. **26:** 70–74.

3330. **Jayakar, Pupul**
Sources of rural arts of India. **22 (1):** 290–308.

3331. **Joshi, M.C.**
Siva temple at Rajamau and the historical paintings of 1857 revolt. **31:** 273–274.

3332. ———
Studies on early Indian art in Uttar Pradesh and neighbouring areas; summary and suggestions. **38(2):** 495–506.

3333. **Joshi, N.P.**
Use of auspicious symbols in the Kusana art at Mathura. **59:** 311–317.

3334. **Joshi, Nibha**
Indian aesthetics and Indian contemporary art. **26:** 158–163.

3335. **Khastgir, S.**
The golden wings. **48:** 68–69.

3336. **Kolte, V.B.**
Rohinkhed. **70:** 1–14. (Marathi).

3337. **Konishi, Masatoshi A.**
A sketch on the tribal masks in India. **91(2):** 373–381.

3338. **Kramrisch, Stella**
The world of art. **91(1):** 129–135.

3339. **Krishnadasa, Rai**
The pink enamelling of Banaras. **22 (1):** 327–334.

3340. **Lipsey, Roger**
Traditional ideas and modern art. **26:** 145–147.

3341. **Lohuizen-de Leeuw, J.E. van**
Humor in Indian and southeast Asian art. **15:** 217–227.

3342. **Mahalingam, T.V.**
Some problems in the study of art and architecture. **92:** 1–9.

3343. **Mate, M.S.**
Art and architecture. **23:** 457–503.

3344. **Meister, Michael W.**
The hero as yogin: A virastambha from Chittor. **46(1):** 283–286.

3345. **Mishra, R.N.**
Artists in the early middle ages. **76:** 65–72.

3346. ———
A profile of Indian artists. **26:** 65–69.

3347. **Mode, Heinz**
European reactions to Indian art. **14:** 189–191.

3348. **Morley, Grace**
On applied arts of India in Bharat Kala Bhavan. **22(1):** 107–129.

3349. **Mukerjee, Ajit**
Tantra art. **48:** 43–50.

3350. **Mukerjee, Sandhya**
Social dimensions of ancient Indian art from Post-Maurya to Kusana period. **20:** 405–413.

3351. **Nagaraja Rao, M.S.**
Memorial stones in Karnataka—recent discoveries. **46(1):** 317–321.

3352. **Pandit, Sneh**
The notion of 'traditional art'. **76:** 61–63.

3353. **Parimoo, Ratan**
Coomaraswamy and Indian art history. **26:** 20–24.

3354. ———
Putanavadha in Indian art. **91 (2):** 263–268.

3355. ———
Sociological and formal problems of modern Indian art: Study of an approach. **75:** 47–53.

3356. **Raman, K.V.**
Hoysala influence on the Vijayanagar art. **92:** 55–58.

3357. **Ray, Niharranjan**
Certain notions relating to form and style in Indan art. **6:** 165–177.

3358. **Riepe, Dale**
A.K. Coomaraswamy, Niharranjan Ray with the assistance of James Marshall Plumer: Reflections on Indian art history and aesthetics. **73:** 19–39.

3359. **Sairam, T.V.**
Contemporary experimentation in Indian art. **46(1):** 375–378.

3360. **Saksena, Jogendra**
Sanjhi: Art and symbolism. **82:** 216–222.

3361. **Sharma, Manohar**
Rajasthani kahavato me kala-prasang. **82:** 272–276. (Hindi).

3362. **Sharma, Ram Charan**
Omens in literature and art. **82:** 223–226.

3363. **Sharma, Savita**
Indian art: The symbolic aspect. **5 (2):** 257–262.

3364. **Shetti, B.V.**
Cornucopia in Indian art. **22 (1):** 350–352.

3365. **Shukla, K.S.**
Basic form and concept of the Srivatsa symbol. **5 (2):** 263–265.

3366. ———
A unique Sunga statuette from Sanchankot. **85:** 75–77.

3367. **Sinha, B.P.**
Origins of art in the central Gangetic valley. **38(2):** 445–450.

3368. **Sivaramamurti, C.**
Indian art against Asian art. **26:** 38–41.

3369. **Smith, R. Morton**
On non-symbolic motifs in Indian art. **42:** 230–240.

3370. **Soundara Rajan, K.V.**
The Satavahana legacy in Indian art. **92:** 10–15.

3371. **Srivastava, A.L.**
Mathura: The cradle of Indian cult images. **85:** 49–66.

3372. **Srivastava, Balram**
Application of western terminology to early medieval art of India. **53:** 218–226.

3373. ———
Resonance and reference in relation to aesthetic experience. **86:** 195–198.

3374. **Srivastava, R.P.**
The art of sculpture in ancient Punjab. **88:** 156–167.

3375. **Tartakov, Gary Michael**
Changing views of orientalism. **46 (1):** 509–522.

3376. **Thakur, Vijay Kumar**
Ancient Indian urban art and culture (c. 600 B.C.—600 A.D.); a framework of inquiry. **36:** 75–86.

3377. **Tippeswamy, P.R.**
Arts and crafts in Mysore city. **92:** 332–334.

3378. **Vatsyayan, Kapila**
The Indian arts: Their ideational background and principles of form. **14:** 11–26.

3379. ———
The Indian arts: Their ideational background and principles of form. **26:** 51–59.

3380. ———
Some terms of Indian arts—an analysis. **94(2):** 783–801.

3381. **Vijay Krishna**
Fantasy in Indian art. **22 (1):** 335–339.

3382. **Wakankar, V.S.**
Rock art of India. **38 (2):** 583–597.

Architecture

3383. **Crowe, Y.**
Some aspects of the tree motif in medieval Indian architecture. **46(1):** 79–83.

3384. **Ghosh, Arabinda**
The architectural and artistic heritage of India. **89:** 125–129.

3385. **Joshi, M.C.**
Vajralepa and its use. **91(1):** 155–158.

3386. **Joshi, S.K.**
Naladurga—a unique fort in medieval Deccan. **74:** 293–299.

3387. **Joshi, S.K.**
Wooden architecture in ancient and medieval Karnataka. **85:** 281–286.

3388. **Lalit Kumar**
Jai Singh's observatory at Banaras—an observation. **82:** 170–171.

3389. **Margabandhu, C.** and **Sharma, R.P.**
Bridges of Delhi region. **93:** 99–104.

3390. **Mehta, R.N.**
Chandravati—capital of the Paramaras of Abu: A study in medieval town-planning. **82:** 161–164.

3391. **Mitragotri, V.R.**
Rock-cut caves of Goa. **32:** 27–36.

3392. **Narasimha Murthy, A.V.**
Vastusastra as described in Lokopakara. **93:** 59–60.

3393. **Raikar, Y.A.**
Forts in Arunachal Pradesh. **91 (2):** 407–412.

3394. **Raman, K.V.**
Ananda Coomaraswàmy on early Indian architecture. **25:** 49–54.

3395. **Roy, Bharati Kumari.**
The prakara of Ayodhya as noticed by Patanjali. **86:** 101–103.

3396. **Shastri, Ajay Mitra**
Varahamihira on the art of exploring underground water-springs. **7:** 79–83.

3397. **Silva, Roland**
Traditional design and modern architecture. **68:** 251–254.

3398. *Tale of the Vivekananda Rock Memorial, Kanyakumari.* **98:** i–lii.

3399. **Trivedi, R.D.**
Kapotika: An architectural term. **93:** 61–63.

3400. **Vyas Mangilal**
Rajlani ki bhoot badavi, **82:** 257–260. (Hindi).

HINDU

3401. **Agrawala, Prithvi K.**
The temple-sikhara as mentioned in the Gupta period records. **43:** 133–138.

3402. **Balasubrahmanyam, S.R.**
The ratha vimana. **72:** 148–150.

3403. **Berkson, Carmel**
An approach towards examining style in the Cave temples. **14:** 57–85.

3404. **Dasgupta, Kalyan Kumar**
Architectural data in the Hayasirsa Pancaratra. **11:** 229–232.

3405. **Dhaky, M.A.**
The "Pranala" in Indian, South-Asian and South-East Asian sacred architecture. **14:** 119–166.

3406. **Ghosh, Devaprasad**
The Chaitya window motif. **6:** 148–164.

3407. **Joshi, M.C.**
James Princep on temple architecture. **93:** 423–429.

3408. ———
Temple architecture in Brihatsamhita and archaeological data. **46(1):** 205–210.

3409. **Kansara, N.M.**
Art notes on architecture in the Tilakamanjari. **16:** 544–553.

3410. **Pereira, Jose**
The plan of the Hindu temple and its impact on the Baroque church. **98:** 623–628.

3411. **Pramar, V.S.**
Origin of the North Indian shikhara form. **47:** 143–147.

3412. **Sarkar, H.**
The ghata-prasadas of ancient texts. **66:** 270–279.

3413. **Shastri, A.M.**
Varahamihira's place in the history of vastuvidya. **59:** 318–335.

3414. **Shukla, D.N.**
Philosophy of Vastu-Brahma and its impact on Hindu temple architecture. **50:** 474–480.

3415. ———
Vastu-Brahma with especial reference to temple-art-cum architecture with advaitic background. **16:** 561–568.

Andhra Pradesh

3416. **Das, D.R.**
Temples at Jayati (Andhra Pradesh). **38(2):** 519–532.

3417. **Krishna Murthy, K.**
Origin of Brahmanical apsidal shrines in Andhra. **93:** 65–66.

3418. **Mazumdar, B.P.**
Endowments to early medieval temples in Andhra Pradesh (c. A.D. 1000—1325). **20:** 420–430.

3419. **Rajendra Prasad, B.**
Telugu Cola temples at Krishnapatnam. **76:** 315–322.

3420. **Sampath, M.D.**
The Siva temple at Attirala. **93:** 95–98.

3421. **Sarma, I.K.**
Brahmanical brick temples and cult objects from Keesaragutta. **91(1):** 233–239.

3422. **Soundara Rajan, K.V.**
Four unique eastern Chalukya temples in Andhradesa. **5(2):** 207–209.

Bihar

3423. **Agrawala, Prithvi K.**
Observations on the Mundeshvari temple. **91(1):** 179–183.

3424. **Narain, H.K.**
Maluti—the village of the Gods and Goddesses. **90:** 397–398.

3425. **Suresh Singh**
Temples in Ranchi district. **62:** 436–442.

Goa

3426. **Mitragotri, V.R.**
The influence of western architecture on the temples of Goa (18th century to 20th century). **74:** 279–287.

3427. **Mitterwallner, Gritli V.**
The rock-cut cave-temples of Arvalem, Goa. **31:** 165–174.

Gujarat

3428. **Buddha Prakash**
Sa'di at Somanath. **50:** 378–384.

3429. **Nagarch, B.L.**
Ancient temples at Sunak. **38(2):** 537–544.

3430. ———
Recent archaeological discoveries from Rudramahalaya and Jami Masjid, Sidhpur. **92 (2):** 395–400.

3431. ———
Siva temples at Desar. **93:** 213–218.

3432. ———
Siva temples at Mankani. **5(1):** 189–190.

3433. **Sompura, Kantilal F.**
The evolution of the superstructure of the garbhagriha of temples in Gujarat. **7:** 68–78.

Himachal Pradesh

3434. **Goswamy, B.N.**
Documents from three Pahari temples. **76:** 251–259.

Karnataka

3435. **Bhatt, P. Gururaja**
The Senesvara temple, Bainduru, S. Kanara. **30:** 140–147.

3436. **Bolon, Carol Radcliffe**
Reconstructing Galagnatha. **91 (1):** 229–232.

3437. **Divakaran, Odile**
The beginnings of early Western Chalukya art. **22 (2):** 59–66.

3438. **Gururaja Bhat, P.**
Temples of Barakuru. **92:** 304–307.

3439. **Halakatti, S.V.P.**
Sabari temple at Sureban: A rare sikhara. **74:** 251–252.

3440. **Kamat, Jyotsna K.**
Depiction of social life in Bhatkal temples. **32:** 59–63.

3441. **Krishna Murthy, M.S.**
Lakshminarayana temple at Mudigonda. **74:** 247–249.

3442. **Maity, S.K.**
Role of artists and technicians in building monuments. **60:** 193–195.

3443. **Mate, M.S.** and **Gokhale, Shobhana**
Aihole: An interpretation. **30:** 501–504.

3444. **Michell, George**
The 'Royal Centre' and great platform at Vijayanagara. **14:** 109–117.

3445. **Nagaraja Rao, M.S.**
Chronology of Papanatha temple at Pattadakal: A reconsideration. **92:** 36–39.

3446. **Nagaraja Rao, M.S.** and **Ramesh, K.V.**
A royal memorial to Chalukya Vikramaditya II. **31:** 175–177.

3447. **Patil, C.S.**
Portrait sculptures in Mahadeva temple at Ittagi. **91(2):** 311–314.

3448. **Rajasekhara, S.**
Identification of the early Chalukyan temples. **92:** 16–22.

3449. **Ramamurthy, K.K.**
Narrative sculptures from Arkesvara temple at Alur. **93:** 187–190.

3450. **Ramaswami, N.S.**
A composite temple. **66:** 225–258.

3451. **Rao, S.R.**
Recent discoveries in Aihole and Pattadakal. **92:** 23–28.

3452. **Sanford, David Theron**
Miniature relief sculptures at the Pullamangai Siva temple, with special reference to the Ramayana sequence. **91 (2):** 277–287.

3453. **Sarma, I.K.**
Brick temples of Western Gangas. **93:** 67–83.

3454. **Settar, S.**
The Hoysala temples. **92:** 40–54.

3455. **Shetti, B.V.**
Aihole Galaganatha temple. **32:** 55–58.

3456. ———
An early Western Chalukyan Durga temple at Bachinagudda. **31:** 185–186.

3457. ———
Ramalingesvara temple at Hungund. **74:** 263–265.

3458. **Soundara Rajan, K.V.**
Two unusual temple models in Mysore area. **30:** 132–139.

3459. **Sundara, A.**
The Ramesvara temple in Kamdolli and bracket figures. **92:** 29–35.

3460. **Tartakov, Gary Michael**
Reassembling an early Calukya Vaisnava temple at Badami. **31:** 179–183.

Kerala

3461. **Gopalakrishnan, M.S.**
A Bhagavati shrine in Kerala. **72:** 188–190.

Madhya Pradesh

3462. **Agnihotri, P.D.**
Khajuraho the pride of Madhya Pradesh. **16:** 539–543.

3463. **Dehejia, Vidya**
A royal temple of the eighty-one yoginis. **46(1):** 93–98.

3464. **Desai, Devangana**
The Visnu-Vaikuntha temple at Khajuraho—placement of images. **46 (1):** 99–108.

3465. **Lascarides-Zannas, Eliki**
Siddhanatha or Siddhesvara temple at Nemawar. **91(1):** 225–227.

3466. **Meister, Michael W.**
The Udayesvara temple plan. **93:** 85–93.

3467. **Misra, R.N.**
Ancient temples of Gwalior revisited. **5(2):** 221–227.

3468. **Nagarch, B.L.**
Mohajamata temple at Terahi. **88:** 385–391.

3469. ———
Siva temple, Chorapura, district Shivapuri (M.P.). **86:** 126–133.

3470. **Spink, Walter M.**
A temple with four uchchakalpa (?) doorways at Nachna Kuthara. **22 (1):** 161–172.

3471. **Trivedi, C.B.**
Late Pratihara temples from Bundelkhand. **31:** 195–198.

3472. **Trivedi, P.K.**
A renovated Pratihara temple in district Guna, M.P. **85:** 401–404.

3473. **Trivedi, R.D.**
Ranamuktesvara temple at Kukarramath. **38(2):** 533–536.

3474. **Zannas, Eliki Lascarides**
The big Sukanasa of Udayesvara temple at Udayapur, Madhya Pradesh. **31:** 187–194.

Maharashtra

3475. **Baikar, Y.A.**
The so-called Hemadpanti temples in Maharashtra. **70:** 258–265.

3476. **Chatham, Doris Clark**
Pratiharas from Pattadakal to Ellora: The early Western Chalukya basis for the sculpture style of the Kailasa temple. **22(2):** 71–79.

3477. **Jamkhedkar, A.P.**
A newly discovered Vakataka temple at Ramtek. Dist. Nagpur. **91(1):** 217–223.

3478. **Pathy, T.V.**
'Verul Sivalayamahatmya' Ms: And some more facts about Ellora. **30:** 105–109.

3479. **Pathy, T.V.** and **Dhavalikar, M.K.**
Daulatabad caves. **91(1):** 191–195.

3480. **Sengupta, R.**
The motif on the facade of the Visvakarma temple at Ellora. **64:** 223–226.

3481. **Tartakov, Gary Michael**
The pratima pratisthapanam in the Kailasa. **91(1):** 201–211.

Orissa

3482. **Bandyopadhyay, Bimal**
A newly discovered minor shrine at Bhubaneswar. **85:** 123–126.

3483. **Banerjea, J.N.**
The Varahi temple at Chaurashi. **59:** 349–354.

3484. **Das, Dipakranjan**
Early bhadra deuls of Orissa. **78:** 182–192.

3485. **Donaldson, Thomas**
Individual styles and workshop participation in the early temples of Bhubaneswar. **22(2):** 80–91.

3486. **Mitra, Debala**
Bhuvanesvara Mahadeva temple, Balia. **36:** 145–147.

3487. ———
Kanakesvara temple at Kualo, District Dhenkanal. **87**: 83–100.

3488. ———
Pancha-pandava temple of Ganeswarpur. **6**: 292–297.

3489.
Svarnajalesvara temple, Bhubaneswar. **38(2)**: 507–518.

3490. **Saraswati, S.K.**
Three old temples at Baudh (Orissa). **30**: 127–131.

3491. **Sarma, Sadasiva Rath**
A living tradition of silpa in Orissa. **14**: 187.

3492. **Stietencron, Heinrich von**
The Lingaraja temple at Balia—an unknown temple of the early Bhauma period. **78**: 68–80.

Rajasthan

3493. **Bhanavat, Mahendra**
Ram-kavad—ek chalta phirta mandir-tirtha. **82**: 261–264. (Hindi).

3494. **Jain, Kailash Chand**
Ancient temples of Rajasthan. **86**: 119–125.

3495. **Meister, Michael W.**
Darra and the early Gupta tradition. **22(2)**: 192–205.

3496. ———
Forest and cave: The temples at Chandrabhaga and Kansuan. **82**: 156–160.

3497. **Soundara Rajan, K.V.**
Temple architecture in Rajasthan. **82**: 148–155.

3498. **Srivastava, Shashi Bala**
Images of Lalata Bimba in Osian temples. **21**: 303–306.

3499. ———
The so-called Sun temple of Osian. **5 (2)**: 229–232.

3500. **Williams, Joanna**
Char-choma and the late Gupta period in Malwa. **22 (2)**: 47–53.

Tamilnadu

3501. **Divakaran, Odile**
Some characteristics of the early Brahmanical caves in the Pandyan country. **91(1)**: 173–178.

3502. **Hari Rao, V.N.**
Wall decorations in Cola temples. **66**: 206–209.

3503. **Mahalingam, T.M.**
Some aspects of early Pandyan architecture. **30**: 121–126.

3504. **Ramamurty, K.K.**
Muktesvara temple—Kanchipuram. **74**: 289–292.

3505. **Raman, K.V.**
Masilamanesvarar temple—Tirumullavayil: An architectural and sculptural study. **31**: 199–200.

3506. **Ramaswami, N.S.**
A portrait of Krishna III? **74**: 229–232.

3507. ———
Saluvankuppam. **32**: 75–81.

3508. **Sarkar, H.**
Tiruppangili and Tandoni: Two less-known cave-temples in the Kaveri Basin. **91(1)**: 169–172.

3509. **Sarma, I.K.**
Beginnings of temple architecture at Kanchipuram; raw materials and religious impacts. **38(2)**: 545–551.

3510. **Soundara Rajan, K.V.**
A Surya shrine at Narthamalai, Tamilnadu, India. **66**: 303–307.

3511. **Srinivasan, L.K.**
Archaeological conservation and resurrection of the Brihadisvara temple, Thanjavur. **91(2)**: 455–466.

3512. **Subbiah, G.**
The rock-cut shrines of Pandinadu—an introduction. **78**: 193–200.

3513. **Wright, G.R.H.**
Restoration of Hindu temples in South India and its conceptual backgrounds. **66**: 315-321.

3514. **Younger, Paul**
The role of landlords, kings and priests in the operation of a South Indian temple. **93:** 243–255.

Uttar Pradesh

3515. **Das, D.R.**
A new temple-type from Jageswar. **90:** 323–330.

3516. **Joshi, Maheshwar P.**
Kapilesvara temple, Kumaon. **36:** 159–162.

3517. **Sharma, Deo Prakash** and **Sharma, Madhuri**
Decorated brick temples of post-Gupta period from Fatehpur district of Uttar Pradesh. **86:** 112–118.

3518. **Sukul, Kubera Nath**
Original sites of some important temples of Varanasi. **61:** 717–724.

West Bengal

3519. **Sanyal, Hitesranjan**
Temple promotion and social mobility in Bengal. **75:** 341–371.

BUDDHIST

3520. **Bandaranayake, Senake**
The recovery of a 'lost architectural style': Some roof from the Ajanta murals and related material. **31:** 139–148.

3521. **Deo, S.B.**
Buddhist remains in Vidarbha. **52:** 59–71.

3522. **Deshpande, M.N.** and **Jamkhedkar, A.P.**
The Buddhist cave at Lonad: A reappraisal. **91(1):** 163–168.

3523. **Dhavalikar, M.K.**
The beginnings of Mahayana architecture at Ajanta. **31:** 131–138.

3524. ———
Mahad Chaitya I—A fresh look. **76:** 53–55.

3525. **Huntington, Susan L.**
The Buddhist stupa at Gyaraspur. **22(2):** 54–58.

3526. **Irwin, John**
The stupa and the cosmic axis (yupa-yasti). **11:** 249–264.

3527. **Khanna, Amar Nath**
Discovery of Buddhist remains at Sanghol. **95:** 64–66.

3528. **Meister, Michael W.**
Sub-urban planning and rock-cut architecture in India. **31:** 157–164.

3529. **Nagaraju, S.**
Cave 3 at Nasik: A restudy. **31:** 149–155.

3530. **Pereira, Jose**
The evolution of the stupa: A summary stylistic history. **38(2):** 351–465.

3531. **Prasad, Hari Kishore**
Terracota sealings and stupas from village Dharawat, Dist. Gaya. **86:** 176–180.

3532. **Ray, Himanshu Prabha**
Bharhut and Sanchi—Nodal points in a commercial interchange. **38(2):** 621–629.

3533. **Spink, Walter M.**
Ajanta's chronology: Cave I's patronage and related problems. **22(2):** 144–157.

3534. ———
A reconstruction of events related to the development of Vakataka caves. **91(1):** 185–190.

3535. **Suresh Vasant**
Ajanta cave 8: A study. **91(2):** 249–253.

3536. **Verma, T.P.**
The question of originality of inscribed vase of Piprahwa. **32:** 85–89.

JAINA

3537. **Dhaky, M.A.**
The Jaina temples in Harasur. **91(1):** 197–200.

3538. **Michael, George**
Two temples from the early Vijayanagara period: Studies in monumental archaism. **91**(1): 213–216.

3539. **Tiwari, Maruti Nandan Pd.** and **Giri, Kamal**
Vaisnava themes in Dilwara Jaina temples. **5**(2): 195–201.

3540. **Tripathi, L.K.**
Jina temple in the Harivamsa purana. **21**: 289–296.

ISLAMIC

3541. **Ahmad, Shamsuddin**
An outline of Muslim architecture in Bengal. **100**: 109–117.

3542. **Asher, Catherine B.**
The Qal'a-i Kuhna mosque: A visual symbol of Royal aspirations. **22**(2): 212–217.

3543. **Desai, Z.A.**
Sidi Bashir Mosque with shaking minarets at Ahmadabad: Its data and history. **38**(2): 553–561.

3544. **Mukhopadhyay, Somnath**
Sibtainabad Imambara of Calcutta. **78**: 213–216.

3545. **Nath, R.**
Padma-kunda of the Rangmahal, Red Fort, Delhi, **76**: 101–105.

3546. **Saran, Parmatma**
Qutb Minar as Vijaya stambh: Super-howlers of the Archaeological Survey of India. **95**: 154–157.

3547. **Saraswati, S.K.**
Muslim architecture in Gujarat. **6**: 190–210.

3548. **Siddiqi, W.H.**
The discovery of architectural remains of a pre-Mughal terraced garden at New Delhi. **38** (2): 573–577.

CHRISTIAN

3549. **Joseph, T.K.**
Inda's St. Thomases in 4 tombs. **39**: 178–185.

Sculpture

3550. **Agrawal, Veena**
Murti kala me adbhot rasa. **85:** 429–432. (Hindi).

3551. **Banerjee, N.R.**
Indian sculptural art tradition. **93:** 169–176.

3552. **Bhattacharyya, A.K.**
Story of Indian sculpture. **1:** 585–601.

3553. **Ganguli, Kalyan K.**
Indian sculpture as viewed by Coomaraswamy. **25:** 11–20.

3554. **Mukherjee, B.N.**
An inscribed Gandhara sculpture. **46(1):** 315–316.

3555. **Parimoo, Ratan**
The idea of form and style in Indian scultpure. **78:** 108–122.

3556. **Sen, Paritosh**
Dynamism in Indian sculpture. **26:** 154–157.

3557. **Sharma, B.N.**
Religious tolerance and intolerance as reflected in Indian sculptures. **61:** 657–668.

HINDU

3558. **Agrawala, R.C.**
Brahmanical sculptures from Bharat Kala Bhavan. **22(1):** 173–177.

3559. **Anand Krishna**
The Gupta style of sculpture from the city of Banaras. **14:** 87–98.

3560. **Bajpai, K.D.**
Some interesting sculptures from Tripuri. **62:** 159–161.

3561. **Banerjee, P.**
A pre-Kushana royal figure from Bhaja. **36:** 141–143.

3562. **Bruhn, Klaus**
The acarya motif at Deogarh. **87:** 179–187.

3563. **Chakravarti, Mathura Mohan**
Sculptural assets of the Gupta period in Gaya. **90:** 311–316.

3564. **Choudhury, R.D.**
Some folk sculptures preserved in the Assam State Museum. **43:** 149–157.

3565. **Chowdhury, R.D.**
Some wooden sculptures newly collected for Assam State Museum. **36:** 279–282.

3566. **Del Bonta, Robert J.**
Brahmasiraschhedakamurti, Brahmahatya and ritualistic suicide in medieval Karnataka. **22(2):** 119–122.

3567. **Desai, Devangana**
Narration of the Ramayana episode—Valivadha—in Indian sculpture (up to A.D. 1300). **76:** 79–89.

3568. ———
Puns and intentional language at Khajuraho. **91(2):** 383–387.

3569. ———
Relevance of tantrism to erotic temple sculpture. **31:** 201–215.

3570. **Dhaky, M.A.**
Cola sculpture. **22(1):** 263–289.

3571. **Dikshit, K.N.** and **Trivedi, P.K.**
Sculptures from Bharat temple, Rishikesh, Uttar Pradesh. **86:** 134–136.

3572. **Dwivedi, V.P.**
A portrait of Tirumalai Nayak on two brass door-jambs. **66:** 188–190.

3573. **Harinarayana, N.**
The material of the Amaravati sculpture. **32:** 21–25.

3574. **Harle, J.C.**
A Gupta ear-ring. **68:** 78–80.

3575. ———
The "pleated" siras cakra. **91(2):** 345–347.

3576. ———
Two Yavana dvarapalas at Aihole. **66:** 210–213.

3577. **Joshi, N.P.**
Early Brahmanical sculptures in Bharat Kala Bhavan. **22(1):** 178–182.

3578. **Kanoria, Gopikrishna**
Ek Mauryakaleen kashtashilpa (A Maurya period Wood carving. **22(1):** 157–160.

3579. **Krishna Deva**
Gupta Ramayana panels from Nachna. **22(2):** 10–14.

3580. **Lakshminarayan Rao, N.**
Portrait sculpture of the Vijayanagara king Mallikarjuna. **30:** 181–182.

3581. **Lerner, Martin**
Early Chola bronzes at the Norton Simon Museum of Art at Pasadena. **22(2):** 109–112.

3582. **Lockwood, Michael**
The Mamallapuram penance panel—its interpretation. **11:** 272–276.

3583. **Lutzker, Mary-Ann**
A reinterpretation of the relief panel at Mamallapuram. **22(2):** 113–118.

3584. **Margabandhu, C.**
Royal sport of love—scenes as depicted in the temple at Abaneri, Rajasthan. **95:** 94–101.

3585. ———
Some notable sculptures from Abaneri, Rajasthan. **82:** 197–199.

3586. **Margabandhu, C.** and **Trivedi, P.K.**
Sculptural representations of Saiva teachers from Southern Rajasthan. **36:** 107–113.

3587. **Michell, George**
Folk tradition in a monumental setting: Sculptures on the great platform at Vijayanagara. **46(1):** 287–290.

3588. **Mishra, Vijayakanta**
A beautiful doorjamb from Mithila. **60:** 176–177.

3589. **Mishra, R.N.**
Sculptures in Dakshina Kosala (A brief survey of stylistic transformations, chronology and artisans). **22(2):** 139–143.

3590. **Mitra, Debala**
Note on two images in the collection of S.K. Saraswati. **64:** 219–221.

3591. ———
Some bronzes from Jaipur. **93:** 191–202.

3592. ———
Some images from Jaipur (district Gaya). **91(2):** 323–333.

3593. **Mukherjee, B.N.**
A note on the Lala Bhagat pillar. **36:** 123–125.

3594. **Nagaraj, Nalini**
Sculpture under the Chalukyas of Badami. **74:** 215–223.

3595. **Nagaraja Rao, M.S.**
A Kiratarjuniya relief sculpture. **30:** 193–195.

3596. ———
Kiratarjuniyam sculptures from Halebidu. **52:** 151–158.

3597. **Nagaswamy, R.**
From Aditi to Kundalini (from prehistoric visirikkal to historic Sricakra). **46(1):** 323–331.

3598. **Nigam, M.L.**
The Ramayana scenes in Andhra sculptures. **91(2):** 269–271.

3599. **Parimoo, Ratan**
On the sculptures from Ellora caves and the problems of Deccan School. **46(1):** 345–353.

3600. **Patel, T. Dayananda** and **Radha, M.**
Jewellery and ornaments in Hoysala period—a sculptural study. **74:** 257–261.

3601. **Pattabiraman, P.Z.**
Portraits of Chola kings and queens. **66:** 467–471.

3602. **Raman, K.V.**
Gopura sculptures from Vriddhagirisvara temple. **93:** 203–212.

3603. ———
Sculptural art of the Pandyas. **20:** 371–375.

3604. **Sagar, A.P.**
The images of Naga 'Muchilinda' and his consort at village Gulgaon, district Raisen (M.P.). **74:** 241–246.

3605. **Sahai, Bhagwant**
An interesting stone panel from the Visnupada temple. **61:** 709–715.

3606. **Sankalia, H.D.**
The Daimabad bronzes. **31:** 23–24.

3607. ———
Saivism and Vaisnavism in early Gujarat (c. 100 A.D.—700 A.D.). **91(1):** 31–34.

3608. **Sarkar, H.**
Beginnings of Saivism in South India with special reference to date of Gudimallam linga. **36:** 115–121.

3609. **Sharma, B.N.**
A Western Chalukya lintel from Hampi. **30:** 167–170.

3610. ———
Ravananugrahamurti: A unique bronze in the National Museum, New Delhi. **31:** 267–268.

3611. ———
Pala sculptures from Bodhgaya. **60:** 188–192.

3612. ———
Rajasthani sculptures: Some recent acquisitions in the National Museum, New Delhi. **82:** 192–196.

3613. ———
Sadyojata theme in Pala art. **47:** 166–168.

3614. **Sharma, R.C.**
The sculptural art of Uttar Pradesh. **85:** 105–109.

3615. ———
Mathura as school of sciupture. **46(1):** 407–416.

3616. **Shetti, B.V.**
Mahakuta sculptures from Kittur Museum. **91(2):** 307–310.

3617. **Singh, Sheo Bahadur**
The Uttarakand art—some special features. **36:** 95–97.

3618. **Sinha, Ajoy Kumar**
Kamadeva images from Bihar. **47:** 157–161.

3619. **Sivaramamurti, C.**
Portrait of Sankara. **98:** 703–705.

3620. **Soundara Rajan, K.V.**
The fair 'town-crier' from Jalasangvi—a symphony of art, literature and history. **48:** 4–8.

3621. **Srinivasan, P.R.**
Four pieces of sculpture. **22(2):** 36–37.

3622. **Stadtner, Donald M.**
A Gupta frieze from Kandava. **22(2):** 187–188.

3623. **Sundara, A.**
A rare Bhavali Ramana Mukhyprana (vayudeva) image from Bennur. **52:** 240–245.

3624. ———
Temples and sculptures from Bilichodu. **74:** 253–255.

3625. ———
Two rare sculptures from Sondur, Bellary district. **73:** 279–284.

3626. **Tewari, S.P.**
Identification of a Naga panel delineated on a door lintel from Sonkh. **46 (1):** 523–532.

3627. **Trivedi, P.K.**
Some observations on a sculpture from Nagda. **36:** 99–101.

3628. **Trivedi, S.D.**
Some rare scultptures from Kalinjar. **46(1):** 543–546.

3629. **Vashishtha, Neelima**
Some aspects of dance as depicted in the Saiva sculptures of Rajasthan. **82:** 200–203.

3630. **Verma, B.S.**
Bronzes from Antichak. **86:** 145–150.

BUDDHIST

3631. **Asher, Frederick M.**
The Sultanganj Buddha. **22(2):** 135–138.

3632. **Asthana, Shashi**
A controversial Buddhist Tantrik deity: Trailokyavijaya vis-a-vis Sambara. **86:** 167–172.

3633. **Bajpai, K.D.**
Ajanta and the contemporary sculpture. **52:** 22–26.

3634. ———
Bodhisattva Maitreya in early art. **36:** 283–285.

3635. ———
Salient features of the early Buddhist art of Central India. **96:** 271–278.

3636. **Bhattacharya, Gouriswar**
Two inscribed Buddhist images from the Museum of Indian Art, Berlin. **87:** 29–45.

3637. **Bhattacharya, D.C.**
Coomaraswamy on Buddhist art and iconograpby. **26:** 62–64.

3638. ———
Dramatic content of tantric Buddhist art and rituals. **85:** 93–104.

3639. ———
Of colour in tantric Buddhist art. **46(1):** 27–34.

3640. **Biswas, T.K.**
A note on six Gandharan sculptures. **90:** 377–382.

3641. **Darian, Jean**
Remarks on Mathuran Buddhist sculpture. **22(1):** 37–42.

3642. **Dikshit, K.N.**
A newly discovered Buddha image from Aurangabad caves. **31:** 235–236.

3643. **Dwivedi, V.P.**
The Kashmir Ivories. **22(1):** 322–326.

3644. ———
Three fragments from Bharhut stupa. **31:** 231–233.

3645. **Dye, Joseph M. III.**
Note on a Gandharan relief in the Bharat Kala Bhavan. **22(2):** 218–220.

3646. **Edwards, Richard**
Towards understanding a Kushan Buddha-type. **22(1):** 130–138.

3647. **Fischer, Klaus**
Interrelations between east and west in the light of newly discovered Gandhara scultprues. **40:** 155–158.

3648. **Giteau, Madeleine**
Note sur quelques images de Buddha laotiens **66:** 479–486. (French).

3649. **Gupta, S.K.**
Cause of the absence of the Buddha image in early Indian art. **47:** 134–139.

3650. **Gururaja Rao, B.K.**
Lord Buddha in Indian art. **73:** 255–262.

3651. **Huntington, John C.**
A section of an early portable shrine from Gandhara. **89:** 81–86.

3652. **Jaini, Padmanabh S.**
On the Buddha image. **49:** 183–188.

3653. **Krishna Deva**
In defence of Gandhara art. **91(1):** 149–153.

3654. **Krishna Murthy, K.**
An early sculpture of Bodhisattva Avalokitesvara from Ramathirtham near Chimakurti hills in Prakasam district, A.P. **21:** 335–338.

3655. **Mitra, Debala**
Images illustrating the Pancha-Dakamandala. **46(1):** 297–308.

3656. ———
A miniature reproduction of the Mahabodhi temple from Jaipurgarh. **31:** 333–336.

3657. **Nagaraja Rao, M.S.**
Sculptural art of Sannati. **91(1):** 159–161.

3658. **Nehru, Lolita**
The narrative reliefs from Gandhara and Mathura of the Kushan period: A broad comparison. **76:** 341–345.

3659. **Parimoo, Ratan**
Buddha's birth scenes in Indian sculpture. **74:** 203–209.

3660. **Pott, P.H.**
The Amoghopasa from Bhatgaon and its parivar. **48:** 30–33.

3661. **Prasad, Ajit Kumar**
Bihar's contributions in the development of the Buddhist art and architecture. **86:** 173–175.

3662. **Sankalia, H.D.**
A unique wooden pala image of Tara from the Kanheri caves, near Bombay. **86:** 143–144.

3663. **Sarkar, Haribishnu**
Beginning of sculptural art under the Guptas: An inscribed image from Baraipur, near Sarnath. **87:** 231–233.

3664. **Schlingloff, Dieter**
The Mahabodhi—jataka in Bharhut. **94(2):** 745–749.

3665. **Shah, Umakant Premanand**
A Buddhist sculpture from Aihole. **5(2):** 203–206.

3666. **Sinha, B.P.**
Some reflections on Indian sculpture (stone or bronze) of Buddhist deities trampling on Hindu deities. **62:** 97–107.

3667. **Sinha, D.K.**
Buddhist sculptures from Bilhari. **93:** 181–186.

3668. **Sinha, Narendra Kumar**
A rare Mathura-head in the Bharatiya Kala Bhawan, Gaya. **90:** 401.

3669. **Sivaramamurti, C.**
A new medallion of the subjugation of Nalagiri. **22(2):** 239–240.

3670. **Smith, R. Morton**
Musings on Mihintale: Locus standi. **68:** 268–274.

3671. **Srinivasan, K.R.**
An interesting sculpture in Tanjavur. **91(2):** 315–321.

3671A. **Thaplyal, Kiran Kumar**
Genesis of the Wheel-and-deer device. **38(2):** 467–469.

3672. **Varma, D.N.**
The problem of sensualism in Satvahana art: The mass communication aspect. **46(1):** 557–565.

3673. **Waterhouse, David**
Value judgements in the study of Buddhist art. **96:** 253–269.

3674. **Zannas, Eliky S.**
Two Gandharan masterpieces. **22(1):** 309–315.

JAINA

3675. **Bajpai, K.D.**
Ancient Indian art and Jainism. **32:** 51–53.

3676. **Bonta, Del**
The Jaina sculpture of Varuna. **91(2):** 273–276.

3677. **Desai, P.B.**
Yaksi images in South Indian Jainism. **59:** 344–348.

3678. **Nagarch, B.L.**
Newly discovered Jaina temple and other sculptures from Udaipur, district Vidisha (M.P.). **85:** 127–140.

3679. **Sarkar, H.**
An evaluation of date of Tirthankara images from Lohanipur. **76:** 39–42.

3680. **Shah, Umakant P.**
Jaina Jataka—stories in art. **91(2):** 289–298.

3681. **Sharma, R.C.**
Art data in rayapaseniya. **16:** 554–560.

ANIMAL

3682. **Chauley, G.C.**
A unique Kadamba sculpture with cow and calf motif. **89:** 87–88.

3683. **Kramrisch, Stella**
The antelope. **14:** 35–39.

3684. **Smith, R. Morton**
Using makaras. **9:** 150–156.

3685. **Welch, Stuart Cary**
A lion-king's lion. **46(1):** 577–580.

Iconography

3686. **Banerjee, J.N.**
Iconography. **23:** 531–545.

3687. **Bhattacharyya, D.C.**
Of murti and pratima. **36:** 43–47.

3688. **Dasgupta, Kalyan Kumar**
Coomaraswamy and Indian iconography. **25:** 55–68.

3689. **Jamkhedkar, Aravinda P.**
Simhakundalas: An appraisal. **31:** 269–272.

HINDU

3690. **Agrawala, P.K.**
The triple yaksha statue from Rajghat. **22(1):** 340–342.

3691. ———
Vedic Goddess Nirrti and the Inamgaon headless figurine. **86:** 97–100.

3692. **Agrawala, R.C.**
Ekapada Siva from Hirapura. **48:** 22–24.

3693. ———
Rock-cut Matrika panels from Deogarh (U.P.). **9:** 157–159.

3694. **Bajpai, K.D.**
Chief traits in the iconography of Devi. **47:** 140–142.

3695. ———
Evolution of the iconography of Siva. **84:** 271–273.

3696. ———
Some salient traits in the iconography of Siva and Sakti. **20:** 155–161.

3697. **Banerjee, N.R.**
The Yakshi from Fyzabad at the Bharat Kala Bhavan, Varanasi. **76:** 73–77.

3698. **Banerji, Arundhoti**
Rare icons of Kubera from Menal (Rajasthan). **82:** 204–206.

3699. **Barrett, Douglas**
The "Chidambaram" Nataraja. **22(2):** 15–20.

3700. **Barua, B.K.**
Kalika purana on iconographical representations of some sakta goddesses and their worship in medieval Assam. **39(3):** 1–18.

3701. **Basham, A.L.** and **Brand, Michael**
The iconography of Santosi Mata. **78:** 37–47.

3702. **Bhattacharya, Gouriswar**
Representation of Nandin in medieval stone sculptures from Bengal. **76:** 131–137.

3703. ———
Three bronze images of the snake-goddess from Bihar. **91(2):** 339–344.

3704. **Billorey, Ramesh Kumar**
Surya image from Siang. **11:** 191–192.

3705. **Biswas, T.K.**
Kinnara—kinnari. **22(2):** 266–269.

3706. ———
A note on three recently acquired Mukhalinga sculptures in Bharat Kala Bhavan. **76:** 163–166.

3707. ———
Sakti images in Bharat Kala Bhavan. **36:** 55–59.

3708. **Bolon, Carol Radcliffe**
A late 8th century Matrka set at Aihole. **46(1):** 51–55.

3709. **Chapekar, B.N.**
Surya in Mahabharata—a study in iconography. **52:** 27–41.

3710. **Chatterjee, Bhaskar**
Mother Goddess in Bengal. **9:** 328–335.

3711. **Chaudhuri, Vijayalakshmi**
The sixty-four Yoginis. **20:** 253–256.

3712. **Chitgupi, Bhimarao**
Nada-Brahma of Pandharpur: An iconographical hypothesis. **30:** 171–180.

3713. **Das, D.R.**
Mahisasuramardini images on Orissan temples. **36:** 61–68.

3714. **De, Bijanbihari**
An unpublished image of Harihara. **88:** 408–410.

3715. **De, Gourisankar**
Mahisamardini images of ancient and medieval India. **90:** 345–353.

3716. ———
The Vaisnava icons found in 24-Parganas. **89:** 69–74.

3717. **Desai, Devangana**
Mother goddess and her partner. **44:** 329–334.

3718. **Dhaky, M.A.**
Yoganarayana and Balamukunda from Huvinahadagali. **30:** 163–166.

3719. **Dhavalikar, M.K.**
Sri Ganesh-Gajanan: Puratattviya magova. **52:** 267–279. (Marathi).

3720. ———
Ganesa in Mathura. **38(2):** 471–478.

3721. **Dwivedi, U.C.**
Ganga and Yamuna in art and literature. **86:** 151–166.

3722. **Filliozat, Pierre-Sylvain**
Two images of Narasimha in Tirukkostiyur. **66:** 239–243.

3723. **Goetz, H.**
Surya as the supreme Godhead: A rare early Cahamana sculpture. **39:** 113–116.

3724. **Gorakshkar, Sadashiv**
A Harihara image recovered from Jogeswari and the problem of dating Gharapuri (Elephanta). **31:** 247–252.

3725. ———
Kalidasa and the Mahayogi at Gharapuri. **91(1):** 145–148.

3726. **Govindarajan, Hema**
The Nataraja image from Asanapat. **46(1):** 143–147.

3727. **Gupta, Chandrashekhar**
Some interesting plaques of Lajja from Paunar. **32:** 45–50.

3728. **Gupta, Chitrarekha**
Background of the iconic conception of Citragupta. **38(2):** 663–669.

3729. **Gupta, Jagdish**
Aaudhaalankrit shirobhusaukta Bali-devi ki rahasyamaya mranamurtiya. **50:** 502–508. (Hindi).

3730. **Gupta, S.P.**
The wine carrying mother goddess at Sanghol. **38(2):** 479–482.

3731. **Handa, Devendra**
Images of Tapasvini Parvati from Haryana. **88:** 179–185.

3732. ———
An inscribed image of Chakrasvami and new light on the Tomaras of Delhi. **36:** 103–105.

3733. ———
An interesting image of Mahisasuramardini. **88:** 311–314.

3734. ———
An interesting Vaikunthamurti from Pehoa. **21:** 297–302.

3735. **Hanumantha Rao, D.**
A Somaskandamurti sculpture from Markanda, district Chanda in Maharashtra. **74:** 275–278.

3736. **Jain-Neubauer, Jutta**
Iconography of sculptures in water-monuments of Gujarat. **44:** 335–341.

3737. **Jash, Pranabananda**
Incarnatory forms of Vishnu-Krishna. **86:** 391–397.

3738. **Jeyechandrun, A.V.**
Measurements in agamic texts. **93:** 107–112.

3739. **Joshi, M.C.**
A note on Sarasvati image of the Kushan period. **95:** 147–148.

3740. ———
A unique Linga from Baijnath in the Kumaun Hills. **48:** 25–29.

3741. **Joshi, Maheshwar, P.**
Siva the auspicious as depicted in some Kumaoni sculptures. **46(1):** 211–220.

3742. **Katti, Madhav N.**
Note on the Mahishamardini panel at Saluvakuppam. **74:** 225–228.

3743. **Khandalavala, Karl J.**
A dated Venugopala image in the collection of Amit Ambalal, Ahmedabad. **91(2):** 335–337.

3744. ———
Two bronzes from Karnataka. **31:** 239–241.

3745. **Kramrisch, Stella**
Siva Bholanatha. **46(1):** 241–245.

3746. **Krishna Murthy, K.**
Mahasadasiva in Hindu iconography. **74:** 267–269.

3747. **Lin-Bodien, Carol G.**
An early yaksha from Aktha near Sarnath (Varanasi district, U.P.). **22(2):** 294–297.

3748. **Lockwood, Michael and Bhat, A. Vishnu**
Siva as Lingin in a Pallava Somaskanda panel. **93:** 131–135.

3749. **Mahalingam, T.V.**
A unique Bhairava image from Nagatti. **72:** 143–147.

3750. **Maitra, Juthika**
Marttanda-Bhairava: The composite form of Siva and Surya. **88:** 211–219.

3751. **Majumdar, M.R.**
Lakulisa images from Western India. **39(3):** 108–120.

3752. **Malaiya, Sudha**
Dancing Ganas in the early art of Central India **5(1):** 177–181.

3753. **Margabandhu, C.**
Early Siva-Parvati plaques. **93:** 117–126.

3754. **Mishra, P.K.**
Some rare Durga icons. **88:** 176–178.

3755. **Naik, D.B.**
Vishnu sculpture in Goa Museum. **74:** 271–273.

3756. **Narain, A.K.**
On the earliest Ganesa. **68:** 142–144.

3757. **Nigam, M.L.**
Early iconography of Vishnu in Andhra. **93:** 127–130.

3758. ———
Two rare Vaisnava sculptures from Andhra—a reappraisal. **46(1):** 333–336.

3759. **Pal, Pratapaditya**
Two syncretistic icons. **6:** 326–335.

3760. **Parimoo, Ratan**
Kaliyamardana Krishna images from South India. **93:** 155–162.

3761. ———
Sculptures of Sheshashayin Vishnu: Some iconological image. **76:** 143–161.

3762. **Pathak, Indu Mati**
A unique image of the Sun-god in Tanjinatha, Ranchi. **60:** 238–240.

3763. **Prahalad Singh**
Images of dancing Ganesa from Bihar. **90:** 383–388.

3764. **Pramod Chandra**
The cult of Sri Lakshmi and four carved discs in Bharat Kala Bhavan. **22(1):** 139–148.

3765. **Purna Iyer, K.**
Iconographic elements of Vishnu in the Rigveda. **30:** 148–154.

3766. **Rahman, Mukhlesur**
The Matrka Varahi. **78:** 92–107.

3767. **Ramachandran, K.S.**
Some Harihara figures from Nepal. **93:** 163–165.

3768. **Ramamurthy, K.K.**
Kshetrapala concept and cult images from South India. **76:** 123–129.

3769. ———
Sati-tandava Siva bronze—an assessment. **32:** 81–84.

3770. **Sahai, Bhagwant**
Balarama in north Indian art. **60:** 217–231.

3771. ———
Parvati in the art of Bihar. **86:** 137–142.

3772. ———
A rare dancing image of Bhairava. **62:** 286–290.

3773. **Sarma, I.K.**
A chaturmukha linga from Amaravati and the spread of Lakulisa Pasupatism. **31:** 221–230.

3774. ———
Some Guhyas and Ganas: their character and prowess. **5(1):** 169–176.

3775. **Schastok, Sara**
The sixth-century Kubera image from Mandasor. **22(2):** 105–108.

3776. **Schmidt, Hanns-Peter**
Mithras the horseman and Revanta the lord of horses. **69:** 132–157.

3777. **Sengupta, Gautam**
Vaisali Mukhalinga revisited. **88:** 336–339.

3778. **Seshadri, M.**
Some unique Mahisasuramardini images from Mysore State. **66:** 297–299.

3779. **Shah, Umakant P.**
A unique Lakulisa sculpture from Chittorgarh. **82:** 176–177.

3780. **Sharma, B.N.**
A unique bronze image of Bharata. **66:** 300–302.

3781. ———
An unpublished Sapta-Matrka relief from Rajasthan in the National Museum of India, New Delhi. **62:** 301–306.

3782. ———
Vainayaki in sculpture and painting. **80:** 496–499.

3783. **Shukla, S.P.**
The early phase of the iconography of Durga Simhavahini. **36:** 69–73.

3784. **Singh, Chitra Lekha**
Sadasiva. **85:** 141–145.

3785. **Sircar, D.C.**
Mahishamardini Durga. **30:** 155–162.

3786. **Siromoney, Gift, Bagavandas, M.** and **Govindaraju, S.**
Iconometric analysis of the sculptures of the Dharmaraja Ratha. **93:** 137–150.

3787. **Sivaramamurti, C.**
Gajendramoksa. **31:** 217–220.

3788. ———
A rare Visvarupa. **14:** 41–47.

3789. **Srinivasan, Doris**
Iconological studies of recent Mathura acquisitions in the Bharat Kala Bhavan. **22(2):** 98–104.

3790. **Srivastava, A.L.**
Conception of Rajya-Laksmi and her plastic representation in Indian art. **43:** 139–148.

3791. **Srivastava, Vijai Shankar**
The iconography of the Ustravahini Devi. **82:** 178–187.

3792. **Subrahmanyam, Padma**
Siva the eternal dancer. **46(1):** 477–480.

3793. **Sundara, A.**
Early sculptural forms of Ganesa in North Karnataka. **91(2):** 255–262.

3794. ———
A unique Virabhadra image from Mulgund. **93:** 151–154.

3795. **Thaplyal, Kiran Kumar**
Tradition and ingenuity in art—A case study of Gajalakshmi motif on a sealing from Nalanda. **46(1):** 533–535.

3796. **Trivedi, S.D.**
Fresh light on some icons of Mathura Museum. **5(2):** 211–215.

3797. ———
Rare representations of Vamana-Avatara from Bundelkhand. **38(2):** 579–582.

3798. ———
Some unique icons from Lucknow Museum. **82:** 188–191.

3799. **Verma, B.S.**
An image of Vaishnavi from Antichak. **60:** 181–182.

3800. **Williams, Joanna**
An Ardhanarisvara-Linga. **91(2):** 299–305.

BUDDHIST

3801. **Bhattacharyya, D.C.**
The meaning of the term sattvaparyankasana. **47:** 171–172.

3802. ———
On some Buddhist asanas. **22(2):** 182–186.

3803. ———
Tradition and innovation in Buddhist iconography. **76:** 139–142.

3804. ———
Transmission of an iconic motif. **90:** 359–364.

3805. **Dasgupta, Kalyan Kumar**
The origin of the Buddha image. **88:** 148–155.

3806. **Klimburg-Salter, Deborah**
Vaisravana in north-west India. **31:** 253–262.

3807. **Mitra, Debala**
Twelve-armed Avalokitesvara. **75:** 169–185.

3808. **Mukherjee, B.N.**
An epigraphic evidence about iconic representation of Buddha. **93:** 113–115.

3809. **Parimoo, Ratan.**
Mahaparinirvana of Buddha in Indian sculpture—an iconological analysis. **90:** 331–336.

3810. **Perera, A.D.T.E.**
The crowned Buddha. **68:** 166–168.

3811. **Sahai, Bhagwant**
Bronze images of Prajnaparamita from Bihar. **47:** 162–165.

3812. **Sen, Asis**
The Buddha and his image. **20:** 37–46.

3813. **Subramonia Ayer, S.**
Depiction of Buddha in the Kushana period. **5(2):** 283–284.

JAINA

3814. **Dhaky, M.A.**
A propos of the image of Jina Rsabha with Nami and Vinami on Satrunjaya-Giri. **78:** 56–67.

3815. **Shah, Umakant P.**
A few Jain images in Bharat Kala Bhavan. **22(1):** 232–234.

3816. ———
A Jain bronze dated in Siddha-Hema-Kumara Samvat from Satrunjaya (Saurashtra). **31:** 237–238.

3817. ———
Origin of the Jaina goddess Ambika. **38(2):** 483–494.

3818. ———
Rare Jaina bronzes in Professor Samuel Eilenberg's collection. **46(1):** 395–405.

3819. **Sinha, Chitta Ranjan Prasad**
Jaina images from Bihar. **47:** 148–156.

3820. **Tiwari, Maruti Nandan Prasad**
Uttar Bharat me Jain pratima vijnana. **82:** 249–256. (Hindi).

3821. **Trivedi, P.K.**
Some metal images from western India. **5(2):** 235–238.

Terracottas

3822. **Auboyer, Jennine**
About an Indian terracotta of the Guimet Museum, Paris. **22(2):** 158–160.

3823. **Bhattacharya, P.**
The unprotected terracotta splendour of Murshidabad. **76:** 335–339.

3824. **Birendra Nath**
A critical study of terracottas from Bihar. **86:** 185–188.

3825. **Biswas, S.S.**
Architectural data in the early terracottas of Bengal. **36:** 149–152.

3826. **Biswas, T.K.**
Early Saivite terracottas in Bharat Kala Bhavan. **46(1):** 45–50.

3827. **Chakraborti, Uma**
Some Bengal terracottas of foreign inspiration. **88:** 243–247.

3828. **Chakravarty, P.L.**
Early terracotta figurines from Bharatpur. **82:** 172–175.

3829. **Chabbra, B.Ch.**
An earthen toy from Sugh. **46(1):** 75–77.

3830. **Das, Ratna**
Terracotta art of Tripura. **88:** 186–188.

3831. **De, Gourisankar**
The Oxford figurine. **9:** 160–165.

3832. **Desai, Devangana**
Pre-Maurya terracottas of the Ganga Valley. **36:** 87–94.

3833. ———
Social background of ancient Indian terracottas (cir. 600 B.C.—A.D. 600). **75:** 143–165.

3834. **Ghosh, Sankar Prosad**
Terracottas of Nadia—their artistic excellence. **5(2):** 217–220.

3835. **Gupta, Kalyan Priya**
A note on terracotta plaque from Kolhua, district Vaisali, Bihar. **36:** 139–140.

3836. **Jayaswal, Vidula**
A new look on the clay bull figurines from Hastinapur in rituals. **91(1):** 111–114.

3837. **Jayaswal, Vidula, Kalyan Krishna** and **Pant, P.C.**
Ethno-archaeological study of ritual terracottas of the Ganga Valley. **46(1):** 189–204.

3838. **Krishna Murthy, K.**
Terracotta toy figurine of horse and elephant from Guttikonda village in Gurzala taluk of Guntur district. **32:** 9–12.

3839. **Lal, B.B.** and **Srivastava, S.K.**
Perhaps the earliest Jaina terracotta so far excavated in India. **31:** 329–331.

3840. **Lohuizen-de Leeuw, J.E. Van**
What was the purpose of the terracotta animal figurines discovered at Kondapur? **91(2):** 369–371.

3841. **Mangalam, S.J.**
Satavahana terracottas from Paithan. **74:** 211–214.

3842. **Mankodi, Kirit L.**
Siva Gangadhara on a terracotta from Rang Mahal. **31:** 243–246.

3843. **Margabandhu, C.**
Early historic terracottas from Gujarat—a study. **31:** 99–112.

3844. ———
Kushana terracottas from Ganga Valley—a chronological and cultural study of the so-called foreign ethnic types. **91(2):** 413–423.

3845. **Mishra, Sudhakar Nath**
Important terracottas from Kakrahta excavations. **5(1):** 71–72.

3846. **Moti Chandra**
Terracottas in Bharat Kala Bhavan. **22(1):** 1–15.

3847. **Nagaswamy, R.**
Ancient terracottas of Tamilnadu. **85:** 67–74.

3848. **Roy, T.N.**
Continuity and change in terracotta discs. **32:** 1–7.

3849. **Sahay, Sachidanand**
Technique of terracotta art. **62:** 404–409.

3850. **Saran, Satish Chandra**
Two rare terracottas from Aguncha. **93:** 177–179.

3851. **Shukla, Vidya Sagar**
Some terracotta figurines from Sirsa (Haryana). **85:** 79–86.

3852. **Singh, Udai Vir**
Some interesting terracottas from Haryana. **5(2):** 191–194.

3853. **Sinha, Chitta Ranjan Pd.**
Some literary references to terracotta art. **86:** 181–184.

3854. **Sivaramamurti, C.**
Naravahanadatta and Madanamanchuka. **48:** 1–3.

3855. **Srivastava, K.M.**
Terracottas from Kapilavastu. **46(1):** 469–476.

3856. **Srivastava, S.K.**
An introduction to Mauryan terracottas in Kedia collection. **22(2):** 270–274.

3857. ———
Technique and art of the Gupta terracottas. **22(1):** 374–381.

3858. **Verma, B.S.**
Temple with terracotta plaques in the village Maluti. **47:** 169–170.

Painting

3859. **Archer, Mildred**
Banaras and the British. **22(1):** 70–74.

3860. ———
George Landseer (1834–78): A forgotten painter of the Indian scene. **36:** 174–177.

3861. **Archer, W.G.**
Banaras and British art. **22(1):** 43–47.

3862. **Bhattacharya, Asok K.**
Line as an element of classical Indian painting. **47:** 173–174.

3863. **Bhattacharya, Asok Kumar**
Silpasastra on depicting objects in Indian painting. **1:** 571–577.

3864. **Biswas, Taran Kumar**
Coomaraswamy's contribution to the study of Indian paintings. **25:** 27–37.

3865. **Chakrabarti, Jayanta**
Fresco-secco painting in India: A fresh technical scrutiny. **78:** 154–161.

3866. ———
Indian miniature painting: Development from east to west. **46(1):** 67–73.

3867. ———
Visual dialogue in Indian painting. **36:** 181–186

3868. **Chandramurti, M.**
Vijayanagar paintings at Thiruvilimilalai. **66:** 472–473.

3869. **Dwivedi, Vinod Prakash**
Madhya yugin laghu-chitro me naayika bhed. **82:** 339–343. (Hindi).

3870. **Fischer, Eberhard**
"Hair" and "shading" in paintings from Orissa. **14:** 183–185.

3871. **Ghosh, D.P.**
Coomaraswamy and Indian painting. **25:** 21–26.

3872. **Goswamy, B.N.**
Illustrations or visual parallels? **46(1):** 133–142.

3873. **Gururaja Rao, B.K.**
Painting in Vijayanagara period. **93:** 419–422.

3874. **Jain, Jyotindra**
Survival of 'Yamapattika' tradition in Gujarat. **46(1):** 173–187.

3875. **Misra, K.K.**
A study of north-eastern school of painting. **71:** 261–265.

3876. **Morley, Grace**
The Rama epic and Bharat Kala Bhavan's collection. **22(2):** 241–251.

3877. **Pandey, Lochan Prasad**
Similarity of the cave-men's art in India and America. **67:** 267–270.

3878. **Parimoo, Ratan**
Kaliya daman in Indian painting—a study in pictorial representation. **5(2):** 239–247.

3879. **Rai, Subas and Gopal, Lallanji**
A study of the rock paints of Mirzapur shelter. **89:** 25–29.

3880. **Seth, M.**
Two Vaisnava mathas of Puri. **76:** 91–94.

3881. **Sharma, R.C.**
The Avadh school of painting. **5(2):** 249–251.

3882. **Singh, Ajaya Kumar**
Wall paintings at Sun-Tsek, Alchi. **22(2):** 308–311.

3883. **Woodward, Hiram W., Jr.**
Burmese sculpture and Indian painting. **22(2):** 21–24.

AJANTA

3884. **Bhat, G.K.**
The vidusaka's cap and an Ajanta Fresco. **59:** 336–343.

3885. **Gupte, Y.R.**
The peculiarities of the art at Ajanta. **39:** 151–154.

3886. **Maity, S.K.**
Our women in Ajanta paintings. **37:** 407–412.

3887. **Spink, Walter M.**
Ajanta's paintings: A checklist for their dating. **46(1):** 457–468.

3888. **Tara Chand**
Ajanta: A unique achievement of the Human spirit. **100:** 50–59.

BENGAL

3889. **Bhattacharya, Asok K.**
Neo-Bengal school of painting. **36:** 187–193.

3890. **Chakrabarti, Jayanta**
Technique and style in Pala painting. **90:** 365–375.

3891. **Dutta, Ajit Kumar**
Some thoughts on Murshidabad painting. **76:** 117–119.

3892. **Ghosh, D.P.**
Eastern school of mediaeval Indian painting (Thirteenth-eighteenth century A.D.). **22(1):** 91–103.

3893. **Moti Chandra**
A pair of painted wooden covers of the Karandavyuha manuscript dated A.D. 1455 from Eastern India. **22(1):** 240–242.

3894. **Parimoo, Ratan**
The chronology of the paintings of Gaganendranath Tagore. **22(1):** 202–217.

3895. **Saraswati, S.K.**
East Indian manuscript painting. **22(1):** 243–262.

BIHAR

3896. **Das Gupta, R.**
The art of painting in Bihar. **60:** 204–216.

3897. **Prasad, H.K.**
The Patna school of paintings. **47:** 175–179.

3898. **Thakur, Upendra**
An introduction to Madhubani painting. **94(2):** 763–781.

DECCAN

3899. **Mittal, Jagdish**
Deccani painting: Golkonda and Hyderabad schools. **100:** 127–133.

3900. ———
An illustrated Deccani manuscript from Rajamundry: A hitherto unknown centre of painting in the Deccan. **26:** 109–114.

3901. **Varma, D.N.**
Socio-economic factors in the shaping of Deccani miniatures. **82:** 312–316.

3902. **Zebrowski, Mark**
Transformations in seventeenth century Deccani painting at Bijapur. **22(2):** 170–181.

MALWA

3903. **Tandan, B.K.**
Two important landmarks in the development of the Malwa school of painting—the Rasikpriya and the Amaru Sataka series. **82:** 307–311.

MUGHAL

3904. **Anand Krishna**
Akbar and his artist—Miskin. **26:** 97–102.

3905. ———
Concept chatura and vichitra in Indian art and culture. **22(2):** 259–265.

3906. ———
A study of the Akbari artist: Farrukh Chela. **22(1):** 353–373.

3907. **Binney, Edwin, 3rd**
Sultanate painting from the collection of Edwin Binney, 3rd. **22(2):** 25–31.

3908. **Chandramani Singh**
European themes in early Mughal miniatures. **22(1):** 401–410.

3909. **Chatterjee, Ratnabali**
European oil painting and the Mughal experience. **76:** 107–116.

3910. **Das, Asok Kumar**
Ananda Coomaraswamy and study of Mughal painting. **25:** 38–48.

3911. ———
Calligraphers and painters in early Mughal painting. **22(2):** 92–97.

3912. ———
Three miniatures from the Razmnama of A.D. 1598. **76:** 261–267.

3913. **Fraad, Irma L.** and **Ettinghausen, Richard**
Sultanate painting in Persian style. **22(1):** 48–66.

3914. **Kalyan Krishna**
Problems of a portrait of Jahangir in the Musee Gumiet, Paris. **22(1):** 392–394.

3915. **Kazmi, Nuzhat**
The discovery of an European painter of Akbari Atelier. **38(2):** 563–566.

3916. **Khandalavala, Karl J.**
Farrukh Beg the artist and the Deccani problem. **36:** 163–173.

3917. **Khare, G.H.**
Mir Khusrau—a misnomer. **39:** 211–214.

3918. **Koch, Ebba.**
Jahangir and the Angels: Recently discovered wall paintings under European influence in the fort of Lahore. **40:** 173–195.

3919. **Pramod Chandra**
The judgement of Khusrau in the garden of Mirza Kamran: An illustration to the Tuzuk-i-Jahangiri. **22(2):** 43–46.

3920. **Sen, Geeti**
Early evidence for Mughal portraiture in the paintings of the Akbar Nama. **76:** 95–100.

3921. ———
The significance of portraits in the paintings of Akbar Nama. **26:** 103–108.

3922. **Vijay Krishna**
Miniature painting ornaments. **36:** 179–180.

PAHARI, KANGRA AND MANDI

3923. **Chandramani**
On Mandi paintings. **22(2):** 206–211.

3924. **Goswamy, B.N.**
The artist Ranjha and a dated set of Ramayana drawings. **22(1):** 224–231.

3925. ———
Ragamala iconography in the Pahari tradition. **14:** 175–182.

3926. **Goswamy, Karuna**
A pahari painting of a Jagannath temple. **22(1):** 235–239.

3927. **Mukandi Lal**
Garhwal ke anayatam kalakaar—Molaram ka vayaktitattva evam chitrashala. **82:** 344–347. (Hindi).

3928. **Randhawa, M.S.**
Kangra painting. **100:** 134–136.

3929. ———
A review of studies in Pahari painting. **82:** 295–306.

3930. **Tandon, R.K.**
Deccani influence on early Pahari painting. **22(2):** 189–191.

PUNJAB

3931. **Goswamy, B.N.**
A matter of taste: Some notes on the context of painting in Sikh Panjab. **26:** 122–133.

3932. ———
On "Tibeti" paintings from the Punjab Hills. **91(2):** 401–405.

3933. **Paul, Suwarcha**
Raja Apurab Singh of Mankot. **86:** 189–194.

3934. **Randhawa, M.S.**
Two Panjabi artists of the nineteenth century Kehar Singh Kapur Singh. **22(1):** 67–69.

RAJASTHAN

3935. **Andhare, Shridhar**
Chronology of Mewar painting **26:** 115–118.

3936. ———
Some dated portraits of Rana Jagat Singh II and Ari Singh II of Mewar. **91(2):** 389–393.

3937. **Bautze, Joachim**
A contemporary and inscribed equestrian portrait of Jagat Singh of Kota. **87:** 47–64.

3938. **Das, Asok Kumar**
An illustrated manuscript of Durga Path of Jaipur school dated 1799 A.D. **46(1):** 85–92.

3939. ———
Ramjidas Chatera: An eighteenth century portrait painter from Jaipur. **82:** 317–323.

3940. **Ganguly, O.C.**
New light on Rajput painting. **1:** 578–579.

3941. **Giriraj Kumar**
Painted rock-shelters from Rajasthan. **82:** 277–285.

3942. **Jagat Narain**
Alnia (Kota) ke pragetihasik shilasra chitra. **82:** 329–331. (Hindi).

3943. **Kalyan Krishna**
Painted pichhavas. **26:** 134–141.

3944. **Khandalavala, Karl**
A note on Thikana paintings from Rajasthan. **82:** 292–294.

3945. ———
A thikana painting from Deogarh. **26:** 119–121.

3946. ———
Two Bikaner paintings in the N.C. Mehta collection and the problem of Mandi school. **22(2):** 301–304.

3947. **Kulshresth, Archana**
Devataji ki haveli (Kota) ke bhiti-chitra. **82:** 348–350. (Hindi).

3948. **Sheikh, Gulam Mohammed**
Coomaraswamy and Rajput painting. **26:** 86–96.

3949. ———
Not by eyes alone: Notes on Shekhawati murals. **46(1):** 425–426.

3950. **Skelton, Robert**
Shaykh Phul and the origins of Bundi painting. **22(2):** 123–129.

3951. **Somani, Ramvallabh**
Early evidence of paintings from Rajasthan. **82:** 286–291.

3952. **Topsfield. Andrew**
Sahibdin's Gita-Govinda illustrations. **22(2):** 231–238.

ILLUSTRATED MANUSCRIPTS

3953. **Anand Krishna**
An illustrated manuscript of the Laur-chanda in the Staatsbibliothek, Berlin. **22 (2):** 275–289.

3954. **Andhare, Shridhar**
The Dhola-maru MS. of the National Museum; a consideration in style and date. **22 (2):** 298–300.

3955. **Das Gupta, R.**
Material culture of medieval Assam as depicted in illustrated manuscripts. **53:** 233–257.

3956. **Goswami, Niranjan**
An illustrated copy of the Ramacarita-manasa. **78:** 142–153.

3957. **Gray, Basil**
The Lahore Laur-chanda pages thirty years after. **22 (2):** 5–9.

3958. **Gupta, Parmeshwari Lal**
The Berlin Chandayan Codex. **22 (2):** 305–307.

3959. **Khandalavala, Karl**
The Mrigavat of Bharat Kala Bhavan. **22 (1):** 19–36.

3960. **Mankodi, K.L.**
A note on the Devimahatmya of Saka 1638 in the Simla Museum. **46 (1):** 279–282.

3961. **Nizamuddin, M.**
A unique illustrated manuscript of Sa' di' s Gulistan. **100:** 121–126.

3962. **Pachner, Regine**
Motifs and designs in the Laur-chanda manuscript from Berlin. **22 (2):** 290–293.

3963. **Tandan, R.K.**
Mediaeval miniature paintings—eleventh to mid-sixteenth century: And a reappraisal of the Mandu and Jaunpur Kalpasutra vis-a-vis origin of the Chaurpanchasika style. **46 (1):** 495–508.

3964. **Vatsyayana, Kapila**
Gita-Govinda and its influence on Indian art. **22 (2):** 252–258.

3965. ———
The illustrated manuscripts of the Gita-Govinda from Orissa. **31:** 275–286.

JAINA

3966. **Andhare, Shridhar**
A note on the Mahavira Samavasarana Pata. **22 (1):** 343–345.

3967. **Bender, E.**
The tigers and the moon revisited. **27:** 29–30.

3968. **Doshi, Saryu**
An illustrated Adipurana of 1404 A.D. from Yoginipur. **22 (1):** 382–391.

3969. ———
Jain miniature painting; an outline. **26:** 77–85.

3970. **Nahta, Agarchand**
Ek aprakashit sachitra vigyapti-patra. **82:** 351–355. (Hindi).

3971. **Shah, Umakant P.**
Two new documents of paintings from Muni Punyavijayaji' s collections. **22 (1):** 151–156.

Handicrafts

3972. **Bhattacharyya, A.K.**
A survey of the art and technique of ivory in India. **100:** 137–144.

3973. **Das Gupta, Kalyan Kumar**
Wood carvings of Arunachal Pradesh and Nagaland. **85:** 287–293.

3974. **Giri, Kamal**
Animal and bird beads. **22 (2):** 312–323.

3975. **Kaus, Hurmuz**
A relic of the British Residency at Hyderabad. **100:** 145–148.

3976. **Khanna, Amar Nath**
The black lustrous ware from Himachal Pradesh. **46 (1):** 237–240.

3977. **Mukhopadhyay, Somnath**
Some aspects of Indian jewellery. **36:** 231–234.

3978. **Ray, Amita**
The bell and brass metal craft of West Bengal—a review based on sample studies. **46 (1):** 359–373.

3979. **Singh, Jagat Pal**
Traditional crafts of Rajasthan: Perspective and prospects. **82:** 227–241.

3980. **Sinopoli, Carla M. and Blurton, Richard**
Modern pottery production in rural Karnataka. **46 (1):** 439–456.

3981. **Subramanyam, K.G.**
Do hands have a chance. **46 (1):** 481–490.

3982. **Wojtilla, Gy.**
Contribution to the Sanskrit sources of the knowledge of precious stones. **80:** 396–402.

TEXTILE

3983. **Ahivasi, Devki**
Bharat Kala Bhavan me sangrahit, kesar se chitrit, ek sari (A sari painted with saffron). **22 (1):** 395–400. (Hindi).

3984. **Chattopadhyay, Kamaladevi**
Kantha embroidery of Bengal. **22 (1):** 75–81.

3985. **Das, Sukla**
A textile heritage of India. **9:** 255–272.

3986. **Das Gupta, R.**
Textiles of mediaeval Assam. **46 (1):** 149–159.

3987. **Irwin, John**
The tree of life in Indian textile. **46 (1):** 161–171.

3988. **Murphy, Veronica**
A note on some recently discovered Tipu Shawl fragments in England and comparative material in the Bharat Kala Bhavan. **22 (2):** 161–169.

3989. **Sharma, Ramesh Chandra**
A Mughal carpet of the early seventeenth century. **36:** 235–238.

3990. **Varadarajan, Lotika**
Figurative kalamkari and its locale. **22 (2):** 67–70.

3991. ———
Indian textiles and early trade routes of the orient. **44:** 343–356.

3992. ———
Kani pashmina of Kashmir. **76:** 231–240.

Preservation and Conservation

3993. **Agrawal, O.P.**
Cleaning techniques of stone objects: Problems and future research. **82:** 62–71.

3994. ———
Conservation of cultural objects in the tropics. **31:** 313–318.

3995. **Bhowmik, S.K.**
Chemical treatment of metallic image of Buddha from Gujarat. **82:** 72–77.

3996. **Mathur, M.S.**
Vegetational growths on monuments and methods of their control. **82:** 84–91.

3997. **Morley, Grace McCann**
Scientific preservation of cultural property: India's contributions. **31:** 309–312.

3998. **Nair, S.M.**
Biodeterioration of palm-leaf, paper manuscripts and miniatures. **82:** 78–83.

3999. **Prasad, Lalan Kumar**
Protecting antiquities of copper and its alloys. **47:** 128–133.

4000. **Ramesh, K.V.**
Preservation of inscriptions. **31:** 319–320.

4001. **Sengupta, R.**
Creativity in conservation. **46 (1):** 389–394.

4002. ———
A plea for better conservation management. **38 (1):** 35–38.

4003. **Srinivasan, L.K.**
Conservation of Kantalingesvara (Kandalisvara)—A Chola temple at Tenneri, district Chingleput. **31:** 321–325.

Mathematics

4124. **Arkasomayaji, D.**
The experience of the 'imaginary' through the glasses of mathematics. **72:** 268–273.

4125. **Bajaj, Prem N.**
Numerals: An invention of the Hindus. **80:** 482–484.

4126. **Bhat, N.R.**
The Kosambi formula for Chromosome mapping. **54:** 296–300.

4127. **Erdos, P.**
On the scarcity of simple groups. **54:** 229–232.

4128. **Gupta, R.C.**
Citrabhanu: A little known mathematician of medieval India. **80:** 485–490.

4129. _______
Formulas for sines of multiple arcs as found in the siddhantatattvaviveka. **71:** 133–136.

4130. **Huzurbazar, V.S.**
Explicit sampling distribution and the posterior probability distribution of the maximum likelihood estimators of parameters of a regular-type distribution admitting sufficient statistics for parameters. **54:** 284–289.

4131. **Kamat, A.R.**
A property of the mean deviation for the Peason type discrete distributions. **54:** 290–295.

4132. **Pingree, David**
The Ganitapancavimsi of Sridhara. **94 (2):** 887–909.

4133. **Saraswathi, T.A.**
Indian methods of calculating the valume of the frustum of a pyramid or cone. **71:** 335–339.

4134. **Shukla, Kripa Shankar**
Series with fractional number of terms. **80:** 475–481.

Botany

4135. **Bedi, Ramesh**
Garlic. **39:** 9–14.

4136. **Kuiper, F.B.J.**
Was the putika a mushroom?. **27:** 219–227.

Medical Science

4137. **Bhattacharya, B.**
Tridosa in Ayurveda. **39:** 15–18.

4138. **Filliozat, Jean**
The expansion of Indian medicine abroad. **98:** 67–70.

4139. **Gopal, Lallanji**
Beginnings of a historical system in ancient India. **5 (2):** 363–371.

4140. ———
Devala and Ayurveda. **9:** 113–123.

4141. **Raison, Alix.**
Le bdellium dans la matiere medicale ayurvedique. **94 (1):** 349–355. (French).

4142. **Sasvadkar, P.L.**
Athravaya shatkateel maratheshahiteel aushdhopachar. **52:** 299–304. (Marathi).

4143. **Sharma, P.V.**
A critical study of the popular text of the Caraka samhita. **56 (2):** 131–138.

4144. **Subba Reddy, D.V.**
Medical lore in yasastilaka of Somadeva Suri (10th century A.D.). **72:** 274–284.

4145. **Sukhatme, P.V.**
The protein problem. **54:** 213–228.

4146. **Thite, G.U.**
Prophylactics in ancient Indian medicine. **56 (2):** 139–154.

4147. **Zysk, Kenneth G.**
Buddhist healing and Ayurveda: Some general observations. **9:** 124–135.

Science and Technology

4148. **Bhardwaj, H.C.**
Indian contribution to steel making in antiquity. **86:** 383–390.

4149. **Chari, C.T.K.**
Thermodynamics, quantum physics and informational entropy. **28:** 48–64.

4150. **Keswani, G.H.**
Some notions of space, time, mass and motion. **54:** 246–272.

4151. **Kosambi, D.D.**
Steps in science. **54:** 193–205.

4152. **Lakshmana Rao, J.R.**
Science writing in Kannada. **92:** 335–341.

4153. **Narlikar, A.V.**
Superconducting magnets. **54:** 273–283.

4154. **Narlikar, J.V.**
Astronomy and laboratory physics. **54:** 233–245.

4155. **Prasad, Lalan Kumar**
A brief note on various kinds of bronzes. **86:** 73–80.

4156. **Rahman, A.**
Science and society: The new phase and tasks. **54:** 206–212.

4157. **Ray, Priyadaranjan**
Science and humanity. **1:** 417–421.

4158. **Riepe, Dale**
Science and contemporary philosophy of science in India. **75:** 571–598.

4159. **Sankaran, C.R.**
On the quantitative and qualitative definitions of the Alpha-phonoid. **54:** 301–305.

4160. **Subbarayappa, B.V.**
India's contributions to the history of science. **98:** 47–66.

4161. **Tobias, Philip V.**
Does the form of the inner contour of the mandible distinguish between Australopithecus and Homo? **83:** 9–17.

Military Science

4162. **Chhabra, B. Ch.**
Navy in ancient India. **80:** 381–384.

4163. **Hariyappa, H.L.**
Strategy and tactics in Indian concept of warfare. **39:** 155–160.

4164. **Pant, G.N.**
Cavalry in ancient India. **5 (2):** 347–351.

4165. ———
Indian horse armour and trappings. **38 (2):** 685–698.

4166. ———
Ornamentation of Indian arms and armour. **36:** 219–230.

4167. **Sharma, Pushpa**
The military system of the Mongols as reflected from their Indian expeditions. **76:** 329–333.

4168. **Sharma, Ravindra Kumar**
Sikh guns and their inscriptions. **76:** 327–328.

Library and Archives

4169. **Agrawal, Govind**
Rajasthan ke agyaat amulaya abhilekh-agar. **82:** 416–419. (Hindi).

4170. **Bal Krishan**
An ideal museum library. **64:** 93–102.

4171. **Gune, V.T.**
Goa Archives. **52:** 95–100.

4172. **Karve, C.G.**
Manuscript-curatorship under the Marathas. **39:** 199–202.

4173. **Khobrekar, V.G.**
Survey of private records in Maharashtra. **52:** 113–117.

4174. **Kulkarnee, Narayan H.**
Archives in India. **32:** 283–290.

4175. **Kuppuswami Sastri, S.**
The library movement as viewed by a classicist. **56 (1):** 178–185.

4176. ———
Kosavan acaryah. **56 (1):** 176–177.

4177. **Parthasarathi, R.K.**
The pauskarasamhita on Library Science. **16:** 629–632.

4178. **Sohoni, S.V.**
Archives in ancient India. **89:** 121–124.

4179. **Tikekar, S.R.**
Indexing of books on Maratha history. **70:** 322–333.

India and the World

4180. **Aalto, Pentti**
On the role of Central Asia in the spread of Indian cultural influence. **98:** 249–262.

4181. **Agrawala, R.C.**
Some aspects of Indian culture in the Kharosthi documents from Chinese Turkestan. **98:** 275–280.

4182. **Amba Prasad**
India's contacts with Africa from the earliest times. **98:** 601–614.

4183. **Bajpai, K.D.**
A study of the past common factors between India and the U.S.S.R. **9:** 218–221.

4184. **Banerjee, Ankul Chandra**
Indo-Tibetan cultural relations. **98:** 393–400.

4185. **Bhattacharya, Chhaya**
India—a major source of central Asian art. **98:** 289–298.

4186. **Bhattacharya, N.N.**
Influence of Indian thought on the West. **90:** 269–281.

4187. **Bhattacharyya, N.N.**
India's contribution to Islamic thought and culture. **98:** 573–578.

4188. **Bongard-Levin, G.M.**
Sanskrit and ancient Indian culture studies in the U.S.S.R. **84:** 299–306.

4189. **Chatterji, B.R.**
Indian cultural heritage in Cambodia. **98:** 493–498.

4190. **Chatterji, Suniti Kumar**
Hindus and Turks from prehistoric times: India—Central Asia contacts and links: The first phase. **29:** 11–29.

4191. **Chhabra, B. Ch.**
Aryan culture abroad. **86:** 525–527.

4192. ———
Indian colonies in South-East Asia. **30:** 275–279.

4193. **Choudhury, P.C.**
Indo-Mongol contact in South-East Asia. **43:** 107–122.

4194. **Christie, Anthony**
The provenance and chronology of early Indian cultural influences in South-East Asia. **58:** 1–14.

4195. **Dalai Lama**
India: The home of Tibetan learning. **98:** 389–392.

4196. **Deshpande, M.N.**
Campa—an outpost of Indian culture. **98:** 475–482.

4197. **Devahuti, D.**
India, Malaya and Borneo—two millennia of contacts and cultural synthesis. **98:** 509–532.

4198. **Dhavalikar, M.K.**
Ganesa beyond the Indian frontiers. **98:** 1–16.

4199. **Francisco, Juan R.**
A survey of Palaeographic relations between India and the Philippines. **98:** 565–572.

4200. **Ghosh, D.P.**
Influence of Indian art on the art of South-East Asia. **78:** 8–15.

4201. **Gregorios, Paul**
Hind and Hellas. **81:** 103–117.

4202. **Gupta, Chandrashekhar**
Depiction of Bharata-Lakshmi in a Roman music. **5 (1):** 165–167.

4203. **Gupta, S.P.**
Prehistoric Indian cultures in Soviet Central Asia. **98:** 239–248.

4204. **Hara, Minoru**
Right in India and left in China? on I-ching's translation of the sudhanakumaravadana. **27:** 159–166.

4205. **Kamata, Shigeo**
Cultural exchange between India, China and Japan. **98:** 315–324.

4206. **Khare, M.D.**
Religio-cultural emissaries from India. **98:** 17–22.

4207. **Kohli, Surinder Singh**
Guru Nanak's travels in the Middle East. **98:** 597–600.

4208. **Leifer, Walter**
India as known to the Germans through the ages. **44:** 391–396.

4209. **Litvinsky, B.A.**
India and Soviet Central Asia. **98:** 263–274.

4210. **Lochan, Amarjiva**
India and Thailand: Early trade routes and seaports. **9:** 222–235.

4211. **Lokesh Chandra**
The cultural symphony of India and Greece. **81:** 89–102.

4212. ———
The cultural symphony of India and Greece. **95:** 38–44.

4213. ———
Indian culture in transbaikalian Siberia. **98:** 629–632.

4214. **Mehrotra, L.L.**
Glimpses of Indian culture in Tibet. **98:** 401–408.

4215. **Misra, B.N.**
Acaryas of Nalanda abroad. **98:** 23–32.

4216. **Mukherjee, Radhakamal**
The glory of Indian art in the eastern seas. **17:** 144–151.

4217. **Mukherjee, B.N.**
The date of the earliest evidence of an overland route for North-Eastern India's communication with China. **43:** 172–182.

4218. **Nakamura, Hajime**
Indian influence on Japanese stories. **98:** 363–370.

4219. **Nigam J.S.**
India and Laos. **98:** 483–486.

4220. **Nirmal, Chiranjivi J.**
Indian studies in the U.S.A. **93:** 437–443.

4221. **Pal, Pratapaditya**
Two Byzantine objects and the Indian connection. **36:** 253–255.

4222. **Pande, B.M.**
Indian religions and the West: Historical perspectives. **98:** 615–622.

4223. **Pandey, C.B.**
Indian influence in Siam. **98:** 453–468.

4224. **Raghuvira**
Cultural relations of India and Korea. **98:** 341–346.

4225. **Raman, K.V.**
Thai India cultural ties. **74:** 331–334.

4226. **Riboud, Krishna**
Animal style in Han dynasty textiles and early Indian sculpture. **22 (1):** 192–201.

4227. **Rinchen, Acad**
Influence of Indian philosophy on Mongolian Shamanism. **98:** 409–412.

4228. **Riviere, Juan Roger**
The study of oriental cultures in Western universities. **17:** 111–120.

4229. **Sarkar, Himansu Bhusan**
The date of the Pali Niddesa and its implications for the history of South-East Asia. **47:** 207–229.

4230. ———
Methods of calculation and measures of Weight in India and South-East Asia: A preliminary survey of links. **88:** 130–139.

4231. **Sarkar, K.K.**
Extent of Indian influence on the ancient religions of Indonesia. **20:** 306–310.

4232. **Sehgal, S.R.**
Sanskritic culture in the South-East Asia. **48:** 464–467.

4233. **Sharan, Mahesh Kumar**
Indian Brahmanas in Cambodian epigraphy. **60:** 166–172.

4234. **Sharotri, G.K.**
The Ramayana and its impact in South-East Asia. **60:** 401–405.

4235. **Shrivastava P.S.**
Cultural influence of India on Tibet. **86:** 528–537.

4236. **Siddiqi, W.H.**
India's contribution to Arab civilization. **98:** 579–588.

4237. **Singer, Milton**
A conversation of cultures: The United States and Southern Asia. **33:** 153–171.

4238. **Singhal, D.P.**
Red Indians or Asiomericans—Indian settlers in Middle and South America. **98:** 633–648.

4239. **Sinha, Arun Kumar**
Indian influence upon the art of Thailand. **80:** 500–512.

4240. **Sircar, D.C.**
Indian influence on the geographical names of South-East Asia. **98:** 41–46.

4241. **Soundara Rajan, K.V.**
Hindu epic and puranic traditions in South-East Asia. **98:** 499–508.

4242. **Srinivasan, K.R.**
The impact of India on the architecture of South-East Asia. **98:** 123–134.

4243. **Sternbach, Ludwik**
Sanskrit niti literature in "Greater India". **98:** 33–40.

4244. **Subhadradis Dis Kul, M.C.**
Indian influences on religious sculptures in Thailand. **26:** 46–48.

4245. **Thakur, Upendra**
Indian Buddhist missionaries in Central Asia and China. **47:** 277–290.

4246. ———
Indian monks in Japan, **80:** 299–308.

4247. ———
Influence of Brahmanism on early Siamese art. **93:** 219–226.

4248. ———
The Manusmrti and the Thai jurisprudence. **9:** 236–241.

4249. ———
Some aspects of religious and literary contacts between India and Thailand. **88:** 108–116.

4250. ———
Some aspects of religious and literary contacts between India and Thailand. **89:** 7–13.

4251. **Xinchuan, Huang**
Hinduism and China, **81:** 125–138.

Other Countries

ASIA

4252. **Buddha Prakash**
From medieval to modern in Asian history. **17:** 1–38.

4253. **Roy, Sailesh Chandra**
Glimpses of Greater India. **17:** 192–202.

4254. **Sinha, Nirmal Chandra**
Man-Chi-Shih-Li: An essay on polity and religion in Inner Asia. **17:** 134–143.

AFGHANISTAN

4255. **Banerjee, P.** and **Agarwala, R.C.**
Hindu sculptures in ancient Afghanistan. **98:** 215–228.

4256. **Dikshit, K.N.**
Buddhist centres in Afghanistan. **98:** 229–238.

4257. **Gardin, J.C.**
Canal irrigation in bronze age Eastern Bactria. **99:** 311–320.

4258. **Klimburg-Salter, Deborah**
Dukhtar-i-Nushirvan: An ideology of Kingship. **91 (1):** 61–76.

4259. **Kohl, Philip**
Prehistoric 'Turan' and Southern Turkmenia: The problem of cultural diversity. **99:** 321–331.

4260. **Mitterwallner, G.V.**
The silver bowl from Swat, its Brahmi inscription and Gupta ornament. **91 (2):** 355–368.

4261. **Narain, A.K.**
The founding date of Ai-Khanum, a Bactrian Greek city in Afghanistan. **9:** 83–89.

4262. **Ojihara, Yutaka**
Sur un manuscrit medico-demonologique en provenance de Bamiyan. **27:** 301–311. (French).

4263. **Sircar, D.C.**
Note on Skandar image inscription. **21:** 5–7.

4264. **Srivastava, V.C.**
Prehistoric research in Afghanistan: Problems and perspectives. **86:** 59–72.

4265. **Upasak, C.S.**
Cultural significance of Udyana (Uddyana). **5 (1):** 93–95.

BANGLADESH

4266. **Pal, Animesh K.**
Phonology of a Dacca dialect. **61:** 537–549.

4267. **Rahman, M.**
A new type of Mahishamardini from Bangladesh. **88:** 168–175.

4268. **Sircar, D.C.**
Copper-plate grant of Viradharadeva of Samatata. **22 (1):** 104–106.

CHINA

4269. **Buddha Prakash**
Social aspects of the spread of Buddhism in China. **98:** 333–340.

4270. **Lokesh Chandra**
Ahimsa in China. **43:** 99–101.

4271. **Goodrich, L. Carrington**
Two notes on early printing in China. **39:** 117–120.

4272. **Hines, Donalds M.**
A brief survey of some textual corruption in some tales from China. **7:** 9–22.

4273. **Leung, Man-kam**
Piracy in South China in the nineteenth century. **42:** 152–166.

4274. **Lokesh Chandra**
The role of tantras in the defence strategy of T'ang China. **79:** 31–44.

4275. ———
The role of tantras in the defence strategy of T'ang China. **91 (1):** 53–59.

4276. **Sarkar, H.**
Buddhist contact of China. **98:** 325–332.

4277. **T'ang-Chun**
Chinese attitude towards world religions. **28:** 395–401.

4278. **Upadhyaya, Bharat Singh**
Dhyaana-sampradaya ki pancha chinisha-khaayen. **95:** 51–53. (Hindi).

4279. **Yun-Hua, Jan**
Chuan-Fa Yuan, the Imperial Institute for Transmission of Buddha-Dharma in Sung China. **17:** 70–93.

4280. **Yun-Shan, Tan**
Chinese religion. **1:** 363–370.

JAPAN

4281. **Aso, Masaru**
Trends in Japanese archaeology. **83:** 73–75.

4282. **Dasgupta, Kalyan Kumar**
Benzai-ten in Indian perspective. **5 (2):** 285–288.

4283. **Kidder, J. Edward**
Ajanta and Horyuji. **98:** 347–358.

4284. **Kidder, J. Edward, Jr.**
Jar-burials of the middle Joman period. **83:** 259–272.

4285. **Mathur, Rames**
Sociology of some Japanese expressions. **18:** 152–162.

4286. **Munsterberg, Hugo**
Dhyana in Japanese art. **98:** 359–362.

4287. **Shashibala**
A Sanskrit manuscript of the Gupta period at the Horyuji monastery in Japan. **80:** 309–314.

4288. **Thakur, Upendra**
Indian Monks in Japan. **74:** 303–310.

MANGOLIA

4289. **Jayaswal, Ayodhya Prasad**
Shak dveep ki khoj. **47:** 331–349. (Hindi).

NEPAL

4290. **Banerjee, N.R.**
The interrelationship of Buddhist and Brahmanical iconography in 18th century, Nepal. **36:** 273–277.

4291. ———
Buddhist art of Nepal. **98:** 385–388.

4292. ———
Did Sri Chaitanya visit Nepal? **91 (2):** 471–472.

4293. **Biswas, S.S.**
A brass lamp from Nepal. **90:** 355–357.

4294. **Chakravarti, Ranabir**
Bhottavisti: Its nature and collection. **90:** 203–207.

4295. **Gorakshkar, Sadashiv**
A bronze sculpture from Nepal in the Prince of Wales Museum. **22 (1):** 346–349.

4296. **Krishna Deva**
Early Buddhism in Nepal, its monumental and iconic manifestations. **9:** 141–149.

4297. **Lanius, Mary**
A note on a Nepali image of Candarosana. **22 (1):** 149–150.

4298. **Macdonald, Alexander W.**
A Tibetan guide to some of the holy places of the Dhaulagiri-Muktinath of Nepal. **49:** 243–253.

4299. **Mitra, Makar**
Two metal images from Nepal. **36:** 127–128.

4300. **Pal, Pratapaditya**
Eight nayikas in Nepali painting. **75:** 187–197.

4301. ———
Some Nepali bronzes in Bharat Kala Bhavan. **22 (1):** 82–90.

4302. **Pandey, R.N.**
An introduction to the handicrafts of Nepal. **46 (1):** 337–343.

4303. **Sharma, Brijendra Nath**
Saiva icons of Nepal. **98:** 371–384.

4304. **Verma, T.P.**
Some new inscriptions of the Lichchhavis of Nepal. **53:** 160–171.

PAKISTAN

4305. **Asthana, Shashi**
Revised chronological frame-work for prehistoric cultures of Northern Baluchistan. **38 (1):** 69–74.

4306. **Banerji, Arundhati**
Terracotta Zhob mother goddess—a study. **38 (1):** 117–134.

4307. **Chatterjee, C.D.**
Taksasila (Taxila). **94 (2):** 627–634.

4308. **Dani, Ahmad Hasan**
A Kusana Kharosthi inscription from North Waziristan (Pakistan) dated year 39. **68:** 48–50.

4309. ———
Prehistoric Pakistan. **35:** 71–76.

4310. **Durrani, F.A.**
Some early Harappan sites in Gomal and Bannu valleys. **99:** 505–510.

4311. **Fairservis, Walter A.**
Archaeology in Baluchistan and the Harappan probelm. **99:** 277–287.

4312. **Ghafur, Muhammad Abdul**
Figural representations on a Muslim tomb at Thatta. **100:** 60–65.

4313. **Jarriage, Jean Francois**
Towns and villages of Hill and plain. **99:** 289–300.

4314. **Khan, Muhammad Ishtiaq**
Metal statuettes from Taxila. **68:** 122–124.

4315. **Mughal, M.R.**
The post-Harappan phase in Bhahawalpur distt., Pakistan. **99:** 499–503.

SRI LANKA

4316. **Bandaranayake, Senake**
Ananda Coomaraswamy and approaches to the study of traditional Sri Lankan art and society. **26:** 27–37.

4317. ———
Sri Lanka and Monsoon Asia: Patterns of local and regional architectural development and the problem of the traditional Sri Lankan roof. **68:** 22–24.

4318. **Bechert, Heinz**
Remarks on astrological Sanskrit literature from Sri Lanka. **68:** 45–47.

4319. ———
Sanskrit subhasites quoted in classical Simhala literature. **94 (1):** 239–246.

4320. **Deraniyagala, P.E.P.**
Some archaeological problems concerning Sri Lanka and its trade routes. **68:** 51–53.

4321. **Deraniyagala, S.U.**
The prehistory of Sri Lanka. **91 (1):** 121–124.

4322. **De Silva, C.R.**
The first visit of the Portuguese to Sri Lanka—1505 or 1506. **68:** 218–220.

4323. **De Silva, K.M.**
Christian missions in Sri Lanka and their response to nationalism 1910–1948. **68:** 221–233.

4324. **De Silva, Lily**
The symbolism of the indrakila in the parittamandapa. **68:** 234–250.

4325. **Dohanian, Diran K.**
Mahayana cult in ancient Ceylon. **98:** 423–436.

4326. **Gunawardana, R.A.L.H.**
Hydraulic engineering in ancient Sri Lanka: The cistern sluices. **68:** 61–74.

4327. **Indrapala, K.**
An inscription of the tenth year of Cola Lankesvara Deva from Kantalai, Sri Lanka. **68:** 81–97.

4328. **Karashima, Noburu**
The Yeh-pa-nai-na problem in the history of Sri Lanka: A review based on new Chinese sources. **68:** 98–106.

4329. **Karunaratne, T.B.**
The Astamangala figure on an Attani pillar of Sena I from Kivulekada, Sri Lanka. **68:** 107–115.

4330. **Kennedy, Kenneth A.R.**
The palaeo-demography of Ceylon: A study of the biological continuum of a population from prehistoric to historic times. **83:** 95–112.

4331. **Kiribamune, Sirima**
The Mahavamsa: A study of the ancient historiography of Sri Lanka. **68:** 125–136.

4332. **Mukherjee, B.N.**
A note on two Lihinimalai records of Kanittha Tissa, the king of Lanka. **11:** 306–310.

4333. **Paranavitana, S.**
Ploughing as a ritual of royal consecration in ancient Ceylon. **58:** 31–39.

4334. **Prematilleke, Leelananda**
The Buddha image of Sri Lanka. **26:** 42–45.

4335. **Prematilleke, L.**
The "Kustarahagala" image at Valigama, Sri Lanka. **68:** 172–180.

4336. **Prematilleke, P.L.**
The Sri Lankan Buddha image. **78:** 139–142.

4337. **Ramaswami, N.S.**
Manikkavachaga in Sri Lanka? **93:** 233–238.

4338. **Samaraweera, Vijaya**
Litigation, Sir Henry Maine's writings and the Ceylon village communities ordinances of 1871. **68:** 191–203.

4339. **Seneviratne, Anuradha**
Kohomba Kankariya: A traditional folk ritual in the hill country of Sri Lanka. **68:** 204–214.

4340. **Srivastava, V.C.**
Hinduism in Ceylon. **98:** 413–422.

4341. **Suseendirarajah, S.**
Vowel splits in Jaffna Tamil. **18:** 254–264.

4342. **Thananjayarajasingham, S.**
The phoneme/k/ in the Jaffna dialect of Tamil. **13:** 196–207.

4343. **Wickramasuriya, Sarathchandra**
The beginnings of the Sinhalese printing press. **68:** 283–300.

TIBET

4344. **Banerjee, Anukul Chandra**
Buddhism in Tibet. **62:** 430–435.

4345. **Dargyay, Eva K.**
Tsong-kha-pa and his relation to Atisa and Padmasambhava. **42:** 16–26.

4346. **Emmerick, R.E.**
Mi-chos. **94 (2):** 883–885.

4347. **Hahn, Michael**
Ajatasatrvavadana—a Gopadatta story from Tibet. **47:** 242–276.

4348. **Lokesh Chandra**
Sanskrit lexicons in Tibet. **17:** 121–133.

4349. ———
Tibetan version of the hymn to Nilakantha. **5 (2):** 293–295.

4350. **Sinha, Nirmal Chandra**
Buddhism in Tibet. **1:** 297–299.

SOUTH–EAST ASIA

4351. **Chang, Kwang-Chih**
Ancient farmers in the Asian tropics: Major problems for archaeological and palaeoenvironmental investigations of South-east Asia at earliest neolithic level. **83:** 273–286.

4352. **Cribb, Joe**
Dating South-East Asia's earliest coins. **87:** 111–128.

4353. **Ghosh, D.P.**
Impact of Indian art on the art of South-east Asia. **66:** 444–451.

4354. **Nagaraju, S.**
The palaeography of the earliest inscriptions of Burma, Thailand, Cambodia and Vietnam. **21:** 67–80.

4355. **Phukan, J.N.**
The thirteenth century and the Tai upsurge. **43:** 183–188.

4356. **Sarkar, H.B.**
Role of Indian epics and dharmasastras in the deification of kings and in the state administration of South-east Asia. **95:** 3–8.

4357. **Sirisena, W.M.**
Sinhalese influences on the architecture of South-east Asia up to the tenth century A.D. **68:** 257–264.

4358. **Solheim, Wilhelm G., II**
Pottery and prehistory in South-east Asia. **83:** 287–298.

4359. **Thakur, Upendra**
Siva in the Brahmanical art of South-east Asia. **36:** 257–271.

BURMA

4360. **Bhise, Usha R.**
A temple of Visnu in Burma. **98:** 445–452.

4361. **Shorto, H.L.**
The Gavampati tradition in Burma. **58:** 15–30.

4362. **Sternbach, Ludwik**
On the influence of Sanskrit dharma and arthasastra-s upon the niti literature of Burma. 1. The rajadharma in the lokasara. **16:** 612–628.

4363. **Thakur, Upendra**
A historical survey of the elements of Hindu culture in Burma. **98:** 437–444.

CAMBODIA

4364. **Bhattacharya, Kamleswar**
Lexicographical gleanings from the Sanskrit epigraphy of Cambodia: **89:** 35–38.

4365. ———
The present state of researches on the Sanskrit epigraphy of Cambodia: Some observations. **27:** 475–484.

4366. ———
Religious speculations in ancient Cambodia. **58:** 78–97.

4367. **Boisselier, Jean**
Nouvelles donne'es sur l'art pre 'Angokrien: Le groupe voisin de Rombang Romeas. **58:** 152–163. (French).

4368. **Chakravarti, Adhir**
Slave labour and free labour in ancient Cambodia: A study in terminology. **11:** 193–204.

4369. **Choudhary, Radhakrishna**
Slaves and serfs in medieval Cambodia (circa 400—1300 A.D.). **62:** 217–229.

4370. **Coedes, G.**
The real founder of the cult of divine royalty in Cambodia. **58:** 63–66.

4371. ———
Le veritable fondateur du culte de la royaute divine au Cambodge. **58:** 56–62. (French).

4372. **Dhaky, M.A.**
Harihara in Cambodian inscriptions and Hieratic art. **31:** 263–266.

4373. **Dwivedi, R.K.** and **Roy, Anamika**
Some observations on the Veal Kantel inscription of Bhavavarman I. **86:** 215–220.

4374. **Ghosh, Manomohan**
Date of the Bayon and the Angkor Vat. **58:** 40–55.

4375. **Mabbett, I.W.**
Divine kingship in Angkor. **11:** 277–285.

4376. **Pou, Saveros**
Subhasit and cpap in Khmer literature. **94 (1):** 331–348.

4377. **Sahai, Sachchidanand**
Indian diplomatic theories in ancient Cambodia (600—1300 A.D.). **66:** 452–460.

4378. **Sinha, Arun Kumar**
The Devaraja cult. **86:** 538–544.

4379. **Srinivasan, P.R.**
Sivasoma's inscription of Saka 80 (.) from Prasat Kandol Dom (North) in Cambodia. **91 (2):** 425–429.

INDONESIA

4380. **Chhabra, Bahadur Chand**
Mulavarman, king of Borneo. **16:** 643–644.

4381. **Dutta, B.**
The Javanese Brahmanda purana. **98:** 533–534.

4382. **Ensink, J.**
Panhidep hati: Some notes on the worship of Sarasvati in Balinese Hinduism. **50:** 400–404.

4383. **Enskin, Jacob**
The old-Javanese Cantakaparwa and its tale of Sutasoma. **58:** 179–223.

4384. **Gonda, J.**
Karman and retributive justice in ancient Java. **58:** 225–237.

4385. ———
Karman and retributive justice in ancient Java. **17:** 94–110.

4386. ———
The presence of Hinduism in Indonesia: Aspects and problems. **98:** 535–554.

4387. **Goudriaan, T.**
Sanskrit texts and Indian religions in Bali. **98:** 555–564.

4388. **Hooykaas, C.**
Kala in Java and Bali. **41:** 133–143.

4389. ———
Pancatantra in Java Bali. **94 (1):** 291–292.

4390. ———
The treasures of Bali. **58:** 67–77.

4391. **Johns, A.**
The enlightenment of Bhima. **58:** 141–151.

4392. **Lohuizen-De Leeuw, J.E. Van**
An Indo-Javanese representation of a bhujanga. **41:** 157–160.

4393. **Lokesh Chandra**
Unto the Siva temple of Indonesia. **48:** 90–96.

4394. **Lokesh Chandra** and **Sharda Rani**
Bali deep ki upasana. **50:** 245–254. (Hindi).

4395. **Mitra, Debala**
Observations on some carved slabs and deposit-boxes in Museum Pusat, Jakarta. **76:** 43–51.

4396. **Puri, B.N.**
Archaeology and the Vaishnava tradition in Indonesia. **60:** 154–160.

4397. ———
Archaeology and Vaisnava tradition in Indonesia. **94 (2):** 679–685.

4398. **Sarkar, H.B.**
The stone of Kanjuruha (Dinaja) 682 saka. **58:** 261–268.

4399. **Sarkar, Himanshu Bhushan**
Survey of some aspects of old-Javanese inscriptions of Central Java. **17:** 39–69.

4400. **Sarkar, Kalyan Kumar**
Dieng temples and the evolution of early Javanese architecture. **9:** 136–140.

4401. **Singh, B.K.**
Muslim sea trade and the rise of Islam in Indonesia. **60:** 604–609.

4402. **Singhal, Sudarshana Devi**
The concept of cetana in Indonesian Saivism. **17:** 158–179.

4403. ———
Glimpses of ancient Indonesian philosophical formulation. **58:** 121–125.

4404. **Teeuw, A.**
Prose and poetry: A contribution to the study of versification in old Javanese. **41:** 208–221.

4405. **Van Naerssen, F.H.**
Sovereignty in early Hindu-Java. **58:** 164–178.

4406. **Wolters, O.W.**
A glimpse of Western Indonesia in the third century A.D. **58:** 126–140.

LAOS

4407. **Raghuvira**
The literature of Lava (Laos). **98:** 487–492.

4408. **Thakur, Upendra**
Elements of Hindu culture in Laos. **11:** 373–385.

THAILAND

4409. **Dhaninivat, Prince**
Allegories of the monsoon in Siamese literature. **58:** 238–244.

4410. **Dhaninivat, H.H. Prince**
The Ramayana in Thailand. **98:** 469–474.

4411. **Griswold, A.B.**
Some iconographical peculiarities in Siam and Burma. **58:** 245–260.

4412. **Lohuizen-De Leeuw, J.E. Van**
An aspect of Sinhalese influence in Thailand. **68:** 137–141.

4413. **Satya Vrat Shastri**
Brahmins in Thailand. **43:** 93–98.

4414. ———
Hindu culture in Thailand. **27:** 501–507.

4415. ———
Panom Rung shrine of Thailand. **3:** 249–259.

4416. **Thakur, Upendra**
Brahmana pandits in Siam. **32:** 273–282.

VIETNAM

4417. **Bombwall, K.R.**
Vietnam: The conditions for peace. **17:** 203–213.

4418. **Majumdar, R.C.**
The Vo-Canh inscription. **17:** 152–157.

IRAN

4419. **Asthana, Shashi**
The place of Shahdad in Indus-Iranian trade. **99:** 353–361.

4420. **Chatterjee, C.D.**
The Aramaic language and its problems in the early history of Iran and Afghanistan. **11:** 205–226.

4421. **Heskel, Denis L.**
Iran-Indus Valley connections: A revaluation. **99:** 333–346.

4422. **Kanga, M.F.**
Datisan i denik-pursishn 35. **16:** 155–161.

4423. ———
Pahlavi version of gatha spanta mainyu yasna has 47–50. **69:** 77–88.

4424. **Kunhan Raja, C.**
Sanskrit in Iran (old and new). **39:** 286–291.

4425. **Morgenstierne, Georg**
Iranian feminines in Ci. **15:** 160–164.

ISRAEL

4426. **Bar-Yosef, O.**
Ubeidiya—a lower palaeolithic site in the Jordan valley, Israel. **83:** 185–198.

LEBANON

4427. **Garrod, D.A.E.**
A pebble industry of early warm age from Abri Zumoffen, South Lebanon. **35:** 41–48.

SIBERIA

4428. **Lokesh Chandra**
The Buddhist temples of Eastern Siberia. **61:** 629–635.

CENTRAL ASIA

4429. **Aquique, Md.**
Elements of Hindu culture in Central Asia. **89:** 49–52.

4430. **Aquique, M.D.**
Studies in the antiquarian remains of Khotan and Chinese Turkestan. **9:** 210–217.

4431. **Banerjee, P.**
Double-headed Buddha (from Central Asia)—an aspect of Agni. **38 (2):** 567–571.

4432. ———
Hindu deities in Central Asia. **98:** 281–288.

4433. **Bhat, M.S.**
A fragment of a frescoed frieze depicting Dipankara Buddha in Miran Central Asia. **61:** 587–589.

4434. **Dhavalikar, M.K.**
Ganesa in Central Asia. **32:** 37–44.

4435. **Dikshit, K.N.**
The beginning of Iron in Central Asia. **5 (1):** 15–22.

4436. **Gardiner, K.H.J.**
Yarkland in the first century A.D. **10:** 42–70.

4437. **Gupta, S.P.**
Some aspects of Buddhist art in Central Asia. **48:** 34–42.

4438. **Lokesh Chandra**
Notes on Central Asian Buddhist iconography. **27:** 255–262.

4439. **Meister, Michael W.**
Silk, technology and Central Asia. **91 (1):** 93–98.

4440. **Panse, M.G.**
Parya: An Indo-Aryan dialect in Central Asia. **98:** 305–314.

4441. **Ranov, V.A.**
Palaeoliths from Soviet Central Asia. **83:** 171–184.

CZECHOSLOVAKIA

4442. **Valoch, Karel**
Bohemian: The lower palaeolithic industry in Czechoslovakia. **83:** 129–134.

FRANCE

4443. **Bordes, F.H.**
Acheulean cultures in Southwest France. **35:** 49–57.

4444. **Bordes, F.**
Bruised blades and flakes in the upper Perigordian at Corbiac, Dordogne, France. **83:** 135–138.

GERMANY

4445. **Kruger, Horst**
Plans for the foundation of an East India Company in Brandenburg-Prussia in the second half of the seventeenth century. **4:** 123–146.

TURKEY

4446. **Bongard-Levin, G.M.** and **Vorbyova-Desyatovskaya, M.I.**
Unknown dharanis from eastern Turkestan. **27:** 485–492.

4447. **Lokesh Chandra**
Sanskrit culture in ancient Turkish. **16:** 633–634.

UNITED KINGDOM

4448. **Sankalia, H.D.**
Unique early stone age finds near Jersey, in the English Channel. **9:** 52–53.

EGYPT

4449. **Smith, Philip E.L.**
The palaeolithic of Egypt, some notes on a centennial. **83:** 157–170.

SOUTH AFRICA

4450. **Davies, Oliver**
The Archeulian industry in relation to the shore lines of Southern Africa. **83:** 139–144.

4451. **Inskeep, R.R.**
Excavations in a South African coastal cave: Reasons, problems and progress. **83:** 145–155.

4452. **Malan, B.D.**
The protection of archaeological and palaeontological objects in the Republic of South Africa. **35:** 64–70.

4453. **Shaw, Thurstan**
Possible Indian origins of ninth century beads excavated in West Africa. **83:** 363–380.

AUSTRALIA

4454. **Charlesworth, Marx J.**
Australian 'aboriginal religion in a comparative context. **51:** 257–263.

4455. **McCarthy, Frederick D.**
Space and superimpositions in Australian aboriginal art. **83:** 113–128.

NORTH AMERICA

4456. **Richards, Horace G.**
A comparison of the marine quaternary mollusks of eastern North America with those of Europe, **83:** 19–24.

UNITED STATES OF AMERICA

4457. **Schneider, Herbert W.**
Religious diversity in America. **28:** 358–361.

MEXICO

4458. **Cornwall, I.W.**
Volcanic deposits and soil in Central Mexico and their pearing on the chronology of prehistoric man in the new world. **83:** 33–46.

SOUTH AMERICA

4459. **Patterson, Thomas C.**
Pachacamac revisited: Some comments on methods of interpreting archaeological evidence. **83:** 65–71.

AUTHOR INDEX

Aalto, Pentti., 599, 4180
Abbie, A.A., 1175
Abhyankar, K.V., 2357
Abidi, S.A.H., 2505, 2525
Acharjee, Jahar, 3215
Acharya, K.V., 1864
Acharya, Ram Krishna, 2042-2043
Acharya, N.N., 836-838
Adippodi, Kamban, 2769
Adrados, Francisco R., 2763, 3007
Agam Prasad, 149
Agesthialingom, S., 2306
Agnihotri, P.D., 1208, 3462
Agrawal, Ashvini Kumar, 9, 600, 3008, 3216
Agrawal, D.P., 538-539, 2774, 2858, 2875
Agrawal, Govind, 1145, 4169
Agrawal, J.N., 601-603, 1585
Agrawal, K.M., 1118
Agrawal, O.P., 3993-3994, 4004
Agrawal, Veena, 3550
Agrawala, Bharat Bhushan, 35
Agrawala, P.K., 1340, 3401, 3423, 3690-3691
Agrawala, R.C., 540, 1209, 2883, 2950-2953, 2977, 3304, 3558, 3692-3693, 4181, 4255
Agrawala, V.S., 463-464, 495, 1341-1342, 1656, 2545, 3217
Ahivasi, Devki, 3983
Ahluwalia, M.S., 3009
Ahmad, Enayat, 465
Ahmad, Khwaja Muhammad, 3218
Ahmad, Nazir, 2534
Ahmad, Nisar, 605, 3219, 3221-3222
Ahmad, Qeyamuddin, 847
Ahmad, Shamsuddin, 3541
Ahmed, Nisar, 604, 3220
Ahmed, Sarharuddin, 3010
Airi, Raghunath, 10
Aithal, K.P., 1343
Aiyappan, A., 1146
Ajai Shankar, 4005
Akhmanova, Olga, 2271
Aklujkar, Ashok, 2546
Alam, Manzoor, 826
Aldrich, Virgil, C., 1865
Ali, Aruna Asaf, 14
Ali, B. Sheik, 1866
Allchin, Bridget, 541, 2776, 2978
Allchin, F.R., 542, 2775, 2860, 2891-2892, 2971
Allchin, Raymond, 2776
Almond, Philip C., 1681
Alsdorf, L., 1830
Altekar, A.S., 848
Altuchow, Nicholas, 426
Alur, K.R., 2777-2778, 2893
Amar Nath Shastri, 1344
Amba Prasad, 4182
Ambardekar, R.R., 2724
Ambasthya, B.P., 747
Anand Krishna, 3559, 3904-3906, 3953, 4006
Anand, Mulk Raj, 15, 156, 187, 223, 409, 1867
Anandasivam, R., 3011
Ananthanarayana, H.S., 2358
Ananthanarayana, S., 413
Anantharangachar, N., 1210
Andersen, Paul Kent, 3012
Andhare, Shridhar, 3935-3936, 3954, 3966, 4007
Andronov, M., 2307
Androssov, V.P., 2044
Aney, M.S., 306
Anjaneyulu, D., 346
Ansari, Hasan Nishat, 787
Ansari, Z.D., 2894
Ansary, Hasan Nishat, 849
Appasamy, Jaya, 303
Apte, P.P., 1345
Apte, Usha M., 1147
Apte, V.M., 1346
Aquique, Md., 606, 1053, 4429
Aquique, M.D., 4430
Arapura, J.G., 1868-1869
Arasaratnam, S., 607
Archer Mildred, 276, 3859-3860
Archer, W.G., 3861
Arguimbau, Lawrence B., 277
Arjun Dev, 748
Arkasomayaji, D., 4124
Aronson, Harvey B., 1682
Arora, Raj Kumar, 1860
Arora, U.P., 1610
Arunachalam, M., 1211
Asher, Catherine B., 3542
Asher, Frederick M., 3305, 3631
Ashraf, Jaweed, 543
Ashrafyan, Klara Z., 749
Askari, S.H., 750, 4055
Aso, Masaru, 4281
Asthana, Shashi, 2779, 3632, 4008, 4305, 4419
Athavale, Sadashiv, 850, 1870
Auboyer, Jeannine, 608, 3822
Avinashilingam, T.S., 453
Awalikar, Pandit, 58
Awasthi, A.B.L., 466, 2211
Awasthi, Brahmamitra, 1347
Awasthi, D., 788

Babar, Sarojini, 2527
Badrinath, G., 4100

Bagavandas, M., 3786
Bagchee, Moni, 2
Bagchi, Kalyankumar, 1871
Bagchi, Subhendu Gopal, 1212
Bahura, Gopal Narayan, 1611
Baikar, Y.A., 3475
Bailey, G.M., 1213, 1632
Bailey, Greg., 274-275
Bailey, H.W., 1348, 1683-1684, 2359-2360, 3013
Bajaj, Prem N., 4125
Bajapai, Hena, 4009
Bajpai, K.D., 467, 932, 1000, 1214, 1685, 2910, 3014, 3223-3226, 3306-3307, 3560, 3633-3635, 3675, 3694-3696, 4183
Bajpai, S.C., 789
Bajpai, S.K., 3015
Balakrishnan Nayar, T., 2780
Balasubrahmanya. N., 2665
Balasubrahmanyam, M.D., 2361-2364
Balasubrahmanyam, S.R., 1215, 3402
Balasubramanian, R., 1872
Baldissera, F., 2547
Bal Krishan, 4170
Balsubramaniam, S.R., 2503
Bandaranayake, Senake, 3520, 4316-4317
Bandyopadhyay, Bimal, 3482
Bandhyopadhyay, Pratap, 2365, 2548, 2666, 4090
Bandyopadhyay, Samaresh, 3227
Bandyopadhyay, Santi, 1349
Banerjea, J.N., 3483
Banerjee, A.K., 278
Banerjee, Anukul Chandra, 1686-1687, 4184, 4344
Banerjee, Biswanath, 2212-2213, 2725
Banerjee, Dilip Kumar, 2532
Banerjee, Hiranmay, 1564, 1873-1874, 4082
Banerjee, J.N., 3686
Banerjee, K.D., 2781
Banerjee, Manabendu, 609, 2549
Banerjee, N.R., 418, 2782, 2911, 3308, 3551, 3697, 4010, 4290-4292
Banerjee, Nitya Narayan, 1216
Banerjee, P., 330, 3561, 4255, 4431-4432
Banerjee, Ramesh Chandra, 4056
Banerjee, S.K., 2496
Banerjee, S.P., 1875
Banerjee, Tarasankar, 146, 1006
Banerji, Adris, 867
Banerji, Arundhati, 3228, 3698, 4306
Banerji, Sures Chandra, 1217, 2550-2552, 4057
Bapat, P.V., 1688-1690, 2214, 2342-2343
Barannikov, P.A., 2312
Bareau, Andre, 1691
Bargohain, Bipin Kumar, 36, 117
Barlingay, S.S., 1876-1878, 2045, 2215
Barrett, Douglas, 3699
Barrier, N. Gerald, 960
Barthakur, Anil Ratan, 37
Barua, B.K., 3700
Barua, Bhaben, 38-40, 118
Barua, Dipak Kumar, 1692-1693
Barua, Rohini Kanta, 41
Bar-Yosef, O., 4426
Basak, Radhagovinda, 1694, 2667
Basavaraja, K.R., 59, 516, 880
Basham, A.L., 42, 193, 279, 610-611, 1218, 3701
Basu, Arabinda, 2046
Basu, G.C., 2272
Basu, Jogiraj, 612, 1022
Basu, Manoranjan, 1879
Batuk Nath, 2553
Baumer, Bettina, 2047
Bautze, Joachim, 3937
Bazi, Smita J., 4011
Bechert, Heinz, 1695-1699, 4318-4319
Bedar, A.R., 1191
Bedekar, D.K., 751
Bedekar, V.H., 372, 4012-4014
Bedekar, V.M., 1612, 2554, 3309
Bedi, Ramesh, 4135
Bender, E., 3967
Berkson, Carmel, 3403
Bernal, J.D., 280
Betal, R.S., 1350
Beyer, Stephan, 1700
Bhadra, Mrinial Kanti, 1880-1881
Bhadri, K.M., 3016
Bhagwan Singh, 1351
Bhanavat, Mahendra, 3493
Bhandari, V.S., 1352
Bhanj Deo, Prafulla Chandra, 1353
Bhardwaj, H.C., 4148
Bharadwaj, K.D., 2048
Bharadwaj, O.P., 11, 613-614, 1354, 1613, 2783-2784
Bharadwaj, Shiv Prasad, 2555-2556, 2668
Bharati, Agehananda, 2049
Bharatiya, Bhawani Lal, 442
Bhargava, Nondita, 963
Bhargava, P.L., 427, 615, 964, 1355-1356, 1583, 2726, 4091
Bhartiya, M.C., 1882-1883
Bhaskar, S., 2864
Bhat, A. Vishnu, 3748
Bhat, G.K., 1219, 1357, 2366, 2669, 3884, 4092
Bhat, M.M., 2331
Bhat, M. Mariappa, 60
Bhat, M. Ramakrishna, 2368
Bhat, M.S., 2367, 4433
Bhat, N.R., 4126

Bhat, S.S., 496
Bhatkhande, S.M., 1565
Bhatnagar, G.D., 752
Bhatt, G.H., 1220
Bhatt, P. Gururaja, 3435
Bhatt, S.R., 2050-2051
Bhatt, Vishnu Prasad, 1566
Bhattacharje, Aparna, 468
Bhattacharjee, Devaprasad, 2052
Bhattacharjee, Jatindra Mohan, 2495
Bhattacharya, Ananta Kumar, 497
Bhattacharya, Ashutosh, 4058
Bhattacharya, Asok K., 137, 3310-3311, 3862, 3889
Bhattacharya, B., 4137
Bhattacharya, B.K., 1884
Bhattacharya, Bhabatosh, 1586, 2557
Bhattacharya, Bhakti, 2053
Bhattacharya, Biswanath, 2369, 2558-2559, 2670
Bhattacharya, Chhaya, 4015, 4185
Bhattacharya, D.K., 2785
Bhattacharya, Dinesh Chandra, 1221
Bhattacharya, Dipak, 1701
Bhattacharya, Gopikamohan, 2054-2055, 2370
Bhattacharya, Gouriswar, 3017, 3636, 3702-3703
Bhattacharya, Kalidas, 2056
Bhattacharya, Kamaleswar, 1192, 1702, 1885, 2057-2058, 4364-4366
Bhattacharya, M., 2998-2999
Bhattacharya, Mandira, 1831
Bhattacharya, N.N., 517-519, 4186
Bhattacharya, P., 3823
Bhattacharya, Rabindra, 1358
Bhattacharya, R.S., 2059-2061
Bhattacharya, Ruby, 224
Bhattacharya, S., 257, 2062
Bhattacharya, S.C., 616
Bhattacharya, Sabyasachi, 1007
Bhattacharya, Sibesh, 1023
Bhattacharya, Sivaprasada, 2671
Bhattacharya, Sudhibhushan, 2273, 2308, 2344
Bhattacharya, Swapna, 1008
Bhattacharya, Vibhuti, 2063
Bhattacharya, Vishnupada, 1222
Bhattacharyya, A.K., 3552, 3863, 3972
Bhattacharyya, Asutosh, 2497
Bhattacharyya, D.C., 3637-3639, 3687, 3801-3804
Bhattacharyya, H.M., 2264
Bhattacharyya, Kalidas, 1886
Bhattacharyya, N.N., 1193, 1223, 4187
Bhattacharyya, Pranab Kumar, 403-404, 3018, 3229
Bhattacharyya, Ramaprasad, 1567, 2064
Bhattacharyya, Sibajiban, 1887-1888
Bhattacharyya, Sivaprasad, 1587, 2560
Bhavani, Sudhindra, 1889
Bhawalpuri, Azad, 16
Bhayani, H.C., 2371, 2539
Bhide, N.K., 151
Bhide, Sudha S., 2561
Bhide, V.V., 1359
Bhise, Usha, 1360, 4360
Bhowmick, Atul Chandra, 3312
Bhowmik, Swarnakamal, 2876
Bhowmik, S.K., 3995
Bhuyan, Laksheswari, 119
Bhuyan, Nakulchandra, 120
Biardeau, M., 1224
Bidya Nand, 790
Biley, H.W., 1703
Bilimoria, Purusottama, 275
Bilimoria, P., 1635
Billorey, Ramesh Kumar, 3704
Bindra, Trilochan Singh, 370
Binney, Edwin, 3rd., 3907
Bipan Chandra, 791-792
Bipin Chandra, 247
Birendra Nath, 3824
Birendra Prasad, 793
Birkhoff, 281
Birwe, Robert, 2372
Bisht, A.S., 4016
Bisht, R.S., 2884-2885
Biswanarayan Shastri, 2373
Biswas, Dilip Kumar, 948
Biswas, S., 2333
Biswas, S.S., 3825, 4017, 4293
Biswas, Sukumar, 2274
Biswas, T.K., 3640, 3705-3707, 3826, 3864
Blurton, Richard, 3980
Bodewitz, H.W., 1361-1364
Boisselier, Jean, 4367
Bokil, V.P., 2065
Bollee, W.B., 1704
Bolon, Carol Radcliffe, 3436, 3708
Bombwall, K.R., 4417
Bond, George D., 1705
Boner, Georgette, 4093
Bongard-Levin, G.M., 1024, 1119, 1225, 4188, 4446
Bonta, Del, 3676
Bool Chand, 1890
Bopardikar, B.P., 2927
Bordes, F.H., 4443-4444
Borooah, Devkanta, 43
Bose, Abinash Chandra, 1365
Bose, D., 1148
Bose, S.K., 1891, 3230
Bose, Subhra, 3000
Bose, Sudha, 188
Botto, O., 1120

Bowers, Faubion, 347
Brahmanand, Swami, 2374
Brajesh Krishna, 3313
Brand, Michael, 3701
Brapaspati, K.C.D., 4059
Breckenridge, Carol Appadurai, 1149
Brockington, J.L., 1226
Bronkhorst, Johannes, 1366
Brook, Peter, 225
Brown, W. Norman, 1367
Bruckner, Heidrun, 2066
Bruhn, Klaus, 3562
Bucca, Salvador, 1568
Buck, Harry M., 1588
Buddhadatta Bhikshu, 1706
Buddha Prakash, 617-619, 1227, 2375, 2562, 3428, 4252, 4269
Buhler, G., 1368
Burnier, Radha, 1892
Burrow, T., 2321, 2376-2380
Burtt, Edwin A., 1893
Bykova, E.M., 2276

Caillat, Colette, 2563
Cantlie, Keith, 121
Cardona, George, 2381-2385
Carter, John Ross, 1707
Caspers, Elizabeth During, 544
Chaitanya, Krishna, 2475
Chaitanya, Deva, B., 4060
Chakrabarti, Dilip K., 545-546, 2786-2787, 3001
Chakrabarti, Jayanta, 365, 3314, 3865-3867, 3890
Chakrabarti, Samiran Chandra, 1369
Chakraborti, Haripada, 1025, 1228
Chakraborti, Kanchan, 3315
Chakraborti, Uma, 3827
Chakraborty, Nirod Baran, 355
Chakravarti, Adhir, 4368
Chakravarti, Chintaharan, 1229-1230, 1370
Chakravarti, Mathura Mohan, 3563
Chakravarti, Pulin Bihari, 2564
Chakrabarti, Ranabir, 1009, 1054, 4294
Chakravarti, Tapo Nath, 2067
Chakravarty, A.K., 4117
Chakravarty, D.K., 3002
Chakravarty, Dhyanesh Narayan, 2727
Chakravarty, P.L., 3828
Chakravarty, S.J., 2068
Chakravorty, Jagannath, 2386
Chakravorty, Tapas Kumar, 2530
Chan, Wing-Tsit, 2216
Chanana, Dev Raj, 256, 1055
Chandel, Bhuvan, 1894
Chandramani, 3923
Chandramani Singh, 3908, 4094
Chandramouli, Jaya, 2672
Chandramurti, M., 3868
Chandra-Ngarm, Saeng, 1708
Chandra Prabha, 2673
Chandrasekharan, K., 1895
Chandra Shekhar Prasad, 1709
Chang, Kwang-Chih, 4351
Chapekar. B.N., 3709
Chapekar, N.G., 498, 1371
Chapekar, Nalinee, 301, 1026
Chari, C.T.K., 3, 4149
Charlesworth, Max J., 4454
Charudeva Shastri, 2565
Chatham, Doris Clark, 3476
Chatterjee, Asim Kumar, 1589, 1614, 2217, 2566
Chatterjee, Asoke, 620
Chatterjee, Bhaskar, 1194, 1633, 3710
Chatterjee, C.D., 4307, 4420
Chatterjee, Chinmayi, 1896
Chatterjee, Chinmoy, 2069
Chatterjee, Ratnabali, 3909
Chatterjee, S.C., 1897, 2070
Chatterji, B.R., 4189
Chatterji, Margaret, 1898
Chatterji, Suniti Kumar, 1231, 1657, 4190
Chattopadhyay, Dipak, 2387
Chattopadhyay, Kamaladevi, 189, 410, 3984
Chattopadhyaya, Alaka, 2476
Chattopadhyaya, B.D., 621, 2728
Chattopadhyaya, Basanta Kumar, 1569
Chattopadhyaya, Debiprasad, 1372-1373, 1899-1900
Chattopadhyaya, K., 1232
Chattopadhyaya, Kshetresachandra, 2388
Chattopadhyaya, Siddheshwar, 2674, 2729-2730
Chattopadhyaya, Sudhakar, 622
Chaturvedi, Harish Kumar, 1590
Chaturvedi, Narmedeshwar, 258
Chaturvedi, P.D., 374
Chaturvedi, Parashu Ram, 212
Chaturvedi, Yugal Kishore, 375
Chaudhary, Ang Raj, 2275
Chaudhary, Radhakrishna, 623-624, 1027
Chaudhary, V.C.P., 851
Chaudhuri, Korak K., 1374
Chaudhuri, Narayan, 2477
Chaudhuri, Roma, 2071
Chaudhuri, Vijayalakshmi, 3711
Chaudhury P.D., 44, 122, 839
Chaudhury,V.C.P., 794
Chauhan, D.V., 469, 2506
Chauley, G.C., 3682
Chavda, V.K., 520

Chawdhry, Radha Krishna, 1233
Chawhan, Devi Singh, 2277
Chemparathy, G., 211, 2072-2074
Chevkina, L.M., 2300
Chhabra, B. Ch., 1056, 2764, 3019, 3231, 3316, 3829, 4162, 4191-4192, 4380
Chidananda Murty, M., 61
Chidananda Murthy, M., 1234, 2567, 3020
Chido, M. D'onza, 2345
Chinchore, Mangala R., 1710
Chinmulgund, P.J., 152, 3232
Chitalwala, Y.M., 547
Chitgupi, Bhimarao, 3712
Chitnis, K.N., 881, 938-939
Chopra, Hira Lall, 1856
Chopra, S.N., 961, 3233
Choudhary, Radhakrishna, 852, 4369
Choudhary, Satya Dev, 2478, 2507
Choudhury, P.C., 2568, 4193
Choudhury, R.D., 840, 3021, 3564
Choudhury, Roma, 1901
Chowdhery, Jayshree, 4018
Chowdhury, Abdul Momin, 3022
Chowdhury, R.D., 3565
Chowdhury, Vasant, 3234-3235
Christie, Anthony, 4194
Christie, William M., Jr., 2433
Chubb, J.N., 1902
Chunder, P.C., 190
Chutia, D., 3023
Clooney, Francis X., 2075
Clothey, Fred W., 1235
Coedes, G., 4370-4371
Cogni, Giulio, 2076
Conlon, Frank F., 940
Corless, R.J., 2218
Cornwall, I.W., 4458
Corvinus, Gudrun, 2928
Coward, Harold G., 336, 1903, 2077
Creel, Austin B., 1236
Cribb, Joe, 4352
Crowe, Y., 3383

Dahiya, B.S., 625
Dalai Lama, H.H., 1711, 4195
Dalal, Katy Feroze, 2954
Dales, George F., 548-549
Damsteegt, Theo., 2278
Dandekar, R.N., 626, 1121, 1237, 1375-1379, 2389
Dange, Sadashiv A., 1238, 1380-1390, 2390
Dange, Sindhu S., 1391
Dani, Ahmad Hasan, 3024, 4308-4309
Danielou, Alain, 135, 4061
Dargyay, Eva K., 4345
Daridan, Jean, 3641
Dart, Raymond A., 2788
Das, Asok Kumar, 133, 3317, 3910-3912, 3938-3939, 4019
Das, Bhuban M., 1176
Das, Binod S., 627, 949-950
Das, D.R., 3416, 3484, 3515, 3713
Das, Jata Shankar, 314
Das, R., 1904
Das, R.M., 1122
Das, Ratna, 3830
Das, S.R., 2391
Das, Sisir Kumar, 2301-2302
Das, Sridhar, 324
Das, Sudhir Ranjan, 1150
Das, Sukla, 628, 871, 3985
Das, Sukumar, 499
Das Gupta, C.C., 3025
Das Gupta, Kalyan Kumar, 1239, 3404, 3688, 3805, 3973, 4282
Das Gupta, N., 1905
Das Gupta, Nupur, 2789
Das Gupta, Probal, 2279
Das Gupta, R., 3896, 3955, 3986
Das Gupta, R.K., 2569
Das Gupta, Rajatananda, 3318
Das Gupta, Sanghamitra, 841
Das Gupta, Santwana, 454
Dash, Prafulla Chandra, 2392
Datta, Asok Kumar, 3003
Datta, B., 1658
Datta, Bhabatosh, 2498
Datta, Bimal Kumar, 191
Datta, K.K., 795
Datta, Kali Kumar, 2731
Datta, V.N., 181
Dave, K.N., 2570
David, M.D., 328-329
Davies, Oliver, 4450
Daye, Douglas Dunsmore, 2219
D'Costa, Anthony, 941
De, Barun, 796
De, Bijanbihari, 3714
De, Gourisankar, 3715-3716, 3831
De, S.K., 2571
Dehejia, Vidya, 3463
De Jong, J.W., 1712-1713, 2220
Del Bonta, Robert J., 3566
De Lippe, Aschwin, 4062
De Mellow, Melville, 248
De Mora, Juan Miguel, 428, 1392, 2393
Deo, S.B., 629-630, 2790, 2929, 3521
Deore, Vijaya, 1393

Deotare, B.C., 2808
Deppert, Joachim, 1028
Deraniyagala, P.E.P., 2791, 4320
Deraniyagala, S.U., 4321
Derrett, J. Duncan M., 96, 1240, 1394-1395, 1714-1716, 1906, 2221, 2572, 3026-3027
Desai, Devangana, 3319, 3464, 3567-3569, 3717, 3832-3833
Desai, P.B., 62, 521, 3028, 3677
Desai, Z.A., 3029-3035, 3543
Deshmukh, C.D., 249, 282
Deshpande, C.R., 1615
Deshpande, G.T., 1241, 1396
Deshpande, M.N., 419, 861, 2792, 3522, 4196
Deshpande, Madhav, 470, 1717
Deshpande, N.A., 1591, 1832
Deshpande, Y.K., 308
De Silva, Anil, 1057
De Silva, C.R., 4322
De Silva, K.M., 4323
De Silva, Lily, 4324
De Silva, Padmasiri, 2222
De Smet, Richard V., 1852, 1907
De Souza, J.P., 797
Devahuti, D., 4197
Devaraja, N.K., 1195, 1908, 2223
Devasenapathi, V.A., 1242
Devasthali, G.V., 1397-1403, 2394-2396, 2573, 2732
Devkar, V.L., 459
De Vreese, K., 2298, 2473
Dhadphale, G.R., 153
Dadphale, M.G., 2574
Dhaky, M.A., 1833-1834, 3405, 3537, 3570, 3718, 3814, 4063, 4372
Dhal, U.N., 1243
Dhaninivat, Prince, 4409-4410
Dharmadhikari, T.N., 1404
Dhavale, D.G., 500
Dhavalikar, M.K., 174, 522, 550, 1058, 2912, 2930-2932, 3320, 3479, 3523-3524, 3719-3720, 4198, 4434
Dhebar, U.N., 1909
Dighe, V.G., 753
Dikshit, G.S., 754, 882-883, 3036
Dikshit, K.K., 1910
Dikshit, K.N., 551, 1010, 2793-2795, 2955-2957, 2979, 2983, 3571, 3642, 4020, 4256, 4435
Dikshit, Moreshwar G., 2796
Dikshit, R.K., 631, 1123-1124
Dinkar, Ramdhari Singh, 234
Divakaran, Odile, 3437, 3501
Diwakar, R.R., 63
Dixit, Prabha, 2078
Dixit, Sadhna, 632
Dobgins, K. Walton, 3236
Dohanian, Diran K., 4325
Donaldson, Thomas, 3321, 3485
Dorson, Richard M., 45
Doshi, Saryu, 3968-3969
Dowling, Thomas L., 1718
Dravid, N.S., 2079
Dravid, Rajeshwar Shastri, 259
Dresden, M.J., 2526
Dubey, Rajendra Prasad, 1911
Dumont, P.E., 1405
Durai Raja Singam, S., 798
During Caspers, E.C.L., 552
Durrani, F.A., 4310
Dutt, Nalinaksha, 1719
Dutta, Ajit Kumar, 3891
Dutta, B., 4381
Dutta, Kali Kumar, 872, 4095
Dutta, P.C., 2859
Dutta, S., 3237
Dutta, S.K., 123
Dviveda, Vrajavallabh, 2080
Dwivedi, R.C., 1406, 1835, 2397, 2675
Dwivedi, R.K., 1029, 1616, 4373
Dwivedi, Srimannarayan, 2081
Dwivedi, U.C., 3721
Dwivedi, V.P., 331, 376, 3322, 3572, 3643-3644, 3869, 4021
Dye, Joseph M. III, 3645

Edgerton, Franklin, 1407
Edwards, Richard, 3646
Eggermont, Pierre H.L., 633
Eimer, Helmut, 2575
Elizarenkova, T.Y., 1408-1410
Embree, Ainslie T., 799
Emeneau, M.B., 2305, 2309, 2676
Emmerick, R.E., 1720, 2576, 4346
Ensink, Jacob, 1244, 4382-4383
Erdos, P., 4127
Esnoul, A.M., 2082
Esteller, A., 1411-1413
Ettinghausen, Richard, 3323, 3913
Ewing, A.C., 1125
Ezhuthachan, K.N., 1126

Fairservis, Walter A., Jr., 553, 4311
Fauza Singh, 523
Fazlullah, S.M., 2535
Fenner, P., 2224
Fentress, Marcia, 554
Ferreira, John V., 1177

Filliozat, Jean, 1659, 2577, 4138
Filliozat, Pierre, 2398, 2733
Filliozat, Pierre–Sylvain, 3039, 3722
Filliozat, Vasundhara, 884, 2479, 3037-3039
Fischer, Eberhard, 3870
Fischer, Klaus, 3647
Fiser, Ivo., 2346
Foote, Robert Bruce, 2972
Forbes, Geraldine, 1151
Fraad, Irma L., 3913
Francfort, H.P., 555
Francisco, Juan R., 4199
Franke, Herbert, 1721
Frankena, William K., 1912
Franklin, R.L., 1913
Fuchs, Stephen, 1178
Fukazawa, H., 1101
Furer-Haimendorf, Christoph von, 1152

Gai, G.S., 885, 3328
Gajendragadkar, P.B., 64
Gajendragadkar, S.N., 452, 1584, 2399
Gambhirananda, 356, 455
Ganda Singh, 524, 800
Ganesan, Saw, 976
Gangadharan, N., 1634
Ganganna, G.M., 65
Gangoly, O.C., 3940, 4083
Gangoly, Srihari, 192
Gangopadhyay, M., 2400
Ganguli, Kalyan Kumar, 1011, 1245-1246, 1660, 3553
Ganguly, J., 1414, 1914
Ganguly, P.G., 1153
Ganguly, Swati, 1915
Gardin, J.C., 4257
Gardiner, K.H.J., 4436
Garg, R.K., 2083
Garnett, A.C., 1916
Garrod, D.A.E., 4427
Gaur, Albertine, 2480
Gaur, G.S., 2890
Gaur, R.C., 1001, 2797-2798, 2933, 2980
Gaur, V.L., 2401
Gaurinath Sastri, 1247
George, K.M., 2337
Gerow, Edwin, 4101
Ghafur, Muhammad Abdul, 4312
Ghatage, A.M., 2402, 2540, 2677
Ghosal, S.N., 2354, 2403, 2578, 3040-3041
Ghosh, Abhijit, 2734
Ghosh, Arabinda, 3384
Ghosh, Asok K., 1012, 2799-2801
Ghosh, Biplab Ranjan, 501
Ghosh, D.P., 3871, 3892, 4200, 4353
Ghosh, Devaprasad, 3406
Ghosh, Manomohan, 2579, 4374
Ghosh, N.C., 3004, 3239-3240
Ghosh, Nirmal K., 157
Ghosh, Oroon K., 634, 1154
Ghosh, Sankar Prosad, 3834
Ghoshal, U.N., 635
Gibson, A. Boyce, 1917
Giri, Kamal, 3539, 3974
Giriraj Kumar, 3941
Giteau, Madeleine, 3648
Godbole, G.H., 1415
Goel, D., 1918
Goetz, H., 3324, 3723
Gogna, Kamal, 176
Gogoi-Chutia, Laksahira, 1722
Gokak, Vinayak Krishna, 66
Gokhale, Balkrishna Govind, 1723-1724
Gokhale, Kamal, 755
Gokhale, Shobhana, 3042-3045, 3241-3242, 3443
Gokhale, V.V., 283-284, 1725
Gomez, Luis O., 1726
Gonda, J., 1416-1425, 1570, 2404-2407, 4384-4386
Goodrich, L. Carrington, 4271
Goonetileke, H.A.I., 341
Gopal, B.R., 415, 525, 886, 3046-3050
Gopal Krishna Kanti, 636, 756
Gopal, Lallanji, 637-639, 1059-1064, 1089, 1155, 1248, 1426, 1919-1920, 2084, 2580-2582, 3051, 3879, 4139-4140
Gopal, Surendra, 1090-1091
Gopalacharya, M.R., 1921
Gopalakrishnan, M.S., 3461
Gopalaswamy Iyengar, K., 1427, 2085
Gopi Nath, 250
Gorakshkar, Sadashiv, 3724-3725, 4295
Gore, N.A., 2678
Gorekar, N.S., 757
Goswami, Asha, 1249, 1617
Goswami, Ashok Kumar, 2280
Goswami, B.N., 3932
Goswami, Golockchandra, 46
Goswami, Krishnagopal, 1250, 2086
Goswami, Kunja Govinda, 1428
Goswami, Mahaprabhu Lal, 2087
Goswami, Niranjan, 3956
Goswami, Praphulladatta, 47, 841A-842
Goswami, R.B.L., 801
Goswami, Sitanath, 2088
Goswami, Upendranath, 2299
Goswamy, B.N., 3434, 3872, 3924-3925, 3931
Goswamy, Karuna, 3926
Goudriaan, T., 4387

Gough, Kathleen, 1156
Gould, Harold A., 1157
Govinda, Lama Anagarika, 1727, 2089
Govindarajan, Hema, 3726, 4984-4085
Govindaraju, S., 3786
Govind Chandra, Rai, 3325
Govind Pai, M., 2735
Goyal, S.R., 556, 640-641
Graefe, W., 2771
Gray, Basil, 3957
Gregorios, Paul, 4201
Griswold, A.E., 4411
Gros, Francoise, 3326
Guenther, Herbert V., 2225-2226
Guha, Amalendu, 1030
Guha, Arti, 1013
Guha, Dinesa Chandra, 2408
Guha, P.K., 169
Gunawardana, R.A.L.H., 1728, 4326
Gunda Jois, K., 3052
Gune, N.P., 2311
Gune, V.T., 802, 1158, 4171
Gunindra Singh, P., 3243
Gunjal, S.R., 67
Gupta, Anand Swarup, 1661
Gupta, Chandrashekhar, 3244, 3727, 4202
Gupta, Chitrarekha, 1014, 3728
Gupta, D.K., 140, 2583, 2679
Gupta, D.P., 366
Gupta, Hira Lal, 1662
Gupta, Jagdish, 3729
Gupta, Kalyan Priya, 3835
Gupta, Lina, 1853
Gupta, M.N., 1429
Gupta, P.C., 803
Gupta, P.L., 642, 1065, 3245, 3958
Gupta, P.S., 1102
Gupta, R.C., 4128-4129
Gupta, S.K., 643, 3649
Gupta, S.P., 557, 2802, 3327, 3730, 4022, 4203, 4437
Gupta, Satadal Kar, 1853
Gupta, Suman, 1922
Gupta, Urmi B., 2736
Gupte, Y.R., 3885
Gurav, R.N., 887
Gurov, N., 564
Gurumurthy, S., 977
Gururaja Bhat, P., 3438
Gururajachar, G., 888
Gururajachar, S., 889-890, 3053
Gururaja Rao, B.K., 2895, 2973, 3650, 3873

Habib, Irfan, 502
Habib, Sayera I., 1103
Habibullah, 285
Habibullah, A.B.M., 1196
Habib-ur-Rahman Shastri, 1857
Hacker, P., 1571
Hahn, Michael, 4347
Halakatti, S.V.P., 3439
Halappa, G.S., 68, 891
Halbfass, Wilhelm, 2090-2091
Haldar, Aruna, 1923
Haldar, Gopal, 503
Hamp, Eric P., 2281
Handa, Devendra, 962, 2958, 3054-3055, 3246, 3731-3734
Handurukande, Ratna, 1729
Hangloo, Rattan Lal, 873
Hanumatha Rao, D., 3735
Hanumantha Rao, G., 1924
Hanumantha Rao, M., 3056
Hanumantha Rao, S., 1730
Haq, S. Moinul, 758
Haque, Intisar-ul, 1925
Hara, Minoru, 1251-1252, 1430, 1592, 1618, 2409, 4204
Hariharan, M., 3075, 4065
Harihara Sastri, G., 1127
Harinarayana, N., 377, 2803, 3573, 4023-4025
Hari Rao, V.N., 3502
Hariyappa, H.L., 4163
Harle, J.C., 3574-3576
Harsh Narain, 1926
Hartel, Herbert, 3057
Hartman, Carl Gustav, 2410
Hasan, Mohibbul, 759-760
Hassan, S. Mahdi, 1927
Hattori, Massaki, 2227
Hawley, John Stratton, 2508
Haye, Chowdhry Abdul, 868
Hayes, Glen A., 2092
Hazra, R.C., 1431, 2680
Heesterman, J.C., 1432
Hegde, K.T.M., 2804-2805
Heinrich, A., 2282
Hejib, Alaka, 1433
Henderson, Edward P., 3323
Heskel, Denis L., 4421
Hines, Donalds M., 4272
Hinueber, Oskar Von, 2347-2348
Hirabayashi, Jay, 1731
Hiranmaya, 69
Hiremath, R.C., 70
Hoenigswald, Henry M., 2283
Hoffman, Karl, 1434
Hondius, J.M., 71

Hooykaas, C., 4388-4390
Horner, I.B., 1732
Howard, Wayne, 1435
Hsu, Francis L.K., 1179
Hulbe, S.K., 1163
Hunashal, S.M., 72
Huntington, John C., 3651
Huntington, Susan L., 3525
Hurvitz, Leon, 1733-1734, 2228
Husain, Shahanara, 1015
Husaini, S.A.Q., 761
Hutchings, P.A.E., 1635
Hutton, J.H., 1180
Huzurbazar, V.S., 4130

Ichimura, Shohei, 1735
Iida, Shotaro, 1731
IM, 73
Imam, Abu, 1016
Inaba, Shoju, 2229
Inagaki, Hisao, 1736
Inamdar, V.B., 2093
Indrapala, K., 1737, 4327
Ingalls, Daniel H.H., 286, 2681
Inskeep, R.R., 4451
Iqbal Singh, 18
Irfan Habib, 1092
Irwin, John, 3328, 3526, 3987
Isri, R., 1738
Ithape, Usha, 345
Iyengar, H.R.R., 2094

Jacobi, Hermann G., 1436
Jagadeb, Sri Lakshmi Narayana Harichandan, 3058
Jagat Narain, 3942
Jagdhari, A.K., 378
Jag Mohan, 158
Jai Dev Vidyalankar, 2584
Jaideva Singh, 1636, 4064
Jain, Dharam Chand, 315
Jain, Jyotindra, 3329, 3874
Jain, K.C., 471, 1836, 3494
Jain, S.P., 195
Jai Narain, 644
Jaini, Padmanabh S., 1739, 1928, 2230, 3652
Jain-Neubauer, Jutta, 3736
Jai Prakash, 3059
Jaiswal, O.P., 327, 2231, 3247
Jaiswal, Suvira, 1031, 1197
Jamindar, Rajesh, 1670
Jamindar Rasesh, 477, 645
Jamkhedkar, A.P., 3477, 3522, 3689
Jamuar, Bipin Kumar, 401
Jan, Yun-hua, 1740-1741
Janaki, S.S., 2481, 2547, 2585, 2737
Janert, K.L., 2586
Jani, A.N., 458, 1437, 2411, 2587-2588
Jansen, M., 558
Jarriage, Jean Francois, 4313
Jash, Pranabananda, 147, 3737
Jassal, H.S., 4026
Jassu Ram, 560
Jauhri, R.C., 762
Javadekar, Pradnya Anant, 222
Javali, V.K., 74
Jayadev, Jani, 2412
Jayakar, Pupul, 447A, 1159, 3330
Jayalakshammanni, M., 4102
Jayaswal, Ayodhya Prasad, 4289
Jayaswal, Sushila, 235
Jayaswal, Vidula, 2868, 3836-3837
Jena, Kurana C., 1160
Jettmar, Karl, 559
Jeyechandrun, A.V., 1253, 3738
Jezic, Mislav, 1637
Jha, Aditya Nath, 260, 340, 804, 4103
Jha, B.K., 4104
Jha, D.N., 1066, 1254
Jha, Dayadhar, 1128
Jha, Harihar, 1638
Jha, Hari Mohan, 165
Jha, J.C., 853, 1017
Jha, Jata Shankar, 1161
Jha, Kishor Nath, 2095
Jha, L.K., 226
Jha, Mangalpati, 2682
Jha, Munishwar, 2472
Jha, Ramakant, 316
Jha, Ramanatha, 2509
Jha, Shailendra Mohan, 2510
Jha, Shaktidhar, 1837
Jha, U.N., 1929
Jha, V.D., 933
Jha. V.N., 2413
Jha, Vivekanand, 1032
Jit, Nabin Kumar, 951
Jiyu, Ren, 1742
Jog, K.P., 1438, 2738
John, K.T., 4027
Johns, A., 4391
Joseph, T.K., 3549
Joshi, D.M., 2414
Joshi, H.M., 1930
Joshi, Hem Chandra, 2096
Joshi, J.P., 560, 2806, 2944
Joshi, L.M., 1743

Joshi, M.C., 196, 456, 1002, 1255, 2097, 3060, 3331-3332, 3385, 3407-3408, 3739-3740, 4028
Joshi, Maheshwar P., 1003, 3061-3062, 3516, 3741
Joshi, N.P., 3063, 3333, 3577
Joshi, Nibha, 3334
Joshi, P.M., 504, 646, 763-764
Joshi, P.S., 765
Joshi, R.M., 460
Joshi, Rasik Vihari, 1439, 1931, 2098-2099, 2415, 2807-2808, 2913-2914
Joshi, S.B., 1440
Joshi, S.D., 2416-2421
Joshi, S.K., 3386-3387
Joshi, S.N., 942
Joshi, Shivnarain, 2232
Joshi, Umashankar, 1932

Kabir, Humayun, 48, 124, 805
Kachhawaha, O.P., 965
Kajiyama, Yuichi, 1744-1745, 2233
Kakati, Banikanta, 125
Kakati, Satish Chandra, 49
Kalagate, B.M., 75
Kalghatgi, T.G., 76
Kalia, Ashok Kumar, 2589
Kaluphana, David J., 2234
Kalyan Krishna, 766, 3837, 3914, 3943
Kalyanov, V.I., 1619
Kamalapur, J.N., 647
Kamat, A.R., 4131
Kamat, Jyotsna K., 3440
Kamata, Shigeo, 4205
Kamath, Jyotsna, 892
Kanavi, Channaveera, 77, 2520
Kane, P.V., 1663
Kanga, M.F., 4422-4423
Kangle, R.P., 1067, 1129
Kanjilal, Dileep Kumar, 2739, 4096
Kanoria, Gopikrishna, 3578
Kansara, N.M., 1441-1442, 3409
Kantawala, S.G., 1443, 1664-1666, 2422, 2740, 2809, 2820
Kapadia, B.H., 1444-1445, 1933
Kapil Deva Shastri, 2423
Kapur, Geeta, 159
Kar, Bijayananda, 1934
Karambelkar, V.W., 2683
Karan Singh, 1256, 1746, 2684
Karashima, Noboru, 648, 978, 4328
Karimashil, K.S., 767
Karmakar, A.P., 1667
Karnik, H.R., 1446
Karunaratne, T.B., 4329
Karve, C.G., 4172
Kashikar, C.G., 1257, 1447-1452
Kasinathan, Natana, 979, 3248
Katre, S.M., 2284, 2322-2323, 2334
Katre, Sadashiva L., 1639, 2590-2591
Katti, Madhav N., 472, 893, 1453, 3064-3067, 3742
Kaul Deambi, B.K., 870
Kaus, Hurmuz, 3975
Kawthekar, P.N., 1454, 1620
Kazmi, Nuzhat, 3915
Kedam, Michael, 2100
Kemp-Ashraf, P.M., 806
Kennedy, K.A.R., 561, 4330
Kenoyer, Jonathan M., 562
Kesarwani, Arun, 563, 649
Keshava Murthy, B.R., 4105
Keswani, G.H., 4150
Khadabadi, B.K., 1838
Khan, Abdul Waheed, 2861
Khan, Ahmad Nabi, 3068
Khan, Benjamin, 1854
Khan, Iqtidar Alam, 768
Khan, Mohd. Israil, 1668
Khan, Muhammad Ishtiaq, 4314
Khan, Namdar, 287
Khan, Shaukat Ali, 379
Khandalavala, Karl J., 3743-3744, 3916, 3944-3946, 3959
Khanna, Amar Nath, 197, 420, 3527, 3976
Khare, G.H., 966, 3917
Khare, M.D., 2913, 4206
Khastgir, S., 3335
Khatri, A.P., 2915
Kher, C.V., 1747
Kher, Chitrarekha, 1748
Khiste, Batuknath Sastri, 1258, 2101
Khobrekar, V.G., 4173
Khomne, S.B., 1163
Khoroche, Peter, 350
Khwaja, Jamal, 1935
Kibe, M.V., 1593
Kidder, J. Edward, 4283-4284
King, Ursula, 1640
Kiparsky, Paul, 2424
Kiribamune, Sirima, 4331
Kirpal Singh, 526
Klimburg-Salter, Deborah, 3806, 4258
Klostermaier, Klaus, 1936-1938
Knorozov, Yu, 564
Koch, Ebba, 3918
Koeningswald, G.H.R., von, 2810
Kohl, Philip, 4259
Kohli, Manorama, 807
Kohli, Surinder Singh, 4207

Kokan, Yousaf, 2494
Koller, John M., 1455
Kolte, S.B., 1163
Kolte, V.B., 3069, 3336
Konishi, Masatoshi A., 565-566, 3337
Kopf, David, 1259
Korti, Vijaya, 2235
Kosambi, D.D., 505, 1162, 4151
Koti, N.N., 2813
Kotraiah, C.T.M., 473, 894
Kramrisch, Stella, 1456, 3338, 3683, 3745
Krasnova, Irina, 2271
Kripalani, K.R., 50, 126
Krishan, Y., 1260, 1749
Krishna, C., 2916-2917
Krishnadasa, Rai, 3339
Krishna Deva, 650, 3188, 3579, 3653, 4296
Krishna Lal, 1457
Krishnamoorthy, K., 78, 651, 1621, 2102, 2236, 2425, 2482, 2592-2598, 2685, 2741
Krishnamurthi, V.G., 808
Krishnamurthy, C., 895
Krishna Murthy, K., 652, 1750, 3417, 3654, 3746, 3838
Krishnamurthy, M.S., 2511, 3070, 3441
Krishnamurthy, R.V., 2774
Krishnamurti, N.S., 4086
Krishnamurty, C., 2896
Krishnamurty, P. Gopal, 2599
Krishnan, K.G., 896, 1261, 3071-3074
Krishnappa, M.V., 897
Krishna Prakash Lal, 380
Krishna Rao, M.V., 1262
Krishnaswamiengar, B.S., 809
Krishna Warriar A.G., 2103
Krishna Warrier, A.G., 1641
Krishnayya, D.N., 898
Kruger, Horst, 22, 4445
Kruse, Cornelius, 254
Kucuradi, Ioanna, 1939'
Kuiper, F.B.J., 1263, 1458-1459, 4136
Kulkarnee, Narayan H., 4174
Kulkarni, A.R., 527, 769-770
Kulkarni, B.R., 1940
Kulkarni, B.S., 1264
Kulkarni, Chidambara, 506
Kulkarni, E.D., 2104
Kulkarni, G.T., 771
Kulkarni, V.G., 79
Kulke, Hermann, 209
Kulli, J.S., 2282
Kulshresth, Archana, 3947
Kulshreshtha, R.B., 2686
Kumar, Suman, 653
Kumara Swamiji, 80
Kunhan Raja, C., 201-202, 4424
Kunjunni Raja, K., 1941, 2105-2106, 2426, 2600
Kunte, B.G., 772
Kunst, Arnold, 1572, 1751
Kuppuswami Sastri, S., 654, 1265-1267, 1573, 1594, 1752-1753, 2107-2115, 2285, 2601-2603, 2687-2688, 2742, 4106-4107, 4175-4176
Kuppuswamy, Gouri, 3075, 4065
Kurl, Shreeprakash, 2313
Kurup, K.K.N., 528
Kusumgar, Sheela, 2774

Lacombe, Olivier, 429
Laddu, S.D., 1460, 2427-2428
Lahiri, A.K., 1461
Lahiri, A.N., 3076, 3249-3251
Lahiri, Bela, 3252
Lahkar, B.C., 51
Lakshmana Rao, J.R., 4152
Lakshminarayan Rao, N., 3077, 3580
Lal, A., 3253
Lal, B.B., 862, 1942, 2811, 2959, 2981-2984, 3078-3079, 3839
Lala Aditya Narayan, 4029
Lalit Kumar, 3388
Lalman, 2874
Lalye, P.G., 357
Lamberg-Karlovsky, C.C., 567, 2812
Lancaster, Lewis, 1754-1755
Lanius, Mary, 4297
Larson, Gerald James, 2116
Lascarides-Zannas, Eliki, 3465
Latifi, Danial, 23
Law, Bimal Churn, 474, 2265
Lawson, Simon, 3254
Leifer, Walter, 4208
Lekha, Indu, 2429
Lele, V.S., 2813
Lerner, Martin, 3581
Leshnik, Lawrence S., 2877
Lethcoe, Nancy R., 1756
Leumann, M., 2430
Leung, Man-kam, 4273
Lewis, Boniface, 1943
Lienhard, Siegfried, 2314, 2689-2690
Limaye, V.P., 1462, 2431
Lin-Bodien, Carol G., 3747
Lindtner, Christian, 3080
Ling, Trevor, 1757-1759
Lipsey, Roger, 3340
Litman, A.D., 4, 1130
Litvinsky, B.A., 4209
Lochan, Amarjiva, 4210

Lockwood, Michael, 3582, 3748
Lohuizen-de Leeuw, J.E. van, 3341, 3840, 4392, 4412
Lokesh Chandra, 1268, 1760-1762, 2237, 4211-4213, 4270, 4274-4275, 4348-4349, 4393-4394, 4428, 4438, 4447
Lokeswarananda, 5
Lorenzen, D., 655
Lorenzen, David N., 1269
Low, Ramesh Kumar, 2286
Lutzker, Mary-Ann, 3583

Mabbet, I.W., 4375
Macdonald, Alexander W., 4298
Machwe, Prabhakar, 52, 127
McKibbin, Penelope M., 1944
McLean, George F., 1945
McLean, M.D., 1270
McLeod, W.H., 507, 1861
Madgavkar, Kusum, 288
Madhav Rao, P. Setu, 773
Madhu Bala, 560, 2814
Madhusudhana Rao, V.V., 2862
Mahadevan, Iravatham, 656, 3081
Mahadevan, T.M.P., 1946, 2117
Mahajan, Malati, 3082
Mahalingam, T.V., 440, 529, 657, 1763, 3342, 3503, 3749
Mahapatra, Khageswar, 2341
Mahapatra, L.K., 952
Mahapatra, Sitakant, 1271-1272
Mahdihassan, S., 2315
Maheshwari Prasad, 1622
Mainariya, Purshottam Lal, 2512
Mainkar, M.G., 2604
Mainkar, T.G., 343, 1463, 1623, 1642, 2743
Mainkar, V.B., 568
Maitra, Juthika, 3750
Maitra, K., 810
Maity, P.K., 1273, 1764
Maity, S.K., 98, 406, 1464, 3255, 3442, 3886
Majumdar, A.K., 863
Majumdar, G.G., 2934
Majumdar, M.R., 3751
Majumdar, R.C., 107, 170, 658, 811, 1274, 2432, 3083, 4418
Majumdar, Santwana, 115
Makkai, Adam, 2433
Makkhan Lal, 2815, 3208
Malaiya, Sudha, 3752
Malan, B.D., 4452
Malaviya, Ram Kuber, 261
Malhotra, K.C., 1163
Malik, D.K., 2979
Malik, S.C., 569, 2816
Malkani, G.R., 1947
Mallappa, T.N., 81
Malledevaru, H.P., 1275-1276, 1948
Mallik, Bhakti P., 2287
Mallik, Madhusudan, 1765, 2349-2350
Mallison, F., 1465
Maloney, Clarence, 508
Malvania, D.D., 1838A
Malvika Singh, 227
Malwad, S.S., 82
Manager Prasad, 475
Manchanda, S.C., 4030
Mangalam, S.J., 3084, 3256, 3841
Mankad, D.R., 659, 1466
Mankodi, Kirit L., 3842, 3960
Manmohan Kumar, 2886, 2945
Manoranjan Shastri, 2118
Manuk, P.C., 237
Marathe, M.P., 1766
Margabandhu, C., 1068, 2817, 2887, 2967, 2985, 3389, 3584-3586, 3753, 3843-3844
Markandeya Sastry, C., 2119
Marneffe, J. de S.J., 1949
Martand Singh, 228
Martinet, Andre, 2228
Marulasiddaiah, G., 83, 1277
Marulasiddaiah, H.M., 899
Masefield, Peter, 1767
Mashi, Y., 1198
Mason, R.J., 2818
Masson, J.L., 2541
Masson, J. Moussaieff, 1643, 2605
Master, Alfred, 2324
Masud, S.A., 1858
Mate, M.S., 570, 943, 3343, 3443
Maten, Erik P., 2765
Mathur, M.S., 381, 3996
Mathur, Rames, 4285
Matilal, Bimal Krishna, 214, 1950-1951, 2120, 2238, 2434-2435
Matsunaga, Yukei, 2239
Mayeda, Sengaku, 1574
Mazumdar, Amiya Kumar, 1952
Mazumdar, B.P., 660, 827, 854, 1669, 3418
Mazumdar, Kanchanmoy, 953
Mccarthy, Frederick D., 4455
Meadow, R.H., 571
Meena, B.R., 2969
Meenakshisundaran, T.P., 1164, 2121
Meghraj, 2513
Mehendale, M.A., 476, 1467-1473, 1624, 1863, 3085
Mehrotra, L.L., 4214
Mehta, J.S., 382

Mehta, M.J., 1069
Mehta, R.N., 477, 572, 864, 900, 1670, 2819-2820, 2878-2881, 3390, 4115
Mehta, Vasistha Dev Mohan, 1575
Meister, Michael W., 3344, 3466, 3495-3496, 3528, 4439
Menezes, Armando, 84
Menon, M.S., 2436
Menon, Narayana, 4097
Michell, George, 3444, 3538, 3587
Mille, Beatrice Diamond, 1181
Mimamsaka, Yudhishthira, 2289
Mirashi, V.V., 116, 478-479, 661-663, 828, 1278, 1625, 2691, 2744-2745, 3086-3092, 3257
Mishra, Adya Prasad, 2122, 2606
Mishra, Baldeva, 262
Mishra, Bhagirath, 2514
Mishra, Gopal Chandra, 2483
Mishra, Hari Mohan, 1474
Mishra, Jagannath, 317
Mishra, Kameshwar Nath, 1768
Mishra, L.N., 1104-1107
Mishra, Madaneshwar, 318
Mishra, P.K., 3754
Mishra, R.S., 2960, 3093
Mishra, Satya Prakash, 2960
Mishra, Shiva Gopal, 2515
Mishra, Shrikrishna, 2484
Mishra, Sudhakar Nath, 3845
Mishra, V., 2290
Mishra, Vijayakanta, 3588
Mishra, V.B., 664, 1279
Mishra, Yugal Kishore, 319
Misra, B.B., 2988
Misra, B.N., 4215
Misra, Gopal Chandra, 2531
Misra, Haripriya, 2325
Misra, J.P., 812
Misra, Jayamanta, 2607
Misra, K.K., 3875
Misra, Om Prakash, 2918
Misra, R.N., 2919, 3094, 3345-3346, 3467, 3589
Misra, Radhey Shyam, 1839
Misra, Satya Deva, 2123
Misra, Satya Swarup, 1644
Misra, Srinarayana, 2124
Misra, V.D., 2986-2988
Misra, V.N., 573, 665, 2961-2964
Misra, Vidya Niwas, 1475, 2692
Misra, Vijaya Kant, 2989
Mitra, Debala, 3486-3489, 3590-3592, 3655-3656, 3807, 4395
Mitra, Makar, 4299
Mitra, Rajyeswar, 4066
Mitra, Sankar Prasad, 6
Mitra, Sisir Kumar, 1280
Mitragotri, V.R., 3391, 3426
Mittal, Jagdish, 3899-3900
Mittal, Kewal Krishan, 13, 2266
Mitterwallner, Gritli V., 3427, 4260
Mizuno, Kogen, 1769
Modak, B.R., 1476, 1645
Mode, Heinz, 2125, 2485, 3347
Modi, P.M., 1646
Moghe, S.G., 1131, 1477, 2126
Mohan, Mehta Vasishtha Dev, 666-667
Mohan, P. Saraswati, 2693
Mohanty, Banshidhar, 843
Mohanty, Gopinath, 954
Mohanty, J.N., 1953
Mohapatra, G.C., 2888, 2889
Mohinder Singh, 480
Moitra, Shefali, 1954
Mokashi-Punekar, Shankar, 1955
Momin, K.N., 574
Mookerjee, Jatil Coomar, 2127-2128
Moore, Charles A., 1956
Moorthy, A.N., 2694
Morgenroth, Wolfgang, 1576
Morgenstierne, Georg, 4425
Morley, Grace, 383, 411, 3348, 3876, 3997, 4031-4034
Moti, Chandra, 3846, 3893
Mudaliar, N. Murugesa, 2129
Muddachari, B., 901
Mughal, M.R., 4315
Mujeeb, M., 1859
Mujumdar, G.C., 2821, 2943, 2990
Mukandi Lal, 326, 3927
Mukerjee, Ajit, 3349
Mukerjee, Hiren, 813
Mukerjee, Radhakamal, 4216
Mukerjee, Sandhya, 3350
Mukerji, A.C., 2130
Mukherjea, Sushil, 1281
Mukherjee, Arun Kumar, 2499
Mukherjee, B.N., 304, 668-669, 1132, 1182, 3095-3096, 3258-3261, 3554, 3593, 3808, 4217, 4332
Mukherjee, Biswadeb, 1770
Mukherjee, D., 3262
Mukherjee, Dilip Kumar, 4067
Mukherjee, Ramaranjan, 2695
Mukherjee, S.N., 99, 1018, 1133
Mukherjee, Swapan K., 1183
Mukherji, Tarapada, 2303
Mukhia, Harbans, 1282
Mukhopadhyay, Biswanath, 1478
Mukhopadhyay, Govind Gopal, 263
Mukhopadhyay, Samir Kumar, 3263

Mukhopadhyay, Somanath, 3544, 3977
Mukhopadhyaya, Bhakti Sudha, 2131
Mukhopadhyaya, Krishnalal, 2500
Mullatti, L.C., 1957
Mullick, C.C., 3097
Mumme, Patricia, 2132
Munda, R.D., 4081
Munsterberg, Hugo, 4286
Murphy, Veronica, 3988
Murthy, P.N.N., 416
Murton, Brian J., 980
Murty, M.L.K., 2863
Mus, Paul, 1479
Muzumdar, B.P., 1070
Mylius, Klaus, 1480

Nag, Arun K., 2822, 3005
Nag, Dilip Kumar, 367-368
Nagar, Malti, 2964-2965
Nagaraj, Nalini, 3594
Nagaraja Rao, M.S., 2823, 2897-2898, 3264, 3351, 3445-3446, 3595-3596, 3657, 4035
Nagaraja Rao, P., 1283, 1595, 1647, 1958-1960
Nagaraj Rao, Nalini, 358
Nagaraju, S., 184, 670, 902, 2899, 3529, 4354
Nagarch, B.L., 3429-3432, 3468-3469, 3678
Nagasaki, Hojun, 2267
Nagaswamy, R., 671, 1284, 2974, 3098, 3597, 3847
Nagendra, 2516
Nahta, Agarchand, 3970
Naik, C.R., 2536
Naik, D.B., 3755
Nair, D. Appukuttan, 2746
Nair, S. Bhaskaran, 371
Nair, S.M., 3998, 4036
Nakada, Naomichi, 1961
Nakamura, Hajine, 1285, 1771-1772, 1840, 1962, 2133-2136, 2240-2242, 4218
Namboodiri, P.E.D., 530
Namboodiripad, E.M.S., 24
Namboodiry, C.P.M., 1963
Nam Joshi, Vijayalaxmi S., 1286
Nandi, R.N., 1287
Nandi, Sudhir, 2137
Nandimath, S.C., 85, 3099
Nanjundaswamy, N., 3100
Naqvi, S., 1033
Narahari, H.G., 1481, 2138
Narain, A.K., 255, 672, 3756, 4261
Narain, H.K., 3424
Narain, Harsh, 2139
Narain, L.A., 2869
Narasimhachary, M., 2140
Narasimha Murthy, A.V., 903-904, 3101-3104, 3265-3267, 3392
Narasimhiah, B., 2975
Narayanababu, P., 2900
Narayanan, M.G.S., 531, 673
Narayana Pillai, P.K., 2338
Narayana Sastry, H.V., 2747
Narayanaswami, V., 2141
Naresh Kumar, 2142
Nariman, Fairbourz, 1482
Narlikar, A.V., 4153
Narlikar, J.V., 4154
Narsingh, K.T., 2696
Narten, Johanna, 1483
Nath, Bhupendra, 1964
Nath, Dwijendra Lal, 393
Nath, R., 3105, 3545
Naudou, Jean, 774
Nautiyal, K.P., 2991
Nawani, N.P., 3106
Nayak, G.C., 1965, 2143
Nayak, H.M., 2521
Negi, J.S., 1034, 2992, 3107
Nehru, B.K., 229
Nehru, Lolita, 3658
Nene, R.P., 289
Neog, Maheswar, 53-54, 128-130, 1165, 1773, 3108-3109
Nigam, J.S., 575, 2920, 4219
Nigam, L.S., 3268
Nigam, M.L., 1288, 3598, 3757-3758, 4037
Nigam, S.B.P., 967
Nikam, N.A., 1577
Nilakanta Sastri, K.A., 509, 674, 1966
Nirmal, Chiranjivi J., 4220
Niyogi, M. Bhavanishankar, 310
Niyogi, Puspa, 1071, 1774
Niyogi, Sumanta, 814
Nizami, K.A., 775, 2537
Nizamuddin, M., 3961
Norman, Dorothy, 230
Norman, K.R., 1775, 2351, 3110
Northrop, F.S.C., 1967

Oates, L.R., 1776
Oberai, K., 1035
O'Connell, Joseph T., 2608
O'Flaherty, Wendy, 180, 1626
Ojha, A.P., 1036
Ojha, Kailas Chandra, 675, 1134
Ojihara, Yutuka, 1484, 2437-2438, 4262
Oleksiw, Susan, 2748
Om Prakash, 676, 1037

Oomen, T.K., 1038
Oturkar, R.V., 776

Pachner, Rgine, 3962
Paddayya, K., 2824, 2901
Pade, J.S., 2609
Padigar, Shrinivas V., 3111
Padoux, Andre, 2144
Pai, Swarnalatha G., 2610
Painter, John, 1855
Pal, A.C., 2825
Pal, Animesh K., 4266
Pal, Jagannath, 2826
Pal, Keshav Ram, 395, 2439
Pal, M.K., 4038
Pal, Pratapaditya, 1671, 3759, 4221, 4300-4301
Palsule, G.B., 1485-1486
Panattoni, E., 2345
Panchamukhi, R.S., 2827
Panda, Shishir Kumar, 955
Pande, B.M., 576-578, 4222
Pande, G.C., 1135, 1968, 2243
Pande, Shyam Narain, 481
Pandey, A.N., 1969, 2611
Pandey, C.B., 677-678, 2612, 3269, 4223
Pandey, D.P., 1289
Pandey, J.N., 492
Pandey, Jagdishwar, 1970
Pandey, K.C., 2749
Pandey, Lochan Prasad, 482-486, 855, 934-935, 956, 1596, 2697-2698, 3112-3130, 3270-3279, 3877
Pandey, M.S., 3280
Pandey, R.N., 4302
Pandey, R.P., 2914
Pandey, Raj Bali, 1487
Pandey, Ramavadha, 2440
Pandey, S.L., 1971
Pandey, Sangam Lal, 443, 2145
Pandey, V.C., 679-680, 3131-3132
Pandey, Yogesh, 264, 2148
Pandeya, R.C., 2146
Pandeya, R.G., 1010
Pandeya, Ramachandra, 1972
Pandeya, Rewati Raman, 2147
Pandeya, Sri Jagdishvar, 2244
Pandeya, Trilochan, 2517
Pandit, Sneh, 3352
Pandurangi, K.T., 2149
Pandya, Suman, 2882
Pandya, Vijay, 2750
Panikkar, R., 1973
Panse, M.G., 4118, 4440
Pant, G.N., 331, 2828, 4039, 4164-4166
Pant, P.C., 3837
Pant, R.K., 2875
Pappu, R.S., 2943
Pappu, Raghunath S., 2929
Parab, L.G., 2699
Parabrahma Sastry, P.V., 1039
Paradkar, M.D., 1648, 2613-2614
Paramashivaiah, J.S., 905
Paranavitana, S., 4333
Paranjpe, V.G., 2150
Parija, Prankrishna, 131
Parimoo, Ratan, 3353-3355, 3555, 3599, 3659, 3760-3761, 3809, 3878, 3894, 4040
Parpola, Asko, 681, 1290, 2770, 3133
Parrinder, Geoffrey, 1777
Parthasarathi, R.K., 4177
Parthasarathi, T.S., 4068
Pas, Julian F., 1778
Patel, T. Dayananda, 3600
Pathak, Indu Mati, 3762
Pathak, R.A., 1488
Pathak, S.K., 1779-1780
Pathak, V.S., 682
Pathan, U.M., 2528
Pathy, T.V., 3478-3479
Patil, C.S., 3447
Patkar, M.M., 203, 1040, 1489
Pattabiraman, P.Z., 3601
Patterson, Thomas C., 4459
Patwardhan, Achyut, 231
Patwardhan, M.V., 2541
Patyal, H.C., 1490
Patyal, Hukam Chand, 2326
Paul, Harendra Chandra, 1291
Paul, R.K., 487
Paul, Suwarcha, 3933
Pavlov, Yuri, 1974
Pawar, A.G., 944
Pereira, Jose, 3410, 3530
Perera, A.D.T.E., 3810
Perera, L.P.N., 1781
Peris, Merlin, 1975
Perrett, Roy W., 1976
Perumal, V., 981
Peter, H.R.H. Prince of Greece and Denmark, 1166
Phadke, H.A., 683, 869
Phadke, Hari Anant Shastri, 2441
Phatak, N.R., 532
Phukan, J.N., 3281, 4355
Piaskowski, Jerzy, 2830
Picron, Claudine Bautze, 3134
Pike, Kenneth L., 2291
Pilania, G.P., 968
Pillai, Poovattoor Ramakrishna, 2700

Pillay, K.K., 533, 982, 3135
Pingree, David, 2615, 4132
Pisani, Vittore, 2486
Pobozniak, T., 430, 1782
Poddar, Arabinda, 2501
Poddar, R.P., 2751
Pollock, S., 1597
Polome, Edgar C., 2329
Poonacha, K.P., 3136
Porcher, Marie-Claude, 2616
Possehl, Gregory L., 579
Potdar, K.R., 1491, 1977
Potdar, Mrinalini K., 1292
Pott, P.H., 3660
Potter, Karl H., 1978
Pou, Saveros, 4376
Prabhavananda, 2151
Prabhu Joseph, 1136
Pradhan, M.C., 182-183, 1184
Prahalad Singh, 3763
Prajnanananda, 2152, 4069
Prajnananda, 684
Pramar, V.S., 3411
Pramod Chandra, 3764, 3919
Pramod Kumar, 396, 2245
Prasad, Ajit Kumar, 3661
Prasad, B.K.R., 290
Prasad, Deo Muni, 1108
Prasad, Hari Kishore, 3531, 3897
Prasad, H.S., 1783, 2246
Prasad, Kunwar Deo, 1109
Prasad, Lalan Kumar, 3999, 4155
Prasad, Rajiva Nain, 777
Prasad, S.K., 2153
Prasad, S.N., 685
Pratap Chandra, 1784
Prebish, Charles S., 1785
Premalatha, V., 4070
Prematilleke, Leelananda, 4334-4335
Prematilleke, P.L., 4336
Prufer, Olaf H., 2831
Punekar, S. Mokashi, 4116
Punekar, Shankar Mokashi, 3282
Puri, B.N., 100, 108, 686-688, 1041, 1293-1294, 1492, 4396-4397
Puri, Ramachandra, 2617
Purna Iyer, K., 3765
Purushottam Singh, 2832
Pusalkar, A.D., 2618, 2752
Pusalker, A.D., 1627, 1672
Puskas, Ildiko, 101, 1199
Pye, Michael, 1786
Radha, M., 3600
Radhey Shyam, 778
Raghavachar, S.S., 1295-1296, 2154
Raghavan, M.D., 2768
Raghavan, V., 204, 298, 1673, 2442, 2518, 2619-2621, 2701-2702
Raghava Varier, M.R., 1841
Raghotham, Venkata, 983
Raghunath, S.N., 580
Raghunathan, N., 1578
Raghunath Bhat, H.R., 359, 3283
Raghuvanshi, V.P.S., 1167
Raghuvira, 4224, 4407
Rahbar, Hansraj, 26
Rahman, A., 4156
Rahman, Mukhlesur, 3766, 4267
Rahula, Telwatte, 2247
Rahula, Walpola, 1787
Rahurkar, V.G., 969, 1493-1495, 2622
Rai, Jaya Chandra, 444
Rai, Subhash, 2833, 3879
Raikar, Y.A., 3393
Raikes, R.L., 581
Raison, Alix, 4141
Rajagopal, T.S., 3137
Rajagopalachar, K., 1297
Rajagopala Shastri, S., 1979
Rajaguru, S.N., 2934, 2943, 2990
Rajamani, M.B., 1168
Raja Rao, M., 4071
Rajasekhara, S., 3448
Rajayyan, K., 984
Rajeevalochana, K., 2155
Rajendra 'Jijnasu', 2773
Rajendra Prasad, 238, 1980-1981
Rajendra Prasad, B., 1298, 3419
Rajendra Ram, 239
Ramachandraiya, O., 3138
Ramachandra Murthy, S.S., 3139-3141
Ramachandran, C.E., 534
Ramachandran, K.S., 582, 689, 985, 1072, 2834, 3142, 3767, 4028
Ramachandra Rao, C.V., 906
Ramachandra Sastry, S., 2156
Ramakrishna, G., 1200
Ramakrishna Bhat, N., 299
Ramakrishna Rao, B.S., 2443
Ramakrishna Rao, K., 2248
Ramakrishna Rao, K.B., 1982
Ramakrishna Rao, K.S., 2157
Ramakrishna Sastry, M., 2444
Ramamurthy, K.K., 3011, 3449. 3504. 3768-3769

Ramamurthy, V., 986
Raman, K.V., 424, 1299, 3143, 3356, 3394, 3505, 3602-3603, 4225
Raman, N.S.S., 1788, 1983
Ram Anant, L.B., 1984
Ramanathan, C., 2754
Ramanna, H.S., 907
Ramanna, Raja, 1985
Ramanujacharyya, Yatindra, 1986
Ramanujam, Chidambaram S., 987
Ramanujan, A.K., 2522
Rama Rao, M., 690, 829
Rama Rao Pappu, S.S., 1987
Ramasubramanian, N., 1169
Ramaswami, N.S., 488, 3450, 3506-3507, 4337
Ramaswami, S., 2487
Ramaswamy, S., 1300
Ramaswamy Sastri, V.A., 2158
Ramesh, K.V., 691-692, 908-910, 3144, 3446, 4000
Ram Gopal, 1496-1498, 1628, 2753
Rami Reddy, V., 2864
Ramjee Singh, 166, 1988
Rana, S.S., 3145
Ranadeva, S.P., 2766
Randhawa, M.S., 3928-3929, 3934
Randle, H.N., 2292
Ranganathan, A., 160, 210
Ranganathananda, Swami, 457, 1201
Rangaswami Aiyangar, K.V., 205
Rangaswamy, C.V., 1110
Ranjit Singh, 1301
Ranov, V.A., 4441
Rao, B.V., 911
Rao, Chalapati, 251
Rao, K.P., 2835
Rao, K.V., 2772
Rao, Raja, 232
Rao, S.R., 583, 1073, 2836, 2935, 3146, 3451
Rao, T.R., 912
Rao, V.D., 945
Rashid, A., 1093
Rastogi, Navjivan, 2159
Rath, Banamali, 2703
Rau, Heimo, 693
Rau, Wilhelm, 1499, 2623
Ravi Prakash, 2352
Ravi Shankar, T.S., 3200
Rawlinson, Andrew, 1789
Ray, Amita, 584, 1019, 1302, 3978
Ray, Aniruddha, 779, 816
Ray, Annada Sankar, 1989
Ray, Dilip Kumar, 3003
Ray, Himanshu Prabha, 3532
Ray, Niharranjan, 161, 510, 3357
Ray, Priyadaranjan, 4157
Ray, Sukumar, 34, 780
Ray, Sunil C., 3284
Rechanna, G.N., 86
Reddy, D. Raja, 3285
Reddy, K. Thimma, 2865
Reddy, P. Chenna, 830
Reddy, P. Suryanarayana, 3285
Redington, James D., 2160
Romon, Joaquin Perez, 1790
Renou, Louis, 1500
Reu, Bisheswar Nath, 936
Reyna, Ruth, 1990
Reynolds, C.H.B., 139
Rhodes, N.G., 3286
Riboud, Krishna, 4226
Richards, Horace G., 4456
Richardson, High E., 1791
Rieppe, Dale, 292, 1991, 3358, 4158
Rimtlen, Fritz-Joachim, 1992
Rinchen, Acad, 4227
Rinpoche, Tarthang Tulku, 1993
Ritschl, Eva, 1501
Ritti, Shrinivas, 178, 913-914, 3147
Riviere, Juan Roger, 4228
Rizvi, S.A.A., 781
Rocher, Ludo, 694, 1303, 1502-1503, 2161, 2624-2625
Rolland, Piere, 1304
Roodbergen, J.A.F., 2445
Roth, Gustav, 1792-1793, 3148
Roth, Phil. Gustav, 1202
Roy, Anamika, 4373
Roy, Bani, 4041
Roy, Bharati Kumari, 3395
Roy, Brajdeo Prasad, 695, 1074-1075, 1579
Roy, J.K., 1994
Roy, Nilima, 4042
Roy, P.C., 3287
Roy, Parimal, 3234-3235
Roy, S.N., 1674-1675
Roy, S.S., 1995
Roy, Sailash Chandra, 4253
Roy, Shashanka Bhusan, 4119
Roy, Sita Ram, 2870
Roy, Somnath, 817
Roy, T.N., 2837-2839, 3848
Roy, Udai Narain, 696-698, 1042-1043, 3149
Roychowdhury, Jyotsna, 1305
Roychowdhury. P.C., 1170
Ruben, Walter, 699-700, 1044, 2626-2627
Rucinski, Tomasz, 2162
Rudrappa, J., 1306
Ruegg, D. Seyfort, 1794
Rule, Paul, 1995A

Rurrow, T., 2446

Saberwal, Satish, 1171
Sadananda Giri, 2163
Saddhatissa, H., 2533
Sadhu Ram, 1598, 1629, 3150-3152
Sadyojata Swamiji, 831
Sagar, A.P., 3604
Saha, Anima, 2355
Saha, P.K., 4043
Saha, Sushil, 102
Sahai, Baldev, 2858
Sahai, Bhagwant, 3605, 3770-3772, 3811
Sahai, Sachchidanand, 4377
Sahai, Yadvendra, 970
Sahasrabuddhe, Madhukar Tryambak, 1504
Sahay, S.N., 701, 2840
Sahay, Sachidanand, 3849
Sahay, Vishnu, 252
Sahu, L.N., 206
Saikia, Jogendranath, 55
Sairam, T.V., 3359
Saklatwala, Beram, 293, 1505
Saksena, B.P., 2538
Saksena, Baburam, 2316, 2327
Saksena, Banarsi Prasad, 782
Saksena, Dwarika Prasad, 511
Saksena, Jogendra, 3360
Saletore, G.N., 782A
Sali, S.A., 585, 2936-2939, 3288
Saloman, Richard, 114, 1506, 3153-3154
Samanta, Biswanath, 3003
Samaraweera, Vijaya, 4338
Sambaiah, O., 1298
Sambamoorthy, P., 4072
Samozvantsev, A.M., 1137
Sampath, M.D., 915, 1076, 3155-3158, 3420
Sampatkumaran, M.R., 2164
Sampurnanand, 265
Samtani, N.H., 450, 1795
Sander, Lore, 1796
Sandesara, Bhogilal J., 3159
Sane, P.S., 1507
Sanford, David Theron, 3452
Sangar, S.P., 1094
Sanghasen Singh, 2767
Sanjivi, N., 535
Sankalia, H.D., 154, 294, 489, 586-587, 844, 865, 946, 1599, 2841, 2940-2943, 2946-2947, 3006, 3606-3607, 3662, 4044, 4448
Sankaran, C.R., 2474, 2503, 4159
Sankaranarayana, N., 3289
Sankaranarayanan, S., 177, 325, 702, 3160-3165
Sankarankutty Nair, T.P., 930
Sankhdher, B.M., 818
Sankrtyana, Rahul, 27, 240-241
Santucci, James A., 437
Sanyal, Hitesranjan, 1020, 3519
Sarabhai, Mrinalini U., 4087
Saran, Parmatma, 512, 1095, 1111, 3546
Saran, S.C., 2966, 2993, 3290, 3850
Sarana, Gopala, 2842
Saraswati, Baidyanath, 2249
Saraswati, Pratyagatmananda, 1996
Saraswati, S.K., 3490, 3547, 3895
Saraswati, Vidyanand, 1508
Saraswathi, T.A., 4133
Sarat Chandran, K., 2165
Sardesai, D.R., 819
Sardesai, S.G., 1307
Sarkar, A.K., 2250
Sarkar, H., 832, 2447, 3166, 3412, 3508, 3608, 3679, 4045, 4276
Sarkar, H.B., 4229-4230, 4356, 4398-4399
Sarkar, Haribishnu, 3663
Sarkar, J.N., 783, 1096-1097
Sarkar, K.K., 4231, 4400
Sarkar, K.R., 1077
Sarkar, Ranajit, 2704
Sarkar, S.S., 1185
Sarkar, V.C., 1045
Sarma *see also* Sharma
Sarma, A.V.N., 588
Sarma, Dimbeswar, 490, 2488, 2705
Sarma, E.R., Sreekrishna, 1509
Sarma, I.K., 2976, 3421, 3453, 3509, 3773-3774
Sarma, I.K., *see also* Sharma, I.K.
Sarma, K.V., 439, 4120
Sarma, M. Madhava Krishna, 344
Sarma, R. Nagaraj, 207
Sarma, R. Thangaswami, 2166
Sarma, Sadasiva Rath, 3491
Sarma, Sreeramula Rajeswara, 1078
Sarma Biswas, A.T., 1676
Sarup Singh, 28
Sastri, Devudu Narasimha, 2448
Sastri, P.S., 1997, 4098
Sastri, Sakuntala Rao, 110
Sastry, B.V.K., 4073
Sastry, M.P.L., 2167
Saswadkar, P.L., 820, 4142
Satish Chandra, 1098
Satswarupananda, 2168
Sattar, Abdus, 215
Satya Prakash, 4046
Satya Vrat, 142, 351, 2449, 2628, 2706, 4415
Satyavrat Shastri, 431, 1649, 4413-4414

Satyavrat Singh, 1510-1511, 2707
Satyavathi, T.S., 4074
Saxena, B.P., 2967
Saxena, K.S., 703
Saxena, Kaushal Kishore, 3167
Saxena, Lakshmi, 1998
Scharfe, Hartmut, 2450
Scharpe, A., 2629
Schastok, Sara, 3775
Schetelich, Maria, 1501
Schlerath, B., 1512
Schlingloff, Dieter, 3664
Schmidt, Hanns-Peter, 1513, 1776
Schmithausen, Lambert, 1797
Schneider, Herbert W., 4457
Schreiner, Peter, 1677
Schwartz, Susan L., 1600
Seetharamaiah, M.V., 1308
Sehgal, S.R., 1514, 4232
Seidal, W., 295
Sen, Amulyachandra, 1842
Sen, Asis, 3812
Sen, Asok, 4108
Sen, D., 2843
Sen, Deba Brata, 2169
Sen, Geeti, 3920-3921
Sen, Indra, 2170
Sen, Nilamadhav, 1601, 2328, 2451
Sen, Paritosh, 3556
Sen, S., 1309
Sen, Sukumar, 1515
Seneviratne, Anuradha, 4339
Sengupta, Anima, 2171
Sengupta, Bratindra Kumar, 1310-1311
Sengupta, Gautam, 3777
Sengupta, Nilakshi, 1172
Sengupta, Pallab, 2504
Sengupta, Pradip Kumar, 1999
Sengupta, R., 704, 3480, 4001-4002
Sengupta, Santosh, 1203
Sen Majumdar, Gayatri, 1798
Sen Sharma, Deba Brata, 1516, 2172-2174
Serebryakov, I.D., 2489, 2630
Serge, Cleuziou, 589
Seshadri, C., 2000
Seshadri, M., 2902-2903, 3778
Seshagiri Rao, K.L., 2175
Seth, M., 3880
Sethi, Rajiv, 233
Sethna K.D., 705
Sethuraman, N., 3168
Settar, S., 3454
Shah, K.K., 706, 1138
Shah, Umakant P., 112, 3665, 3680, 3779, 3815-3818, 3971
Shanbhag, D.N., 2001, 2176
Shanmugam, P., 1079, 1312
Shantakumari, Leela, 916
Shapeti, S.B., 87, 1139
Sharan, Mahesh Kumar, 707, 1650, 4223
Sharda Rani, 4394
Sharma *see also* Sarma
Sharma, Arvind, 1799, 2268
Sharma, B.D., 971
Sharma, B.N., 1313, 3557, 3609-3613, 3780-3782, 4047, 4303
Sharma, B.N.K., 1517, 2002
Sharma, B.R., 1518
Sharma, Brahmadatta, 2755
Sharma, Brijbhanu, 3169
Sharma, D.D., 2317, 2756
Sharma, D.P., 2994
Sharma, Dasharatha, 708-709
Sharma, Deo Prakash, 3517
Sharma, G.R., 144, 2844
Sharma, Ganesh Datta, 1651
Sharma, GAnesh Dutt, 2631
Sharma, Hazari Lal, 386
Sharma, I.K., 1843, 3170, 3291
Sharma, I.K., *see also* Sarma I.K.
Sharma, Jagdish P., 1844
Sharma, Jajneswar, 216
Sharma, K.L., 1519
Sharma, Kadambri, 1602
Sharma, Krishna Kant, 2871
Sharma, M.J., 3171
Sharma, M.R., 1314
Sharma, Madhuri, 2994, 3517
Sharma, Manohar, 3361
Sharma, Mukunda Madhava, 56, 132, 1520, 2632-2635
Sharma, Narendra Nath, 2636
Sharma, P.V., 2637, 4143
Sharma, Pushpa, 710, 4167
Sharma, R.A., 2921
Sharma, R.C., 2887, 2995, 3172, 3614-3615, 3681, 3881, 4048
Sharma, R.G., 387
Sharma, R.K., 2177-2178, 2922
Sharma, R.N., 2003, 2183
Sharma, R.P., 2967, 3389
Sharma, R.S., 711-714, 856, 1046, 1204, 2845
Sharma, Ram, 715, 1521, 3173-3174
Sharma, Ram Charan, 3362
Sharma, Ramesh Chandra, 3989
Sharma, Ram Murti, 2179-2182
Sharma, Ravindra Kumar, 972-973, 4168
Sharma, S., 332
Sharma, Savita, 3363

Sharma, T.C., 2846-2847
Sharma, Umesh Chandra, 392,1522-1523
Sharma, Y.D., 2948-2949, 2968
Sharotri, G.K., 4049, 4234
Sharpe, E.J., 1652
Shashi, S.S., 1173
Shashi Bala, 4287
Shashi Kant, 2356
Shastri, Ajay Mitra, 311, 353, 399, 716-718, 833, 917, 937, 957-958, 1315, 3175-3178, 3292-3296, 3396, 3413
Shastri, Balacharya, Khuperkar, 1316
Shastri, Biswanarayana, 217, 1603, 1678
Shastri, D.N., 266, 1524, 2452
Shastri, H.G., 866
Shastri, Raja Ram, 2004
Shastry, A.K., 918
Shaw, J.L., 2005
Shaw, Thurstan, 4453
Sheik Ali, B., 417, 919
Sheikh, Gulam Mohammed, 3948-3949
Shende, N.J., 1525-1526
Sheo Shanker Prasad, 2453
Sherwani, H.K., 1099, 4109
Shetti, B.V., 3364, 3455-3457, 3616
Shintri, Sarojini, 88
Shivaganesha Murthy, R.S., 920, 1527, 2638
Shivaji Singh, 1528
Shivanna, 1080
Shivanna, K.S., 921
Shivaramaiah, B.K., 2639-2640
Shivarudrappa, A.L., 1317
Shorto, H.L., 4361
Shraddhananda, 1318
Shri Nivas Shastri, 2184
Shripaty Sastry, K., 922
Shrivastava, M.C.P., 719, 874, 1081
Shrivastava, P.S., 4235
Shukla, Badri Nath, 2185
Shukla, Bhawani Shanker, 1800
Shukla, D.N., 3414-3415
Shukla, Govardhan Nath, 267
Shukla, J.M., 2186
Shukla, K.S., 3365-3366
Shukla, Karunesha, 1801, 2006, 2251
Shukla, Kripa Shankar, 4134
Shukla, N.S., 2252
Shukla, S.P., 3297, 3783
Shukla, Uma Kant, 2490
Shukla, Vidya Sagar, 3851
Shulman, David, 1319
Shute, Clarence, 2007
Shyam Prakash, 2454
Siddiqi, M. Raziuddin, 296
Siddiqi, W.H., 3548, 4236
Silva, Roland, 3397
Simons, Elwin L., 2848
Sinari, Ramakant, 2008-2009
Singer, Milton, 4237
Singh, A.D., 1653
Singh, Ajaya Kumar, 3882
Singh, B.K., 4401
Singh, Bhagwati Prasad, 268-269
Singh, C.D., 1112
Singh, Chitra Lekha, 3784
Singh, Ghanshyam Narain, 1113
Singh, Hari Sahay, 1082
Singh, J.D., 2455
Singh, Jagat Pal, 3979
Singh, Jai Prakash, 720, 845-846
Singh, K.S., 1140
Singh, L.P., 1186
Singh, Lal Rama Yadupal, 2708
Singh, Madan Mohan, 1083
Singh, Nawal Kishore, 1114
Singh, P.N., 253
Singh, R.C. Prasad, 2849
Singh, R.P., 4110
Singh, R.R., 2923
Singh, R.S., 2456
Singh, Rajeshwar Prasad, 1529
Singh, Ram Bhushan, 1845
Singh, Ravindra N., 2850
Singh, S.B., 821
Singh, S.P., 2187
Singh, Sarjug Prasad, 3298
Singh, Satya Prakash, 1530
Singh, Sheo Bahadur, 1320, 3617
Singh, Udaya Narayan, 2335
Singh, Udai Vir, 3852
Singh, Umrao Bist, 2010
Singh, Y.B., 721, 875-876, 1321, 3299
Singhal, D.P., 4238
Singhal, G.D., 491
Singhal, Sudarshana, 4402-4403
Sinha, A.K., 2969
Sinha, Ajit Kumar, 2011
Singh, Ajoy Kumar, 3618
Sinha Arun Kumar, 4239, 4378
Sinha, Atul Kumar, 1141
Sinha, B.C., 974
Sinha, B.K., 857, 4111
Sinha, B.P., 103, 242, 590, 722, 2851, 3367, 3666
Sinha, Chitta Ranjan Prasad, 243, 402, 2873, 3819, 3853
Sinha, D.K., 3667
Sinha, Debabrata, 2012
Sinha, Gopal Chandra, 270, 432, 723
Sinha, H.P., 2852

Sinha, J.P., 433-435
Sinha, Jadunath, 2188
Sinha, K.P., 1531
Sinha, Narendra Kumar, 3668
Sinha, Nirmal Chandra, 4254, 4350
Sinha, Prabhakar, 2336
Sinha, Priti, 2641
Sinha, R.C. Prasad, 2872
Sinha, Sachidananda, 244
Sinha, Satya Prakash, 1115
Sinha, Surendra Prasad, 724
Sinha, Tarkeshwar Nath, 1142
Sinopoli, Carla M., 3980
Sircar, D.C., 111, 923, 1021, 1205, 1322-1324, 1532, 1846, 3179-3187, 3785, 4121, 4240, 4263, 4268
Siridhamma, Ven L., 1802
Sirisena, W.M., 4357
Siromoney, Gift, 3786
Sitaraman, B., 2293
Sitaramayya, V., 1604
Sivaramamurti, C., 333, 1047, 1605, 2013, 2642, 3188, 3368, 3619, 3669, 3787-3788, 3854, 4075
Sivaraman, K., 2014
Skelton, Robert, 3950
Slater, Robert Lawson, 2015
Sluszkiewicz, E., 2457, 2643
Smart, Ninian, 1206
Smirnov, G.L., 2016
Smith, Bardwell L., 1803
Smith, Philip E.L., 4449
Smith, R. Morton, 1533-1534, 1654, 3369, 3670, 3684
Smith, W.L., 2304, 2502
Sogani, Kamal Chand, 2017
Sohoni, S.V., 407, 725, 2644-2645, 2709, 2757, 3189-3190, 4178
Solheim, Wilhelm G., II, 4358
Somani, Ramvallabh, 3951
Somasundaram, S., 89
Somasundara Rao, C., 784, 988, 3138, 3191
Someshwar Prasad, 2253
Sompura, Kantilal F., 3433
Sonawane, V.H., 2970
Sontheimer, Gunther D., 1187, 1325-1326
Sood, R.K., 2858
Soundara Rajan, K.V., 412, 591, 726, 1327, 1606, 2853, 2904, 3370, 3422, 3458, 3497, 3510, 3620, 4241
Spellman, J.W., 2018
Spencer, George W., 989
Spink, Walter M., 3470, 3533-3534, 3887
Sprung, Mervyn, 1804, 2254
Sreedhar, B.H., 513
Sreekantaiya, T.N., 2491
Sreekrishna Sarma, E.R., 1535, 2646
Sreenivasa Murthy, H.V., 1048
Sreeramamurti, P., 2458
Sri Nivas, 1536
Srinivasan, C.R., 3192
Srinivasan, Doris, 3789
Srinivasan, G., 2019
Srinivasan, K.R., 990, 3193, 3671, 4242
Srinivasan, L.K., 199, 3194, 3511, 4003
Srinivasan, P.R., 3195-3196, 3621, 4379
Srinivasan, S., 991-992
Sri Niwas Shastri, 2020, 2255
Sriramamurti, P., 2710
Srivastav, N.M.P., 822-823
Srivastava, A.L., 3371, 3790
Srivastava, Avinash Kumar, 1805
Srivastava, Balram, 3372-3373
Srivastava, D.N., 2519
Srivastava, Dharma Bhanu, 1116
Srivastava, Hari Shankar, 1100
Srivastava, J.S., 2021
Srivastava, K.M., 592, 2996-2997, 3855
Srivastava, Narendra Pratap, 1537
Srivastava, O.P., 1084
Srivastava, R.N., 2294
Srivastava, R.P., 3374
Srivastava, S.K., 2984, 3839, 3856-3857
Srivastava, Shashi Bala, 3498-3499
Srivastava, V.C., 145, 1328-1329, 4264, 4340
Srivastava, Vijai Shankar, 388, 975, 3791
Sriyan, Ratna N., 2459
Staal, Frits, 1538-1540
Stall, J.F., 1330
Stacul, Giorgio, 593
Stadtner, Donald M., 3622
Steinkellner, Ernest, 1806-1807
Sternbach, Ludwik, 727, 1143, 1541-1542, 1607, 2647, 2711-2712, 4243, 4362
Sthapathy, Ganapathy, 425
Stietencron, Heinrich Von, 3492
Stone, James H., 1580
Subbanna, N.R., 2758
Subbarayalu, Y., 993-994
Subbarayappa, B.V., 4160
Subba Reddy, D.V., 4144
Subbiah, G., 995, 3512
Subhadradis Diskul, M.C., 4244
Subrahmanian, N., 1543
Subrahmanyam, B.R., 2866
Subrahmanyam, Padma, 3792, 4088
Subrahmanyam, R., 2867
Subrahmanyam, V.S., 3197
Subrahmanya Sastri, P.S., 1544
Subrahmanya Sastri, S., 1545, 2189
Subrahmanya Sastri, Vepattur, 2022
Subramani Aiyar, N., 1331

Subramania Iyer, K.A., 2190, 2460-2462, 2713
Subramanyam, K.G., 3981
Subramanyam Sastri, A., 2191
Subramanyan, K.G., 162
Subramonia Ayer, S., 3813
Subramonia Iyer, S., 3144, 3198-3200
Subramoniam, V.I., 2310
Sud, P.D., 4050
Sudarshan, E.C.G., 2023
Sudhanshu, Brahmachari, 8
Sukhatme, P.V., 4145
Sukhvir Singh, 2714
Sukul, Kubera Nath, 3518
Sullerey, S.K., 1004
Sundara, A., 179, 2905-2909, 3459, 3623-3625, 3793-3794
Sundaram, C.S., 4089
Sundaram, J., 3201
Sundaram, R.M., 2474
Sundara Rajan, R., 2024
Sundar Raj, M., 1546
Sunkapur, M.S., 90
Suraj Bhan, 2854
Surendra Rao, B., 924
Suresh Singh, 3425
Suresh Singh, K., 785
Suresh Vasant, 3300, 3535
Suri, C.L., 3202
Surya Kanta, 728, 1547, 2330
Suryanarayana Rao, M.K., 2648
Suryanarayana Sastri, Peri, 2025
Suseendirarajah, S., 4341
Sushil Malti Devi, 4112
Sushma, 2649
Swaminathan, V., 1548, 1581
Syamchaudhuri, N.K., 1117
Sylvan, R., 2026

Takeuchi, Shoko, 2256
Talbot, Cynthia, 3203
Talukdar, Nanda, 218
Talukdar, Phanindranath, 57
Tanaji, B., 445, 2192
Tandan, R.K., 3903, 3930, 3963
T'ang Chun, 4277
Tara Chand, 3888
Tarlekar, G.H., 4076
Tartakov, Gary Michael, 3375, 3460, 3481
Tatacharya, D.T., 2193
Tatia, Nathmal, 2027, 2269
Tatz, Mark, 1808
Teeuw, A., 4404
Tejasananda, 4113
Templeman, David R., 1809
Tewari, S.P., 729, 3204-3207, 3626, 4077
Thakur, Anantalal, 441, 730, 1810, 2028, 2194-2195
Thakur, Umakant, 1005
Thakur, Upendra, 320, 408, 731-732, 858-859, 1085-1086, 1332-1333, 1847, 3898, 4245-4250, 4288, 4359, 4363, 4408, 4416
Thakur, Vijay Kumar, 733-737, 860, 1087, 1811-1812, 3376
Thakur, Vishnu Singh, 339
Thammaiah, Bandaru, 91
Thananjayarajasingham, S., 4342
Thapar, B.K., 594, 738, 2855
Thapar, Romila, 514, 739-740, 1049, 1088, 1608, 2856
Thaplyal, Kiran Kumar, 438, 3208, 3301-3302, 3671A, 3795
Theodore, A. Sunderaraj, 92
Thieme, P., 2463, 2650
Thipperudraswamy, H., 1334
Thirujnanasambandhan, P., 2295
Thirunavakkarasu, K.D., 535
Thiruvengadathan, A., 1335
Thiruvenkatachari, S., 998
Thite, G.U., 4146
Thite, Ganesh, 1549-1550
Thompson, I., 2818
Thosar, H.S., 947
Thrasher, Allen W., 2651
Tikekar, S.R., 4179
Tilakasiri, J., 2652
Tipnis, S.N., 2029
Tipperudraswamy, H., 93
Tippeswamy, P.R., 3377
Tirumalai, R., 999, 3209-3210, 4078
Tiwari, A.R.G., 1336
Tiwari, Bhola Nath, 2318-2319, 2464
Tiwari, Lakshmi Narayan, 1813
Tiwari, Lalit Shanker, 389
Tiwari, Mahesh, 2257
Tiwari, Maruti Nandan Prasad, 3539, 3820
Tiwari, Nand Kishor, 339
Tiwari, Pratibha, 2653
Tiwari, Ramakant,, 644
Tiwari, Ramanand, 1551
Tiwari, S.P., 400
Tobias, Philip V., 4161
Tomos, Jindrich, 1050
Tonki, Saiyed Mohammed, 29
Topdan, 877
Toporov, V.N., 1410
Topsfield, Andrew, 3952
Trautmann, Thomas R., 741
Triloki Nath, 143
Tripathi, C.L., 2030

Tripathi, Chandrabhal, 2654
Tripathi, Gaya Charan, 1337-1338, 1552
Tripathi, K.K., 4051
Tripathi, L.K., 3540
Tripathi, R.K., 2031
Tripathi, Rammurti, 271, 2196
Tripathi, Ram Narain, 2197, 2655
Tripathi, Ram Narayana, 436
Tripathi, Ram Shankar, 1814
Tripathy, Snigdha, 959
Trivedi, C.B., 2924, 3471
Trivedi, H.V., 2925, 3211
Trivedi, P.K., 3472, 3571, 3586, 3627, 3821
Trivedi, R.D., 3399, 3473, 4052
Trivedi, S.D., 3628, 3796-3798
Trumalai, R., 931
Tsering, Migmar, 2258
Tulku, Doboom, 1815
Tulpule, S.G., 2529
Tyagi, B.S., 397
Tyagi, N.C., 1144

Uberoi, J.P.S., 515, 1862
Ucida, Norihiko, 2296
Udaya Vira Shastri, 1553, 2198-2199
Uday Shankar, 4114
Uma Shankar, 245
Uniyal, Indra Datt, 2715
Unni, N.P., 2656, 2716-1717, 2759
Upadhyay, R., 492
Upadhyaya, Baldev, 272, 4122
Upadhyaya, Bharat Singh, 4278
Upadhyaya, Jagannath, 2259
Upadhyaya, K.N., 2260
Upadhyaya, P., 2465
Upadhyaya, R., 2760
Upadhyaya, Ramji, 2718
Upadhyaya, S.A., 1554
Upadhyaya, U.P., 2297
Upadhyaya, Vachaspati, 113
Upadhye, A.N., 451, 493, 1848-1849, 2523, 2542-2543, 2657-2658
Upadhye, P.M., 1679, 1850
Upasak, C.S., 1816, 2659, 4265
Upreti, Jayadutt, 1555
Ursekar, H.S., 2761
Usha Dev, 1680

Vadnerkar, S.V., 4079
Vahiduddin, Syed, 2032
Vaidya, P.L., 1630
Vaidyanathan, S., 2466
Vajpeyi, Raghavendra, 1655
Valoch, Karel, 4442
Vanaja, R., 742
Van Buitenen, J.A.B., 1631
Van Naerssen, F.H., 4405
Varadachari, K.C., 2033, 2200-2204, 2719
Varadarajan, Lotika, 3990-3992
Varadaraja Rao, G., 925
Varenne, J., 1582
Varma, Birendra, 824
Varma, D.N., 390-391, 3672, 3901, 4080
Varma, Kailash Chandra, 595, 743, 1556, 4123
Varma, R.K., 2857
Varma, R.L. 3303
Varma, Siddheshwar, 2034, 2205, 2467
Varma, V.K., 1557
Varma, Vishwanath Prasad, 273, 744, 1817-1818, 2261
Vasantha, R., 926
Vasantharaj, M.D., 2544
Vashishtha, Neelima, 3629
Vasudeva Murthy, A.R., 297
Vatsyayan, Kapila, 334, 363, 1207, 3378-3380, 3964-3965, 4099
Ved Kumari, 878, 2660, 2720
Ved Vyas, 398, 596
Velankar, H.D., 1558-1559
Veluppillai, A., 3212
Venkatachalam, V., 2661
Venkatachala Sastry, T.V., 1851, 2332, 2524
Venkatacharya, T., 2468
Venkatakrishna Rao, U., 2662
Venkatarama Aiyar, T.L., 352
Venkataramanayya, N., 834, 927
Venkataramani, M.S., 825
Venkata Rao, Shivananda, 3194
Venkataratnam, A.V., 928
Venkatarayacharya, 300
Venkatarayacharya, S.K., 2663
Venkateswara Rao, K.V., 1051
Venkitasubramonia Iyer, S., 2339, 2469-2470, 2721
Verma, B.S., 3630, 3799, 3858
Verma, D.N., 4053
Verma, K.C., 1560
Verma, O.P., 745
Verma, S.K., 2035, 2320
Verma, T.P., 3213, 3536, 4304
Vidyalankar, Kailash Chandra, 1561
Vij, Brij Bhusan, 597
Vijayan, K., 2722
Vijayaraghavan, K.R., 4054
Vijaya Rani, 2262
Vijay Krishna, 3381, 3922
Viney Kumar, 1052
Vireswarananda, 2206

Vishnu-Mittre, 494
Vishva Bandhu, 208, 1339, 1562
Visswanathan, E.Sa., 1174
Viswanathan, K., 2492, 2762
Vittal, Rao, Y., 835
Vohra, Durga Devi, 446
Volchok, B., 564
Vora, P.R., 2471
Vorobyova-Desyatovskaya, M.I., 4446
Vyas, Mangilal, 3400
Vyas, N.J., 2036, 2270
Vyas, S.N., 1609

Wadia, A.R. 167
Wadiyar, Jayachamaraja, 94
Wakankar, V.S., 2926, 3382
Waldschmidt, Ernst, 1819
Wani, M.B., 2723
Warder, A.K., 1820
Warnekar, Shridhar Bhaskar, 2664
Waterhouse, David, 3673
Watwe, K.N., 2493
Wayman, Alex, 746, 1821-1822, 2207, 2263
Weedon, William S., 2037
Weiler, Royal W., 1823
Weiner, Sheila, 598
Welch, Stuart Cary, 3685
Werkmeisters, W.H., 2038
Wezler, A., 2208-2209
Wickramasuriya, Sarathchandra, 4343
Wijeskera, O.H. de A., 2353
Williams, Joanna, 3500, 3800
Wilson, J.V. Kinnier, 3214
Wodeyar, Sadashiva, 929
Wojtilla, Gy., 3982
Wolters, O.W., 4406
Woodward, Hiram W., Jr., 3883
Woolner, A.C., 1563
Wright, G.R.H., 3513
Wuerfel, Alfred, 136

Xinchuan, Huang, 4251

Yadava, B.N.S., 786
Yajnik, J.A., 2039
Yamunacharya, M., 95
Yash Pal, 2858, 3152
Yasoda Devi, V., 536-537
Yazdani, Ali, 461
Yazdani, Masood, 462
Yogendra, Jayadeva, 2040
Younger, Paul, 3514
Yudhistar Mimansak, 2210
Yun-Hua, Jan, 879, 4279
Yun-Shan, Tan, 2041, 4280
Yuyama, Akira, 1824-1826

Zaheer, S., Sajjad, 30
Zannas, Eliki, 186, 3474, 3674
Zebrowski, Mark, 3902
Zelinsky, A.N., 1827
Zelliot, Eleanor, 1828
Zide, Norman H., 2340, 4081
Zwilling, Leonard, 1829
Zysk, Kenneth G., 4147

KEY-WORD INDEX

Abaneri, 3584-3585
Abdali, Ahmad Shah, 824
Abdu'llah, Qutbshah, 1099
Abhasa, 2123
Abhayakaragupta, 1794
Abhidhamma, 2253
Abhidharma, 2228, 2251
Abhidharmakosa, 2225
Abhijnana-Sakuntala, 2730, 2739
Abhinavabharati, 2733
Abhinavagupta, 2607, 2619
Abri Zumoffen, 4427
Abu, 3390
Accounting, 1108
Achaemenid, 635
Acintya-bhedabheda, 2053
Aciravati, 474
Adamgarh, 2913
Adhyaraja, 2539
Adhyasa-bhasya, 1509
Adil Shahis, 914
Adipurana, 3968
Aditi, 3597
Adityas, 1355, 1525
Adiyaman, 3155
Administration, 735, 782, 985
Advaita, 1317, 2052, 2117-2118, 2152, 2156, 2163, 2167-2168, 2179, 2183, 2190, 2196
Advaitic, 2109, 2123, 3415
Advaitic ethics, 2103
Aesthetics, 1873, 1903, 1905, 2102, 2137, 2478, 3314, 3334, 3358, 3373
Afghanistan, 4420
Africa, 4123, 4182
Agam, 1258
Agamasastravivarana, 1571
Agamic, 2121
Agate, 1069
Agni, 1537, 4431
Agraharas, 916
Agrarian system, 921
Agriculture, 1055, 1080, 1089, 1096, 1112, 1148, 2785
Aguncha, 3850
Ahacca, 1850
Ahalaya, 1544, 1603
Ahar, 2955
Ahichchhatra, 3297
Ahimsa, 1890, 1928, 2017, 2270
Ahmadabad, 477, 2878, 3543, 3743
Ahmadnagar, 2941
Ahwal-i-Khawaqin, 773
Aihole, 3443, 3451, 3455, 3576, 3665, 3708
Ai-Khanum, 4261
Air, 1927
Aisvaryas, 1920
Ajanta, 3520, 3523, 3533, 3535, 3633, 4283
Ajatasatrvavadana, 4347
Ajay-Damodar Valley, 3005
Ajivika, 2293
Akasa, 1416
Akbar, 755, 766, 768, 3904, 3906, 3915
Akbar Nama, 747, 3920-3921
Akhyana, 1470
Aktha, 3747
Alchi, 3882
Ali-namah, 2506
Allahapur, 2979
Alnia, 3942
Alur, 3449
Allur, 3209
Alwars, 1210
Amarakosa, 4084
Amaravati, 3573, 3773
Amarja Valley, 2899
Amarsimha, 2369
Amaru Sataka, 3903
Amber, 4094
Ambhiyas, 1970
Ambika, 3817
America, 3877
Amir Khan, 971
Amit Ambalal, 3743
Amma I, 3158
Amoghapasa, 3660
Amrdanga-natakanka, 2752
Amrtkar, 2510
Amudanka-nadaa, 2752
Amusements, 701
Anahilavad Patan, 3159
Anandamath, 2498
Anantamukhanirharadharanitika, 1736
Anantapala, 887
Anantavarma, 3138
Anatmavada, 1788, 2261
Anattavada, 1790
Andhaka, 660
Andhra Pradesh, 1051, 1750, 3165, 3278-3279, 3285, 3598, 3654, 3757-3758
Anegondi, 3084
Anekarthakairavakarakaumudi, 2372
Angkor Vat, 4374-4375
Anguttara Nikaya, 1798
Anhilwad Patan, 2879
Animal sacrifice, 1219, 1680
Animals, 647, 2789, 2893, 2920, 4226
Anna-mantri, 3191
Annual Register, 818
Antelope, 3683

Antichak, 3630, 3799
Anumeya, 1950
Anviksiki, 2139
Apabhranshapuram, 1839
Apastamba, 1257
Apilaka, 3278-3279
Aprameya's Jayastambha, 3056
Aprapti, 1915
Apratigha, 3247
Apsaras, 1292
Apurab Singh, Raja, 3933
Arab, 1196, 3086, 4236
Arabic, 2315
Aramaic, 3095
Arang, 3112, 3128
Aranyani, 1363
Aravalli, 540
Aravanavatikal, 1753
Archives, 802
Ardhamagadhi, 2354
Ardhanarisvara, 3800
Argumentation, 2066
Arikamedu, 3081
Arikesari, 671
Ari Singh II, 3936
Aristas, 1919
Arjuna, 1889
Arkesvara temple, 3449
Art, 650, 1207, 1271, 1776, 1976, 2040, 2294, 4291, 4353, 4359, 4437
Arthasastra, 727, 1118, 1120, 1127, 1131-1132, 1134, 1141, 2136, 2564
Arti, 1558
Artisans, 1093, 3589
Artists, 3345-3346, 3442
Arunachal Pradesh, 3317, 3393, 3973
Arunagiri, 1235
Arvalem, 3427
Aryaka, 2759
Arya-Mahasamghika-Lokottaravadin, 1793
Aryamanjusrimulakalpa, 3216
Aryans, 592, 643, 647, 649, 738, 964, 1028, 1185, 2787, 2802, 2947, 4123, 4191
Aryavarta, 1222
Asanapat, 3726
Asanga, 1961, 2244, 2251
Asaval, 477
Ascaryacudamani, 2742, 2746
Ashmolean Museum, 3254
Ashraf, K.M., 868
Asia, 687, 1083, 1590, 1776, 2810, 2843, 3368
Asiatic Society Library, 2549
Asoka, 610-611, 666, 724, 746, 1000, 2354, 3007, 3012, 3080, 3085, 3095-3096, 3110, 3148, 3166, 3171
Assam, 1117, 1165, 1176, 2568, 3010, 3021, 3023, 3219, 3237, 3700, 3955, 3986
Assam State Museum, 3564-3565
Assamese, 1773
Assemblies, 1121
Assurance, 1111
Astadhyayi, 2383, 2421
Astamangala, 4329
Astasahasrika, 1789
Astrological, 912
Astronomical, 500
Astronomy, 2613, 3168
Asuvika, 2293
Asvaghosa, 2558
Asvalayana, 1343
Asvasena, 1834
Aswapati, 3117
Atharagarh, 956
Atharva Veda, 1121, 1348, 1376, 1379, 1396, 1398, 1402, 1407, 1409, 1429, 1476, 1487
Atidana, 1251
Atisa, 4345
Atitapas, 1251
Atiyajana, 1251
Atman, 2012
Atri, 1444
Attha, 1724
Attirala, 3420
Atudkhas, 2918
Aurangabad, 3642
Aurangzeb, 752, 772
Aurobindo, 82, 1879, 1899, 1934
Australia, 1175, 4123
Authority, 1987
Avadh School, 3881
Avalokitesvara, 3654, 3807
Avidheya, 3089-3090
Avikrita-parinamavada, 1948
Avikrta-parinama, 1442
Awliya, Shaykh Nizam al-Din, 758
Ayas, 1374, 1459
Ayodhya, 2981, 3395
Ayub, 804

Babur, 3033
Babylonian, 3207
Bachinagudda, 3456
Bactria, 3236, 4257, 4261
Badami, 3460, 3594
Badaraya, 1565
Badrayan, 2042
Badarayanekakrtaktava, 2043
Bagor, 2964

Bahawalpur, 4315
Bahur, 3194
Baijaladeva II, 855
Baijnath, 3740
Bailey, Harold, 1754
Bainduru, 3435
Bairam Khan, 780
Bairat Valley, 2967
Balädityas, 641
Balaghat, 3175
Balakesari, 3270
Balamukunda, 3718
Balapur, 3270-3271, 3276
Balarama, 3770
Balarjuna, 3124-3125
Bali, 1416, 4382, 4387-4390, 4394
Balia, 3486, 3492
Bali-devi, 3729
Balirajgarh, 2870
Ball-game, 1224
Baluchistan, 4305, 4311
Bamhani, 3176
Bamiyan, 4262
Bana Bhatta, 1074, 2637
Banaras *see* Varanasi
Banas, 3064
Banas Basin, 2961
Banasvasi, 3266
Banawali, 2884-2885
Bandhuvarman, 3186
Bank, 1112
Bankim Chandra, 2496, 2498
Bannu Valleys, 4310
Banswara, 3244
Bara Culture, 2949
Barahum, 1917
Baraipur, 3663
Barakuru, 3438
Baramasi, 2531
Barkachha, 2978
Barmurtiya-bil copper plate, 3108
Barque, 3410
Basava, 883
Basav Kalyan, 3032
Baudh, 3490
Bauls, 1239
Bayon, 4374
Beads, 3974
Beg, Asad, 764
Beg, Farrukh, 3916
Belan Valley, 2990
Belgaum, 2909
Bellary, 3625
Bengal, 810, 940, 1071, 1150, 1217, 1229, 1259, 1270, 1322, 1324, 1758, 1774, 2092, 3022, 3134, 3187, 3219, 3312, 3541, 3702, 3710, 3827, 3984, 4056, 4067, 4108
Bengali, 517-519, 1414
Bennur, 3623
Benzai-ten, 4282
Berlin, 2575, 3636, 3953, 3962
Berlin chandayan, 3958
Betel, 1340
Betwa, 3225
Bhadanakas, 708
Bhaddilapura, 471
Bhadralok, 1018
Bhagavadgita, 78
Bhagavan, 2046
Bhagavata Cult, 2102
Bhagavatapurana, 1659, 1676
Bhagavati, 3461
Bhairava, 3749-3750, 3772
Bhaja, 3561
Bhakti, 1288, 1310-1311, 1677, 2029, 2053, 2156, 2518-2519
Bhakti-cult, 1222
Bhakti movement, 1282
Bhamaha, 2236, 2425
Bhandarkar, D.R., 661
Bharat Kala Bhavan, Varanasi, 3093, 3348, 3558, 3577, 3645, 3697, 3706-3707, 3764, 3789, 3815, 3826, 3846, 3876, 3959, 3983, 3988, 4301
Bharata, 2595, 2599, 2724, 2741, 3780, 4090-4091, 4096, 4098
Bharata-Lakshmi, 4202
Bharatiya Kala Bhavan, Gaya, 3668
Bharatpur, 3828
Bharat Temple, 3571
Bharhut, 3148, 3532, 3644, 3664
Bhartrhari, 1366, 1903, 1941, 2077, 2416, 2460-2461, 2712
Bhartrmitra, 2670
Bhasa, 2600, 2656, 2732, 2754
Bhasa-yogavasisthasara, 2622
Bhashaparichheda, 1994
Bhaskaracharya, 469
Bhaskararaya, 2100-2101
Bhasma, 3216
Bhatgaon, 3660
Bhatheli, 841A
Bhatkal, 3440
Bhatta, Jayanta, 2621
Bhatta, Kaunda, 2417-2418
Bhatta Ranachoda, 969
Bhattacharyya, Kalidas, 1954
Bhauma, 3492
Bhavabhuti, 478, 2683

Bhavali Ramana Mukhyprana, 3623
Bhavanukirtanam, 4090
Bhavarman I, 4373
Bhava Somesvara, 3173
Bhiksu-pratimoksa-sutra, 1793
Bhima, 4391
Bhishma Chandra, 3062
Bhitari, 3019, 3131-3132
Bhoja, 2680, 2758, 3150, 3208
Bhojadeva, 3015
Bhojpur, 777
Bhubaneswar, 3482, 3485, 3489
Bhusundopakhyana, 1587
Bhutan, 790
Bhuvanekavira, 3248
Bhuvanesvara Mahadeva temple, 3486
Bible chapati, 803
Bihar, 468, 475, 1114, 1774, 3134, 3618, 3661, 3667, 3703, 3763, 3771, 3811, 3819, 3824-3825, 3835, 3896
Bijapur, 764, 914, 2907, 3902
Bikaner, 966, 3946
Bilichodu, 3624
Binjor, 2954
Biroba, 1326
Birudas, 689
Bodhayana, 2108
Bodhgaya, 3179, 3611
Bodhisattva, 1683, 1726, 1756, 1808, 1825, 3634, 3654
Bodo, 1176
Boehme, Jacob, 1937
Boghazkoi, 649
Bombay, 797, 941, 946, 1110, 3662
Boons, 1591
Borneo, 4197, 4380
Bradley, F.H., 1995, 2011
Brahma, 1213, 1259, 1577, 1668, 3414-3415, 3566, 3712
Brahmadeya, 978
Brahmadeyas, 999
Brahmadhiraja, 3100
Brahmagiri, 2903
Brahmanas, 1037, 1174, 1233, 1388, 1415, 1474-1475, 1525-1526, 1533, 1550, 1702, 1765, 2071, 4233, 4413, 4416
Brahmanayudu, 1298
Brahmanda purana, 4381
Brahmanical, 1014, 4290, 4359
Brahmanism, 4274
Brahmasiddhi, 2110
Brahmasutrakara, 1646
Brahma-sutras, 1285, 1500, 1517, 1565, 2043, 2162, 2206
Brahmavaad, 2196
Brahmendraswami, 820
Brahmi, 3120, 3128, 3136, 3163, 3180, 3195, 3199, 3201, 4260
Brahui, 2309
Brajanatha Simha, 846
Brandenburg, 4445
Brass, 3978
Brhadaranyaka Upanishad, 1573
Brhadarnyakopanisadbhasya, 2066
Brhaspati, 2369
Brhaspati smrti, 1489
Bridges, 3389
Brihadisvara temple, 3511
Brihatkathamanjari, 2653
Brihatsamhita, 3408, 4122
Brindavan, 3136
British, 794, 818, 821, 930, 1013, 1017, 1110-1111, 1116, 2302, 2497, 3859, 3861, 3975
British Baptist missionaries, 953
British Museum, 2537
Budget, 1077, 1105
Buddha, 87, 712, 1704, 1738, 1768, 1771, 1795, 1805, 2996, 3631, 3642, 3646, 3648-3650, 3652, 3659, 3805, 3808-3810, 3812-3813, 3995, 4334, 4336, 4431, 4433
Buddhaghosha, 1752
Budha Gupta, 606
Buddhasena, 3179
Buddhavacana, 1968
Buddha-yana, 1780
Buddhism, 640, 1192, 1334, 2068, 2150, 2985, 4269, 4279, 4296, 4344, 4350
Buddhist, 13, 633, 1181, 1202, 1589, 2267, 2347, 3253, 4147, 4245, 4256, 4276, 4290-4291, 4428, 4437-4438
Bundelkhand, 3471, 3797
Bundi, 3950
Burj, 2945
Burma, 3883, 4354, 4411
Burton, Major, 963
Byzantine, 3264, 4221

Cahamana, 3723
Caitya, 652, 1729
Capitalism, 796
Calcutta, 3544
Cambay, 1069
Cambodia, 670, 4189, 4233, 4354
Campa, 4196
Campbellpur, 3024
Canakya, 1607
Candagavejjhaya, 2563
Candarosana, 4297

Candellas, 706, 1004
Candesvara, 767
Candi, 1291
Candra, King, 3145
Candragomin, 1808
Candragupta, 3280
Candragupta Vikramaditya, 2757
Capitalist Class, 791-792
Caraka Samhita, 4143
Cartridge, 803
Carudattam, 2726
Castes, 952, 1022, 1040, 1167
Cattle, 572
Caturbhani, 2611
Causality, 2011, 2052
Caves, 3391, 3403, 3427, 3479, 3501, 3508, 3522, 3529, 3533, 3535, 3599, 3642, 3662
Cedi, 3114
Central Asia, 1089, 1796, 4180, 4185, 4190, 4245
Central Museum, Indore, 3030
Ceramic, 2840
Ceylon *see* Sri-Lanka
Chahamana, 3287
Chaitanya, 1259, 2002, 4292
Chakmas, 1695
Chakra, 3325
Chakrasvami, 3732
Chalukyas, 670, 691, 829, 893, 903, 3063, 3422, 3437, 3446, 3448, 3456, 3460, 3476, 3594, 3609
Chamargora, 3003
Chamba, 870
Chamber tomb, 2907
Champaner, 2880
Champawat copper plate, 3061
Chanda, 3735
Chandala hill, 3199
Chandella, 3016
Chandogya Upanisad, 1565, 1576
Chandrabhaga, 3496
Chandra Bhan, 2538
Chandragupta IV, 3220
Chandravati, 2970, 3390
Chaopha Su-hum-mung, 836
Char Chaman, 2538
Char-choma, 3500
Chatera, Ramjidas, 3939
Chaturddanta, 3204
Chatvarimsa Brahmana, 1521
Chaudadanapura, 3099
Chauhan, 855
Chaurashi, 3483
Chaurpanchasika, 3963
Chen wei Shih lun, 1915
Chidambaram, 3699
Chieh-shen-mi-ching-Shu, 2229
Chhatrapatis, 945
Chhatra Shah, 3151
Chhattisgarh, 934, 3120
Chilas, 559
Chimakurti Hills, 3654
China, 648, 1688, 1740, 1742, 1774, 2041, 2226, 2239, 4204-4205, 4217, 4245, 4251
Chinchani plates, 3086
Chingleput, 4003
Chintalapalem, 2864
Chirki, 2928
Chirwa, 3202
Chitrameli, 1076
Chittor, 3344
Chittorgarh, 3197, 3779
Cholas, 648, 989, 994, 1079, 1312, 3113, 3419, 3502, 3570, 3581, 3601, 4003, 4327
Chorapura, 3469
Chos-Grub, 2229
Chota-Nagpur, 853
Christ, 84
Christian, 1202
Christian missions, 4323
Christianity, 1179, 1943
Chrit, 861
Chronology, 500, 598, 604, 615, 937, 957
Church, 3410
Citrabhanu, 4128
Citragupta, 3728
Coiffure, 1047
Coins, 3076, 4352
Colonialism, 796
Colvin, Auckland, 812
Communalism, 1963
Confederacy, 919
Confucius, 86
Congress, 812, 817
Consciousness, 1945
Coomaraswamy, A.K., 210, 798, 1193, 1873, 2569, 3249, 3310, 3314-3315, 3318-3319, 3353, 3358, 3394, 3553, 3637, 3688, 3864, 3871, 3910, 3948, 4318
Coopertive movement, 1114
Coorg, 898
Coromandel, 607
Coronation, 612
Cornucopia, 3364
Corruption, 1085-1086
Corvee, 1101
Cosmogony, 1518
Council of Ministers, 880
Cow and Calf, 3682
Crafts, 1667
Credit, 1053, 1059

Credit laws, 1059
Criminal law, 1350
Cuddapah basin, 2865
Curses, 1591
Cust, Robert Needham, 2340
Cyavana, 1352
Cyrus, 618

Dacca, 4266
Dadu Dayal, 1282
Dahala, 933
Daimabad, 585, 2936-2938, 3288, 3606
Daksina, 1491
Daksinamurti stotra, 2119
Dalavaipuram plates, 3135
Damoh, 3029
Dana, 664, 1248
Dance, 4057, 4080, 4097
Danda, 1037
Dandin, 2567, 2765
Danseuses, 1253
Dantidurga, 3181
Dantura, 2322
Darbhanga, 859
Darora, 3239
Darra, 3495
Dasakumaracarita, 2765
Dasapura, 3185
Dasarupa, 2669
Dasas, 3167
Dashrooplaksana, 2718
Dasopanta, 2590
Daspur, 2926
Daughter-in-law, 1395
Davis Samuel, 4117
Daulatabad, 3035, 3479
Death, 2032
Deccan, 764, 778, 1730, 2281, 2937
Deer, 2671A
Deity, 1231, 1261, 1837
Delhi, 3389, 3545
Demetrius II, 3236
Democracy, 1125,2030
Deogarh, 3562, 3693, 3945
Dependency, 799
Desais, Lakshmeshwar, 938-939
Desar, 3431
Devadasi, 1052
Devagiri, 479, 763
Devala, 1248, 1919, 4140
Devaladharmasutra, 1426, 1920
Devapala, 620
Devapi, 1494
Devaraja cult, 4378
Devasena, 3069, 3178
Devi, 3694
Devimahatmya, 3960
Devipurana, 1671
Dhammapada, 1715, 2215
Dhangar god, 1326
Dharawat, 3531
Dharma, 1136, 2013, 2075
Dharmadasa, 2620
Dharmakirti, 1766
Dharmamitra, 1794
Dharmapadas, 1769
Dharmaraja Ratha, 3786
Dharmasastra, 727, 1477, 1507, 1529, 1666, 2136, 3027
Dharmasutras, 1040
Dharma Thakur, 1223
Dharwar, 881
Dhaulagiri, 4298
Dhenkanal, 3487
Dhola-maru, 3954
Dhruvadevi, 685
Dhule, 580
Dhulia, 2939
Dhvaja, 651
Dhvani, 1903
Dhvanyaloka, 2541
Digambaranucara, 2590
Dignaga, 2250
Digvijaya, 658
Dijjinnavisaya, 3023
Diksita, Appayya, 2638
Dilwara Jaina temples, 3539
Dinnaga, 1710, 1950
Diplomacy, 799
Dirghatamas, 1522
Dive-Agar, 3156
Diwan-e-Mubadi, 1191
Dohada, 1043
Domeli, 2948
Donors, 989
Dramidacarya, 2108
Dravidanatha, 620
Dravidian, 900, 2298, 2345, 2473
Dravya, 2090
Dream, 1782
Dream-consciousness, 1188
Drsti, 1739
Duhkha, 2060, 2215
Dukhvada, 2122
Durga, 1247, 3754, 3783, 3785
Durgacharya, 1496
Durga Path, 3938
Durga temple, 3456

Durkheim, Emile, 1168
Durvinita, 3156
Dvadasaha, 1451
Dvaidhibhava, 1120
Dvaita, 2093, 2149, 2176

Earth, 1927
Earthquakes, 845
East India Company, 818, 824, 941, 4445
East Nimar, 2918
Economy, 1033
Education, 841, 1013, 1492, 1579, 2065
Eilenberg, Samuel, 3818
Ekayana, 1751, 1794
Elephant, 741, 3838
Elephant Corps, 973
Elephanta, 3724
Ellora, 3181, 3476, 3478, 3480, 3599
Embroidery, 3984
Emotion, 2040
Employee, 1081
Employer, 1081
Engineering, 774, 783
England, 3988
Epic, 4241
Epigraphy, 404, 517, 522, 531, 536, 650, 664, 739, 742, 2479, 4233
Error, 2077, 2231
Ethical, 1940, 1981
Ethics, 1912
Europe, 1992, 2712, 2843
European, 693, 1007, 1167, 1338, 3347, 3908-3909, 3915, 3918
Euthydemus II, 3236
Evil, 1913
Existentialism, 1992
Export, 1094

Faith, 1913, 1946
Famine, 857, 965, 1100
Farrukh Chela, 3906
Fatehpur, 3517
Fawcett, Henry, 814
Feasts, 1230
Female names, 1169
Feudalism, 623-624, 657, 711, 756, 1050, 1820
Fire, 1927
Folk, 2497
Folk art, 1325, 3312
Folk-cult, 1273
Folk-custom, 1043
Folklore, 905, 1454, 2551
Folktales, 842, 2485
Folk-traditions, 1383
Foreign influence, 1194
Foreign relations, 799
Foreign trade, 1075
Fortification, 734
Forts, 3393
Fortunatov, 2281
Frederic, Caesar, 907
Freedom, 811, 823, 1939, 1945, 1966, 1988
French, 779
Fyzabad, 3697

Gachtal, 3183
Gadag region, 2891
Gajalakshmi, 3795
Gajendramoksa, 3787
Galagnatha, 3436
Galaganatha temple, 3455
Gamal, 4310
Ganapati, 1238
Ganapati cult, 1293
Ganas, 3752, 3774
Gandaraditta, 1211
Gandhara, 3554, 3640, 3645, 3647, 3651, 3653, 3658, 3674
Gandharvas, 1292
Gandhi, M.K., 79, 825, 1130, 1909, 1964, 2516, 4100
Gandhi-stotra-gatha, 2558
Ganesa, 1293, 1313, 1329, 3719-3720, 3756, 3763, 3793, 4198, 4434
Ganeshwar, 2950
Ganeswarpur, 3488
Ganga, 692, 1332, 1843, 3156, 3721
Ganga Basin, 1980
Ganga period, 1080
Gangas, 3064, 3453
Ganga Valley, 2817, 2826, 2844, 2994, 3832, 3837, 3844
Ganga-Yamuna doab, 2794
Gangetic-Basin, 675
Gangetic Valley, 590, 3367
Gangoly, O.C., 4069
Ganitapancavimsi, 4132
Ganjam, 1160
Garbhadhatu Mandala, 1761
Garhwal, 2991, 3927
Garlic, 4135
Garo hills, 2847
Garta, 1384
Garuda, 1168
Garudapurana, 1634
Garuda upanisad, 1582

Gathasaptasati, 1026
Gauri, 1341
Gauriya Samaj, 1018
Gaudavaho, 2541
Gautamiputra Satakarni, 622
Gavampati, 4361
Gaya, 491, 2872, 3303, 3531, 3563, 3592
Gaya trial, 823
Genealogy, 604, 659, 913, 939, 957
Geography, 1030
German, 1983, 2389, 4208
Gharapuri, 3724-3725
Gharma, 1558
Ghatika, 977
Ghaznavi, Mahmud, 709
Gift, 1671
Gigantopithecus, 2848
Gilgit, 1796
Gita-Govinda, 2703, 3952, 3964-3965
Gladstone, 814
Goa, 802, 3391, 4171
Goa Museum, 3755
God, 1534, 1550, 1958, 1977, 2096, 2188, 2203, 2260
Godana, 1417
Godavari, 3225
Goddesses, 1207
Golaki Matha, 3203
Gold, 1056, 1078
Golkonda, 3899
Gopaladaraka, 2759
Gopas, 1639
Gopis, 1639
Gorakhnath, 69
Goravas, 1308
Gotra, 1794
Gotra-bhumi, 2006
Gotra system, 1162
Govardhana, 1001
Government Museum, Madras, 4025
Govindabhisheka, 1660
Gour Archaeological Museum, 4051
Gramani, 1781
Grammar, 1878
Grassmann, Hermann, 1433
Greece, 2763, 4211-4212
Greek, 186, 638, 678, 1338, 2456-3457, 3007, 3095, 4261
Grihya sutras, 1514
Grtsamada-suktas, 1495
Gudimallam linga, 3608
Gudnapur, 3046, 3189
Guenther, H.V., 2089
Guhyas, 3774
Guilds, 735, 830, 1070, 3059
Guimet Museum, Paris, 3822
Gujarat, 520, 574, 587, 2536, 3159, 3547, 3607, 3736, 3843, 3874, 3995
Gujjar, 1173
Gulbarga, 2899
Gulgaon, 3604
Gulistan, 3961
Guna, 3472
Gunavratti, 1536
Guntur, 3838
Guptas, 9, 606, 609, 616, 619, 626, 641, 661, 673, 696, 705, 720, 725, 1066, 2097, 3019, 3088, 3131, 3145, 3186, 3216, 3220, 3228, 3258, 3280, 3293, 3401, 3495, 3500, 3517, 3559, 3563, 3574, 3579, 3622, 3663, 3857, 4260, 4287
Gurjara-Pratihara, 3150
Gurucarita, 1773
Guru Nanak, 4207
Gurusamhita, 2581-2582
Gurzala, 3838
Guttikonda, 3838
Gwalior, 3033, 3150, 3467
Gyaraspur, 3525

Haihaya, 3114, 3272, 3275, 3277
Hala, 1026
Halebid, 3067
Halebidu, 3596
Haleri Rajahs, 898
Halhed, 2302
Hampi, 473, 894, 3037, 3609
Hamsa Vidya, 1516
Han dynasty, 4226
Hansi, 2883
Hanumana, 3273
Haraha, 3177
Haramekhala, 2543
Harappa, 538-539, 541-542, 544, 551, 553-555, 557, 561, 563-566, 569-570, 572, 574-580, 583-585, 587-588, 590-593, 596, 1290, 2797, 2954, 3079, 3301, 4310-4311, 4315
Harasur, 3537
Haribhadra, 1736
Haricaritra, 2515
Harichandra, 2565
Haridasas, 1262, 2019
Hari-Hara, 1760, 3714, 3724, 3767, 4372
Harisena, 679, 725, 3091
Harisvami, 1560, 2612
Hariti, 1750
Harivamsa, 1625
Harivamsa purana, 3540
Harivrddha, 2539

Harsa, 628, 640, 2688, 2727
Harsacarita, 728
Haryana, 1320, 3731, 3851-3852
Hastinapur, 2982, 3836
Hayasirsa Pancaratra, 3404
Heart sutra, 1821
Heidegger, Martin, 1992
Hellas, 4201
Hellemistic, 633, 635
Hemadpanti temples, 3475
Hemadri, 745, 2518, 2685
Himachal Pradesh, 3976
Himalayan, 465, 559, 807, 2991
Hindi, 375
Hindu, 744, 952, 1147, 1149, 1169, 1837, 4125, 4190, 4241, 4255, 4363, 4405, 4408, 4414, 4429, 4432
Hindu-Muslim, 813
Hinduism, 4251, 4340, 4382, 4386
Hir and Ranjha, 2525
Hirapura, 3692
Hisse-Borala, 3069, 3178
Historiography, 851, 1006, 1011, 1329, 1723, 2301
Hitopadesa, 2764
Hiuen-Tsang, 695, 705
Honey, 1062
Horoscope, 609
Horse, 1626, 3838
Horyuji, 4283, 4287
Hoysala, 911, 921, 2511, 3356, 3454, 3600
Hsuan-Tsang, 1733, 1915
Hua-Yen, 2226
Hui Ch'ao's, 879
Humanism, 1283
Human rights, 1136
Human sacrifice, 838, 1160, 1680
Human values, 1314
Hume, 1980
Huna, 675, 731-732
Hungund, 3457
Huvinahadagali, 3718
Hyderabad, 826, 835, 3899, 3975

I-Ching, 4204
Iconography, 4085, 4290, 4438
Idealism, 1983
Idol worship, 1208
Ikkeri, 898
Imbroglio, 819
Immediacy, 1995
Immortality, 1929
Imperialism, 791, 1013
Inamgaon, 2930, 3691
Incarnation, 1197
Inclination, 1971
Indian History Congress, 25
Indian Museum, 3263
Indigo, 1096
Indo-Aryan, 649, 964, 1185, 2308, 2454, 2798, 4440
Indo-Caspian, 1185
Indo-China, 793, 819, 1231
Indo-European, 1338, 2453
Indo-Greek, 678, 3250
Indo-Hellenistic, 739
Indo-Muslim, 778
Indo-Pakistan, 801
Indo-Persian, 2505
Indo-Tibetan, 2328
Indologists, 743
Indonesia, 1231, 4231
Indore, 3030
Indra, 1356, 1364, 1440, 1461, 1603, 1704
Indra-Dhvaja, 651
Indrajit-kavya, 2678
Indrapur, 3092
Induraja, 2387
Indus, 4419, 4421
Indus script, 3133, 3146
Indus seal, 3160, 3290
Indus Valley, 618, 1429, 3068
Inscriptions, 404, 486, 489, 521, 529, 559, 564, 827, 841, 870, 1792, 1796, 4000, 4260, 4263, 4304, 4327, 4354, 4373, 4379, 4418
Institutions, 744
Insurance, 1095
Intelligence system, 771
Internationalism, 806
Intuition, 1953
Irrigation, 889, 1117
Isanamangalam, 3209
Isanavarman, 3177
Islam, 1202, 1274, 1862, 4401
Isopanisad, 1567-1568
Isvara, 2072, 2180, 2191
Isvaradatta, 3241
Isvaradvavaad, 2196
Isvara Krsna, 2204
Isvara-pranidhana, 2059
Isvaravaad, 2148
I-Tsing, 2235
Ittagi, 3447
Ivory, 3643, 3972

Jacobi, Professor, 1368
Jagadisa, 2435
Jagannatha, 1228, 1281, 2587, 2715
Jagannath culture, 1272

Jagannath temple, 3926
Jagat Singh, 3937
Jagat Singh II, Rana, 3936
Jahangir, 3914, 3918-3919
Jaimini, 2075
Jaiminiya Brahmana, 1361-1362, 1499
Jaina, 630, 1202, 1589, 2230, 2706, 3001, 3055, 3180, 3839, 4063
Jainism, 1192, 1264
Jaipur, 3591-3592, 3939, 4094
Jaipurgarh, 3656
Jaipur School, 3938
Jaisalmer, 3009, 3169
Jai Singh, 968, 3388
Jajmani system, 1321
Jakarta, 4395
Jalalladeva, 3273
Jalasangvi, 3620
Jalgaon, 2927
Jami Masjid, 3430
Jangambadi, 3303
Japa, 2144
Japan, 1786, 4205, 4218, 4246
Jara, 1406
Jat, 1184
Jata-choda Bhima, 3161, 3164
Jataka, 3680
Jatara, 3200
Jati, 1426, 1529, 2051
Jaunpur, 3963
Java, 4381, 4383-4385, 4388-4389, 4392, 4399-4400, 4404-4405
Javadekar, A.G., 2039
Jayantabhatta, 2138
Jayantia, 3234
Jayaraja, 3115
Jayaraksita, 1715
Jayasekhara, 2628
Jayati, 3416
Jewellery, 3600, 3977
Jhukar pottery, 2825
Jibanananda, 2500
Jinendrabuddhi, 1807
Jivadaman, 3292
Jivagosvamin, 2188
Jivaka, 1738
Jivakartrtva, 2132
Jnanagarbha, 1736
Jnanasrimitra, 1806
Jogeswar, 3515
Jogeswari, 3724
Jonai, 840
Jonaraja, 871
Jordan, 4426
Jorwe Culture, 2931, 2936
Junagarh, 3152
Junnar, 3043, 3300
Justice, 637, 1124
Jyotisa-ratna-mala, 4118

Kabir,2519
Kabul, 603
Kachchhapaghat, 936
Kadamba, 692, 3046, 3049, 3147, 3682
Kadavas, 986
Kaifiyats, 925
Kailasa, 3481
Kailasa temple, 3476
Kakanada, 633
Kakrahta, 2922, 3845
Kalachurya Bijjala, 3067
Kalacuri, 353, 617, 718
Kaladgi, 2907
Kalamukha, 1269, 1287
Kalanjara Fort, 1004
Kalantaka myth, 1319
Kalapriyanatha, 1278
Kalhana, 874
Kali, 1217, 1322
Kali age, 1046
Kalibangan, 2959, 2968, 3290
Kalidasa, 479, 2085, 2550, 2553, 2559, 2566, 2573, 2579, 2583, 2586, 2589, 2611, 2613, 2619, 2628-2629, 2631, 2636, 2644-2645, 2652, 2679, 2686, 2713, 2724, 2736, 2757, 2911, 3725
Kalighata, 1212
Kalika purana, 1680, 3700
Kalingas, 3130
Kalinjar, 3628
Kaliya-daman, 3878
Kaliya mardana Krishna, 3760
Kaliyur, 3056
Kalpasutra, 1556, 3963
Kalyana Chandra, 3061
Kamadeva, 3618
Kamandaka, 1123-1124
Kamandakiya, 631
Kamandakiya-nitisar, 2647
Kamarupa, 2118, 3259
Kamarupa Anusandhan Samiti, 122
Kamarupa School, 2373
Kambalapada, 1801
Kambar, 2769
Kamboja, 1021
Kambuja, 990, 3167
Kammalas, 3027
Kampannas, 3038

Kamran, Mirza, 3919
Kanada, 2819
Kanakadurga-Mallesvara temple, 3139
Kanakesvara temple, 3487
Kanchi, 657, 977
Kanchipuram, 3161, 3504, 3509
Kandahar, 3096
Kandalisvara temple, 4003
Kandava, 3622
Kangra, 3008
Kangra Valley, 2889
Kanheri, 2935, 3662
Kaniska, 3207
Kanittha Tissa, 4332
Kanjuruha, 4398
Kannada, 516, 525, 925, 3070, 3103, 4152
Kansuan, 3496
Kant, 1957
Kantalai, 4327
Kantalingesvara temple, 4003
Kanti, 1689
Kanyadana, 3074
Kanyakubja, 3302
Kanyakumari, 3398
Kapalle, 3070
Kapilavastu, 2997, 3855
Kapil-Dhara, 2966
Kapilesvara temple, 3516
Kapotika, 3399
Kapur Singh, 3934
Karanavaisnava, 2615
Karandavyuha, 3895
Kariristi, 1554
Karma, 1260, 1279, 1718
Karma-mimamsa, 2112
Karman, 1557
Karna, 1610
Karnataka, 83, 93, 521, 754, 1079, 1110, 1187, 1283, 1308, 1838, 2154, 2544, 3053, 3065, 3171, 3222, 3264-3265, 3267, 3351, 3387, 3566, 3744, 3793, 3980, 4072-4073, 4078
Karnavati, 477
Karpuramanjari, 2728
Karuna, 1780
Karuppu, 1299
Kashmir, 703, 2172, 2174, 3299, 3643, 3992
Kashmir Saivism, 1306
Kathasaritsagara, 1678, 4089
Kathaupanisad, 1570
Katra, 2871
Katyayana Smrti, 1489
Kausambi, 1000
Kautilya, 679, 1067, 1118, 1120, 1126-1127, 1129, 1131, 1140-1141, 2564
Kaveri Basin, 3508
Kaveripakkam, 3034
Kaveri Valley, 2896
Kavyalamkarasutravrtti, 2438
Kayasthas, 1154
Keesaragutta, 3421
Kehar Singh, 3934
Keladi, 918, 3052
Kerala, 439, 1156, 1841, 2700, 2717, 2746, 2976, 4120
Kerehalli, 3283
Keshub, 1259
Khajuraho, 3462, 3464, 3568
Khalji, Ala-ud-Din, 763
Khalji, Ghiyathu'd-Din, 3030
Khandavalas, 859
Khandoba myth, 1325
Khanti, 1689
Kharosthi, 4181, 4308
Khasas, 1002
Khataoli, 2887
Kheda, 574
Khilji, 3169
Khmer, 4376
Khotan, 4430
Khotanese, 1720, 1754
Khuda Bakhsh Library, 1191
Khusro, Amir, 2277
Khusrau, Amir, 750
Khusraw, Amir, 4055
Khusraw, Mir, 3917, 3919
Kikkuli, 649
King, 1037
Kinjar, 3298
Kinnara-Kinnari, 3705
Kiratarjuniya, 3595-3596
Kirticandrodaya-kavya, 2591
Kirtimukha, 3320
Kirttistambha-prasati, 3105
Kisan Bilas, 2966
Kittur Museum, 3616
Kivulekada, 4329
Knowledge, 1972, 2171
Kodaikanal, 2971
Kolhapur, 944-945
Kolhua, 3835
Kondapur, 3840
Kongu, 908, 3064, 3157
Konidena, 3191
Korea, 4224
Kosala, 485, 605, 1596, 3113, 3118, 3589
Kosam, 3041
Kosambi, D.D., 1050
Kota, 2966, 3937, 3947
Krama, 1399

Kratu, 1463
Krishna, 1214, 1227, 1246, 1249, 1269, 1288, 1294, 1614, 1639, 1660, 3506, 3737, 3760
Krishna basin, 2829
Krishna Cult, 1245
Krishnapatnam, 3419
Krishna Valley, 2905
Kriyakalpa, 2702
Kroeber, 1866
Krsnananda Vagisa, 1221
Ksanti, 1689
Kosalananda kavyam, 2697
Ksetrajna, 1548
Kshatrapa, 645, 3292
Kshemendra, 2653, 2660
Kshetrapala, 3768
Kualo, 3487
Kuan-wu-liang-Shou Foching, 1778
Kubera, 2554, 3698, 3775
Kudarkot, 3205
Kudumiyamalai, 3075
Kujula Katphisa, 3013
Kukarramath, 3473
Kulakundalini, 2049
Kulinism, 1324
Kumaon, 1003, 3062, 3516
Kumaradevi, 3280
Kumaragupta, 3088, 3186, 3293
Kumaramatya, 3302
Kumaravarman, 3185
Kumaun, 3741
Kumaun Hills, 3740
Kumbhakara, 3297
Kumbhakarna Virdauli, 2512
Kumbhaswamin-Alaya, 3105
Kundakunda, 1851
Kundalini, 3597
Kundalini-yoga, 2142
Kundamala, 2744-2745
Kuntaka, 2695
Kuntapa, 1385
Kura, 3283
Kural, 2772
Kurukshetra, 1613, 2886
Kusananula, 3044
Kushanas, 645, 668-669, 687, 2890, 3024, 3163, 3233, 3245, 3333, 3350, 3561, 3646, 3658, 3739, 3813, 3844, 4308
Kustarajagala image, 4335
Kutch, 591
Kutsana, 1613
Kutsa Trita Aptya, 3282
Kuvalayamala, 2542, 2657
Labour, 1066, 1102
Laddigam, 3155
Ladkhan temple, 3111
Ladnun, 3031, 3054
Laghusabdaratna, 2367
Laghu yogavasistha, 2701
Lahore, 3918, 3857
Lajja, 3727
Lakshmana samvat, 848
Lakshmanasingh, 3244
Lakshminarayana temple, 3441
Lakshmipur, 3066
Lakshmi-Vidambanam, 2545
Laksmi, 3790
Lakulisa, 3751, 3773, 3779
Lala Bhagat pillar, 3593
Lalitaditya Muktapida, 644
Lalitasahasranamabhasya, 2100
Lampsacos Dish, 1058
Land, 996, 1071, 1092
Land-grants, 609
Land settlements, 1116
Landscape art, 1776
Landseer, George, 3860
Language, 2010, 2246
Lanka, 1593
Lankavatara sutra, 1779
Lankesvara Deva, 4327
Landscape, 2594
Laos, 2533, 4219
Latin, 3007
Laur-chanda, 3953, 3957, 3962
Law, 1124, 1137, 1143, 1303
Lepakshi, 831
Liberation, 822, 1872, 2181-2182
Lichchhavis, 4304
Life, 2026
Linga, 3740, 3773, 3777, 3800
Lihinimalai, 4332
Likhanavali, 1034
Lingaraja temple, 3492
Linguistic, 2105
Lion, 3685
Local government, 1142
Lodhia, 3119
Logic, 1985, 2099
Lohanipur, 3679
Lokayatikas, 1779
Lokesvara, 1760
Lokopakara, 3392
Lonad, 3522
Lothal, 2876, 2882
Lotus sutra, 1825

Lucknow Museum, 3798

Maccocalingae, 1182
Machenes, 3295
Machiavelli, 1140
Mackenzie, 808
Madanamanchuka, 3854
Madan Mohan temple, 3136
Madanapala, 2667
Madanavarman, 3016
Madhava, 1400
Madavarman I, 828
Madhava Vidyaranya, 2596
Madhubani, 3898
Madhuravijaya, 2673
Madhva, 1283, 2001
Madhvacarya, 1621, 1864
Madhyamagama, 1688
Madhyamika, 1731, 1804, 2224, 2251
Madhyantanugamasastra, 1961
Madhya Pradesh, 3029
Madhyodesa, 702
Madras, 987, 1169, 2972
Madras Government Museum, 3289
Madras University, 4106
Madura, 3256
Madurai, 984, 998
Magadha, 3017
Magadhisms, 2351
Magha, 2635, 2707
Mahabharata, 490, 1029, 2554, 2590, 2676, 2806, 2982, 3309, 3709
Mahabhasya, 1208
Mahabodhi temple, 3656
Mahad Chaitya I, 3524
Mahadeva, 3045, 3221
Mahadeva temple, 3447
Mahakosala, 483-484, 486, 934-935, 3120-3121, 3272-3273, 3275, 3277
Mahaksatrapa, 3300
Mahakuta, 3616
Mahanandi, 484
Mahanadi Basin, 2914
Mahaprajnaparamitasutra, 1684
Mahapuran, 1839, 2459
Maharaja Sawai Man Singh II Museum, Jaipur, 4019
Maharashtra, 532, 580, 1158, 1181, 1187, 1326, 2590, 2614, 3082, 3735, 4173
Maharavala, 3244
Mahasivagupta I, 948
Maha-Sudevaraja, 3112
Mahasukha, 2213
Mahavagga, 1773
Mahavamsa, 4331
Mahavastu-Avadana, 1694
Mahavira, 76, 3966
Mahayana, 1698, 1700, 1740, 1744, 1789, 1820, 2243, 4325
Mahayogi, 3725
Mahendra, 2372, 3098
Mahinda, 1763
Mahisasuramardini, 3713, 3715, 3733, 3742, 3778, 3785, 4267
Mahishmati, 2917
Mahmud Begada, 865
Mahorana, 2949
Mainamati, 3187
Maine, Henry, 4338
Maithial, 860
Maithila smrti, 1414
Maithili, 2509
Maithuna-Virati, 1714
Makaras, 3684
Maktab Khana, 781
Malaya, 4197
Malayalam, 528, 530-531
Mallar, 3122, 3125, 3176
Mallari myth, 1325
Mallikarjuna, 3580
Mallinatha, 2552, 2699
Maluti, 3424, 3858
Malwa, 715, 866, 2912, 2925, 2932, 3030, 3260, 3500
Mamallapuram, 3582-3583
Manahali copper-plate grant, 2667
Manasa, 3321
Manasollasa, 2119, 4074
Manava-dharmasastra, 1542
Mandala, 1727
Mandana, 1567, 2064, 2106, 2110, 2646
Mandasor, 3775
Mandelbaum, 1894
Mandi School, 3946
Mandu, 3963
Mandukyopanisad, 1571
Mandya, 1843
Manegaon, 2927
Mangala-symbols, 1792
Mangalesa, 3048
Mangulam, 3201
Manickavasagar, 92
Manipur, 3243
Manipura-purana, 1657
Mankani, 3432
Mankot, 3933
Mantra, 1540, 1996, 2158
Mantrarthamukramani, 1400
Manu, 1122, 1250, 1393, 1548

Manusmrti, 1350, 1662, 4248
Manyakheta, 910
Maratha, 527, 753, 800, 938, 982, 1098, 1101, 4172, 4179
Marathi, 522, 527
Maratipalem, 2864
Maritime, 1072
Markanda, 3735
Marketing organisation, 1097
Marriage, 1025, 1045, 1147, 1161, 1172, 1503
Marutura, 3162
Marx, 1033
Marxian, 1113
Marxist, 502, 1899, 2016
Masala, 942
Masilamanesvarar temple, 3505
Masks, 3337
Matak, 3237
Materialism, 2027
Mathura, 1001, 2985, 3057, 3172, 3180, 3284, 3333, 3371, 3615, 3641, 3658, 3668, 3789
Mathura Museum, 3796, 4048
Matli, 834
Matrka, 3693, 3708, 3766
Matsya-purana, 1664
Matter, 2067
Matvan plates, 3042
Maves, 3295
Mauryas, 615, 632, 635, 666, 677, 701, 703, 721, 724, 739, 741, 746, 1066, 3350, 3578, 3832, 3856
Maya, 2152, 2165
Mayakonda, 782A
Mayavada, 2044
Measurement, 1071
Measures, 897
Meat-eating, 1709, 2247
Medhatithi, 1492
Megasthenes, 639
Meghaduta, 479, 2559, 2674, 2679, 2689, 2694, 2704-2706, 2709, 2724
Mehrauli iron pillar, 3014, 3145
Mehta, N.C., 3946
Mekala, 716
Meluhha, 599
Memorial stones, 3351
Memory, 2001
Menal, 3173-3174, 3698
Menander, 3040
Merchants, 830, 1091, 1093
Merutungacharya, 2879
Mesopotamia, 2763
Metallurgy, 1064
Metta, 1800
Mewar, 2965, 3935-3936
Mewat, 868
Mexico, 2415
Middle East, 4207
Midnapur, 3003
Milinda-panha, 1782
Milindapanha-atthkatha, 1717
Military, 783, 972
Milk, 1538
Mill, James, 924
Mimamsa, 1442, 1491, 1507, 2075, 2086, 2105, 2112, 2158, 2191
Mimamsakas, 1977
Mina and Lurka, 2505
Mind, 1420, 2177
Mining, 1064
Miran, 4433
Miris, 842
Mir Jumla, 927
Mirzapur, 3879
Mishra, L.N., 4104
Miskin, 3904
Misra, Mandana, 2115
Misra, Vacaspati, 1911, 2186, 2195, 2255
Missionaries, 2480
Mithila, 852, 858-859, 1161, 1324, 2081, 3588
Mithras, 3776
Mitra, 742
Mlechchas, 704
Modi, 939
Moggaliputta, 746
Mohajamata temple, 3468
Mohen-jo-daro, 548-549, 554, 558, 562, 571, 581, 1429
Mohils, 3031
Moksa, 1871, 2009
Momins, 787
Monarchy, 1121
Mongolia, 1721, 4227
Mongol, 710, 4167, 4193
Monkeys, 729
Monks, 1706
Montagu, Edwin, 797
Moon, 1420, 1538, 2713
Morality, 1140, 1152
Mother Goddess, 3710, 3717, 3730, 4306
Mother-in-law, 1395
Motion, 2057
Mountains, 1226
Mratuanjayamantrathavimarsha, 1510
Mrcchakatika, 2725-2726, 2748, 2750-2751, 2759, 2761
Mrigavat, 3959
Mrsa-vada-virati, 2221
Muchilinda, 3604
Muddesvari, 3153
Mudigonda, 3441
Mudraraksasa, 2730, 2735

Mughal, 757, 771, 777, 1097, 2535, 3033, 3989
Mukhalinga, 3706
Muktesvara temple, 3504
Mukti, 2181-2182
Mukuta Manikya, 3215
Mulavarman, 4380
Mulgund, 3794
Multan, 709
Mundari, 4081
Mundeshvari, 3423
Munjeru plates, 3138
Muralidharadasa, 1220
Murshidabad, 3823, 3891
Murunda, 600
Musalimadugu, 2867
Musee Gumiet, Paris, 3914
Museum of Indian Art, Berlin, 3636
Museum Pusat, 4395
Mushroom, 4136
Music, 684, 4202
Muslims, 3324
Mutua Museum, 3243
Mysore, 905, 919, 2521, 2639, 3377, 3458, 3778, 4035
Mysore Representative Assembly, 922, 928
Mysticism, 1679, 1777
Myth, 740, 1207
Mythology, 1297, 1338, 1378, 1546

Nabhagarista, 659
Nachna, 3579
Nachna Kuthara, 3470
Naciketas-legend, 1443
Nadia, 3834
Nadinagar, 2924
Nadoda, 476
Naga, 1152, 3246, 3321, 3604, 3626
Naga tribes, 1180
Nagaland, 3973
Nagarjuna, 2044, 2057, 2254
Nagarjunakonda, 2447, 4045, 4054
Nagatti, 3749
Nagda, 2920, 3627
Nagpur, 3477
Nahush ka tila, 2992
Naisadham, 2688
Naisadhacarita, 2671, 2676
Naladurga, 3386
Nalagiri, 3669
Nalanda, 3097, 3795, 4215
Namalingnusasana, 2369
Namdinagar, 2924
Nami, 3814
Namipavvajja, 1830
Namputiris, 1435
Nana, 3207
Nandantara, 698
Nandi, 3702
Nandi Ksamasramana, 1833
Narada smrti, 1489
Narasimha, 3722
Narasimha Cult, 1323
Narasimha purana, 1673
Narasinghanath, 3116
Narasipur, 2902
Narasipur Sangam, 2892
Naravahanadatta, 3854
Naravarman, 3144
Narayana, 464, 2698, 2764
Narayanabali, 3048
Narendra, 3127
Narmada, 3225
Narmada Valley, 2915
Narsingh, 3208
Narthamalai, 3510
Narwar, 3246
Nasik, 3190, 3529
Nataraja, 1284, 3699, 3726
Nationalism, 794, 796, 798
National Museum, New Delhi, 330-331, 3610, 3612, 3781, 4034, 4049
Nature, 2146
Natyasastra, 4091, 4096
Naubandhana, 1354
Navasahasankacarita, 682
Navyanyana, 2054
Navya-nyaya, 2050-2051, 2106
Nayaka, 898, 955, 984, 988
Necessity, 1957
Nehru, Jawaharlal, 792
Nemawar, 3465
Nepal, 3229, 3767
Netti-pakarana, 1705
Newspapers, 851
Neytal, 995
Nibandhas, 854
Nibbana, 1775
Nietzche, 1250
Nietzsche, 2254
Nilakantha, 2126, 4349
Nilakantha Lokesvara, 1760
Nilakantha-vijaya Campu, 2687
Nilapatas, 1234
Nilgiris, 681
Nirrti, 3691
Nirvana, 1743
Nisadas, 1032
Nitidvisastika, 2711

Nitisara, 1124
Niti-sataka, 2712
Nittur, 2894
Nivedita, 501
Nolambas, 915, 3064
Non-violence, 2247
North Arcot, 2972
Norton Simon Museum, 3581
Nude, 1389
Numismatic, 742
Nyaya, 1887, 2005, 2050-2051, 2106, 2238
Nyayabhasya, 1427
Nyayakandali, 2072
Nyayamanjari, 2138
Nyaya sutra, 1536
Nyaya-Vaisesesika, 2073, 2111, 2124
Nyayavarttikatatparyatika, 2195

Obligation, 1971, 1987
Oddiyana, 2237
Offences, 1118
Om, 1796
Oman, 1558
Oman Peninsula, 589
Omens, 3362
Omniscience, 1988, 2264
Orientalism, 1951, 2302
Orion, 1368
Orissa, 843, 3058, 3321, 3713, 3870, 3965
Ornament, 3600, 3922, 4260
Osian, 3055, 3499
Osmania University, 4109

Pacaratra-samhitas, 1345
Padacandrika, 2369
Padmabandha, 3197
Padmapada, 1933
Padma purana, 1670
Padmasambhava, 4345
Padyacudamani, 1752
Pagalatek, 3259
Pagara, 2916
Pahari, 2317
Paintings, 3331
Paippalada samhita, 1490
Paithan, 3841
Pakbira, 3001
Pakistan, 801, 2843
Paksata, 2054
Pala, 1014, 3611, 3613, 3662, 3890
Pala-Sena, 1831
Paleru Valley, 2862
Pali, 1188, 1702, 1765, 4229
Palimpsest, 1411-1413
Pallava, 656-657, 692, 976, 986, 3011, 3196, 3748
Pampa Sarassu, 473
Panca kancuka, 2169
Panca kosa, 2169
Pancamahasabda, 636, 3104
Pancaratra, 2048
Pancasikha, 1969
Pancha-Daka-mandala, 3655
Panchala, 487
Pancha-pandava temple, 3488
Panchatantra, 2545, 2763, 4389
Pandarangapalli, 3089-3090
Pandavas, 480, 716
Pandharpur, 943, 3045, 3712
Pandikkovai, 671
Pandinadu, 3512
Panduvamsins, 937
Pandya, 671, 931, 3501, 3503, 3603
Pangoraria, 3166
Panhala, 772
Panini, 1401, 1521, 2362-2363, 2368, 2375, 2381, 2384, 2388, 2394, 2396, 2401, 2407, 2414, 2419-2420, 2431, 2433, 2437, 2441, 2452, 2455-2456, 2470-2471, 4110
Panjabi, 1861
Panji-prabandha, 860
Pao-Ssu-Wei, 1762
Papanatha, 3445
Parama-laghu-manjusa, 2423
Paramara, 715, 3063, 3144, 3211, 3390
Paramasiva, 2046
Paramitayana, 2258
Parantaka Viranarayana, 3135
Parathanumana, 2028
Parikshita, 698
Paris, 3822, 3914
Partnership, 723
Parvati, 3731, 3753, 3771
Pasadena, 3581
Pastoral Communities, 1187
Pasupata, 1239, 1252
Pasupata-Saivism, 1320
Pasupata sect, 1328
Pasupatica, 1430
Pasupatism, 3773
Patanjali, 1208, 2357, 3395
Patanjalayogastravivarana, 2208
Patiala, 2945
Patna, 855, 3897, 4111
Patna University, 236
Patna Yuvak Sangh, 822
Pattadakal, 3445, 3451, 3476

Paunar, 3727
Pehoa, 3734
Pekkandru, 830
Penukonda, 784
Peshwa, 881
Persia, 780
Persian, 3007, 3060, 3913
Perumal hills, 2971
Philippines, 4199
Philosophy, 1195
Pink city, 970
Pipalda copper plates, 3015
Pipardula, 3127
Piplya Lorka, 2923
Piprahwa, 3536
Pischel, 2355
Plumer, James Marshall, 3358
Pokaran, 2958
Poland, 431
Polanyi, Michael, 1949
Political party, 1156
Polity, 713, 911, 984, 1121, 1138-1139, 1153
Polyandry, 1166
Pondichery, 3194
Poona, 2933-2934, 2940, 2942-2943
Portuguese, 770, 802, 884, 2341, 4105, 4322
Potter, 1036, 2936
Pottery, 2892, 2898, 2912, 2951, 2965, 2971, 3980, 4358
Prabhakara, 2112, 2149
Prabodha-candrodaya, 2734
Pragjyotisa, 490
Prajapati, 1415
Prajna, 1739, 1744, 1780
Prajnaparamita, 1683, 1713, 1754, 1756, 1789, 1794, 1797, 1824, 1826, 2263, 3811
Prakamodya, 1470
Prakasam, 3654
Prakasananda, 2002
Prakrit, 493, 1279, 2403, 2610, 2690, 2743
Prakrti, 1944
Pramana, 1835, 2001, 2166
Pramanya, 2050
Prameyacarcamrta, 2710
Pranagnihotra, 2076
Pranala, 3405
Prapti, 1915, 2164
Prasannamatra, 3274
Prasastapada, 2090
Prasasti, 725
Prasat Kandol Dom, 4379
Pratapamalladeva, 3271
Pratihara, 683, 3313, 3471-3472, 3476
Pratimanataka, 1138
Pratimoksa-sutra, 1793
Pratyaya-sarga, 2116
Pravaraja, 3129
Pravara river, 2928
Prayascita, 1037, 1906
Prayogaratnamala-Vyakarana, 2373
Precious Stones, 3982
Prehara, 3077
Prestige, 1152
Press, 960
Preta, 1767
Priesthood, 2003
Priests, 723, 827
Prince of Wales Museum, Bombay, 4007, 4295
Princes, 794, 952
Prinsep, James, 3407
Prithvideva, 3273
Prithivishena II, 3175
Prithivivallabha, 3162
Professions, 1667
Proprietary rights, 1155
Providence, 2007
Public opinion, 680, 719, 793, 817, 874
Pudukkottai, 999
Pujyapada, 3101
Pulakesi I, 691
Pulankurchchi, 3071, 3168
Pullamangai Siva temple, 3452
Pulumavi, 3190
Punjab, 3221, 3231, 3374
Punjabi, 523-524, 526
Punishment, 1122
Punyavijaya, Muni, 3971
Puranas, 615, 1837, 1845, 1847, 3540
Purandaradasa, 2520, 4073
Puranic, 4241
Puri, 3880
Purnaism, 2113
Purna river, 2927
Purulia, 3001
Pururava, 613, 1386, 1505
Pururavas-Urvasi, 2481, 2585
Purusa, 2047, 2200
Purusa-sukta, 1342
Purusottama, 2373
Purvamimamsa, 2166
Puspadanta, 2459
Pusyamitra Sunga, 678
Putanavadha, 3354

Qal'a-i Kuhna mosque, 3542
Qutb Minar, 3546
Qutb Shahi, 3218

Radha, 1639
Ragamala, 3925
Ragavartmacandrika, 2608
Raghavan, V., 2574
Raghunatha-deva, 2678
Raghuvamsa, 2699
Rail Transport Museum, New Delhi, 4030
Railway, 1105-1107
Rain, 1554
Rain-imagery, 1383
Raisen, 2923, 3604
Rajadharma, 875, 1741
Rajamau, 3331
Rajamundry, 3900
Rajaraja, 3161, 3164
Rajaram, Chhatrapati, 765
Rajaprasastimahakavya, 969
Rajasekhara, 470, 2562, 2728
Rajasimha, 689
Rajasthan, 378-379, 382, 573, 575, 1209, 1245, 3063, 3304, 3361, 3584-3586, 3612, 3629, 3698, 3781, 3979, 4189
Rajasthani, 2397, 2513
Rajatarangini, 871-872, 874
Rajgad, 769
Rajghat, 3263, 3690
Rajlani, 3400
Rajpur, 3144, 3211
Rajput, 777, 972-974
Rajyapala, 3093
Ramabhadra, 683
Ramabhyudaya-kavyam, 2698
Ramacarita, 2667
Ramacaritamanasa, 3956
Ramachandra, 1595
Rama epic, 3876
Ramagiri, 467, 476
Ramakantasimha, 3235
Ramakrishna, 1266, 1270
Ramakrishna movement, 1318
Ramalingesvara temple, 3457
Ramanand, 2654
Ramanuja, 1567, 2108, 2140, 2155, 2164, 2203
Ramapala, 1009
Ramapanivada, 2610
Rama's finger-ring, 1599
Rama's paduka, 1599
Ramathirtham, 3654
Ramayana, 490, 1847, 3452, 3567, 3579, 3598, 3924, 4234, 4410
Ramendravana, 2654
Ramesvara temple, 3459
Ramtek, 3477
Ranadhavala, 3211
Ranamuktesvara temple, 3473
Ranchi, 3425, 3762
Rang Mahal, 3842
Ranjha, 3924
Rasa-sutra, 2724
Rasikpriya, 3903
Rastrakuta Indra III, 3066
Rastrakutas, 617, 718, 910, 947, 959, 3090, 3238
Ratna, 3215, 4121
Ratnadeva II, 3114
Ratnakarasanti, 1885
Ratnakirti, 1885
Ratnavali, 2044, 2733
Rattapadi, 896
Ravana-bhasya, 2114
Ravananugrahamurti, 3610
Ravivarma, 3046, 3189
Rayapaseniya, 3681
Rayavacakamu, 906
Razmnama, 3912
Rbisa, 1444
Real, 1897
Reality, 1993, 2010, 2246
Reason, 2183
Rebirth, 2212
Red Fort, 3545
Reh, 3213
Religion, 583, 640, 1140
Religions policy, 821
Renaissance, 940
Renigunta, 2863
Republics, 700, 707, 730
Revanta, 3776
Revelation, 2066, 2183
Revolt of 1857, 963
Revolutionaries, 823
Rewa, 3195
Rgveda, 1346, 1351, 1355, 1357, 1360, 1363, 1367, 1371, 1384, 1397, 1401, 1405-1406, 1408, 1411-1413, 1421-1423, 1433, 1436, 1438, 1440-1441, 1445, 1454-1457, 1463-1464, 1479, 1483, 1493-1494, 1497-1498, 1514, 1525-1526, 1530, 1539, 1546, 1559, 1563, 2394, 2431, 2820, 3765
Rishikesh, 3571
Ritual, 1271, 1302, 1325, 1330, 1380-1381, 1388, 1432, 1447, 1449, 1455, 1540, 1549, 1569, 3329, 3638
Rock, 559, 3879
Rock art, 3382
Rock painting, 2966
Rohtas, 492
Roman, 1065, 2974
Rome, 4202
Ropar, 2968
Ror, 2889

Roy, Raja Rammohun, 1133
Rsabha, 1478, 3814
Rtu-samhara, 2686
Rudradaman I, 3152
Rudramahalaya, 3430
Rudrasimha I, 3242
Rudra-Siva, 1286
Rural art, 3330
Russia, 1090, 2429

Sabari, 3439
Sabha, 1369
Sachchidananda, 2071, 2083
Sacrifice, 723, 1244, 1449, 1491, 1543, 1550, 1566, 1680
Sadasiva, 3784
Saddantavadana, 2220
Sad-gunya, 2161
Sadhana, 2167
Sa'di, 3961
Sadyojata theme, 3613
Safvids, 757
Sagaranandin, 2755
Saharanpur, 2977
Sohibdin, 3952
Sahis, 603
Sahodarasnehah, 2747
Saint, 1283
Saiva, 1284, 1311, 3203, 3586, 3629, 4303
Saivagamas, 1275
Saiva-Siddhanta, 1276
Saivism, 1241, 1320, 3607-3608, 4402
Saivite, 1287, 3826
Saka, 681
Sakara, 2725
Sakkayaditthi, 1822
Sakta, 1270, 3700
Sakta pitha, 1243
Sakta-tantrism, 2097
Sakti, 3696, 3707
Saktibhadra, 2746
Sakti Cult, 1209
Saktikumara, 3296
Saktism, 1218, 1241
Sakti-worship, 1331
Sakuntala, 2355, 2738, 2758
Salabhanjika, 718
Salar Jung Museum, 391
Sala-suktas, 1396
Salem, 980
Saluvakuppam, 3742
Samadhimarana, 1838
Samanya, 2051
Samara Kolahala, 3248
Samarasimha, 3202
Samatala, 3259, 4268
Samavayi-karana, 1883
Samaveda, 1435
Sambalpur, 956
Sambara, 3632
Sambhaji, 755
Samhita, 1404, 1411-1413, 1423, 1481, 1490
Samkaracarya, 2145
Samkhya, 2067-2068, 2084, 2098, 2116, 2122, 2131, 2171, 2193, 2197-2198, 2207
Samskara-duhkhata, 2230
Samskrtalaksana, 1783
Samudragupta, 619, 673, 725
Sanchankot, 3366
Sanchi, 633, 3532
Sandhyakaranandin, 2667
Sandilya bhakti sutras, 1220
Sangam age, 981, 1543, 1753
Sanghol, 3527, 3730
Sanjan, 946, 3149
Sanjhi, 3360
Sankara, 1509, 1567, 1571, 1648, 1943, 1985, 2011, 2045, 2066, 2077, 2079, 2085, 2148, 2196, 2615, 3619
Sankarappadiyar, 979
Sannati, 3657
Sanskars, 1289
Sanskrit, 85, 186, 625, 865, 914, 920, 1190, 1279, 1768, 1792, 1807, 1818, 2338-2339, 2347, 2809, 2827, 3073, 3142, 3159, 3253, 3982, 4101, 4188, 4232, 4243, 4287, 4318-4319, 4348, 4364-4365, 4387, 4424, 4447
Santanu, 1494
Santosi Mata, 3701
Saora pictograms, 1271
Saptamatri Cult, 1312
Saptamatrka, 3781
Sapta-sindhava, 1553
Saptavadhri, 1444
Sarabhapura, 482, 3115, 3123, 3127, 3129
Sarakupa, 2996
Saranas, 1210, 1262
Sarangarh, 3123, 3151
Sarasvata School, 2412
Sarasvati, 1668, 3739, 4382
Sarasvati river, 1616, 2858
Sarasvati Valley, 2854
Saraswati, Kavindracarya, 2614, 2622
Saraswati, S.K., 3590
Saratbari, 3183
Sarhindi, Ilahdad Faizi, 747
Sarnath, 2989, 3663, 3747
Sarngaka legend, 1628
Sarvajnasiddhih, 1806

Sarvastivad, 1915, 2233
Sa-Skya, 1728
Satakarni, 622
Satapaha Brahmana, 1349, 1446, 2612
Satavahana, 630, 642, 713, 717, 2539, 3269, 3296, 3370, 3672, 3841
Sat-cakrani, 2100
Sati, 1465
Sati-pratha, 1145
Satrunjaya-Giri, 3814, 3816
Sattasambandha, 2091
Sattra, 650
Satyagraha, 2030
Saundarnand, 2714
Saundarya, 1984
Saundaryalahari, 2178
Saura Cult, 3233
Sautrantika, 1814
Savalda Culture, 2937
Sawai Jai Singh, 968
Sayana, 1404, 1460, 2596
Scepticism, 2254
Schwartz, 982
Sculpture, 3304, 4226, 4255
Seals, 546, 1429
Sea-ports, 1068
Sectarian, 899
Secular, 899, 1963, 2004, 2024
Semathan, 2890
Sena I, 4329
Sendrakas, 885
Senesvara, 3435
Sensation, 2034
Separatism, 1153
Settlement, 1110
Seunas, 913
Sevunas, 904
Sexualism, 1381
Shah, Abdullah Qutb, 3034
Shahbad, 4419
Shahji, 901
Shakespeare, 2736
Shakuntala, 2684
Shankuk, 2617
Shaykh Phul, 3950
Shekhawati, 3949
Sher Afgan, 760
Shinkot Steatite Casket, 3040
Shipping, 1063, 1073
Shivaji, 751, 754, 769-770, 779, 1098
Shivapuri, 3469
Shorapur Doab, 2901
Shortughai, 555
Shu-Klen-Mung, 3281
Siam, 4223, 4247, 4409, 4411, 4416
Siang, 3704
Siberia, 4213
Sibtainabad Imambara, 3544
Siddavatam, 834
Siddham, 1796
Siddhanatha temple, 3465
Siddhantalaksana Jagadisi, 2058
Siddhantamuktavali, 2160
Siddhantatattvaviveka, 4129
Siddhapur, 2978
Siddhasiddhantapaddhati, 1955
Siddhesvara temple, 3465
Siddhis, 2178
Sidhpur, 3430
Sidi Bashir Mosque, 3543
Sikh, 800, 4168
Sikkim, 3229
Silk, 1057, 4439
Silpa, 1385
Simhakundalas, 3689
Simla Museum, 3960
Sindhu, 667, 3078
Sindhu durga, 493
Singabhupala, 2722
Singers, 1283
Sinhala, 1728
Sinhalese, 1803, 3081
Sirkurmanatha temple, 3141
Sirpura, 3115
Sirsa, 3851
Sisna-Deva, 1389
Sisyahitaisini, 2706
Sittannavasal, 3193
Siva, 1286, 1300, 3331, 3420, 3431-3432, 3452, 3469, 3478, 3692, 3695-3696, 3741, 3745-3746, 3748, 3750, 3753, 3769, 3784, 3792, 3842, 4359, 4393
Sivagupta, 3119, 3122, 3124-3125
Sivasoma, 4379
Skanda Cult, 1215
Skandagupta, 3019, 3088, 3131
Skanda-purana, 1005, 1678
Skander image, 4263
Skandhaka, 1770
Slavery, 1034, 1050
Smrtis, 639, 1393-1394, 1414, 1477, 1489, 1506, 1528, 1541-1542
Snake, 1626, 3703
Social structure, 852
Sodasa, 3172
Soddhala, 2691
Sohan culture, 2857
Sonadeva Suri, 4144
Somanatha, 709, 3428

Somaskandamurti, 3735
Somavamsins, 957
Someshwar Deva, 3113
Sondur, 3625
Sonkh, 2995, 3626
Sonpur grant, 948
Sooron, 2921
Sopatma, 488
Sori, 841A
Sothi, 2956-2957
South America, 4123, 4238
South Asia, 3154, 3405
South-East Asia, 1094, 1293, 3065, 3341, 3405, 4192-4194, 4200, 4229-4230, 4232, 4234, 4240-4242
South India, 1148-1149, 1174, 1222, 1254
South Kanara, 3137
South Kosala, 937, 1685
Soviet Central Asia, 4203, 4209
Space, 2011
Spengler, 1866
Sphutartha Srighana-Carasangroha-tika, 2767
Spice, 1057
Spiritualism, 2027, 2065
Sri, 1255
Sridhara, 4132
Srighanacara-Sangraha-tika, 1715
Sriharsa, 2676
Sri Lakshmi, 3764
Sri Lanka, 139, 902, 1698-1699, 1763, 2485, 4115
Srimukapanacasati, 1265
Sringeri matha, 918
Srinivasanallur, 996
Sripati, 4118
Sriranga-Raya I, 3039
Srisukta, 2104
Srivatsa symbol, 3365
Srngararasodaya-Bhana, 1051
Srngaravairagyatarangini, 2677
Sruti, 2066
Staatsbibliothek, 3953
State formation, 712, 714, 785
Stein, M.A., 1405
Sternbach, L., 2630
Sthavira Srona Kotivimsa, 1819
Struggle, 823
Subhadraharana, 2436
Subhasitaratnakosa, 1015
Subhasita-samgrahas, 727, 2647
Subrahmanya Iyer, 1985
Suci, 1425
Sudevaraja, 3123
Sudhanakumaravadana, 4204
Sudraka, 2725
Suffering, 2230
Sufism, 1901
Sugar, 475
Sugatipa, 3086
Sugh, 3829
Suhadevi, 3174
Sukanya, 1352
Sukasandesa, 2716
Sukla Yajurveda, 1452
Sulka, 1084
Sultanganj, 3631
Sumerian, 544
Sum-Tsek, 3882
Sumukhadharani, 2576
Sun, 1612, 3762
Sun temple, 3499
Sunak, 3429
Sundarapandya, 2711
Sunet, 3231
Sunga, 605, 667, 678, 3366
Suns, 1226
Sunyata, 1735
Surabala Udirnavaira, 3176
Surangama-sutra, 1799
Sur Das, 2508
Sureban, 3439
Suresvara, 2646
Surya, 1357, 3510, 3704, 3709, 3723, 3750
Surya Verman, 3117
Suttapitaka, 1790
Suvikrantavikramipariprccha, 1713
Svadharma, 1928
Svalpaksara prajnaparamita, 1826
Svarnajalesvara temple, 3489
Svarnamukta-samvada, 2737
Svarupabheda, 2149
Svasru-snusadhana-samvada, 1395
Svati Tirunal, 2721
Svetasvatara Upanisad, 1572
Swat, 593, 4260
Syadvada, 2268
Syananduraprabandha, 2721
Syenaciti, 1257
Symbol, 1792, 2294, 3325, 3333, 3365
Symbolic, 3317, 3363, 3369
Symbolism, 608, 1172, 1429, 2788, 3360
Syncretism, 1305

Tagore, Debendranath, 1952
Tagore, Gaganendranath, 3894
Tagore, Rabindranath, 1965, 1967, 1976, 1999, 2157, 2287
Tai, 4355
Taittiriya-Brahmana, 1419, 1486

Taittiriya samhita, 1404
Takkolam, 991
Talcher, 3058
Tambula, 1039, 1165
Tamil, 89, 533-535, 681, 983, 992, 995, 1235, 1543, 2129, 2466, 3142, 3194, 3212
Tamil movement, 1335
Tamilnadu, 529, 1174, 1299, 3073, 3193, 3847
Tamils, 1031, 1737
Tamil Society, 981
Tamralipta, 1764
Tandoni, 3508
Tanjavur, 982, 3671
Tanjinatha, 3762
Tanjore, 988
Tanmatra, 2207
Tantra, 1217-1218, 1996, 2048, 2081, 2235, 2263, 3349
Tantrasara, 1221
Tantric, 1809, 1813, 2089, 2234, 2239, 2252, 3638-3639
Tantrism, 1204, 2097, 2232, 3569
Tapasvini Parvati, 3731
Tapti Basin, 2939
Tara, 1711, 3662
Tarafeni Basin, 3003
Tarikh-i-Assam, 1180
Tarka, 2066
Tathagatagarbha, 1794, 1815
Tattva, 2121, 2173
Taxation, 712, 1109
Taxila, 4307, 4314
Tcum-Ttechi, 1703
Teacher, 1526
Tekkalakota, 3100
Telugu, 91, 536-537, 927, 3034
Temple, 827, 1253-1254, 1280, 1841
Tenkalai, 2132
Tennari, 4003
Terahi, 3468
Terracotta, 3288, 3531, 4306
Terrorist movement, 810
Textile, 1094, 4226
Thailand, 4210, 4225, 4239, 4244, 4248-4250, 4354
Thakurdiya, 3129
Thalner, 3091
Thanjavur, 3511
Thar desert, 2958
Thaton Mingun Zetawun Sayadaw, 1717
Thatta, 4312
Theravada, 1682, 1687, 1707, 1787
Thiruvilimilalai, 3868
Tibet, 1166, 1728, 1768, 1827, 2226, 2575, 4184, 4195, 4214, 4235
Tikotiparisuddha, 1709
Tilak, B.G., 1368
Tilakamanjari, 3409
Time, 2011
Tippuru, 1843
Tipu Sultan, 816, 924
Tirtha, 1506
Tirthankara, 3679
Tiruchirapalli, 2973, 3098, 3196
Tiru-isaippa, 1211
Tirukkadavur, 1319
Tirukkostiyur, 3722
Tirumalai Nayak, 3572
Tirumullavayil, 3505
Tiruppangili, 3508
Tiruvalluvar, 60, 2770
Tiruvanaikka, 3192
Tiruvarur, 1242
Tiruvorriyur, 997
Todas, 681
Toilet, 1035
Tolerance, 1708, 1924
Tomaras, 3732
Tonnur, 926
Tools, 562
Toponyms, 900
Town, 699, 736, 886, 3390
Trade, 886, 1065, 1075, 1083, 1085-1086, 1088, 1090, 1111, 1115
Trade Union, 1115
Traikutaka, 3042
Trailokyamalladeva, 3198
Trailokyavijaya, 3632
Transoxiana, 2535
Transport, 2817
Travel accounts, 907
Travellers, 646
Tree, 3383
Tribal, 785, 853, 954, 1147, 1170, 3337
Trikalinga, 486, 958
Trika philosophy, 2172, 2174
Trikaya, 2226
Trilocana, 2184
Tripitaka, 1762
Tripura, 1552, 3215, 3830
Tripura-rahasya, 1979
Tripuri, 353, 3560
Trivikramabhatta, 2719
Trsna, 2215
Truth, 1964
Tsong-kha-pa, 4345
Tughluq, 3029, 3035
Tughluq, Ghiyathu'd-Din, 762
Tughluq, Muhammad Bin, 3032
Tukaram, 58
Tun-huang, 1791

Turfan, 1721
Turkestan, 4181, 4430
Turkish, 749, 2502, 3009
Turks, 849, 4190
Tuzuk-i-Jahangiri, 3919
Tyagaraja, 4068

U.S.A., 825, 1991, 4220, 4237
U.S.S.R., 4183, 4188
Ubeidiya, 4426
Udaharana, 2693
Udaipur, 3678
Udaiyarkoyil, 3072
Udayana, 1810, 2096
Udayapur, 3474
Udayasundarikatha, 2691
Udayesvara temple, 3466, 3474
Udbhandapura, 603
Udbhata, 2597
Udbhattasiddhasvamin, 1829
Uddyana, 4265
Udyana, 4265
Ujjain, 935
Ujjainiya rajputs, 777
Ujjayini, 2911
Ukkal, 978
Umasvati, 3102
Universality, 1957
Unmattananda, 2104
Upadana-karana, 1883
Upadhyaya, Narahari, 2055
Upagupta, 746
Upanisad, 1535, 1857, 1968, 2085, 2151, 2232
Ur, 993
Urban, 832, 864
Urban art, 3376
Urbanization, 733, 1019
Urdhva Saivas, 1284
Urdu, 2312, 4109
Uruvela passapa, 1816
Urvasi, 1505
Ustravahini Devi, 3791
Uttaradhyayanasutra, 1850
Uttarakhand, 1002
Uttarakuru, 481
Uttaramerus, 3326
Uttararamacarita, 2672, 2683, 2730, 2745
Uttar Pradesh, 1116, 3332, 3571, 3614

Vacaspati, 2064
Vaddamanu, 3170
Vaddaradhane, 2523
Vadgaon-Madhavapur, 2909
Vadiraja, 2176
Vaibhasika Abhidharma, 1739
Vaikunthamurti, 3734
Vainayaki, 3782
Vainyagupta, 3261
Vaira, 2215
Vairagya, 2712
Vaisali, 850, 3777, 3835
Vaisesika, 2073-2074, 2195, 2205, 2208-2209
Vaishnavi, 3799
Vaisnava, 2092, 3143, 3460, 3539, 3716, 3758, 3880, 4396-4397
Vaisnavism, 1259, 1296, 1315, 1335, 1511, 3607
Vaisravana, 3806
Vajapeya, 1451
Vajracchedika, 1720
Vajralepa, 3385
Vajrayana, 1801, 2258-2259
Vajresvari Devi temple, 3008
Vak, 1475
Vakataka, 604, 661, 917, 3069, 3091, 3094, 3175, 3178, 3477, 3534
Vakparusya, 1502
Vakya-kanda-tika, 2546
Vakyapadiya, 2623
Valabhi, 572
Valentijn, Francois, 607
Validity, 1972, 2171
Valigama, 4335
Vallabhadeva, 2699
Valmiki, 1585, 1588, 1592-1597, 1602, 1847
Values, 2018
Vamana, 2438
Vamana-Avatara, 3797
Vaman purana, 1656
Varadaksina, 1164
Varaha-katha, 1622
Varahamihira, 3396, 3413
Varaha purana, 1661
Varaha school, 1450
Varaha srauta sutra, 1448, 1451
Varahi, 3483, 3766
Varanasi, 752, 1005, 1055, 1691, 2987, 3339, 3388, 3518, 3559, 3747, 3859, 3861
Varendri, 1009
Varna, 1426, 1529
Varnamalika, 1078
Varna-samkara, 1655
Varsus, 580
Varuna, 903, 1356, 1584, 3676
Vasistha, 1559
Vasisthiputra, 3300
Vasishthiputra Sivasri Pulumavi, 833

Vastu, 2092
Vastu-Brahma, 3414-3415
Vasubandhu, 1710
Vasudeva-Krsna, 1214, 1614
Vatsyayana, 1427
Vayu purana, 1675
Vayu rupabhavavan, 1914
Veal Kantel, 4373
Vedabhasyas, 1460
Vedanta, 1840, 1901, 2070-2071, 2093, 2133-2136, 2148, 2152, 2154, 2163, 2175, 2182-2183, 2187
Vedanta desika, 2132, 2155, 2201
Vedas, 3160
Vedic, 614, 719, 723, 737, 1075, 1147, 2854
Velaikkarar, 992
Vemabhupala, 2444
Venad, 931
Vena-sukta, 1379
Venkaatmakhi, 4059
Venugopala, 3743
Vernacular, 851
Verul Sivalayamahatmya, 3478
Vibhramaviveka, 2115
Vibhuti-Yoga, 1642
Vidagdhamukhamandana, 2620
Vidarbha, 2929, 3521
Viddanacarya, 2710
Viddha, 718
Vidisha, 3226, 3678
Vidusaka, 3884
Vidyabodhini, 2104
Vidyapati, 1034
Vidyaranya, 1982
Vidyasagor, Iswar Chandra, 4108
Vietnam, 4354
Vijayadhvajacharya, 2663
Vijaya durga, 493
Vijayanagar, 884, 894, 988, 1048, 1277, 3038, 3324, 3356, 3444, 3538, 3580, 3587, 3868, 3873
Vijjalavida, 469
Vijnanavad, 1915
Vijnaptimatratasiddhi, 1722
Vikramaditya II, 3446
Vikramasena, 3042
Vikramendravarman II, 690
Vikramorvasiyam, 2740, 2743, 2757
Vikramsila University, 2993
Vinami, 3814
Vinasana, 2783
Vinaya, 1785
Vinayaditya, 670
Vindhyas, 1074, 2994, 3166
Vinnakota, 3158
Vira Ballala II, 3067
Vira-Bananjus, 890
Virabhadra, 3794
Viradharadeva, 4268
Viraja-ksetra, 1243
Virasaivism, 1264, 1269, 1276-1277, 1296, 1306, 1317, 1334
Virastambha, 3344
Viravaishnavism, 1298
Visakhavijaya, 2700
Visalamalavati, 1807
Visesa, 2062
Visesastva, 1829
Vishishtadvaita, 1986
Vishnudasa, 3231
Vishnukundin Madhavarman I, 828
Visistadvaita, 2033
Visnu, 491, 1263, 1602, 2048, 3134, 3464, 3737, 3755, 3757, 3761, 3765, 4360
Visnukundi, 3291
Visnukundins, 3257
Visnukundin Vikramendravarman II, 690
Visnupada temple, 3605
Visnu purana, 1658, 1677
Visnusahasranama stotra, 1267
Visnuvardhana, 662
Visual art, 1999
Visvakarma temple, 3480
Visvamitra, 1523, 1559
Visvanatha Cakravartin, 2608
Visvarupa, 3788
Viswanatha, 2490
Vitanda, 2128
Vivarta, 1442
Vivekananda, 73, 810, 2078, 3398
Vjnaptimatra, 2256
Vo-Canh, 4418
Vohara, 1690
Vopadeva, 2518, 2685
Vratya, 1431, 1561
Vriddhagirisvara temple, 3602
Vrttikara, 2621
Vyaghra, 3246
Vyaghra-smrti, 1477
Vyahara, 1690
Vyavahara, 1690
Vyomasiva, 2091

Wang Yang-Ming, 2216
Waqiat-i-Azfari, 967
Water, 1927
Water-monuments, 3736
Water-springs, 3396
Weber, 1547

Weights, 897
Wellesley, 924
West Bengal, 1273, 2477, 3978
West Dinajpur, 3018
Western impact, 953
Wheel, 1487, 3060, 3671A
Whitehead, 1958
Widow, 1391
Wills, C.U., 956
Wisdom, 1971
Women, 1151, 1170, 1173, 1207, 1393, 1464-1465
Wood carvings, 3973
Wooden, 3387, 3565, 3662
Working class movement, 806

Yabgus, 672
Yadava, 3045
Yadava Simhana, 933
Yajna, 1463
Yajnaparsve, 1452
Yajnavalkya, 1067, 1393
Yajnavalkya-smrti, 1542
Yajurveda, 1452
Yaksha, 1309, 3690, 3747
Yakshi, 3677, 3697
Yamaka poems, 2717
Yamapattika, 3874
Yama-Yami, 1390
Yamuna, 3721
Yamunacarya, 2140
Yantra, 1996
Yapaniya, 1849
Yasastilaka, 2645, 4144
Yaska, 1390, 2385
Yasodharman, 662-663
Yasovarman, 602
Yatis, 1364
Yatra, 1506
Yatu, 1463
Yaudheya tribe, 707
Yavana, 702, 3576
Yavati Mahasivagupta I, 948
Yeleswaram, 2861
Yoga, 2040, 2153
Yogacara, 1731, 1741, 2251
Yoganarayana, 3718
Yogasanas, 2141
Yogasutras, 2177-2178
Yoga-therapy, 2142
Yogavasistha, 2449, 2723
Yogin, 3344
Yoginipur, 3968
Yoginis, 3463, 3711
Yueh-Chih, 672
Yuktidipika, 2116
Yukti-kalpataru, 2680

Zaman Shah, 816
Zanskar, 877
Zen, 1787, 2222